I0199661

Licentious
GOTHAM

Licentious GOTHAM

Erotic Publishing *and* Its Prosecution *in* Nineteenth-Century New York

Donna Dennis

HARVARD UNIVERSITY PRESS
Cambridge, Massachusetts · London, England
2009

Library of Congress Cataloging-in-Publication Data

Dennis, Donna.
Licentious Gotham : erotic publishing and its prosecution in
nineteenth-century New York / Donna Dennis.
p. cm.
Includes bibliographical references and index.
ISBN 978-0-674-03283-5
1. Pornography—New York (State)—New York—History—19th century.
2. Pornography—Law and legislation—New York (State)—New York—
History—19th century. 3. Pornography in popular culture—
New York (State)—New York. I. Title.
HQ471.D46 2009
364.1′7409747109034—dc22 2008036466

For Nancy

Contents

Licentious Gotham

Introduction

In the winter of 1855, a New York police officer entered the basement-level bookstore of John Atchison on Nassau Street in lower Manhattan, just below City Hall. To many observers, Nassau had an odd, old-world feel. "Crooked, contracted, unclean, with high houses and low houses, marble palaces and dingy frames," it reminded the author of one nineteenth-century guidebook "more of a street in an old Continental town than of a popular thoroughfare in the new Republic." With a "strange stream of humanity" continually "flowing and overflowing" through the street, it rated as "one of the most peculiar and striking" spaces in the city. Among its other distinctions, Nassau had long served as the center of New York's printing and publishing trade, especially at the northern end of the street, where it intersected with Fulton, Ann, Beekman, Spruce, and Frankfort, in the area where Atchison's shop was located. These blocks housed a dark, congested warren of bookstores, print shops, secondhand and antiquarian book dealers, engravers, lithographers, stationers, job printers, newspaper offices, and small and midsize publishing firms. Since at least the 1840s, they had also functioned as the heart of the city's

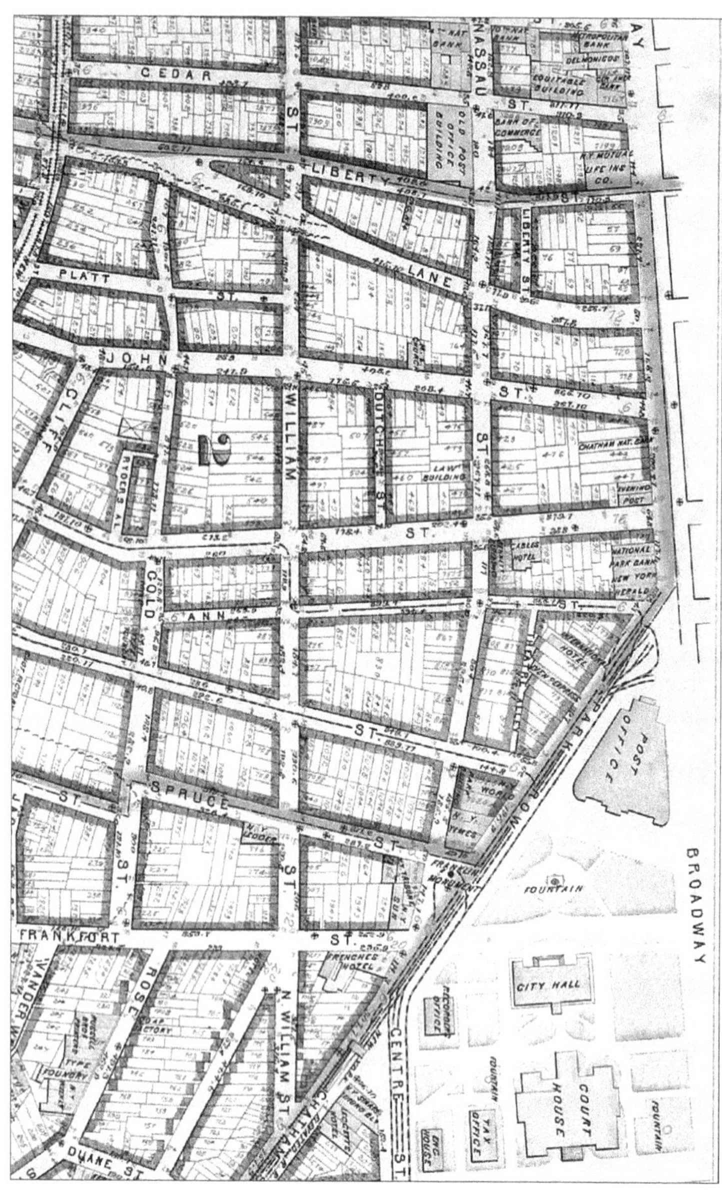

I.1 Nassau Street. Starting just below City Hall, Nassau Street was the main artery of New York's nineteenth-century erotica trade. Running from north to south, it crossed Frankfort, Spruce, Beekman, Ann, Fulton, John, Maiden Lane, Liberty, and Cedar streets. Bromley's Atlas of New York City (New York, 1879), plate 2. The J. Clarence Davies collection, 34.100.772.

MUSEUM OF THE CITY OF NEW YORK.

erotic print trade, a New York version of London's infamous Holywell Street.[1]

While in Atchison's store, the policeman found a "trunk filled with certain lewd, wicked, scandalous, infamous and obscene printed books, many in numbers and of divers titles." Only a month before, a new Democratic mayor had taken office, the flamboyant, charismatic Fernando Wood. Looking to placate middle-class critics who feared he would be soft on vice, Wood ordered the members of his police force to investigate and report all violations of morals laws in the city directly to him. Complying with the mayor's decree, the officer arrested Atchison, confiscated his chest of books, and delivered them to the mayor's office. Among the "infamous and obscene printed" works seized, all of European origin, were *Memoirs of a Woman of Pleasure* (better known today as *Fanny Hill*), *The Curtain Drawn Up*, and *The Life and Adventures of Silas Shovewell.* Described in one nineteenth-century American catalogue of erotica as "standard works of the voluptuary," they represented best-selling titles in New York's antebellum pornography market.[2]

Shortly after Atchison's arrest, the district attorney, A. Oakey Hall, asked the grand jury of the Court of General Sessions, the city's main criminal court, to return an indictment against the bookseller. Since there was no governing statute prohibiting the sale of obscene literature at that time, the indictment relied on the unwritten common law that the state of New York had inherited from England. Under common-law precedents, the sale of obscene publications had been illegal for more than a century, although officials in New York did not begin to prosecute significant numbers of obscenity cases until the early 1840s.

Unfortunately for Atchison, the foreman of the grand jury happened to be James Harper. As a principal of Harper Brothers, New York's largest and most prominent publishing firm, the foreman presumably took a dim view of booksellers who sullied the reputation of the "respectable" publishing trade by trafficking in obscene books. Even more ominously for Atchison, Harper, a devout Methodist and a former mayor of the city, had been elected in 1844 by running on an anti-alcohol, pro–moral reform platform. The grand jury swiftly indicted the bookseller for obscenity. Fortunately for the defendant, however, Atchison was a family friend of the new mayor. The charges were dismissed when Wood wrote to the district attorney vouching for Atchison's character, stating that he believed the accused would refrain from selling obscene books in the future, and asking that the charges be dropped.[3]

Tellingly, before Atchison was released, his case provided the occasion for a tawdry tabloid, the *New York Atlas,* to call attention to his arrest. The paper's account succinctly captures the ways in which nineteenth-century obscenity prosecutions often generated publicity for the trade in erotica and served as a vehicle for fueling, rather than suppressing, commerce in obscene books:

> OBSCENE BOOKS.—James Tivner . . . made an affidavit . . . setting forth that he had called at the store of one John Atcheson, 76 Nassau street, and purchased a book called "The Mysteries of Venus; Or, The Amatory Life and Adventures of Miss Kitty Pry" . . . The collection of books and prints seized were presented at the office of the Mayor. They were of the most beastly and revolting nature. There are other shops of the kind in the city, which we hope may soon be similarly visited. Such panders to the most degrading of vices, should be severely punished.[4]

Despite its own reputation for publishing morally indecent content, the *Atlas* made a show of endorsing arrests for obscenity and advocating severe punishment for the sale of "beastly and revolting" publications. At the same time, the paper conveniently disclosed the address of the bookseller and the title of the allegedly obscene book, thereby providing curious readers with information about the forbidden text and precisely where to purchase it. If other obscenity prosecutions from the 1850s serve as any guide, Atchison's case may have increased the circulation of obscene books in a more immediate way. Policemen, court employees, and other municipal officers were often accused of pilfering confiscated books for their private perusal, sharing them with friends, and even selling them on the open market.

Despite Mayor Wood's assurances to the contrary, Atchison was still doing business in obscene books seven years later. In 1862, in the midst of the Civil War, he ran this thinly veiled advertisement for erotica in the *New York Clipper*, a paper for sporting men, the back pages of which pornography dealers favored: "BOOKS ON LOVE, AS USUAL.—Catalogues sent free."[5] Significantly, by this time Atchison had graduated from selling such books over (or probably more accurately under) the counter to offering them by mail order. In this respect, his practices followed the trend in the metropolitan erotica trade as a whole. In the years leading up to the war, New York dealers, in an effort to free themselves from the costs and constraints of municipal obscenity regulation, had engineered a major reorientation of their business toward sales by mail.

One New York publisher, a savvy former bookbinder named George Akarman, was particularly responsible for this transformation. By the mid-1850s, working out of a series of offices in the vicinity of Nassau Street, Akarman was well on his way to becoming one of the century's largest producers of pornography, second only to a legendary publisher of bawdy books named William Haines. The prominence Akarman had in the erotic print trade meant that he operated in the constant shadow of the law, where he was continually confronted with raids on his publishing firm and with the threat of police harassment, arrest, indictment, and imprisonment for obscenity. As a way out of these legal difficulties, Akarman conceived a visionary scheme to circumvent existing prohibitions on obscenity. Instead of marketing his erotic publications within the metropolis, he resolved to employ the U.S. mail as the exclusive vehicle for advertising and distributing books, pictures, and other merchandise that New York officials were likely to condemn as obscene. (At the time, Congress had not yet banned the sale of obscene materials through the mail.)

As a resident of a federal America, Akarman understood that regulation of morals took place at the state and local levels. Accordingly, he believed his commerce could not be impeded if it relied on the U.S. mails or private systems of interstate transportation. By shifting business away from New York City and toward the mail, Akarman gained a safe, inconspicuous means of selling publications that metropolitan authorities considered obscene; at the same time, he laid the groundwork for what would soon become a sweeping, nationwide market for pornography. In this respect, municipal restrictions on obscenity had the unintended effect of dramatically abetting the proliferation of obscene literature throughout the United States.

Rather than suppress the output of sexual writing, prohibitions against obscenity inspired bold new genres of erotic print. Pornographers like Akarman paid careful attention to the laws on obscenity and how they were enforced: erotic texts were classified according to their relative risk of instigating prosecution and their relative attractiveness as more or less "forbidden." In 1856, for instance, Akarman decided to launch a new venture, a highly risky, innovative periodical called *Venus' Miscellany*. Calculating that he could not sell the magazine in New York without triggering prosecution for obscenity, Akarman planned to market it solely to an upscale audience of out-of-town subscribers, the sort of people who possessed the financial resources and sophistication to negotiate mail-order subscriptions and purchases.

Given the tenor of the publication, Akarman had ample reason for concern. Carving out a novel niche, *Venus' Miscellany* offered a thrill of transgression by focusing on precisely the representations that years of New York obscenity prosecutions had singled out as the most illicit: expressions by women of sexual passion and pleasure. To intensify the sense of taboo, Akarman chose to highlight the carnal desire of seemingly "average," middle-class women. To this end, he included a regular column of letters to the editor from purported subscribers, in which he showcased married women who wished to share their sexual experiences with other readers. The writers recounted the excitement that subscribing to *Venus' Miscellany* had added to their marriage, their enthusiastic erotic adventures with female neighbors, and their involvement in ménages à trois in which their husbands passively followed their lead. In this way, the prohibitions expressed in obscenity prosecutions did not silence representations of female lust so much as create the conditions for new forms of textual titillation.

Through the contributions of publishers like Akarman, late antebellum New York became a focal point for what dealers in erotica styled "fancy" literature—their own marketing term for sexually arousing publications. Other New Yorkers—especially those who wished to suppress the trade or were otherwise critical of it—typically referred to such texts instead as obscene, lascivious, lewd, libidinous, or licentious. The last adjective had a particularly powerful resonance for citizens of a republic, where "license" often stood in stark opposition to "liberty." In this worldview, sexual license or "licentiousness" posed a special risk of harm because it represented the antithesis of rational, ordered liberty. To call a publication licentious therefore meant not only that it was indecent and immoral, but also that it threatened the safety and stability of the republic through an excess of freedom and a seeming perversion of liberty.[6]

In condemning obscene and licentious literature, advocates of moral and civic reform in New York undoubtedly found comfort in the strictures of the law. Legal treatises routinely declared that states and localities had inherent power to regulate morality. Indeed, such legal works often described the protection of morality as a central function of state and local governments. More expressly, nineteenth-century jurists made clear that government officials had wide-ranging authority to suppress any speech or writing that had a tendency to corrupt public virtue, including the authority to punish the sale of obscene publications.[7] Looking solely at these doctrinal formulations of the law, one might well conclude that state and local governments worked forcefully and consistently to police morality and suppress indecency in nineteenth-century America.[8]

The history of erotic publishing and obscenity law reveals a much more ambiguous picture, however. Obscenity prosecutions in antebellum New York tended to occur only sporadically, at punctuated moments. Interest in obscenity regulation, as in other efforts to enforce conventional moral standards, occurred in bursts, before and after which most people did not seem to view sexually explicit publications as a major social problem or public concern. Moreover, municipal authorities never enforced prohibitions on obscenity as rigorously as official norms would suggest. Instead, officials chose to tolerate many forms of writing that moral reformers denounced as indecent and obscene. Important mid-nineteenth-century genres that escaped prosecution for obscenity despite such condemnation include health manuals that provided advice on birth control and abortion and sensational novels that combined graphic accounts of violence with euphemistic depictions of sex.

Most significantly, participants in the erotica trade, far from being cowed by the forces of decency or by threats of imprisonment, repeatedly turned ostensible conditions of repression into opportunities for promotion and profit. Through the ingenuity and persistence of its major erotic entrepreneurs, New York produced a prodigious array of lewd prints, engravings, lithographs, pamphlets, and licentious books before the Civil War. Other urban locales, including New Orleans, Boston, and Philadelphia, though they also generated sexual publications, never approached the astounding productivity of New York. By the time John Atchison was advertising his mail-order catalogue for "Books on Love" in 1862, the city in general, and the Nassau Street area in particular, had solidified a position of preeminence in the field of erotic publishing. During the war, New York dealers gained particular notoriety for exploiting the heavy demand for mail-order pornography, including the wildly popular new medium of erotic photography, among Union soldiers.

It was no accident, then, that the New York milieu also spawned the country's most aggressive and influential censor, Anthony Comstock, as well as its most powerful antivice society, the New York Society for the Suppression of Vice, which moral reformers cannily located at 150 Nassau Street, in the thick of the industry they sought to eradicate. Just as obscenity prohibitions shaped and inspired the city's mid-nineteenth-century erotica trade, the trade itself could be said to have "created" Comstock. Indeed, the former dry goods salesman's surge to power in the early 1870s was directly predicated on the success of New York publishers and dealers in establishing a flourishing market for sexually arousing material, first in New York and eventually in the nation at large, during the middle part of the century. For it was their pioneering turn to mail-order marketing that galvanized Comstock's crusade against interstate traffic in obscene literature and led Congress to pass the so-called Comstock Act of 1873, which banned a broad range of alleged obscenity from the mails.[9] The pornographers' success also paved the way for Comstock's appointment as a special agent of the U.S. Postal Service in charge of enforcing the ban on purveying obscene publications by mail. This position catapulted him onto the national stage and endowed him with the power and resources of a vast federal agency.

The commercial activities of New York erotica dealers also laid the foundation for radical, far-reaching innovations in the structure and scope of obscenity regulation. Widespread use of the mails to market and deliver erotic goods, itself a tactic designed to evade local prohibitions, ultimately brought about a critical shift in the primary venue for obscenity prosecutions during the last three decades of the nineteenth century. What had once fallen within the exclusive purview of localities and states now became a function of the federal government. This ascension from the local to the national forum represented a striking regulatory move during a century in which crimes of all kinds, but especially crimes involving morals, were prosecuted at the local level.

New York in the nineteenth century constituted a locus of tremendous cultural experimentation and commercial possibility, especially during the middle decades. In this period, the city established itself as the financial, manufacturing, and cultural capital of the young nation. By the 1850s it had attained the stature of a metropolis, a "great organization of powers and skills that strengthened its commercial and cultural dominance of the nation while making it a major presence in world society." At the same time, thanks to its burgeoning book and newspaper publishing industries, New York came to enjoy an unrivaled position as a communications center.[10]

For all these reasons, the young metropolis attracted a steady stream of daring, entrepreneurial individuals who hoped to capitalize on the dizzying opportunities the city seemed to offer. Among these ambitious newcomers was a cadre of enterprising publishers, journalists, printers, authors, and illustrators, who pioneered the production and marketing of erotic materials in the two decades before the Civil War. Because of his pathbreaking part in developing the American pornography trade, George Akarman plays a leading role in this book. He is joined by a host of other protagonists, including the "fancy" book publishers William Haines, Thomas Ormsby, and Frederic Brady, the "flash" newspaper editors William Snelling, George Wooldridge, and George Wilkes, the "fancy" lithograph publisher Henry Robinson, and the writer of "racy" novels George Thompson. These men (and a few women who assisted them), together with the moral reformers and law enforcement officials who sought to suppress them, form the central cast of characters in our story.

The lives of these individuals demonstrate the manifold ways in which the world of obscenity law and the domain of erotic publishing influenced, sustained, and promoted each other during the formative periods of their development in the United States. Again and again, prohibitions against obscenity gave rise to innovative ways of creating, marketing, and distributing pornography. In turn, new forms of pornography generated new prohibitions, including unprecedented techniques for regulating, investigating, and prosecuting pornographers. This history testifies to the persistent contradictions that early efforts to censor sexual expression in the name of moral necessity engendered—paradoxes that offer lessons for our own time.[11]

Chapter 1

"Beware of Print and Fancy Goods Stores"

In 1830 a zealous missionary named John McDowall, fresh from his studies at the Princeton Theological Seminary, began work as an agent for the American Tract Society. Upon his arrival, the twenty-nine-year-old McDowall beheld a city that, to his fervent young mind, teemed with lust and sin. Not content with promoting Bible study in municipal almshouses, prisons, and hospitals, he soon became obsessed with publicizing what he saw as the rampant sexual corruption in the city. In 1831, with the aid of wealthy merchants Arthur and Lewis Tappan and a band of socially prominent evangelical women, he was instrumental in founding the New-York Magdalen Society, an organization dedicated to reclaiming and reforming "fallen women." The same year, a study prepared by McDowall for the executive committee of the Magdalen Society, known as the *Magdalen Report*, charged that New York contained not fewer than ten thousand prostitutes. This remarkable assertion was tantamount to declaring that one in every ten female residents was a harlot.[1]

To McDowall, widespread prostitution was not the only sign that Gotham was suffering from an epidemic of sexual license. In *McDowall's Journal*, a monthly periodical he founded in 1833 with support from the Female Benevolent Society, he railed, "Our great cities . . . are inundated with a flood of books and pictures vile enough to make even licentiousness blush to look at them." Surveying this urban scene, "one would think the devil had turned editor, and converted hell itself into a printing office." Such vile, satanic publications, McDowall elaborated, contained the "most lust-exciting representations and illustrations of pleasure that it is possible to invent." To protect against such evils, he cautioned parents to keep their children away from traveling salesmen peddling books. "Beware of the common pedlars who visit your abodes." For city dwellers, he added a special warning: "Beware of dashing dandy-youth. Beware of print and fancy goods stores."[2]

In New York, McDowall's claims that prostitution and licentious literature had reached epic proportions were widely denounced from several quarters as grossly exaggerated. Indeed, rather than provoking communal soul-searching or legal action against brothel keepers and smut dealers, the moralist's passion for exposing sexual wrongdoing led to charges that *he* was guilty of indecency. The New York elite thought that McDowall exhibited an improper, even perverse, interest in revealing the inner workings of libertinism and in reciting stories of "seduction, rape, and incest," especially when he went so far as to distribute his journal to the private residences of well-to-do citizens. In a dramatic turn of events, after McDowall threatened to publish the names of men who patronized brothels in 1834, a grand jury condemned *McDowall's Journal* (and by implication McDowall himself) as a public nuisance for revealing "odious and revolting details" that were "offensive to taste, injurious to morals, and degrading to the character of our City."[3]

From then on, the popular press frequently cited *McDowall's Journal* as a notorious example of a "filthy, foul mouthed, indecent, immoral" and "obscene" publication. Toward the end of his short life,

McDowall, who remained obsessed with the dangers of licentious books and prostitution, carried "about a valise of works like *Fanny Hill* to prove their full horror to doubters." He died of tuberculosis in 1836 at the age of thirty-five, a broken and impoverished man.[4]

His name quickly became a symbol of the alleged excesses and hypocrisies of evangelical moral reform, a shorthand term for a pruriently zealous, prying moralist. Novelists even began to produce satirical treatments of "dark reform," as the literary scholar David Reynolds has termed it—religious fervor that revealed an unseemly fascination with vice, scandal, and tabooed subjects. These takeoffs were sometimes explicitly modeled on McDowall. "The hero of Henry Junius Nott's 'Biographical Sketch of Thomas Singularity' (1834)," notes Reynolds, "is a pious Magdalen Society member who nevertheless writes popular pornographic poetry; he is also a temperance advocate who guzzles rum in private." By the 1840s such "immoral reformers" had become standard figures in American popular literature.[5]

Given the grand jury's rebuke to McDowall and his subsequent humiliation, could there have been any substance to his claim that "lust-exciting representations and illustrations of pleasure" were readily available in 1830s New York, or to his suggestion that fancy goods stores and print shops were often the places to find them? Evidently, both these assertions contained a kernel of truth.

One of the first erotic works to be sold in the United States was an illustrated edition of *A Sentimental Journey*, by Laurence Sterne (1768). It was published in New York as early as 1795, more than three decades before McDowall began ranting against licentious print. Sterne's novel related the amorous adventures of an English parson on his journeys through France and Italy. The New York edition of 1795 featured seven copperplate engravings, many of a highly sexual nature, which could be removed from the text and sold separately. Three images, such as the frontispiece shown in Figure 1.1, depicted the exposed breasts of different women in various states of dishabille. Two other engravings graphically portrayed the parson engaged in sexual intercourse with females he encountered during his travels, one scene being set in a riding coach and one in a bedchamber.[6]

By the early nineteenth century, the most popular erotic book sold in New York was undoubtedly another eighteenth-century English novel, *Memoirs of a Woman of Pleasure,* also known as *Fanny Hill.* John Cleland had completed the book while confined in debtors' prison, perhaps in a successful effort to have a publisher purchase his release in exchange for the rights to the manuscript. While the author was still in jail, the work was issued in two volumes in London in 1748 and 1749. After his release, Cleland embarked on a largely unsuccessful career as a Grub Street writer, trying his hand variously at journalism, plays, poetry, other erotic novels, paramedical tracts, and even treatises on linguistics. But he never equaled the success of *Memoirs of a Woman of Pleasure,* which enjoyed a steadily increasing notoriety throughout Europe and America, especially after his death in 1789.[7]

By today's standards, one of the most striking features of *Fanny Hill* is the way in which it couples sexual entertainment with anti-aristocratic, republican politics. At the time Cleland was writing, however, explicit erotic literature ("pornography" as a term had not yet been invented) often employed the shock of sex to serve radical political ends. French philosophes, such as Diderot and Voltaire, as well as Mirabeau later in the century, were especially drawn to graphic sexual language as a vehicle for attacking royal, religious, and aristocratic authorities.[8] Similarly, through the carnal adventures of Fanny, Cleland thematized the decadence and corruption of the aristocracy, while celebrating the more honest, "authentic" sensual-

1.1 Frontispiece, Laurence Sterne, A Sentimental Journey . . . Ornamented with Elegant Engravings *(New York, 1795).*

COURTESY OF THE AMERICAN ANTIQUARIAN SOCIETY.

A

SENTIMENTAL JOURNEY

THROUGH

FRANCE and ITALY.

BY

Mr. YORICK.

Ornamented with Elegant Engravings.

NEW-YORK:

PRINTED FOR THE BOOKSELLERS.

1795.

1.2 Title page, Laurence Sterne, A Sentimental Journey . . . Ornamented with Elegant Engravings *(New York, 1795).*

COURTESY OF THE AMERICAN ANTIQUARIAN SOCIETY.

ity of workers and the self-made bourgeoisie.[9] At the same time, *Memoirs of a Woman of Pleasure,* which was intended for the developing middle-class audience of British novel readers, distinguished itself from the French erotic tradition by merging a radical, libertine message about sexual freedom with bourgeois aspirations for marriage and domesticity. Surprisingly, Fanny's life as a prostitute ends not with her painful demise, but with her attaining middle-class status as a wife and mother in a happy, secure marriage to her true love.[10]

Within the English literary landscape, *Fanny Hill* served as an irreverent rejoinder to Samuel Richardson's pious *Pamela* (1740–41), which had used the emerging genre of the English novel to celebrate female chastity.[11] In pointed contrast, Cleland's work portrayed a woman's longing for sexual pleasure. Consisting of two lengthy confessional letters, each making up a volume of the book, the novel recounts the life of the eponymous heroine, a humble country girl forced to move to the city after the death of her parents and become a prostitute. Through the device of having Fanny disclose her experiences in letters to an unnamed woman, *Memoirs of a Woman of Pleasure* provides explicit descriptions of a wide range of sexual activities reputedly practiced by prostitutes in the eighteenth century. Among its many offerings were scenes of sex between women, cross-dressing, flagellation, orgies, and public sex.[12]

We know that Cleland's fictional classic was available in New York by at least 1824. In that year, a man walked into the fancy goods emporium of one Joseph Bonfanti on Broadway, a store with a reputation for high fashion and exclusive taste in imported wares, and asked for a copy of the book.[13] Throughout the antebellum era, numerous merchants' emporiums and fancy goods stores like Bonfanti's lined Broadway, the city's main commercial thoroughfare. They specialized in selling finished goods produced in Britain and France: fine linens, silks, china, jewelry, and books of diverse styles and genres. Many of the books arrived as bound volumes ready for sale, while others were shipped as printed sheets that needed only to be assembled by a binder before being dispatched to import shops, book and print stores, periodical depots, and street corner bookstands.

Faced with the request for *Memoirs of a Woman of Pleasure,* Bonfanti replied "without any hesitation" that he had it in stock. Given his reputation as an importer, it is likely that the copy purchased at his store was of English rather than American provenance. Although the original London edition of *Memoirs of a Woman of Pleasure* did not include pictures, English publishers commonly produced illustrated versions by the 1760s. The edition sold by Bonfanti was no exception: his indictment indicates that the sale of obscene engravings furnished the basis for a separate charge against him. Specifically, the indictment states that the book included certain "wicked, false, feigned, lewd, impious, impure, bawdy, and obscene prints." These were said to represent "men and women with their private parts in most indecent postures and attitudes and . . . in the act of carnal copulation in various attitudes and postures." For this illustrated edition, Bonfanti charged $3.50. That high price, equivalent in today's terms to roughly $65, signaled that it was a relatively luxurious commodity, intended for the well-heeled customers of his fancy goods store.[14]

Bonfanti's sale of Cleland's erotic classic was not an isolated event, either in New York or in neighboring states of New England. As early as 1786, perhaps with the intention of printing his own edition, the master printer Isaiah Thomas, Sr., of Worcester, Massachusetts, sought to buy a copy from an English bookdealer. In 1817 the final inventory of a New Hampshire bookseller named Anson Whipple, who was affiliated with the Thomas firm, disclosed that he had 293 copies of the book in stock. In 1818 a resident of Concord, New Hampshire, penned a complaint to the state governor asserting that several Vermont men had recently published "*Two Large Editions* of a very improper Book, with very obscene plates," which were "circulating in all parts of this and the adjoining States." A second letter identified the improper book as *Memoirs of a Woman of Pleasure.* The same year, another printer from the Worcester area, Peter Holmes, was indicted for publishing Cleland's work. In 1820 a wheelwright named Stillman Howe, likewise from Worcester County, was sentenced to six months at hard labor for selling copies of *Fanny Hill.* Also in 1820, three men from Boston received hundred-dollar fines and one month in prison for selling unidentified obscene books, in all probability *Memoirs of a Woman of Pleasure.* Moreover, on the same day in 1824 that Joseph Bonfanti sold his copy of Cleland's novel at his fancy goods store, a New York printer and bookseller named Joseph McLelland also offered it for sale—a transaction that led to McLelland's arrest as well.[15]

Sexually explicit books like *Fanny Hill* were not the only source of "lust-exciting representations" available in New York markets by McDowall's day. In 1833 a New York commercial paper lamented the proliferation of indecent pictures in store windows around the city. Attributing such displays to unbridled profit seeking, it called on the police to intervene if a sense of modesty did not prevail. "If tradesmen have not sufficient consideration or self-respect to prevent them from descending to such measures for gain, in our opinion the evil should be remedied by the interference of the police." The next year, a New York printer named James Bailey was indicted for "exposing indecent prints in an open window." In 1835 a lithographer by the name of Desobry was accused of selling dozens of obscene pictures from his Broadway print shop to boys, who then peddled them on nearby streets.[16]

A second lithographer, Henry R. Robinson, also began to experiment with the manufacture of lubricious pictures in the 1830s. Rob-

1.3 A. H. Hoffy, Ellen Jewett, *published by H. R. Robinson, 1836.*

COURTESY OF THE AMERICAN ANTIQUARIAN SOCIETY.

inson, who owned a successful store on Courtlandt Street in downtown Manhattan, was active in the New York lithography trade from 1831 until his death in 1850. He was especially well known for his ardent support of the Whig Party and for producing biting caricatures of such Democratic politicians as Andrew Jackson and Martin Van Buren. Many of the political cartoons he created are still admired by collectors today for their exceptional humor, artistry, and sophistication.[17] Along with political caricatures, Robinson published a hand-colored lithograph of the murdered prostitute Helen Jewett in 1836 (Fig 1.3), displaying her in bed after the crime with her breasts and nipples prominently exposed, an image that captured the imagination of New York's tabloid journalists. Another Robinson lithograph that survives from 1837 depicts a dancer named Madame LeComte performing topless. By the following decade this aspect of Robinson's trade in sexual titillation had ballooned into a major segment of his business, enabling him to offer thousands of bawdy prints to customers who patronized his store.[18]

In addition, McDowall's failed campaign against licentious print provided the unwitting inspiration for a novel erotic genre, the metropolitan guide to brothels and prostitutes, at the end of the 1830s. Admittedly, the concept behind such publications was not new. London publishers had begun to produce tour guides to the sexual underworld several years earlier.[19] But the oldest extant guide of this sort to emerge from the New York scene was a short pamphlet passing itself off as a "moral reform directory," along the lines of McDowall's *Magdalen Report.* Published in 1839, it was titled *Prostitution Exposed; or, A Moral Reform Directory, Laying Bare the Lives, Histories, Residences, Seductions &c. of the Most Celebrated Courtezans and Ladies of Pleasure of the City of New York.*[20]

The anonymous author identified himself only as "A Butt Ender." This pseudonym, in part a coarse sexual joke, had important political connotations as well. The slang clearly referred to a defiantly boisterous, unruly faction of egalitarian, prolabor Democrats in the late 1830s (generally known as Locofocos) that was closely linked to emerging machine politics.[21] The Butt Enders probably took their name from the workingmen's style of continually chomping on the "butt end" of a "segar," as popularized by the character Mose, the famous Bowery B'hoy. The rowdy, seemingly brutal style of this gang within the Democratic Party horrified the city's "respectable" classes. One Whig paper bemoaned the thuggish consequences of Butt Endism after the Locofocos captured the mayor's office in 1839: As a "procession of Butt-enders, Rowdies and Loafers, was passing through Broadway . . . one of the young men fell down, and was run over and trampled upon, and bruised so badly as to deprive him of all sensation or signs of life."[22] George Wooldridge, who managed a popular saloon that allegedly also furnished prostitutes for patrons, was a leader of the Democratic Butt Enders.[23] He would become a key player in the "flash" press that surfaced in the city in the early 1840s, and may well have been the anonymous Butt Ender who wrote *Prostitution Exposed.*

Ridicule of moral reform, and particularly of McDowall and the evangelical women who organized in the 1830s to oppose prostitution and the sexual double standard, generated the humor in this pocket-sized pamphlet.[24] Waggishly dedicated to the "Ladies Reform Association for the Suppression of Onanism," it provided reviews of the city's best-known prostitutes, bawdy houses, and places of assignation. In a further mockery of purity reformers, the guide claimed to expose the "evil" of prostitution and began with a table listing the number of known and occasional prostitutes among eighteen occupations of working-class women.[25] But the self-proclaimed Butt Ender quickly moved on to the business at hand: reporting addresses, names, prices, and physical assessments of prostitutes.

Prostitution Exposed guided readers to a gamut of options, from cellar rooms in the Five Points to elegant townhouses on Church Street, from streetwalkers working out of back alleys to courtesans living in grand mansions. The author's choice of pseudonym linked him to the workers' culture of the Bowery and Locofoco politics, but the ironic introduction suggested that his target audience may have been out-of-town businessmen. "This will be an interesting work for those residing at a distance from the city," he advised, "not only because it displays the amount of evil practiced therein, but if they ever visit our busy Gotham, it may be used as a guide to direct them how to shun the dangers." It is even possible that the guide was produced at the behest of successful New York brothel madams. The initial entry was for "Mother Miller," aka Adeline Miller, a prosperous businesswoman who ran a first-class brothel for customers able to pay an

1.4 *Frontispiece, A Butt Ender,* Prostitution Exposed *(New York, 1839).*

COURTESY OF THE AMERICAN ANTIQUARIAN SOCIETY.

FIFTH EDITION—WITH MANY ADDITIONS.

PROSTITUTION EXPOSED;

OR, A

MORAL REFORM DIRECTORY,

LAYING BARE THE

Lives, Histories, Residences, Seductions, &c.

OF THE MOST CELEBRATED

COURTEZANS AND LADIES OF PLEASURE

OF THE CITY OF NEW-YORK,

Together with a Description of the Crime and its Effects,

AS ALSO, OF THE

Houses of Prostitution and their Keepers,

HOUSES OF ASSIGNATION,

THEIR CHARGES AND CONVENIENCES,

AND OTHER PARTICULARS INTERESTING TO THE PUBLIC.

BY A BUTT ENDER.

NEW-YORK:

PUBLISHED FOR PUBLIC CONVENIENCE,

1839.

1.5 Title page, A Butt Ender, Prostitution Exposed *(New York, 1839).*

COURTESY OF THE AMERICAN ANTIQUARIAN SOCIETY.

eye-popping ten to twenty-five dollars a night, exclusive of alcohol ("Champagne $3. Breakfast Free"). Another high-end brothel was described as "a splendid nunnery . . . furnished in the mostly costly style, with pianos, centre-tables, and other furniture, which render it a voluptuous retreat." Yet another was touted as a "splendid establishment . . . well known to the Bowery and Grand-street Dry Goods merchants and their clerks." Allegedly, it was not uncommon for "one of the former to meet his clerk at this house, indulging himself at the expense of his employer's till." While the most select houses known for their "good order" and elegance were described in fawning terms, establishments catering to laborers, sailors, and black men were limned as "unclean" and "wretched." The author noted that the poor Five Points neighborhood held ninety-one bawdy houses and seventeen houses of assignation, which he condemned as "complete hovels of wretchedness" populated by "an indiscriminate mixture of whites and blacks."

In short, *Prostitution Exposed* testified to the increasing visibility of both commercial sex and sexual print in 1830s New York. It also has the distinction of being the earliest surviving book dealing with material of a plainly libidinous nature to be both written and published in the city.[26]

What was the legal climate in which New York's early vendors of erotica operated? The relevant legal concepts, like many of the indecent texts and images that circulated in the city, migrated to the New World from England. Following the American Revolution many state legislatures enacted statutes in which they "received" the English common law, a vast body of precedents and principles, as it existed before the Declaration of Independence. Other states, such as New York, formally accepted the common law in their new state constitutions. The New York constitution of 1777, for instance, declared, "such parts of the common law of England . . . and Great Britain, and of the acts of the legislature of the colony of New York, as together did form the law of the said colony" on April 19, 1775, "shall be and continue the law of this State, subject to such alterations and provisions as the legislature of this State shall, from time to time, make concerning the same." The New York constitution of 1821 reaffirmed the reception of English common law, excluding only those parts that were "repugnant" to the constitution, such as laws relating to the monarchy, an established church, and inherited nobility. In coming to terms with the emergence of a metropolitan market in erotic print, New York officials therefore turned to English law for guidance and ultimately a road map on how to proceed.[27]

For municipal officials who sought a basis for suppressing publications they viewed as morally improper, one alternative was the longstanding common-law tradition of criminal nuisance. Writing in 1769, William Blackstone, the leading authority for nineteenth-century Americans on English law, defined criminal nuisance as a "species of offences against the public order and economical regimen of the state; being either the doing of a thing to the annoyance of all the king's subjects, or the neglecting to do a thing which the common good requires." Criminal nuisances, he continued, were "such inconvenient or troublesome offenses, as annoy the whole community in general," as opposed to private, civil nuisances, which annoyed "merely some particular person." Among the activities cited by Blackstone as public nuisances were obstructing or failing to repair highways, bridges, and rivers, keeping hogs in any city or market town, running a lottery, setting off fireworks, eavesdropping, and keeping a disorderly house.[28]

Early on, American courts agreed with their English predecessors that public displays that violated a community's norms of decency and morality could be punished as criminal nuisances. The Connecticut Supreme Court of Errors, for instance, declared in 1808: "Every public show and exhibition, which outrages decency, shocks humanity, or is contrary to good morals, is punishable at common law." A Boston judge, in ordering the burning in 1835 of hundreds of dollars' worth of imported snuffboxes and music boxes with lascivious pictures inside their lids, likewise made clear that "the law doth not protect obscene prints or other publications injurious to good morals; nor allow them to be sold as an article of traffic, or exhibited for money or for any base purpose—and . . . they ought to be destroyed as a common nuisance." By 1850 the U.S. Supreme Court strongly affirmed not only the power but the obligation of states and localities to suppress moral nuisances: "The suppression of nuisances injurious to public health or morality is among the most important duties of government."[29]

Moreover, local officials had the authority to suppress moral nuisances on the basis of relatively minimal evidence. As one American treatise writer explained, "there are a class of nuisances arising from . . . one's personal conduct that are nuisances *per se,* irrespective of their results and location, and the existence of which only need to be proved in any locality . . . to bring them within the purview of public nuisance." Such nuisances, he continued, involve "those intangible injuries which affect the morality of mankind, and are in derogation of public morals and public decency." Unlike with other forms of criminal nuisance, then, no demonstration of inconvenience or annoyance to the general public, aside from morally offensive conduct, was technically required to substantiate nuisances of a moral nature.[30]

Another option for municipal officials who sought to suppress indecent publications lay in the English common law regarding obscene libel, one of three derivatives of the crime of libel against individuals.[31] In England the royal courts first permitted actions for seditious libel, designed to punish disparaging statements against the monarchy and crown officials, during the seventeenth century. In 1676 they also endorsed an action for blasphemous libel, which was understood as an offense against religion and the established church. About fifty years later, in 1727, the Court of King's Bench first recognized the crime of obscene libel in *Rex v. Curll.* The occasion was the conviction of a notorious British publisher named Edmund Curll for printing an English translation, seductively titled *Venus in the Cloister; or, The Nun in Her Smock,* of Jean Barrin's 1683 work about a group of sexually overheated nuns. Curll's obscenity indictment was also based on his 1718 edition of *A Treatise on the Use of Flogging in Physical and Venereal Affairs.* Just twenty years earlier, the English court had rejected an opportunity to treat the publication of an indecent book as a criminal offense, by ruling that libels against public morality were not actionable in the royal courts, only in ecclesiastical ones. In the *Curll* case, however, the Court of King's Bench reversed course, perhaps motivated by publisher Curll's unabashed flouting of conventional standards of morality.[32]

Nonetheless, some confusion remained within the eighteenth-century English judiciary about whether the publication of a morally indecent book was in and of itself a crime, or whether publications of a criminal nature would need to contain some other kind of blasphemy or heresy, as *Venus in the Cloister* clearly did. Perhaps owing to this uncertainty, English prosecutions for obscene libel were uncommon for most of the century. It was not until the end of the eighteenth century that indictments for expressions of sexual immorality, unconnected with threats to religious orthodoxy, occurred in any significant number. One impetus for the change was a 1787 proclamation by George III, urging authorities to "suppress all loose and licentious prints, books and publications, dispensing poison to the minds of the young and unwary, and to punish publishers and vendors thereof." To enforce the king's will, the moral reformer and abolitionist William Wilberforce established the Proclamation Society, which instituted prosecutions for obscene libel, though with only mixed success. In 1802, however, a more rigorous, scientific organization was launched, the London Society for the Suppression of Vice, which vigorously pursued publishers and dealers of "loose and licentious" literature. In its first fifteen years, it obtained dozens of convictions on charges of obscene libel. During its first half century, the society initiated a total of 159 prosecutions and obtained 154 convictions. Many of the books involved, such as *The Frisky Songster* and *The Voluptuarian Museum*, posed no specific threat to religion.[33]

During the early nineteenth century, English jurists developed a broad definition of obscene libel. Francis Ludlow Holt, a leading English authority, included a chapter titled "Libels against Morality and the Law of Nature" in his influential treatise *The Law of Libel* (1816). As a general matter, Holt explained, "an indictment at common law may be supported for any offence which is against public morals, decency, and good manners." Obscene libel, by extension, "comprehended every species of representation, whether by writing, by picture, or by any manner of sign or substitute, which is indecent and contrary to public order and natural feeling." While blasphemous and seditious libels were understood as attacks on religion and the state, respectively, an obscene representation was perceived as an affront against "public morals" and "good manners," as well as "public order and natural feeling."[34]

English common-law doctrines supporting the prosecution of indecent speech soon insinuated themselves into the law of the new American republic. In 1811, for instance, one John Ruggles challenged the reception of the English common law of blasphemy. Ruggles had been convicted for declaring: "Jesus Christ was a bastard, and his mother must be a whore." In his appeal he relied on a provision in the original New York constitution of 1777 protecting religious liberty, by arguing that it prevented prosecutions to enforce religious orthodoxy.[35]

In deciding *People v. Ruggles,* James Kent, chief judge of the Supreme Court of New York, vigorously defended the reception of the English law of both blasphemous and obscene libel. Although the *Ruggles* case dealt specifically with blasphemy, Kent insisted that the need to prevent liberty from lapsing into licentiousness made the crime of obscene libel, like blasphemy, an indispensable part of the common law that New York had received from England. In the view of a conservative Federalist like Kent, the safety of the republic depended on state enforcement of "moral discipline, and of those principles of virtue, which help to bind society together." In all the countries of the "civilized world," he asserted, "things which corrupt moral sentiment, as obscene actions, prints and writings, and even gross instances of seduction, have . . . been held indictable." Without sanctions against offensive speech such as blasphemy and obscenity, Kent reasoned, civil government would be destroyed, leaving "semi-barbarous" licentiousness to reign in its place.[36]

Four years after the ruling in *Ruggles,* the highest court in Pennsylvania was called upon to decide explicitly whether that state recognized the English common-law crime of obscene libel. In this case of first impression for an American appellate court, a man named Jesse Sharpless and five other men were indicted for obscene libel after they invited several paying customers to view "a certain lewd, wicked, scandalous, infamous, and obscene painting, representing a man in an obscene, impudent, and indecent posture with a woman," which they had on display in a private home.[37]

In appealing their convictions in 1815, the first recorded targets of an American prosecution for obscene libel did not assert, as a modern reader might expect, that their conviction for exhibiting an obscene painting conflicted with their right to freedom of expression under the Pennsylvania constitution. Rather, their lawyer argued that obscene libel was not an indictable offense in Pennsylvania. Taking a narrow view of the most analogous English precedent, *Rex v. Curll*, he argued that a licentious or otherwise immoral exhibition, standing alone, was not actionable under the inherited common law. In England, the lawyer contended, only ecclesiastical courts had the power to penalize moral "improprieties" of the sort Sharpless had committed; the lack of such tribunals in Pennsylvania meant that the state could not punish mere indecency in the absence of specific action by the legislature. Unless and until the legislature chose to act, only the "frowns of society," not the criminal justice system, could discipline Sharpless and his ilk.[38]

Even if one assumed that common-law courts had the power to restrain immorality, Sharpless's counsel argued, they could punish only *public* conduct, not a *private* exhibition like the one Sharpless and his friends had mounted. In this respect, the defense posited a foundational distinction between the authority of governments to regulate public immorality and their inability to regulate private vice. As Blackstone had explained, open and notorious offenses against public decency (like being drunk in public) could be prosecuted criminally, but private vices and immoralities (like being drunk at home) were "beyond the reach of human tribunals."[39]

In an effort to point up the vagueness of the charges and probably also to embarrass the prosecutors by compelling them to describe acts of sexual intercourse, Sharpless's lawyer further asserted that the indictments failed to describe the allegedly obscene content of the picture in question with sufficient specificity. It was not enough to say that the painting represented "a man in an obscene, impudent, and indecent posture with a woman." Rather, "the posture ought to have been so described as to enable the Court to judge, whether or not it was obscene." The obscenity of the picture displayed by his clients, he suggested, was only in the eye of especially "fastidious" beholders. Introducing an argument about the distinction between art and obscenity that would reverberate throughout the nineteenth century (and to the present day), he suggested: "In every public exhibition there are pictures which are viewed with pleasure and approbation, by many respectable and pure minded persons, as noble productions of art, while others more fastidious, consider them improper to be presented to the public eye."[40]

The Pennsylvania Supreme Court decisively rejected each of the defendants' arguments. On the baseline issue—the power of common-law courts to regulate morality—Chief Judge Tilghman broadly proclaimed that under the inherited common law any offense "may be punishable, if in its nature and by its example, it tends to the corruption of morals." Citing *Rex v. Curll,* he ruled that it was not necessary for the Pennsylvania legislature to pass a law specifically banning obscene exhibitions or obscene libel. Nor was it necessary to prove that the immoral picture was actually exhibited in a public place, given that it was shown to "sundry persons for money." As the court explained: "The law is not to be evaded by an artifice of that kind. If the privacy of the room was a protection, all the youth of the city might be corrupted by taking them one by one into a chamber, and there inflaming their passions by the exhibition of lascivious pictures." The essence of the crime lay not in the public or private nature of the display, but in its bad effect—in other words, its tendency to corrupt morality. In addition, Tilghman dismissed the notion that an indictment should have to describe in any detail the obscenity alleged. In a rather futile attempt to protect jury chambers and courtrooms from being sullied by evidence of carnality, he complained, "Must the indictment describe minutely, the attitude and posture of the figures? I am for paying some respect to the chastity of our records."[41]

Though *Sharpless* involved a painting, it was not long before the highest court of Massachusetts, also applying the common law regarding obscene libel, sustained a conviction for selling an obscene printed book—none other than *Memoirs of a Woman of Pleasure.* In 1819 a trial court convicted the Worcester area printer Peter Holmes of publishing Cleland's novel, as well as for printing an obscene picture contained in the book. He was fined the large sum of three hundred dollars and forced to post five hundred dollars' bond to guarantee future good behavior. In challenging his conviction on appeal, Holmes did not raise a constitutional challenge to state censorship, as Ruggles had in New York, or question the legitimacy of common-law morals regulation, as Sharpless had in Pennsylvania. Rather, he argued only that his indictment failed to describe the portions of the book that were alleged to be obscene. In *Commonwealth v. Holmes* (1821), the Supreme Judicial Court of Massachusetts denied Holmes's appeal. Following *Sharpless,* the court declared that it "can never be required that an obscene book and picture should be displayed upon the records of the court."[42] By 1821, then, the appellate decisions in *Ruggles, Sharpless,* and *Holmes* established a broad foundation for government officials in the new republic to pursue common-law prosecutions for obscene libel.

Starting in the 1820s, many state legislatures also began to codify previously unwritten prohibitions on obscenity. Vermont adopted an early criminal statute banning obscenity in 1821, followed by Connecticut in 1834 and Massachusetts in 1835. New York, however, did not enact an antiobscenity statute until 1868, instead relying on the wide-ranging common-law offenses of criminal nuisance and obscene libel.[43]

Despite the heated diatribes of moral reformers like McDowall and the clear-cut legal authority in neighboring states confirming the legitimacy of moral censorship, the circulation of obscene books and prints failed to make much of an impression on criminal justice officials in early nineteenth-century New York. The city's principal criminal court was the Court of General Sessions, which had jurisdiction over all felonies except for capital offenses, as well as over all indictable misdemeanors, including obscene libel and criminal nuisance. Yet the first obscenity prosecution does not appear in the records of the Court of General Sessions until 1824, with the cases against the store proprietor James Bonfanti and the printer Joseph McLelland for selling *Memoirs of a Woman of Pleasure.*[44] Even then, it is unclear exactly what inspired the district attorney at the time, Hugh Maxwell, to pursue these unusual prosecutions. The files in the Bonfanti case include an oath by one Thomas T. Ryder stating that he had gone to Bonfanti's fancy goods store to ask about buying *Memoirs of a Woman of Pleasure* and that Bonfanti had readily replied that he had multiple copies in stock. Although we do not know how openly Bonfanti displayed the book or whether he offered other kinds of erotica for sale, his lack of hesitation suggests he was not concerned about the possibility of arrest.

Under the circumstances, Bonfanti's openness was understandable. At the time the storekeeper made his sale, neither New York authorities nor private antivice societies in the city were devoting energy to sexual censorship, so vendors of erotic books had little cause to engage in subterfuge. A similar candidness had characterized the erotic book trade in London at the beginning of the nineteenth century, when William Wilberforce and other moral reformers founded the London Society for the Suppression of Vice. A member of the society recalled that prosecutions for obscenity were virtually unknown when it first began to investigate the licentious print trade, and therefore "little disguise and concealment were used by dealers of this class."[45]

In drafting the indictments for Bonfanti and McLelland, District Attorney Maxwell undoubtedly was aware not only of the *Sharpless* decision in Pennsylvania but also of the *Holmes* case, especially since Holmes had also been prosecuted for selling *Memoirs of a Woman of Pleasure.* Though the impetus for Maxwell's prosecution of Bonfanti and McLelland remains somewhat mysterious, his reliance on the common law of obscene libel in drawing up the charges is unsurprising, given the available precedents. The essential parts of the bills, copied out in careful handwriting in the original documents, charged that each man:

> being a person of a wicked and depraved mind and disposition and most unlawfully, wickedly and impiously devising contriving and intending to vitiate and corrupt the morals of the citizens of this state and debauch poison and infect the minds of the youth of this state and to bring them into a state of wickedness lewdness, debauchery and brutality . . . did unlawfully, wickedly and impiously sell and publish and cause and procure to be sold and published a certain wicked, nasty, bawdy and obscene libel entitled 'Memoirs of a woman of pleasure" in which said libel are contained amongst other things, divers wicked, false, feigned, lewd, impious, impure, gross, bawdy and obscene matters . . . to the high displeasure of Almighty God to the scandal and reproach of the Christian Religion in contempt of the People of this State and their laws to the evil example of all others in like

> case offending and against the peace of the people of the State of New York and their dignity.

This language followed word for word the precedent included in an 1816 English guide for criminal law practitioners, Joseph Chitty's *A Practical Treatise on the Criminal Law.* Chitty in turn borrowed his formulation from the prosecution of a London bookseller named Edward Rich, who had also been indicted for selling *Memoirs of a Woman of Pleasure.*[46]

In the Bonfanti case, the accused initially pleaded not guilty and was released on bail. A few months later, his counsel, a future district attorney for New York County named Thomas Phoenix, substituted a guilty plea. Phoenix consequently made no effort to challenge Bonfanti's prosecution on constitutional or other grounds. Eight months after his arrest, Bonfanti received a suspended sentence and was released without fine or imprisonment on a promise that he would behave himself in the future. The other defendant indicted for selling *Memoirs of a Woman of Pleasure,* Joseph McLelland, followed the same strategy and also received a suspended sentence. Thereafter, the two men either stopped selling the condemned book or became more circumspect about how they offered it.[47]

For the next decade, obscenity cases in the Court of General Sessions were nonexistent. Indeed, from the Bonfanti and McLelland cases in 1824 to the early 1840s, the only other obscenity indictment in the records of the Court of General Sessions was the prosecution of the printer James Bailey for the exposure and sale of indecent pictures in 1834. Though Bailey was tried and convicted on the charge, the outcome was the same as in the Bonfanti and McClelland cases a decade before—a thirty-day sentence, which the Court of General Sessions suspended.[48] The negligible level of prosecutorial activity in the area of obscenity contrasted with a far greater number of prosecutions for other perceived offenses to morals. In the period between 1820 and 1840, for instance, the case files of the Court of General Sessions contain dozens of indictments each year related to gambling and prostitution.[49]

How do we account for this relative lack of interest in suppressing or punishing commerce in erotic representations? The answer lies in two factors, one related to the general structure of law enforcement and the other to the nature of the erotic print trade. In general, criminal justice in early nineteenth-century New York was heavily dominated by private prosecution of crime. In other words, criminal prosecutions usually arose when a private citizen who had suffered a physical injury or pecuniary loss filed a complaint. Rather than independently pursuing government interests, constables, marshals, district attorneys, and other agents of law enforcement simply reacted to the initiatives of private parties. The strength of private prosecution and the relative weakness of public instruments of law enforcement meant that cases involving larceny and assault and battery far outweighed morals prosecutions in the early nineteenth century. A contemporaneous estimate by the antebellum court reporter Jacob Wheeler stated that prosecutions for keeping a disorderly house (usually a brothel) constituted 5 percent of all indictments for 1823 and 1824, whereas cases involving larcenies totaled nearly 45 percent and those relating to assaults and batteries constituted 40 percent. A recent scholarly sampling of prosecutions in the New York Court of General Sessions between 1800 and 1865 similarly found that only 5 percent involved "public order prosecutions and quality of life offences," while a full 65 percent involved property cases and 30 percent involved crimes against the person, such as assault and battery.[50]

The few morals offenses that were prosecuted, such as keeping a disorderly house, selling liquor without a license, and insuring numbers in a lottery, were usually pursued by individuals who claimed to have suffered tangible harm. These individuals might include neighbors disturbed by noise from adjacent bawdy houses; government officials deprived of fees by unlicensed saloons and grog shops; or people who lost money gambling on cards and lotteries. By comparison with prosecutions for property offenses, the penalties imposed in morals cases were generally light or nonexistent, an outcome suggesting that the central function of such actions was primarily administrative, not criminal or moral.[51] In other words, early nineteenth-century morals prosecutions were more akin to civil suits to abate particular local nuisances or to achieve private settlements of disputes between victims and defendants than to public actions to punish criminals or reform morality on a grand scale.

The circulation of obscene publications, then, had no clear place within this system of law enforcement. It differed from property crimes, and even other morals offences, in that it failed to produce a readily identifiable victim of the type recognized in the everyday practice of criminal law in New York courts: a person who had lost money or goods, an individual who had suffered a battery, or a neighbor who had been deprived of peace and quiet.[52] The evidence from the Bonfanti case, for instance, suggests that lewd books were available primarily to men of means who knew how and where to inquire for them. Because of the absence of concrete physical or monetary injury from the sale of erotic publications, private parties had little practical motivation to pursue obscenity prosecutions. Rather, the harm inflicted by obscenity implicated more ephemeral, amorphous categories: public decency, public morality, public order. In theory, of course, the common-law principles elucidated by jurists like James Kent in the *Ruggles* blasphemy case provided strong support for sanctions against publications that had a tendency to corrupt morality regardless of whether they had caused injury to any particular person. Indeed, the doctrines of obscene libel and criminal nuisance were specifically designed to allow government officials to suppress indecent expression even in the absence of tangible injury, in order to protect "morality, or the law of nature."[53]

These formal legal principles had little effect, however, on the reality of New York life. Before the institution of a salaried police force in 1845, constables, marshals, and night watchmen often received a substantial part of their income from rewards for recovering stolen property. As a result, those workers had little economic motivation to pursue such nonproperty crimes as selling obscene literature. Moreover, in an era of limited municipal resources, the main function of New York prosecutors was to facilitate the redress by private parties of specific economic and physical injuries and the abatement of particular neighborhood nuisances, not to protect public decency. The lack of tangible injury from the sale of sexual publications, coupled with a government apparatus ill equipped to enforce public morality, created a legal culture that offered few incentives for the prosecution of obscenity.[54]

The behavior of the city legislative body, the Common Council, underscores the general tolerance for, or at least indifference to, the circulation of lewd publications in early nineteenth-century New York. The only time the council addressed the issue of obscenity was in 1837, when the Joint Select Committee on the Reorganization of the Police Department, convened by the Board of Aldermen, recommended that the council ask the state legislature to adopt an "Act for the More Effectual Punishment of Crime in the City and County of New York." An animating principle of the committee's report was the need to expand municipal morals enforcement by adding a police force dedicated to prevention rather than simply detection of crime.[55]

Along with banning gambling dens, brothels, houses of assignation, and "any other disorderly house or any public nuisance," the proposed statute would have outlawed the display of "obscene books, paintings or prints . . . kept for sale in any house or premises." Offenders faced proposed fines of up to five hundred dollars and a year in prison, a rather steep penalty, given the rarity of municipal obscenity prosecutions up to that point. In certain respects, the recommended law was a nonevent, in that it simply codified preexisting common-law doctrines allowing government officials to punish obscenity. But it also gave the police significant new powers to search, seize, and destroy obscene publications on a summary basis. Solely on a sworn complaint about an alleged public nuisance, magistrate judges were authorized to issue search warrants empowering any constable or marshal to enter a disorderly house and "take possession of all [obscene] books, paintings or prints, and the plates used in making them." Police officials were directed to take the seized items to the Court of General Sessions, which could order that they be destroyed. Still, the presence of obscenity was clearly not a legislative priority for municipal politicians in 1837. The Joint Select Committee tabled the proposal, and the Common Council took no further action.[56]

In the coming years, enterprising New York newspaper editors, taking their cue from the enduring popularity of *Memoirs of a Woman of Pleasure* and the recent success of *Prostitution Exposed*, would further develop the thrills and agonies of prostitution as a subject of commercial writing. The new print culture was spearheaded not by high-end importers like Bonfanti, who catered to the elite, but by young men of the Butt Ender variety, often Democratic Party hoipolloi, who were associated with the New York world of lowbrow entertainment and raunchy sporting life. This was a milieu where workingmen cavorted with prizefighters, pimps, gang leaders, and an assortment of disreputable "loafers" and "rowdies." In the process, these men (and at least one brothel madam who financed them) created a new genre of sexual journalism. Their innovations would also provoke the city's first sustained efforts to mobilize the common law of obscenity against an ascendant commercial culture of "licentious" and "obscene" print.

Chapter 2

Flash Weeklies

The decade following publication of John McDowall's 1831 *Magdalen Report* brought profound changes in the culture and politics of the fledgling metropolis. In the cultural sphere, a thriving marketplace for salacious commercial entertainment came into being. The city teemed with rowdy theaters, saloons, dance halls, and oyster cellars—where female sexual charms were often on display and sometimes for sale—not to mention an abundance of brothels designed to appeal to men of a variety of classes, tastes, and occupations. New forms of politics emerged as well. Before 1840 an older political order held sway, in which working-class men generally deferred to the leadership of upper-class merchants and other wealthy men who were charged with promoting the "common good." Even during the 1830s, when universal suffrage theoretically opened the polity to virtually all white males, the patrician class continued to dominate municipal offices. By the early 1840s, however, a prolonged economic depression and widespread unemployment stemming from the Panic of 1837 helped unravel the old-line elites' monopoly on political power and usher in an age of mass party politics.[1]

A vivid manifestation of the changing styles of culture and politics that had surfaced in New York in the early 1840s was the appearance of a new genre of male-oriented, sexually suggestive newspapers, collectively known as the flash press. In the parlance of the day, to be a "flash man" was to flaunt a flamboyant, flashy, devil-may-care personal style, a rakish approach to women, and an intimate knowledge of the urban demimonde. In addition, the term suggested an association with shady or criminal elements of sporting culture, such as gamblers, counterfeiters, pimps, and panel thieves (who robbed men while they were having sex with prostitutes). Categorizing a newspaper as "flash" therefore signaled not just that the proprietors had stepped outside the bounds of respectable society by embracing sexual hedonism. It implied also that they willingly rubbed elbows with elements of the criminal underworld, and perhaps directly participated in it.[2] Indeed, the editors of the flash press soon became outlaws themselves, when they sparked the city's first wave of obscenity prosecutions in the early 1840s.

At their inception, flash papers defiantly flouted middle-class standards of respectability, temperance, and discipline, by promoting instead a libertine ethic of sensual pleasure for the male reader. Beginning with the *Sunday Flash* in 1841, they championed a variety of popular, rough-and-tumble male leisure activities: drinking in saloons, mingling in the pits of Bowery theaters, heckling at bare-knuckle boxing matches and cock fights, hanging out in gambling "hells," and frolicking at firemen's balls. Papers of this kind also promoted prostitution by featuring biographies of notorious New York courtesans and offering detailed descriptions of the city's many brothels. In this way, flash newspapers served as erotic tour guides for young men on the prowl for sexual pleasure, both in real life and as imagined through reading. In addition, such publications routinely trafficked in sexual gossip, often as a prelude to blackmail.[3]

In essence, the rise of the flash press reflected a deep cultural conflict over the meaning of manhood, especially young manhood, in a rapidly expanding capitalist economy.[4] Just as new middle-class constructions of gender presented a domesticated, somewhat feminized paradigm of masculinity focused on the need for self-restraint, self-discipline, and moral conduct as a key to economic success, the flash weeklies stoked a desire for its opposite. They represented a public sphere of male entertainment in which men obtained unfettered sensual gratification, free from the dictates of market capitalism and evangelical moral reform. In this world, moreover, women figured not as moral authorities, but as barmaids, cigar girls, or prostitutes.

Although the tone of the flash papers was rarely explicitly political, their emergence around 1840 was closely linked to the political empowerment of non-elite men and the increasingly egalitarian, anti-aristocratic ethos of the city's official culture. Intense competition between the Whig and Democratic Parties for voters in the early 1840s decisively oriented the Democratic political stronghold, Tammany Hall, away from placating the forces of wealth and aristocracy and toward securing the votes of workingmen and the poor. The rise of a Jacksonian Democratic political machine, rooted in ward-level political organizing, also created opportunities for men of humble origins, including unsavory party hacks and political gang leaders, to play a role in public life. Whig political organizing soon followed suit, creating its own machine of colorful gang leaders, street toughs, and ward-level party faithful.[5]

The irreverent, rabble-rousing editors of the flash press sought to capitalize on this antielitist, democratic momentum in the city's political life. George Wooldridge of the *Sunday Flash* personified the cross-pollination between the sporting world of commercial recreation and the public sphere of machine politics. A key figure in both arenas, he played multiple roles as the manager of Ellsler's Saloon, a drinking establishment and occasional brothel popular among Tammany regulars, the leader of the rowdy political gang the Butt Enders, and the editor of at least five sporting papers. (Under Wooldridge's aegis, the *Sunday Flash* and *True Flash* of 1841 morphed into the *Whip and Satirist of New York and Brooklyn* and the *Libertine of New York* in 1842 and then the *New York Sporting Whip* in 1843.) And yet it was clear that flash editors were first and foremost in the business of entertainment, not political activism. They rarely espoused political positions in their papers. Instead, they channeled their libertine energies into satirical cultural critiques of emergent middle-class values that emphasized domesticity, privacy, male self-control, and female purity.

In stylistic terms, the flash papers represented a mixture of imitation and innovation. A chief inspiration came from lubricious London journals like William Benbow's *Rambler's Magazine* (1822), Edward Duncombe's *Original Rambler's Magazine* (1827), and Renton Nicholson's *Town* (1837–1842). These papers printed articles on prostitution, biographies of prostitutes, transcripts of sensational trials involving allegations of sodomy, adultery, and other sexual transgressions, bawdy jokes, notices about entertaining goings-on in the metropolis, and comic engravings with sexual undertones.[6] Indeed, some of the early illustrations in the New York flash press were shamelessly pirated from London sources. Two issues of the *Whip*, for instance, featured on their front pages the engravings *Females in Masquerade*, accompanied by an article warning men about prostitutes who cross-dressed as dandies, and *The French Barmaid*, accompanied by a story about fashionable nightlife in the city. Both pictures had appeared in earlier issues of the *Town*.[7]

The other major inspiration came from a distinctively American product, the mass penny dailies.[8] With the arrival of the *New York Sun*, founded by the twenty-three-year-old printer Benjamin Day, in 1833, the *New York Transcript* in 1834, and James Gordon Bennett's

New York Herald in 1835, sex became a focus of journalistic attention for the first time. The city's previous dailies, generally known as the commercial press, mainly represented the interests of an elite group of merchants and professionals who had dominated both commerce and politics in the early decades of the nineteenth century. Most readers purchased commercial periodicals by subscription; at ten dollars a year, the cost of a subscription, which equaled one week's wages for even well-paid, skilled artisans, made such papers a luxury. In addition, the stodgy mercantile papers strenuously avoided risqué topics, humorous anecdotes, and sexual scandals (unless they related to a prominent political figure) in favor of dry political and economic news. Nor did they cover sporting events, theater openings, or local criminal proceedings.[9]

The penny press made a sharp break with its staid commercial competitors, developing in the process a new mass audience for newspapers.[10] An entrepreneurial editor like James Gordon Bennett realized that he could attract readers by enlivening the conventional business and political news with urban stories of sexual titillation, erotic scandal, and sexual violence culled from legal cases. He pioneered the practice of assigning beat reporters to scour police offices and courtrooms for material on criminal prosecutions involving sex, such as murders inspired by jealousy. Civil suits for seduction, criminal conversation (in other words, when a husband sued for damages from his wife's seducer), and divorce also provided fodder for scores of sensational, voyeuristic articles, in which the intimate lives of New Yorkers were laid bare to public gaze.

Political figures had long experienced unwelcome journalistic attention directed to their private lives. Thomas Jefferson and Andrew Jackson had come in for particularly rough treatment on this score, though they used such tactics themselves against their political enemies.[11] But the penny press extended the subjects of sexual gossip beyond political figures holding public office, to include private citizens who had somehow become caught up in the legal system. Charles Dickens, in his novel *Martin Chuzzlewit* (1843–44), famously satirized the prurience and intrusiveness of the New York tabloids by imagining this street scene among urban newsboys: "'Here's this morning's New York Sewer!' cried one. 'Here's this morning's New York Stabber! Here's the New York Family Spy! Here's the New York Private Listener! Here's the New York Peeper! Here's the New York Plunderer! Here's the New York Keyhole Reporter! Here's the New York Rowdy Journal! Here's all the New York papers!'"[12]

Reporting of this sort soon prompted a storm of criticism that the penny dailies were indecent and obscene.[13] Rather comically, the rival editors of the leading penny papers even took turns accusing one another of immorality and obscenity for their criminal reports. The *Herald*, for instance, early on charged the *Sun* with printing "filth, indecency, immorality and obscenity under the name of the Police Reports."[14] All the while, the *Herald* served up more and more titillating police news that scandalized genteel merchants, professionals, and publishers. Nonetheless, though Bennett was frequently accused of printing obscenity under the guise of police reports and was in and out of court on both civil and criminal libel charges, he never faced an indictment for obscenity. Nor did any of his colleagues in the 1830s penny press.

By the end of the decade, the reading public that had been created for periodical entertainment by papers like the *Herald* opened up novel opportunities for literate young men hoping to turn a profit by putting out a newspaper. But the same improvements in printing technology that facilitated the mass circulation of the penny papers in the first place caused an increase in the amount of capital necessary to purchase the most sophisticated equipment, such as steam-driven cylinder presses. For instance, while Bennett launched the

Herald in 1835 with only five hundred dollars, the start-up costs for a daily paper in 1840 could run as high as ten thousand dollars. As a result, the price of running a mass-produced daily became too steep for men without access to conventional sources of financing.[15] By comparison, the capital needed to found a small weekly paper was much lower. In other words, the high capitalization of penny dailies like the *Sun* and the *Herald* drove aspiring but underfinanced newspaper entrepreneurs who were eager to capitalize on their success to develop smaller niche weeklies with content that was riskier and even less respectable. One product of this dynamic was the creation of a new class of flash journals that specialized in reporting on the city's thriving sexual underworld.

The flash weeklies, although they drew on aspects of the penny dailies, were distinctive in discussing sex much more openly and expansively. They specialized in lavish descriptions of the milieu of New York prostitution, for which they provided a veritable directory to the best and worst prostitutes, brothels, and madams in the city. Many articles dwelled on the splendid physiques and charming personalities of individual courtesans. A typical item from the *Weekly Rake* praised several harlots who had paraded by its office window that week:

> Maria J___s was decked in all the finery the dry goods and jewelry stores of this city can afford. Her residence is Green street, and she has, (we have her word for it) only three gentlemen visitors. She is a very fine looking woman of thirty, about the middle size . . . Sarah F___h is a lovely, light, tripping little flaxen-haired, blue-eyed Cyprian, about four months on the *pave*, and of so innocent a look and manner, that you would suppose her of any other profession, dressed in the right manner, tasty and not gaudy.[16]

In the case of "Maria J___s," the writer informed readers (and her potential clients) not only of her location and age but also about the number of customers she already serviced. Similarly, an 1842 issue of the *Whip* included an admiring description of New York's finest prostitutes during one of their frequent promenades in the public park along the Battery: "The elegant Mary Smith was there—dressed in the most splendid costume we ever saw . . . The superb Mary Capito, far more blooming than ever, dressed in the height of fashion."[17] The life stories of celebrity courtesans seemed to hold a special fascination. The *Sunday Flash*, for instance, ran an eighteen-part series, Lives of the Nymphs. Each number featured a lengthy biographical sketch of a prominent New York prostitute.

Flash weeklies also delivered sexual entertainment through ribald humor that subverted bourgeois standards of female modesty and decorum. These jokes often came in visual form, emblazoned on the covers of the papers. A characteristic engraving on the first page of Thomas Meighan's *Weekly Rake*, bearing the caption "A Street View" (shown in Figure 2.1), portrayed a prostitute after she had been run down in the street by a pig, an incident that caused her to fall on her back with her bare thighs and legs thrust in the air.[18] While a top-hatted "gentleman" bends over the woman's splayed legs for a better view, the unruly pig dashes off. Under the caption "Nuisances," the adjacent article complained: "There are a number of nuisances at present existing in this city which should be abated. Look at the horrible situation of that poor female, and behold her agonized countenance. Years will not efface the remembrance of the occurrence from her mind, or soothe the pangs inflicted by that hog."[19] In effect, the paper ridiculed municipal authorities for wasting their time suppressing harmless sexual entertainment like the *Weekly Rake*, instead of preventing *real* nuisances in the city—wild hogs that assaulted women in the street. Another image, in Charles Scott's *Flash*,

2.1 *"A Street View,"* Weekly Rake, *July 9, 1842, 1.*

COURTESY OF THE AMERICAN ANTIQUARIAN SOCIETY.

depicted a man consorting with a "celebrated married lady, of this city," under an umbrella in Hoboken's Elysian Fields, a popular tryst-ing place for working-class New Yorkers and for courtesans and their customers. In the picture and accompanying story, the woman's cuck-olded husband stumbles upon the couple in flagrante delicto and shoots his wife's paramour in the buttocks. Under their umbrella, but clearly visible, lies a copy of the *Flash*.[20]

Flash papers did not simply disseminate embarrassing personal information culled from police offices or court proceedings, as legal reporters for the penny press did. Rather, such publications circulated sexual gossip about private citizens gathered through contacts in brothels, saloons, and houses of assignation. Even more scandalously, flash editors repeatedly threatened individuals with publication of details of their "private" indiscretions unless they paid hush money. Testifying before a committee of the British Parliament on newspaper regulation in 1851, the *New York Tribune* editor Horace Greeley highlighted the role of blackmail in the operations of the flash press. As he pointed out, "there are weekly papers got up from time to time, called the *Scorpion*, the *Flash*, the *Whip*, and so on," whose modus operandi was "to extort money from parties who can be threatened with exposure of immoral practices or for visiting infamous houses."[21]

William Joseph Snelling (1804–1848) and George Wilkes (1817–1884) launched the first entry in the flash genre in August 1841, the *Sunday Flash*. Soon thereafter, they invited George Wooldridge (1818–1868) to join their partnership. Together, they appeared on the masthead as "Scorpion, Startle, & Sly, Editors and Proprietors." Over the next two years, a succession of imitators followed in the path of the *Sunday Flash*, among them Wooldridge's and George Washington Dixon's *True Flash*, Wooldridge's *Whip and Satirist of New-York and Brooklyn*, *Libertine of New York*, and *New York Sporting Whip*, Thomas Meighan's *Weekly Rake*, and Charles Scott's *Flash*. Circulation statistics vary, but they evidently ranged from a low of four thousand to a high of ten thousand for the *Whip* in the summer of 1842.[22]

Snelling, the oldest of the founding editors at thirty-seven years of age, had already had a varied literary and journalistic career. Among other things, his life conveys something about the difficulties of making a living as a professional writer in the antebellum era. Born in

Boston in 1804, he attended West Point for three years before dropping out, then traveled to the Northwest, where he lived with Indians and worked as a fur trapper and a translator of Dakota. Upon his return to Boston, the highly literate Snelling published a well-received collection of short stories, *Tales of the Northwest* (1830), about his experiences on the frontier and among Indian tribes. While working from time to time as a Whig editor and freelance writer, he became an early ally of William Lloyd Garrison and David and Lydia Maria Child in the antislavery cause. In 1831, enraged by the duplicitous conduct of his employer, a wealthy publisher, the feisty author wrote a scathing poetic satire on the literary establishment called *Truth: A New Year's Gift for Scribblers.* In the years that followed, Snelling's luck turned, as he fell prey to alcoholism, became the target of a battery of libel suits stemming from his journalism, and as a final blow suffered imprisonment for public drunkenness.[23]

Finding his way to New York, Snelling emerged in 1838 as the co-editor of George Washington Dixon's artisan-oriented weekly, the *Polyanthos and Fire Department Album.* Dixon, a native of Richmond, Virginia, was then in his mid-thirties and was already a well-known character among urban workingmen. He was especially popular for his famed portrayals of "Zip Coon," a black dandy, which earned him a posthumous reputation as the "father of blackface minstrelsy."[24] Under Dixon and Snelling's editorship, the *Polyanthos* provided additional entertainment for working-class audiences by printing comic reports on alleged sexual wrongdoing among the city's religious and economic elite. It took an especially harsh stance toward wealthy libertines who seduced and betrayed lower-class women.[25]

Wilkes, a twenty-four-year-old man about town, had far less literary experience than Snelling had but was eager to pursue a career in journalism. The son of an obscure New York cabinetmaker of Irish descent, he, like Snelling, probably had little in the way of financial resources when starting the *Sunday Flash.* He was affiliated with radical working-class circles in the Democratic Party through his involvement with the labor activist and proletarian political hero Mike Walsh, and he later became a reporter and editor for Walsh's journal, the *Subterranean.* Wilkes was also a clever writer, with a temperament that was at once ambitious, adventurous, and entrepreneurial.[26]

The third editor, Wooldridge, also twenty-four, came from a family that operated refectories. He apparently had no literary background, but he was the manager of Ellsler's Saloon, the drinking establishment, oyster bar, and occasional assignation house frequented by Democratic Party operatives and principals in New York's commercial vice trade. (In 1842, the district attorney for New York County marked an advertisement for Ellsler's Saloon in the *Sunday Flash* with the notation "Bawdy House.") As such, Wooldridge brought extensive contacts among Democratic politicos, "shoulder-hitters" in political gangs, prostitutes, and brothel madams.[27]

In court testimony in 1842, Wooldridge shed light on the business practices employed at the start-up stage of the *Sunday Flash,* as well as on its marginal financial condition. He recalled that Wilkes had visited him after a couple of issues of the paper had been printed and had told him that it needed additional investment to stay afloat. According to Wooldridge, Wilkes also explained that he and Snelling (whom Wilkes touted as a talented writer) had established the *Sunday Flash* in order to levy blackmail. They had already obtained fifty dollars from a Mr. Wyckoff, who was described as "an ardent friend" of Fanny Elssler, a famous Viennese ballerina whose name graced the saloon and adjoining assignation house that Wooldridge ran; another blackmail scheme against a Mr. Levison was already under way. Wilkes added that if Wooldridge would contribute a small amount of capital, he could become a partner and receive a share of the profits.

The three men evidently obtained financing for major expenses from a wealthy brothel madam, Adeline Miller. When Snelling retained the services of a job printer named William Applegate (the printer of choice for many of the flash papers), it was Miller who provided a guarantee of payment. As Wooldridge told the jury, the next day he gave Wilkes "$7 or $8 . . . , became a partner, and did the outdoor business."[28]

In effect, the three partners allocated the tasks of running the paper according to their abilities. Snelling and Wilkes handled the writing and editing, with Snelling as lead writer and Wilkes as lead editor. Wooldridge was responsible for marketing, bookkeeping, and researching background material for the stories. Snelling later charged that Wooldridge, in his capacity as the proprietor of a saloon and part-time bawdy house, was mainly supposed to collect evidence for blackmail or, as Snelling put it, "to do the dirty work of the Flash."[29] The partners then split whatever profits they reaped from sales of the paper and from their probably more lucrative blackmail schemes.

Within a matter of months, the appearance of the new medium precipitated an unusual municipal effort to suppress it. After several decades of restraint and de facto protection for commerce in erotic books and pictures, the district attorney and grand jury for New York County began to take an interest in restraining the circulation of sexually themed newspapers in the fall of 1841. Over the next two years, the authorities instituted a series of indictments for obscenity against the publishers and editors of the flash press.

The *Sunday Flash* initially came to the attention of public officials through a complaint by a Wall Street broker named Myer Levy that he had been libeled in an October 17, 1841, issue. The article in question, "Big Levy," consisted of an antisemitic rant invoking race, class, and religion, in a volatile mixture. Among other things, the article accused Levy of patronizing many prostitutes and of being a "practical amalgamationist," because of his alleged predilection for sex with women of color.[30] Following the longstanding tradition of private prosecution, Levy had responded by swearing out a complaint of libel against the editors before a police magistrate. As was typical in such cases, the complaint was referred to the district attorney, James R. Whiting, for further action. Whiting then drafted an indictment charging the three editors with criminal libel arising out of the "Big Levy" story.[31]

Up to now, nothing out of the ordinary had occurred in the chain of legal events. In addition to the libel indictment, however, Whiting included an unusual second count charging the three proprietors with "Publishing an Obscene Paper." The basis of the obscenity claim was a second article, a biography of New York courtesan Amanda Green. This piece presented Green as a victim of seduction, forced to turn to prostitution at a brothel on West Broadway after her mother threw her out of the house for having sex with her lover in the attic.[32] Five days after the October 17 issue of the *Sunday Flash* hit the streets, the grand jury returned indictments on both the libel and obscene libel counts that led to the arrests of Snelling, Wilkes, and Wooldridge.

Emboldened by his success with the obscenity charges against the *Sunday Flash* editors, Whiting swiftly went after Snelling's former colleague, George Washington Dixon, the editor of *Dixon's Polyanthos,* by securing an indictment against him for publishing an obscene paper.[33] Like the *Sunday Flash, Dixon's Polyanthos* had begun to run biographical features on celebrity prostitutes. It even reprinted excerpts from *Prostitution Exposed,* the erotic tour guide of 1839, which provided the names, locations, and descriptions of numerous New York whorehouses.[34]

After the dearth of obscenity cases in preceding decades, the floodgates of moral censorship seemed to have opened. Over the next year and a half, Whiting obtained more than a dozen additional obscenity indictments against the editors of six different flash periodicals—the *Whip & Satirist of New-York and Brooklyn*, the *Libertine of New York*, the *Whip*, the *Weekly Rake*, the *New York Sporting Whip*, and a new incarnation of the *Flash*.

What caused the district attorney to initiate obscenity prosecutions against the publishers and editors of the flash press? After all, the records of the New York Court of General Sessions document only three indictments for obscenity over the preceding half-century.[35] Moreover, municipal authorities had never instituted obscenity charges against the proprietors of newspapers, including the publishers of the penny press, despite widespread outcry that they trafficked in scurrilous and licentious material.

An important part of the answer lies in the background of the district attorney and the grand jurors who were responsible respectively for drafting and presenting the indictments. Although the right to vote for the mayor and the common council was no longer limited to property owners, the city's legal system continued to reflect a strong class bias. In 1841, rather than being a popularly elected official, the district attorney for New York County was still appointed by the Governor's Council of Appointment, subject to the approval of judges on the Court of General Sessions.[36] The officeholder at the time, James Whiting, was a conservative Democrat who had been a lawyer and director for a powerful local bank before his selection as district attorney. As a representative of banking interests, he had close connections with the city's professional and commercial elite. Indeed, his appointment to the office of district attorney in 1838 had outraged the populist, antibank factions of the municipal Democratic Party. With prominent business allies but little record of public service,

Whiting seemed to symbolize the dominance of capital over labor and the antithesis of egalitarian, Locofoco politics.[37]

Similarly, the grand jurors for the Court of General Sessions were not selected randomly from an extensive jury pool, as they are today. Rather, the city's Board of Supervisors, which consisted of the mayor, the recorder, and the aldermen, drew up a list of six hundred eligible citizens, all of whom were required by law to be substantial property holders. Officials selected potential grand jurors by lot from the list and empaneled a body comprising between sixteen and twenty-four qualifying individuals. The property requirements for eligibility, together with the secrecy of the proceedings, led to frequent charges that grand juries were biased in favor of commercial and professional elites. As one egalitarian critic protested, "we demand *open sessions,* that we may know hereafter how the fourteen hundred wealthy men in the city of New York, who alone are eligible to the service, deal with the lives, the liberties, and the sacred honors of the remaining quarter million of their poorer fellow citizens."[38]

Other important clues appear in an article titled "Scurrilous Prints," which appeared in a self-consciously high-minded penny paper just a few days before the grand jury indicted the editors of the *Sunday Flash.* It complained that the city was currently teeming with "a loathsome herd of venal and licentious scribblers," who were more than willing "to disturb the peace of the best man in the community" for cash. As a result, even "persons of the most undoubted honor, perfectly free of all vice," could become "objects of attack" for these "ruffian robbers of private character" and their "libidinous sheets" if the citizens behaved indiscreetly or displayed an "excess of levity." Calling on criminal authorities to take legal action, the author expressed hope that "two vigilant ministers in the temple of justice, Mayor Morris and District Attorney Whiting, [would] promptly adopt measures to prevent the city from being longer polluted and disgraced by the publication of these obscene and disgusting newspapers, and to punish all those concerned in any way in publishing them."[39]

Of the factors precipitating obscenity prosecutions against the flash press, anxiety about the ways in which this new medium of communication invaded elite conceptions of privacy, especially for the purpose of blackmail, took center stage. The ability of a defiantly disreputable underclass with access to printing presses to destroy the reputations of prominent citizens weighed on the mind of the district attorney as he prepared his first obscenity case against the editors of the *Sunday Flash* in 1841. Next to an apology in the paper for slurs it had printed about Hiram Marsh, another stockbroker, Whiting made the notation "Hush money probably paid." A second article, threatening to reveal the illegitimate business of an auctioneer, "Mr. Jones of Broad street," prompted the district attorney to write, "For black mail" in the margins. At the subsequent trial of the editors of the *Sunday Flash*—the first trial of an obscenity case in New York County—Whiting got Wooldrige, who had turned state's evidence in exchange for dismissal of the charges against him, to admit on the stand that the paper had been conceived as an instrument for blackmail.[40]

But what could authorities do about this practice? Though it was regarded as an unsavory way to make a living, extorting money by threatening to injure a person's reputation was not yet recognized as a crime in New York State.[41] As a result, public officials and private citizens who wished to prevent it had no clear legal recourse. One indirect way to seek redress for embarrassing items published in scandal-mongering newspapers was to initiate charges for criminal libel; the strategy was quite common. Alluding to the frequency of libel prosecutions against newspapermen in the antebellum era, sensational novelist and occasional flash editor George Thompson remarked: "An editor who has never been imprisoned for libel, may be considered a green-horn in his profession."[42]

Whiting, however, had recently learned the limitations of libel prosecutions for taming unruly journalists. In 1839 he had obtained an indictment against minstrel star and tabloid editor George Washington Dixon for printing sexual gossip in his spicy proletarian weekly, the *Polyanthos and Fire Department Album.* In the offending article, the raffish Dixon poked fun at the "criminal conversation" of a wealthy auctioneer and middle-aged bachelor, Roland Minturn, with a Mrs. Roome, the wife of a sea captain. Auctioneers were regarded as aristocratic figures in the antebellum urban economy and Minturn was a member of one of New York's most prominent commercial families. As a result, he made an attractive target for popular abuse. Here is the wry notice that Dixon published about the Minturn affair:

> *Crim Con.*—An auctioneer handling the wrong goods . . . Last week we gave our readers the piquant case of the Roman Priest, and now we have an auctioneer to dish up. A certain knight of the hammer, and whose cry of going, going, going is well exercised, whose *Mint* of money might be supposed to have a tendency to *Turn* him to temptation . . . was seen leaving a certain married lady's apartment, she and he being in dishabille . . . The unfortunate husband was an eyewitness of the departure of our hero of the hammer.[43]

Note how Dixon pointed out the "piquant" quality of the lewd gossip he had to "dish up" for his readers, his thinly veiled accusation of Minturn's adulterous connection with another man's wife, and his saucy, sarcastic treatment of Minturn as "our hero of the hammer."

Tragically, Minturn, "while in a state of mental depression" brought on by Dixon's exposé, jumped to his death from a roof. When Minturn's enraged brothers filed a police complaint against Dixon, Whiting quickly produced an indictment. Significantly, despite the salacious tenor of the article, he classified the offense only as libel, not as obscene libel. But if Whiting and the Minturn family intended to use the law of libel to suppress scandal and teach insolent newspaper editors a lesson, they got exactly the opposite result. By the end of the case, Dixon's cheeky journalistic puns paled beside the explicit evidence of sexual indiscretion that New York's daily papers reproduced in detail from the three-day trial.[44]

The indicted editor organized his defense around a provision of the state constitution of New York establishing truth, good motives, and justifiable ends as a defense to criminal libel charges. "In all prosecutions or indictments for libels," it declared, "the truth may be given in evidence, to the jury; and if it shall appear to the jury that the matter charged as libelous is true, and was published with good motives, and for justifiable ends, the party shall be acquitted."[45] Ever the performer, Dixon gave his own opening, delivering "a long harangue" in which he "attempted to show that the libel had been published by him for justifiable ends, and out of pure and innocent motives." As he argued, he had a constitutional right to discuss the details of Minturn's affair with Mrs. Roome not only because the story was true, but also because the public had a legitimate interest in preventing "female honor" and the sanctity of marriage from being mocked by wealthy sybarites like Minturn. Conveniently siding with Dixon, James Gordon Bennett, the standard bearer of the penny press, agreed that libel prosecutions should not permit immoral acts such as adultery to be cloaked in secrecy. If so, "fashionable libertines, by their political connections with the courts, lawyers and juries, can at any moment stifle the voice of truth—and make black white, or white black, whenever it suits their purposes to conceal their wickedness."[46]

Enthralled readers consumed lengthy trial reports full of titillating revelations.[47] To prove the truth of the accusations of criminal conversation between Minturn and Mrs. Roome, Dixon's counsel called Mrs. Roome's neighbor to the stand. He testified that he had witnessed Minturn and Mrs. Roome having sex while her husband was out of town. The testimony included this exchange between Robert Morris, the city recorder who presided over the Court of General Sessions, and the neighbor:

> Recorder—Now, Mr. Bowman, you say Mrs. Roome lay on the front side of the bed?
>
> Witness—Yes.
>
> Recorder—And two feet from the edge of the bed?
>
> Witness—Yes.
>
> Recorder—And the bed a narrow one?
>
> Witness—Yes.
>
> Recorder—Now, Mr. Bowman, pray where could Mr. Minturn have lain?
>
> Witness (looking steadily over his spectacles at the Recorder)—Right on top of her.

Dixon's defense team then called Mrs. Roome's husband. A pathetic figure, he still had a shaved head and other marks from a recent stay in a mental hospital. He testified that he and his wife no longer slept together, that he had once hidden under her bed to catch her in the act of adultery, and that he had become so "deranged" by her sexual escapades that he had to be institutionalized. To rebut this testimony, the prosecution called Minturn's brother to introduce his dying declaration denying illicit intercourse with Mrs. Roome.[48]

At the close of evidence, both the defense and the prosecution invoked the New York constitution to support their contending interpretations of freedom of the press. Dixon's counsel, John A. Morrill, read the sections protecting liberty of the press and citing truth, good motives, and justifiable ends as a legitimate defense against a libel charge. Whiting emphasized the dangers that unbridled freedom posed to society "if the law of the land did not step in to stay the plague which was raging" in the popular press. In his view, publication of scurrilous gossip amounted to nothing more than licentiousness, which represented the antithesis of liberty. By the same token, libel prosecutions constituted a defense of, rather than a threat to, individual freedom and republican government.[49] Following the language of the state constitution, the recorder, Robert Morris, instructed the jury that it was to determine whether "the publication *was true*, and then if made from good motives and justifiable ends."[50]

Faced with this task, the jury could not reach a verdict. The jury members agreed that the article was accurate, but they differed on the motive for which it had been published. Whiting elected to drop the case rather than fuel scandal even further by retrying it. The *Herald* published (and Dixon proudly reprinted) an editorial observing that Dixon's trial had created "a greater sensation and a more marked curiosity than any trial that has taken place" since the spectacular prosecution of Richard Robinson, a clerk accused of brutally murdering the well-known prostitute Helen Jewett three years before. As the *Herald* made clear, the intense public interest in the Minturn affair stemmed from the "extraordinary disclosures made by the witnesses—the glimpses which the evidence affords us of the morals of certain classes of society." Dixon claimed to be producing a pamphlet of the trial testimony to capitalize on the enormous publicity.[51]

A fascinating outgrowth of Dixon's prosecution was the forum it provided for tabloid editors to challenge prevailing legal rules governing the scope of legitimate subject matter for the press. In defending their right to print sexual gossip despite laws against libel, they insisted that republican politics and personal morality were intimately interconnected. In a hard-hitting editorial criticizing Morris's charge to the jury, the *New York Herald* complained about judges who construed all discussions of the morality of private parties as unjustified: "One of the most remarkable points in this case is the opinion given by the Judge that because 'the individuals were all private the public could have no interest in their affairs, and, therefore, the publication was not a good motive.'" Instead, the paper urged courts to recognize that private sexual morality was an appropriate topic of public concern. "The principle on which the institutions of a republic are founded, is a principle of morals in official as well as in private life," it asserted. "Every thing that affects this great basis, is public, and of the most momentous public character too."[52]

For that reason, the public interest demanded press coverage of more than party politics. "The Judge supposes that nothing is public but that which may be called political—either dirty whig or dirtier locofoco," wrote the *Herald*. "Here lies his mistake in applying the law." Alluding to Minturn's seduction of Mrs. Roome, the paper argued that libel law should not be used to hide moral transgressions: "Another man seduces his neighbor's wife—or at least meets her clandestinely and breaks up the peace of a family, and because both the parties are not in official life, the motive of the press in commenting upon such acts, is to be considered unjustifiable and therefore libelous." In the *Herald*'s view, such an opinion was a "way to fritter away by inference the broad principle of the constitution, guaranteeing the liberty of the press."[53] Needless to say, this lofty rhetoric on behalf of a constitutional right to expose sexual immorality conveniently served Bennett's self-interest as the ringleader of the scandal-conscious penny press.

A year and a half later, when Whiting was confronted with the *Sunday Flash*'s sexual libel against the businessman Myer Levy, he was probably still smarting from his disastrous prosecution of Dixon for libeling Roland Minturn. Certainly, he had learned the hard way that libel prosecutions involving sexual gossip had the potential to spiral out of control, creating nasty public spectacles that damaged reputations more than the libelous publications themselves did. And the fallout from the Minturn trial probably made New York's elite increasingly wary about using libel suits to redress invasions of their privacy.

Nonetheless, Whiting was determined to punish "licentious scribblers" and "ruffian robbers of private character" who destroyed reputations and employed predatory blackmail techniques. As a creative solution to the shortcomings of libel prosecutions and the absence of a criminal ban on procuring money through threats to damage an individual's reputation, Whiting mobilized the common law of obscene libel. Though it had been very rarely invoked in the past, the doctrine was especially attractive to someone in Whiting's position. Most advantageously, prosecutions for obscene libel shifted the focus of any trial: the question was no longer whether specific statements were true, but whether they had a tendency to corrupt public morality. According to the leading treatise writers, truth was irrelevant in actions regarding obscene libel. Indeed, as British authority Thomas Starkie remarked, with respect to "libels against religion, or morality, . . . permitting such a defense would be attended with consequences almost too absurd to mention." He went on to ask rhetorically: "Would proof that indecent transactions have actually occurred, supply any excuse for the public exhibition of them in a print or pamphlet?" By sidestepping the question of truth, prosecutions for obscene libel, unlike those for plain libel, had the potential, without destroying the victims' reputations in the courtroom, to punish individuals who printed sexual gossip in the press.[54]

Court records show that almost all the obscenity indictments engineered by Whiting between 1841 and 1843 involved some degree of defamation against individuals, accompanied by evidence of blackmail. An 1842 case against the *Whip* editor George Wooldridge was typical. Three of the five articles named in the indictment either directly or indirectly sought hush money: "The Libertine Dr. B." attempted to extort money from an "upper-crust soaplock" by threatening to expose love letters he had written to a married woman; "Poughkeepsie Rakes" related coded gossip from an out-of-town correspondent about the sexual philandering and adulteries of various men about town in Poughkeepsie, New York, probably as a prelude to a blackmail attempt; "Seduction—Conviction of the Libertine" accused a man in Newark, New Jersey, of repeated acts of seduction and libertinism and also made a veiled request for payment.[55] A second indictment handed down at the same time, involving an issue of Thomas Meighan's *Weekly Rake*, followed the same pattern. Whiting highlighted eight articles in the July 9, 1842, issue as obscene. Half of them contained overt demands for money in exchange for future silence about sexual wrongdoing. A fifth included a more oblique ultimatum to a brothel madam whom the editor threatened to turn over to the police.[56]

Although the desire to punish blackmail was a critical factor, it was not the only motive authorities had for turning to obscenity law. A second factor lay in the blatant visibility of the flash papers and their aggressive public distribution. As the middle-class *New York Tribune* complained in 1842, "the virtuous and refined" were constantly "insulted in passing through our streets by the vagabond venders of licentiousness and filth."[57] Another outraged observer argued that flash weeklies posed a much greater harm to public morality than the sale of more graphic books and prints. In contrast to explicit erotica, which at least was expensive and generally kept out of sight, the six-penny flash weeklies were "open, bold, and shameless advocates of licentiousness, and faithful directories to the lair of our most abandoned prostitutes." Public circulation meant that flash papers could be easily viewed by women and children. They seemed to be everywhere, constantly hawked by newsboys on all the city's streets ("Here's the Rake, Libertine, Whip, Flash"), "displayed to the eager eyes of every lad who chose to loiter on his way to school or to work" and "*thrust into the very face* of every young lady who ventured out for the purpose of taking a walk or making a purchase."[58]

For men of the "respectable" classes, flash papers seemed to raise the specter of an entirely sexualized city, where increasingly dense, crowded streets were overrun with sexually aggressive youths literally thrusting obscene materials into the faces of their wives and daughters. Alarm about obscene newspapers was part of a larger struggle over control of the city's public sphere. In the minds of members of the urban elite, the street scene was becoming distressingly chaotic and promiscuous, forcing them to have encounters with people of different classes and races and creating a persistent anxiety about the ability of wealthy men to shape and control public spaces.[59] Prosecutions against the flash press thus stemmed less from a desire to limit working-class access to sexual representations than from fear that lower-class males would use new forms of commercial print to invade bourgeois conceptions of privacy and assault middle-class families with such material in the streets.[60]

In a further affront to established codes of propriety, the flash papers were published and sold on Sundays, at a time when state Sabbatarian laws mandated the closing of most businesses. The *Sunday Flash* even flaunted its violation of the Sabbath on its masthead. As a grand jury protested in October 1841, just before its successor handed down the first obscenity indictment against the publishers of the *Sunday Flash:*

> The Grand Inquest respectfully present as a nuisance, and an evil of no ordinary magnitude, the *public* CRYING of newspaper venders through the streets on the Sabbath . . . It is a wrong also to that portion of our community who consider the Sabbath a divine institution. We are a Christian community, and have a right to claim that our consciences and feelings as Christians be not constantly outraged. The outrage complained of, is one from which we cannot escape. The shrill cries of these boys penetrate to our firesides, to our family altars, and to our places of public worship.[61]

In other words, the flash weeklies were not considered obscene solely or even primarily because their language was immoral per se. Rather, the boisterous sale of the papers rudely and even violently disrupted the decorum and decency of the city streets on Sundays. Perhaps most disturbingly, the unruly shouts of their vendors had even "penetrated" to the ultimate symbol of the bourgeois private sphere, the family hearth. (With characteristic naughtiness, the *Sunday Flash* proposed to cure any public disturbance related to Sunday papers by hiring a bunch of street toughs to ring the doorbells of the moralistic grand jurors, just after the stroke of midnight on Sunday, asking them to buy Monday papers.)[62]

Another factor underlying the rise of obscenity prosecution was the way in which flash papers openly discussed prostitution and extramarital sex. The basis of the very first obscenity charge involving a newspaper, the *Sunday Flash*'s biographical sketch of the New York prostitute Amanda Green, included a description of her height, complexion, and build, as well as the address of the brothel where she resided. Many other articles identified as obscene disseminated information about the amenities offered at various bawdy houses in the city and the physical attributes of particular prostitutes. In still other cases, obscenity indictments condemned articles and images that advertised the sexual availability of even seemingly proper women. A *Weekly Rake* story cited as obscene went so far as to suggest that "thousands and thousands of women who pass as respectable—married—virtuous—chaste in this modern Sodom" were in fact "kept mistresses." By asserting that not only actual prostitutes but also ostensibly chaste women engaged in sex outside marriage, stories such as these brazenly flouted middle-class conventions of female purity and piety.[63]

A final motivation for the resort to obscenity prosecution arose from an acute frustration among the propertied classes with the operation of the city's criminal justice system and its lax enforcement of morals. In the months leading up to the first *Sunday Flash* indictment, members of grand juries repeatedly complained about being overwhelmed with "trifling cases of assault and battery" generated by petty disputes and drunken barroom brawls. Grand jurors wanted government officials to reorient municipal priorities away from essentially private prosecutions on behalf of low-status victims of assault and battery and toward morals enforcement on behalf of the "public" at large. Jurors particularly wanted officials to take action against new forms of moral nuisance—flash weeklies, proliferating grog shops, street gatherings of unruly youths—that disturbed the orderly quality of life for Christians of the propertied classes.[64] Shortly after hearing these protests, Whiting, having devised a claim that turned on general harm to public morality rather than on any individualized complaint, brought the proposed indictment of the *Sunday Flash* editors to a newly convened grand jury.

In short, the origin of obscenity regulation in antebellum New York cannot be attributed to any single cause. Rather, it grew out of a cluster of concerns raised by the arrival of the flash press. Most scandalously, flash editors humiliated private figures and attempted to blackmail prominent citizens. They also violated public order and offended Christian sensibilities by brazenly marketing their papers in public spaces and on Sundays. And by openly discussing prostitution and extramarital sex, they shone an unwanted, embarrassing light on licentiousness in Gotham.

Faced with unprecedented charges of obscenity, the editors of flash weeklies were suddenly forced to defend and negotiate their understanding of the meaning of freedom of speech and freedom of the press. The most revealing insight into the legal consciousness of the indicted editors can be gleaned from the columns of the flash papers, which carried a barrage of vitriolic editorials challenging the arrests. One thing was clear: obscenity prosecution did little to intimidate the pugnacious journalists or quell their temerity. On the contrary, the threat of incarceration seemed to inspire them. When the editors of the *Sunday Flash* were first arrested for "publishing an obscene paper" in October 1841, they sarcastically pretended to heed the grand jury's demand to cease publication by renaming their paper the *Flash* and describing it as a "new weekly." Then the chief writer for the paper, William Snelling, mischievously skewered the grand jury and its foreman, William Boggs, who was the respectable publisher of the stodgy *New York Evening Post,* as a group of "Bogs, Snobs," and "Gobs."[65] A new grand jury was not amused, and it quickly approved a second indictment against Snelling for publishing an obscene paper, the October 31, 1841, issue of the restyled *Flash.* Having no money for bail, he was committed to the city's recently constructed penitentiary, nicknamed the Tombs.[66]

Even prison failed to silence writers for the *Flash*. Until his release on bail, thanks to the aid of his then patron, the brothel madam Adeline Miller, Snelling continued to pen stories for the paper in which he savaged the grand jurors and the district attorney.[67] Wilkes too mocked the grand jurors as the picture of self-righteous obsolescence. In a pamphlet he wrote from prison while later serving time for publishing the *Sunday Flash*, he ridiculed them as old, prudish, and hopelessly out of touch with the fun-loving sporting life. The grand jury, he wrote, consisted of "twenty-three individuals, mostly old gentlemen in brown wigs, white neckcloths and red bandanna handkerchiefs—parrot-faced old fellows, who wear nightcaps when they go to bed" and "stand in the front place in the pew on Sunday." Wilkes quipped that this collection of dreary, sexless old men was "honestly down on licentiousness, because licentiousness has long been honestly down on them."[68]

But the flash editors also articulated a number of somewhat more serious arguments in response to their prosecutions. Perhaps most vehemently, they condemned the hypocrisy of the parties demanding censorship. In the editors' view, claims that flash papers should be suppressed to protect public morality were disingenuous—propagated by sanctimonious hypocrites who preached morality in public, while secretly (or not so secretly) indulging in vice in private.[69] In the *Weekly Rake*, Thomas Meighan ridiculed the double standard applied by publishers of the supposedly respectable press, who frequently lambasted the flash press as obscene: "The proprietor of one of the papers which have furiously attacked us, we have seen prowling about Broadway, night after night, in company with prostitutes of the lowest grade . . .—and he a married man!" The worst hypocrites were religious leaders: "Watch the professor of religion. With trembling hands he snatches one of the 'obscene' papers, rushes to his room, and pores over it—gratified and amused." But when the same man hears the paper spoken of in public, "he assumes his mask, and bellows most lustily—*'put them down.'*"[70] By the same token, the grand jury that indicted the editors of the *Sunday Flash* included "several sinners and one fornicator," who sought to suppress the *Flash* in the vain hope of avoiding exposure.[71]

Another critique targeted the internal inconsistencies of morals regulation in New York State. As flash editors tirelessly pointed out, the law of New York (unlike the law of many other states) did not prohibit sexual misconduct in the form of adultery or fornication. Drawing an analogy to the English common law of individual libel, which punished defamation because it had a tendency to incite a breach of the peace or an assault, they asked how obscene libel could possibly be a crime, when the feared results of perusing lewd publications, namely, fornication and adultery, were not themselves criminal offenses. As Snelling asserted: "How weak and wretched to punish the sale and exposure of licentious prints and pictures, on the pretence that they lead to the growth of those very crimes, the commission of which is not punishable by law."[72]

In his prison pamphlet, *Mysteries of the Tombs*, Wilkes reiterated this theme. He pointed out that obscene publications were subject to prosecution under the common law on the ground that they "tend to promote licentiousness." But licentious conduct was not even illegal in New York, as evidenced by the fact that the state had no laws against adultery or fornication, "the very evils" that obscenity prosecutions were "intended to prevent." This inconsistency led Wilkes to remonstrate: "Is not this supremely absurd?" Can "the proposition stand that it is criminal to *incite* to an act, the *actual commission* of which is innocent by law?" Though Wilkes did not develop this line of reasoning, it was not without force. Claims that obscene papers should be suppressed because they might induce men to consort with prostitutes or engage in extramarital sex had little logical power in terms of public policy. Owners of brothels could be prosecuted for "keeping a disorderly house," but merely patronizing a house of prostitution was not a crime in New York for either single or married men. (Indeed, even keeping a brothel, provided the owner maintained a quiet, orderly house to outward appearances, was rarely treated as illegal.) If it was legally permissible to visit a bawdy house, commit adultery, or seduce an unmarried woman, why should reading things that might incite such acts be criminal? In other words, why was *representation* of immoral practices more objectionable than the immoral practices themselves?[73]

Flash editors further resisted their indictments for obscenity by appealing for honesty and candor in writing about urban existence. As they maintained, street prostitution, brothels, houses of assignation, saloons, and gambling dens were all omnipresent facts of life in 1840s New York. They therefore professed a determination not to ignore or sugarcoat these "evils," but instead "to speak the truth about them." Observing that flash writers were "too coarse it seems, in our language, for the refined taste of this very moral community—we call things too plainly by their right names," one questioned: "How are things to be known, if they are not named?"[74]

Paradoxically, by "speaking the truth" about prostitution and other forms of vice, flash editors contended that they were serving the cause of public virtue. As they repeatedly (if preposterously) proclaimed, their stories about prostitution were designed to deter rather than promote traffic in sex. When the editors of the *Sunday Flash* were indicted for publishing the eleventh installment in their biographical series about New York prostitutes, Lives of the Nymphs, they refused to halt production. Instead, they produced seven additional installments. At the conclusion of the series, Snelling archly defended it as a public service: "We have now published the lives and adventures of eighteen notorious prostitutes, and by our indignant denunciation of their profligate career, have, under God, with reverence be it said, effected a reformation in the demeanor and practices of several who were before desperate in vice." This reformation, he boasted, was sufficient reward for his "virtuous labors."[75]

Likewise, when flash editors divulged secrets about Christian merchants who cheated on their wives by visiting luxurious brothels, or about married upper-class women who met their lovers at houses of assignation, or about zealous ministers who had affairs with their parishioners, the journalists insisted they were not behaving irresponsibly. As Wooldridge maintained, one issue of his paper did "more good in correcting vice and shaming profligacy than all the sermons preached by all the paid and pretended moralists of the church put together."[76]

Even as they faced indictment for obscenity, flash editors declared their purported bona fides by advocating stricter regulation of morals. Snelling, for one, vigorously urged the legislature to pass bills making seduction and adultery criminal offenses.[77] In this respect, the world of the flash press collided in curious ways with the world of evangelical moral reform. In the early 1830s, female purity activists in New York had begun to campaign against the sexual double standard that they believed fueled the prostitution trade. Like John McDowall, they sought to punish male licentiousness by threatening to publish the names of married men and churchgoers who visited brothels in their newspaper, the *Advocate of Moral Reform*.[78] By the late 1830s, they had turned to political action, commencing a successful petition drive that ultimately led the legislature to outlaw seduction and abduction for the purpose of prostitution in 1848.[79] In effect, the flash press, by printing its own exposés of male licentiousness and conducting its own campaign for laws against seduction, was mimicking the platform of female moral reform.

In announcing the launch of his fourth flash paper, the *Libertine of New York,* Wooldridge pithily summarized the avowed ethics of the flash press. "It will be a record of not only the doings but the misdoings of the world of fashion, and is intended to operate as an agent of reform. If a wife goes astray, it will lead her back to the right path. If a clergyman sin[s], it will spread the pages of the bible before him. If a husband neglects his 'responsibilities,' it will remind him of them." Driving home the point, he explained that "The Libertine is not itself a libertine but a chronicler of libertinism." But in virtually the same breath, he promised that each issue would offer exciting biographies of celebrated courtesans and would be "embellished with a splendid wood engraving, illustrating a pleasure picture."[80]

The flash editors' shameless juxtaposition of "pleasure pictures" and other libidinous content with strident defenses of female chastity and the sanctity of marriage creates a puzzling impression, as they zigzagged between enticements to the gratification offered by beautiful "nymphs" and condemnation of prostitution as a moral and social wrong. But these contradictions become less perplexing when one realizes that flash editors intended their professions of morality to operate simultaneously on a number of different cultural and legal planes, each of which was designed to promote and protect their interests.

On a key level, the sanctimonious claims of the flash editors functioned as a comic parody of the moral reform movement and the upsurge in religious fervor engendered by the Second Great Awakening (1795–1837). First and foremost, the object of the flash press was to sell papers by amusing its audience. To do so, flash editors repeatedly promised readers that they would offer exceptional "wit," "humor" and "satire." In a typical offering, while poking fun at municipal reformers who had lobbied for the city's first professional police force, the writers facetiously predicted that urban crime and vice would magically evaporate:

> We can, without fear, leave our hall doors gaping—bolts and bars will be dead property—locksmiths will emigrate to Texas for want of sufficient employment here—scamps, prowlers, pilferers, blackmail editors, publishers of licentious and obscene novels, and others will starve or take up an honest course of life . . . Thank God for the preventive police.[81]

If nothing else, the tongue-in-cheek reference to "blackmail editors" and "publishers of licentious and obscene novels" seemed certain to elicit a smile of recognition. An even more surefire way for flash editors to demonstrate their comic capabilities was to ridicule their nemesis: moral reformers, especially female moral reformers. Indeed, much of the output of the flash press can be read as a sarcastic response to the increasing visibility of evangelical proselytizing and bourgeois assertions of female moral authority. When the flash editors postured as self-righteous citizens determined to police moral virtue, they expected their audience—men well versed in the city's manifold types of commercial leisure and sexual pleasure—to be in on the joke. They certainly suffered from no moral ambivalence about prostitution or other forms of entertainment that proponents of purity condemned as indecent or improper. After all, the flash editors were men who regularly consorted with prostitutes and whiled away their time at saloons, brothels, gambling dens, and other places of ill repute.[82]

The feigned moral superiority of the flash editors also served less lighthearted ends. In particular, their professions of moral outrage provided a darkly comic pretext for extorting money from victims of their blackmail plots. An early issue of the *Sunday Flash* revealed how this game would be played. "The work of reform goes bravely on," it declared in an article, "Interesting to Christians." "Our straightforward and unflinching course is effecting wonders in the field of morals . . . We will not truckle to the false delicacy of the age. We shall call things, ay, *and persons too,* by their right names."[83]

At the same time, the feigned moralism of the flash papers functioned as an audacious legal strategy. Flamboyant flash editors, even as they assertively rejected the dictates of respectable, law-abiding society, nonetheless sought to position their publications within the framework of conventional legal standards and structures. Understanding their strategic maneuvering requires revisiting the world of libel law, a world that antebellum journalists confronted in a visceral way almost every day. More than any other aspect of the law, newspaper publishers and editors affiliated with the emerging tabloid press were intensely aware of the rules of libel and their available defenses. Virtually all of them had faced not only civil but criminal libel charges multiple times in their careers. Many of these men had also served the standard sentence—thirty days in the Tombs—for defaming someone in print.[84]

Even so, flash editors assumed the risk of reporting on such immoral conduct by private parties as visits to prostitutes, seductions, and adulteries. The editors did so because they knew such stories would entertain readers, sell papers, and abet their blackmail schemes. In defending the right to print such material, flash editors did not contest the state's right to restrict speech on the basis of immorality or indecency. Even George Wilkes, a strong critic of restrictive libel laws, admitted that obscenity "very often" was "deserving of punishment," though not of course in his case. Rather, the newspapermen tried to work within the system as they understood it to justify their practices.[85]

This strategy of accommodation may have reflected a lack of ideological commitment to broad freedom of the press, as well as a more general disavowal of political activism.[86] But it also stemmed from the absence of a constitutional framework for defending speech that offended moral orthodoxy. After all, flash editors plied their trade in a legal environment in which freedom of speech and liberty of the press were tightly constrained by majoritarian standards of morality. Even the free speech clause of the New York constitution contained an exception for "abuse": "Every citizen may freely speak, write, and publish his sentiments on all subjects, being responsible for the abuse of that right; and no law shall be passed to restrain or abridge the liberty of speech or of the press." "Abuse" in this context alluded to the continuing legitimacy of prohibitions against libel. In turn, the state constitution required defendants in libel prosecutions to prove not only truth but also "good motives" and "justifiable ends" to establish a defense. In other words, even while flash editors in their writing lampooned bourgeois moral norms and mocked religious authorities, their political consciousness reflected the moralistic underpinnings of the legal doctrine of their day. The reigning standards of freedom of speech and freedom of the press seemingly left them with little choice but to emphasize the virtuous content of their writing and to pander to conventional notions of morality.[87]

To the extent that the claims of flash editors to champion chastity and virtue were offered as serious legal defenses, they were obviously deeply cynical. And yet, without staking out new doctrinal ground, the strategy revived a topic that had captured media attention during the Dixon-Minturn trial: Did journalists, even assuming that their statements were true, ever have a right to discuss the sexual morality of nonpolitical figures? In the opportunistic logic of the flash editors (and their mentors in the penny press), sexual exposés, because they safeguarded public morality, were just as legitimate as conventional forms of political speech. Indeed, because the success of a republic was said to rest on a foundation of morality, the editors insisted that "speaking the truth" about sex and exposing moral hypocrisy were themselves forms of political advocacy.[88]

Though professions of truth and good motives filled the editorial pages, flash editors and their lawyers were far less ambitious about pursuing this line of defense in the courtroom. Rather than challenge their indictments in court, they often put up no defense at all and simply forfeited their bail to avoid a trial. The editors of the *New York Sporting Whip*, several of whom had recently served prison sentences for publishing obscene papers, comically alluded to this strategy in an illustration depicting two newspaper editors balancing a bale of hay between their heads. The column below explained: "Editors and publishers are famous for Getting Bale Between Them and forfeiting their recognizances, and we can play that game with the most skillful."[89] At other times, flash editors resisted conviction on narrow, nonconstitutional grounds—for example, by denying responsibility for the articles or papers in question or challenging the credibility of prosecution witnesses. In part, this approach may have reflected their lawyers' recognition of the inherent implausibility of attributing good motives to journalists whom jurors of the propertied classes were more likely to regard as blackguards than as models of propriety; however, the evasion also underscored the unwillingness of flash editors to fight for free speech as a matter of constitutional right.

In a sign that obscenity trials involving the flash press would rarely take the high road of legal principle, the first obscenity indictment to come to trial in the Court of General Sessions pitted the squabbling editors of the *Sunday Flash* against one another. Before the proceedings began, Wooldridge, in exchange for a dismissal of the indictments against him, agreed to testify against Snelling and Wilkes.[90] That action led the former colleagues of Wooldridge to dismiss him as an untalented thug. They reported that they had taken him on "principally on account of his services as a pimp and collector of scandal."[91] When the case against Snelling and Wilkes was called in January 1842, the city recorder Frederick A. Tallmadge (1792–1869) presided. In the 1840s the Court of General Sessions consisted of a rotating panel of varying numbers of judges. Usually, the city recorder, who was an appointed state official until 1847, served as chief judge. He was joined by some combination of state-appointed judges and popularly elected aldermen from the Common Council.

Tallmadge, a graduate of Yale College and the Litchfield Law School, was a conservative Whig from a distinguished Connecticut family with a long history of public service. Later in the decade he solidified his reputation as a supporter of law and order by playing a key role in calling up the state militia to quell the notorious Astor Place disturbance of 1849, a theater riot in which troops fired point-blank into a large working-class crowd and killed twenty-two people.[92] Two appointed judges joined Tallmadge on the panel for the *Sunday Flash* case. One was a newspaper editor and playwright named Mordecai Noah. Originally a Democrat, he had recently been rewarded with a judicial appointment by the Whig governor William Seward, in exchange for switching to the Whig Party. The other member of the panel was James Lynch, who was often described as an unaccomplished and incompetent judge.[93] Shortly before the trial, Snelling and Wilkes pleaded guilty to the individual libel against Myer Levy and printed a formal apology to him in the *Sunday Flash* and the *New York Herald*, probably in return for a suspended sentence.[94]

The editors decided to resist the obscene libel count, however. They hired a charismatic criminal specialist named James Topham Brady (1815–1869) to represent them at trial. Brady was the son of Thomas Brady, an Irish scholar and lawyer who, having immigrated to the United States during the War of 1812, became a justice of the peace and an alderman in the city. At the time of the *Sunday Flash* trial in 1842, James Topham, though only twenty-six years old, was said to be a magnetic presence in the courtroom and "almost irresistible before a jury." He was also on his way to becoming one of the most renowned criminal defense lawyers of his day. Known for his courtly manner and sparkling conversation outside the courthouse, he displayed a literary bent as well and later in his life contributed stories to the *Knickerbocker* magazine.[95] Unfortunately, we have no way of knowing what Brady advised the *Flash* editors or what strategy he recommended. Perhaps he told them that a "truth-plus" defense was a losing cause, because there is no evidence that he pursued that tack at the trial.

In court, Whiting asserted that the prosecution had to prove only two things to obtain a conviction for obscene libel. First, it had to establish that the defendants were the actual publishers of the paper. Second, it had to show that the *Sunday Flash* contained "obscene matter, such as should not be allowed to appear in a public print." As a result, the truth of the allegedly obscene statements and the intent of the defendants in publishing them were not at issue. In making the prosecution's case, Wooldridge was the star and only witness. He admitted that he had gathered research for the allegedly obscene biography of prostitute Amanda Green but testified that Snelling and Wilkes were the writers and editors of the paper.[96]

For the defense, Brady called several witnesses to challenge the character and veracity of Wooldridge. He also suggested that Wooldridge, rather than Snelling or Wilkes, was responsible for the paper's indecency. Summing up to the jury, Brady reportedly "made an able speech in defense of his clients."[97] Still, no indication appears in any of the newspaper reports of the trial that he sought to establish the moral purpose of the *Sunday Flash*. Almost certainly, he did not mount a libertarian challenge to the state's power to punish speech that municipal officials deemed to be immoral.

Fortunately for Snelling and Wilkes, one of the twelve jurors held out for acquittal. It is telling that this juror was a talesman—that is, a bystander hired to fill out a jury on an emergency basis who did not need to meet the usual property qualifications for service.[98] Undaunted by this defeat, Whiting refused to drop the case and decided to retry Snelling and Wilkes in April 1842. Tallmadge, Noah, and Lynch continued as judges with a new jury. Snelling failed to appear, and thus his surety forfeited the bail he had paid. Wilkes, who did show up, argued that the case against him should be dropped because "the paper had been discontinued" and "he had devoted his time to different pursuits."[99] Whiting and the panel of judges resisted this arrangement. Instead, after consultation with his attorney, Wilkes agreed to plead guilty and accept a suspended thirty-day sentence, offered on the condition that he sever his ties with obscene papers.

Soon thereafter, the surety for Snelling turned him in and he was committed to prison, to stand trial on the old indictment.[100] When he was finally tried in September 1842, the prosecution identified three additional articles from the October 31, 1841, issue of the *Sunday Flash* as obscene—"Thomas S. Hamblin, the Patriarch of the Slaughter House" (a lengthy exposé of the sexual misdeeds of a New York theater impresario), "Jane Dixon, Alias Fisher, Alias Smith" (a biographical account of a lustful young seamstress's willing resort to prostitution), and "Adultery and Fornication" (an editorial challenging the logic of penalizing obscenity in a state without laws against adultery or fornication). Wooldridge, again testifying for the prosecution, told the jury that Wilkes was the chief editor of the paper and that Snelling had written the offending pieces.

Snelling, conducting his own defense this time, did not deny responsibility for the articles. Instead, he invoked the defense the New York constitution provided in libel prosecutions—proof of truth, good motives, and justifiable ends. He "admitted that the article headed Thomas Hamblin was written by him," for instance, but insisted that "it was true, every word of it."[101] Denying any ill intent, he submitted to the jurors "whether the articles he had written were obscene and indecent or not." His argument failed to carry the day with the jury, which convicted him for publishing an obscene paper. Perhaps in recognition of time he had spent in jail awaiting trial, the Court of General Sessions suspended his sentence.[102]

The largest legal confrontation involving the flash press took place on September 14, 1842, when a series of obscenity trials were scheduled at the Court of General Sessions before Tallmadge, Judge Lynch, and an alderman named Calvin Balis.[103] The most significant involved Wooldridge, who had been indicted for publishing an issue of the *Libertine of New York* dated July 1, 1842. This was the first of four separate obscenity indictments on which the incorrigible editor faced trial that day.[104] Wooldridge retained James M. Smith, Jr., to represent him. Smith would later win election as a Democrat to the office of recorder, the second highest political post in the city after the mayor's office. When Wooldridge admitted his connection with the *Libertine*, the district attorney stated that the only issue to be proved was whether or not the paper was obscene. He proposed simply handing it to the jury. Smith objected that the district attorney needed to call witnesses to establish its obscenity. Whiting replied that decent men would refuse to read the paper and that he personally refused to do so "as he thought it too obscene and unfit to be read in court." Astutely, he also argued that if he read the *Libertine* into evidence, "it would become part of the record, and the reporters of other papers, if they saw fit, could re-publish the articles he might read." Relying on the *Commonwealth v. Holmes* case in Massachusetts as precedent, Whiting contended that it was not necessary for the prosecution to specify which passages were obscene. Rather, the "title of the paper itself, 'The Libertine,' sufficiently indicated its character." In his view, the captions of many of the articles named in the indictment provided additional evidence of the *Libertine's* obscenity, such as "Seduction and Abandonment," "Sappho," and "Wife v. Mistress."[105]

Wooldridge's counsel resisted the prosecution's reliance on titles alone and insisted that the district attorney read the challenged articles to the jury and call witnesses to prove their obscenity. Here, Smith spelled out the principal line of defense presented in the flash editorials: "It might be the opinion of the majority of the public that these very articles, the titles of which had been read by the District Attorney," were designed to serve "the cause of virtue, by pointing out the effects of vice." Smith also introduced a second argument, one that obscenity defendants would press for the next century. He charged that no literature was safe from censorship if the court permitted the prosecution to rely on isolated words or phrases rather than the character of the work as a whole. "If a book or publication was to be judged by its title, or the selection of isolated passages," he asserted, "there is scarcely a publisher but would be liable to prosecution for obscene publications, and many of the works of Moore and Byron could not be defended with as much propriety as the articles named by the District Attorney." In response, Whiting threatened to resign rather than read "every filthy, lewd, and obscene matter that might be brought before the court." Smith sarcastically rejoined that the district attorney's refusal to read the articles in the *Libertine* showed that he "wished to skulk from doing the dirty work, for which he got paid, and throw it upon the jury, who were compelled to attend here gratuitously."[106]

After the theatrics subsided, the court ruled that the district attorney was indeed required to introduce the parts of the *Libertine* on which the indictment was based, to establish its obscenity. Whiting selected two biographical sketches of prostitutes: "Matilda Rollins, *alias* Daniels, *alias* Dutch Till," and "Catherine Alley, *alias* Kate Hall." After reading them to the jury, he rested his case. The defense called no witnesses, though Smith reportedly gave a "speech abounding in eloquence," during which he read several extracts from the paper in yet another effort to show that they were printed with good motives and for the purpose of revealing the harmful effects of vice.[107]

According to newspaper accounts of the Wooldridge trial, Whiting delivered a powerful closing "in which he forcibly depicted the consequences that must ensue if these licentious papers were countenanced and allowed to exist." Recorder Tallmadge delivered the charge to the jury. Perhaps sensitive to concerns about censorship, he drew the jury's attention to the traditional distinction between liberty and license by adverting to the "blessings of a properly conducted press, and of the evils of an abandoned and profligate press." The jury was out less than five minutes, returning with a verdict of guilty.[108] Seeing the writing on the wall, Wooldridge, along with fellow flash editors Henry McVey and George Colburn, withdrew their pleas of not guilty and confessed to obscenity in the indictments pending against them in connection with April 1842 issues of the *Whip & Satirist of New-York and Brooklyn*. Wooldridge also pleaded guilty to a separate indictment for publishing the *Whip* in July 1842.[109]

A panel of the Court of General Sessions chaired by Recorder Tallmadge issued the sentences two weeks later. Wooldridge, McVey,

Colburn, and Charles Scott were sentenced to sixty days in prison on the first indictment to which they entered a guilty plea, and to a fine of six cents on the other indictments.[110] The minutes of the Court of General Sessions indicate that the *Weekly Rake*'s Thaddeus Meighan, indicted twice in the summer of 1842, was never brought to trial along with the other flash editors. It appears he may have taken the helm at the *Whip* while Wooldridge served his sixty-day sentence for publishing the *Libertine*. In any event, Meighan's two prior indictments failed to suppress his licentious writing. In the spring of 1843, Meighan was again indicted for "publishing an obscene paper," this time a March 4, 1843, issue of the *Whip*, now in its third incarnation, as the *New York Sporting Whip*. Arrested on a bench warrant, he was committed to prison. After pleading guilty and serving twelve days, the wily Meighan was somehow able to obtain a suspended sentence.[111]

After his release from prison, Wooldridge continued his association with the flash press as the publisher of the *New York Sporting Whip*. With typical bravado, he claimed that his prosecution had only increased his tenacity. Though "we have suffered imprisonment and persecutions at the hands of our enemies," he bragged, "we still survive, prosperous and conquering."[112] The district attorney's files from March 1843 show that he was indicted a fifth time, along with his old colleague George Colburn, on the basis of a complaint by a dancer, Eliza "Madame" Trust, for an alleged libel against her in the *New York Sporting Whip*. The article in question shows that Wooldridge sometimes dropped his guard, by admitting that the purpose of his revelations was not to reform morals but to extort money: "Now, the drift of this is that we have on hand a queer, funny, and explicit *expose* of the doings of a quack who married this *madame*—of her transactions—and of the secret affairs of both. If we can make any black-mail by suppressing it we will. There! we, more daring than

Bennett, openly avow that we extort hush-money."[113] Despite his brazen methods, Wooldridge managed to avoid further punishment. The minutes of the Court of General Sessions show no proceedings in his case after the initial indictment. It is likely that he skipped out on the warrant for his arrest by signing on as an agent for the acclaimed minstrel group the Virginia Minstrels and accompanying them on tour to England.[114]

The 1843 indictment against Thomas Meighan of the *New York Sporting Whip* was the last obscenity charge instigated by Whiting, and in fact the last obscenity indictment against a newspaper editor for the next seven years. The decline in newspaper prosecutions after 1843 may at first suggest that New York authorities succeeded in suppressing the dissemination of vulgar, sexually titillating weeklies, or at least in sequestering them from public view. This was not the case, however. Within a few years, municipal officials had come to tolerate the blatant display of disreputable papers in newsstands and periodical depots throughout the city. Though indictments were occasionally brought against the publishers of obscene papers over the next two decades, these prosecutions failed to stem the tide of sex and crime-filled weeklies, often known generically as the weekly press or the Sunday papers. Indeed, they soon became something of a New York institution. By 1850, the *New York Tribune* reporter George Foster summed up the New York periodical scene by referring to the "immense mass of nonsense, wit, originality, trash and obscenity circulating through all classes of the community under the generic title of the 'weekly press.'" The same year, journalist Lambert Wilmer lamented, "nothing is read now by young people, but pamphlet novels and the New York weekly papers." Likewise, the author of an 1855 article in the *Brooklyn Eagle* rued the pervasiveness of "vehicles of obscene filth, in the shape of flash weekly newspapers," still trying "to pull the wool over the eyes of simpletons" by claiming to "expose vice and crime and so conserve virtue and morality."[115]

Although the prosecutions of the early 1840s failed to suppress New York's unsavory periodical press, the threat of obscenity charges played a critical role in defining the style and substance of later incarnations of the flash weeklies. The career of George Wilkes, one of the founders of the *Sunday Flash* who was jailed for obscenity, illustrates the ways in which obscenity prohibitions helped to shape subsequent versions of the tabloid press.

Recall that at his 1842 obscenity trial Wilkes received a suspended sentence on the condition that he cease his association with obscene papers. But he soon ran into trouble when the bank lawyer turned district attorney James Whiting spotted him working as a court reporter for Mike Walsh's vitriolic working-class paper, the *Subterranean*, in 1843. At the time, Whiting was prosecuting Walsh for criminal libel and Wilkes was in the courtroom covering the case. The district attorney took the extreme position that the prolabor *Subterranean* was an obscene paper, and that Wilkes had violated the terms of his suspended sentence by writing for it. Recorder Tallmadge, who was presiding over Walsh's trial, ultimately agreed, sentencing Wilkes to thirty days in prison. While recognizing the "youth of the accused, his talents," he hoped the sentence "would serve not only as a warning" to Wilkes, but to others engaged in "publishing sheets of an infamous and libelous character." In his view, such men deserved severe punishment for "their personal attacks" on private citizens and for "harrowing up the feelings of families, and innocent and unoffending persons."[116]

On his release, the anger Wilkes felt over his incarceration initially led him to toy with the idea of becoming a criminal defense lawyer. He arranged to study as a law clerk under one Enoch Camp, who had recently been admitted to practice before the Court of General Sessions. But Wilkes soon jumped back into fray of the tabloid newspaper business, teaming up with Camp in 1845 to become the mastermind behind one of the most notorious of the next generation of New York flash papers, the *National Police Gazette.* This long-running illustrated weekly served up a spicy stew that included trial reports of seductions, criminal conversations, incest, and bigamy, shocking biographies of famous criminals of both sexes, and an assortment of true crime stories about violent acts like murder, sexual assault, and highway robbery.[117]

From the paper's office, Wilkes, who was acting as chief editor, ostensibly eschewed his former association with obscene papers and ostentatiously donned the mantle of law enforcement. In an effort to distance itself from its predecessors, the *National Police Gazette* made a specific point of printing the particulars of obscenity cases, including the names of men charged with the crime, their addresses, and the content of their inventory. Given the newspaper's location at the corner of Nassau and Ann and Wilkes's past associations, this call for evidence against purveyors of obscene books, which appeared in the tenth issue, must have struck readers as decidedly amusing: "We particularly request all persons, who have knowledge of the printing, publishing, stitching, binding, or sale of obscene books in this city, to give us notice, in order that the infamous authors of the numerous publications that flood our country should be exposed to the public authorities." Another early number bragged that its staff had "communicated information to the Mayor of this city, of an extensive obscene publication depot," thereby leading to at least one arrest. Within a short time, Wilkes and Camp had perfected the art of condemning obscene books while broadcasting information about them.[118]

In a further effort to deflect obscenity charges, Wilkes deliberately shifted the emphasis of his new venture from the sexual to the criminal underworld. In particular, the *National Police Gazette* substituted sensational biographies of criminals from around the country for salacious biographies of New York courtesans. In place of Lives of the Nymphs, it offered a series called Lives of the Felons, which appeared on the front page of each issue and featured lurid woodcuts of the lawbreakers. Stories such as these thrilled readers with detailed renditions of gruesome crimes and the life stories of outlaws.

The editors of the *National Police Gazette* also renounced the practice of blackmailing individuals over their sexual indiscretions, in an attempt to sever the link between flash journalism and extortion. Instead of revealing gossip overheard in assignation houses or saloons, they derived news of sex scandals from court records, police reports, and other official publications. Building on the prurient crime reporting of early penny dailies like the *Sun* and the *Herald*, the *National Police Gazette* printed especially extensive excerpts from prosecutions of sex crimes. As one caption highlighted a lengthy transcript from a police court investigation of incest: "Alleged Incest of a Father on Two of His Daughters—Brutality and Obscenity upon a Third . . . Wonderful and Surprising Details."[119] Like the original flash weeklies, the *National Police Gazette* reported with relish on the seamy side of urban life, such as abductions of young virgins by debauched libertines or unscrupulous brothel madams for the purpose of prostitution. By contrast with its forerunners, though, the new paper presented lascivious details about prostitution and other morals offenses through the filter of police blotters and trial transcripts.[120]

Thus, instead of either internalizing bourgeois moral norms or resisting moral censorship, Wilkes and his accomplices seized on the opportunity to profit from morals regulation. While paying lip service to the need for rigorous moral policing, they manipulated the law to serve their own ends, by using it as a platform for sensationalized treatments of sex and especially of violence. In this way, latter-day flash weeklies at once inscribed prohibitions on direct sexual representation in their texts and seduced readers with eroticized accounts of crime.

Thanks to this strategy, Wilkes escaped further prosecution for obscenity during five enormously successful years at the helm of the *National Police Gazette,* where he saw its circulation grow from fifteen thousand in 1845 to more than forty thousand in 1850.[121] Throughout the 1850s, New York officials continued to condone titillating flash weeklies focused on crime and violence, despite persistent charges from arbiters of respectable culture that such sheets were licentious and immoral. Official toleration for the indecent content of flash journalism was bolstered by the shift to general election of the district attorney in 1847, which put a series of Tammany Democrats in office and made the criminal justice system more responsive to popular tastes.[122]

Although the lifespan of the founding generation of flash weeklies was short, their salacious, titillating, voyeuristic style continued to thrive in its repackaged, crime-oriented form, for decades to come. In a sign of changing times, the man who served as New York's police chief during the late 1840s and '50s, George Matsell, took over as the publisher of the *National Police Gazette* in 1857. A decade later, the *Atlantic Monthly* declared that the city was "deluged" with flash papers, describing ubiquitous newspaper stands where "idle men and women are grouped, improving their minds . . . by the inspection and perusal of the flash police papers and other obscene trash." By 1870, an article in *Godey's Lady's Book,* a middle-class fashion magazine published in Philadelphia, condemned what had become a national onslaught of indecent New York weeklies. "New York, the source of most of the filthiest immorality with which the country is afflicted, sends to this city every week thousands of copies of each of five or six flash picture papers, which are devoted to glorification of vice, to illustration of scenes of debauchery and crime, and to lewd representations of the human figure." Reflecting a new concern with children, it complained that such journals were "exposed to view in shop windows and upon newspaper stands," where they were "studied with absorbing interest, not only by grown persons, but by children of both sexes and all ages." In 1873 the *New York Times* glumly noted, "Everybody is familiar with the name of the *Police Gazette* as a synonym for everything that is foul and indecent in journalism."[123]

The sensibility of the original flash periodicals migrated not only to scandalous weekly "flash picture papers" like the *National Police Gazette,* but also to the new genre of graphically violent, sexually suggestive "pamphlet novels," as the critic Lambert Wilmer lamented. Wilkes himself became an early contributor to this field with an 1849 story about the murder of prostitute Helen Jewett, a work that blended soft-core sex and explicit violence in a style that would come to be known as "racy."[124] Meanwhile, a vanguard of antebellum New York book publishers was venturing toward the hardcore, laying the foundation for the emergence of an American pornography industry.

Chapter 3

Fancy Books and Racy Pamphlets

In the decades leading up to the Civil War, the United States witnessed an unprecedented burst of book production—an outgrowth of the communications and reading revolutions that swept the United States in the first half of the nineteenth century. New York was at the center of this surge of activity, with its publishers issuing nearly 40 percent of the total value of all American-produced books by 1856.[1] Custodians of traditional morality considered much of this new literature—ranging from lurid crime pamphlets, sensational city mysteries, and romance novels to sex and reproductive advice manuals, lay medical guides, sexually provocative poetry, and domestic reprints of European erotica—not only immoral but also criminally obscene. Certainly, those demanding censorship found ready support for their views in the official doctrines of the common law, which permitted government authorities to suppress any writing or illustration that had a tendency to promote indecency as illicit obscenity.

Had criminal justice officials chosen to suppress the publication of every book that was regarded as impure or had a tendency to corrupt morality, however, they might have had time for little else. In the midst of New York's burgeoning print culture and the moral controversies it provoked, how exactly did antebellum authorities draw a boundary between permissible and forbidden expression, between books that were vulgar, lamentable, and even indecent and those which had to be cordoned off as illicit and obscene? The fragmentary nature of the legal records and the fact that many condemned works were destroyed or have since disappeared make it difficult to answer this question with any precision. Fortunately, despite the archival lacunae, obscenity indictments have preserved a significant number of extracts from obscene texts, providing valuable clues for reconstructing the meaning of obscenity in the legal culture of antebellum New York. These court records, together with rare surviving examples of books banned as obscene, sensational pulp novels, the catalogues of publishers operating in the literary sex trade, newspaper articles about obscenity prosecutions, moral reform tracts, and other primary documents from the period, help illuminate the distinctions that unfolded between obscene and non-obscene speech.

These sources show that municipal authorities, rather than accept the open-ended invitation offered by the common law, and urged on by strict moralists to engage in sweeping censorship, defined obscenity in fairly limited, restrained terms. To be sure, official conceptions of obscenity were never entirely stable or coherent. Nonetheless, in the years between 1840 and the Civil War, certain basic guidelines separating licit from illicit print emerged, distinctions that were understood by prosecutors, publishers, and authors alike.

Whereas the city's first wave of obscenity indictments in the early 1840s targeted sexually suggestive newspapers, obscenity prosecutions for the remainder of the antebellum period focused on lewd books. A review of the case files of the Court of General Sessions between 1840 and the Civil War discloses that New York grand juries condemned twenty separate books as obscene.[2] Most of these works were originally printed in England or France. New York publishers probably pirated the texts, set them on stereotype plates, and reprinted them at will, common practices in the publishing industry in an era before the United States adopted an international copyright law.[3] Whatever their provenance, publishers' circulars and other advertisements indicate that antebellum dealers commonly marketed these titles as "fancy," a nineteenth-century term for what we might now describe as extreme or "hard-core."

What in particular made a book "fancy" in the eyes of publishers and "obscene" in the eyes of regulators? One feature of such books was that they tended to be expensive by comparison with other indecent texts available in the mid-nineteenth-century literary market. Significantly, they generally cost two dollars or more and were bound in cloth rather than enclosed in cheap paper covers. As such, fancy books were aimed at an audience likely to consist of middle- and upper-class readers who could afford to purchase luxury goods. In addition, such works were typically advertised as containing numerous "elegant" engravings. A circular from one New York pornography dealer captioned "Genuine Fancy Books" characteristically described the offerings as "richly bound in cloth" and "handsomely illustrated with expensive COLORED PLATES." Even at discounted prices, the cost per book ranged from one to four dollars (the latter sum for an oversized edition of *Fanny Hill*).[4]

As for content, almost all the books condemned as obscene described or directly referred to sexual conduct. Many of the activities they portrayed would have been regarded as quite transgressive at the time, such as sex between women, orgies, masturbation, and public sex. The book that gave rise to the greatest number of prosecutions, *Memoirs of a Woman of Pleasure,* included graphic accounts of no fewer than thirty-nine different sexual encounters.[5] Judging from the language of the indictments, many of the volumes in question also contained fancy pictures—that is, explicit illustrations of the nude body or of miscellaneous sexual couplings and group sex. Typical language in a prosecution charged that the book contained "bawdy and obscene prints, representing and exhibiting men and women with their private parts in most indecent postures and attitudes, and representing and exhibiting men and women in the act of carnal copulation, in various attitudes and postures."[6]

Moreover, obscenity indictments reveal that the specific elements of fancy works that authorities found most offensive were often representations of female sexual desire or sexual pleasure, usually narrated by women in the first person. As new middle-class norms arose in the first half of the nineteenth century prescribing sexual purity and "passionlessness" for women, the bourgeoisie came to regard its construction of fundamental sexual differences between men and women as one of its paramount cultural achievements. By highlighting female pleasure, erotic tales narrated by women directly clashed with middle-class sensibilities and flew in the face of bourgeois conventions enshrining feminine piety and chastity.[7]

One of the earliest obscenity indictments brought against a New York book publisher, *People v. Richard Hobbes* (1842), provides an excellent guide to the inventory of bawdy books available in the city before the Civil War. Joining the by then ubiquitous *Memoirs of a Woman of Pleasure* were *Memoirs of the Life and Voluptuous Adventures of the Celebrated Courtesan Mademoiselle Celestine of Paris; The Cabinet of Venus Unlocked; The Curtain Drawn Up; or, The Education of Laura; The Confessions of a Voluptuous Young Lady of High Rank; The Amorous Songster or Jovial Companion; The Lustful Turk; The Amorous History and Adventures of Raymond De B— and*

Father Andouillard; and *The Auto-Biography of a Footman.*[8] Notably, all of the named works were published initially in England, though several purported to be translations of French originals.

The Hobbes indictment also demonstrates how the district attorney and the grand jury constructed the legal meaning of obscenity at the outset of municipal efforts to regulate sexual publications. Perhaps because Hobbes was thought to be the most prolific publisher of erotic books in early 1840s New York, the district attorney drafted the charges against him with unusual thoroughness and provided numerous excerpts deemed to be obscene.

The indictment began with three passages from *Memoirs of a Woman of Pleasure,* the prototypical fancy book for nineteenth-century New Yorkers. Even several decades later, *Fanny Hill* was still being touted in erotica catalogues as "*the* Fancy Book, having never been surpassed in the splendor of its illustrations, or the style in which it was written."[9] Each excerpt in the indictment related one of Fanny's sexual confessions. The first depicted an early scene in which young Fanny describes how her heterosexual desires are initially aroused when she spies on an Italian customer having sex with one of her brothel companions:

> The young Italian (still in his shirt) stood gazing and transported at the sight of beauties that might have fired a dying hermit; his eager eyes devoured her, as she shifted attitudes at his discretion; neither were his hands excluded their share of the highest feast, but wandering, on the hunt of pleasure over every part and inch of her body, so quali[fied] to afford the most exquisite sense of it.[10]

The second, which broke off abruptly in midsentence, had been plucked from a later portrayal by the much more highly experienced

Fanny of an orgy that she enjoys both participating in and observing: "And as he kissed, he gently inclined his head, till it fell back on a pillow disposed to receive it, and leaning himself down all the way with her, at once countenanced and endeared her fall to her. There, as if he had guessed our wishes, or meant to gratify at once his pride in being the master, by title of present possession, of beauties delicate beyond imagination." As the sentence continued in Cleland's original, "he discovered her breasts to his own touch and our common view." It was probably no accident that the district attorney truncated this passage right before the moment of revelation, with the "gratifying" "discovery" of the woman's breasts.[11]

The final selection, though intended as comedy, was also the most explicit. It presented a scene in which Fanny, while working at a "refined" brothel for rich gentlemen, becomes frustrated with her effete clients' increasingly elaborate sexual fetishes (her last customer had been a weak, dissipated man who was obsessed with deflowering virgins) and offers herself free of charge to a sailor in a public house. When he attempts anal intercourse, she at first protests. In rejoinder to her complaint, the sailor makes a nautical quip: "Any port in a storm." According to the indictment, Hobbes's edition of *Memoirs of a Woman of Pleasure* also contained several "wicked . . . bawdy and obscene prints, representing and exhibiting men and women in the act of carnal copulation, in various attitudes and postures."

The indictment transcribed additional excerpts from three of the other obscene books manufactured by Hobbes. Destroyed by censors during the course of the nineteenth century, no copies of any of these titles survive today. One was chattily entitled *The Cabinet of Venus Unlocked in a series of Dialogues between Louisa Lovestone and Mariana Greedy, Two Cyprians! of the most Accomplished Talent in the Science of Practical Love.*[12] The graphic passage chosen by the district attorney conveyed a woman's "rapturous" enjoyment of sexual intercourse:

> Oh, what rapturous exquisite delight as I took it, when it rushed in and filled the whole deep cavity, where I felt it swell and throb as if it would burst with its exertions within. I strained and struggled with him to the utmost of my strength, and seemed inspired beyond my natural powers in every effort. I screamed with excessive extacy [*sic*], and, oh! god of burning lust! At the last flush and overwhelming flow of bliss that gushed into me from him, my senses were wholly entranced and the whole world of love seemed swallowed up in the heavenly sweet delirium.

With its quasi-religious first-person narration of a woman's experience of mutual orgasm, this selection dramatically flouted prevailing bourgeois prescriptions concerning female indifference to the power of lust.

Another part of the indictment quoted a graphic scene from *The Confessions of a Voluptuous Young Lady of High Rank.* The full title of this book, *The Confessions of a Voluptuous Young Lady of High Rank. Disclosing Her Secret Longings and Private Amours before Marriage. Forming a Curious Picture of Fashionable Life and Refined Sensuality,* also emphasized the theme of female ardor. According to the nineteenth-century bibliographer Henry Spencer Ashbee, *The Confessions* consisted of thirty-nine pages of letters written by a "heroine-authoress," named Tilly Touchitt, to the editor of a London gentlemen's magazine, *The Rambler.* In her epistles, "Tilly explains the inclination she always had for the opposite sex, and the curiosity which a man excited in her." Among other things, her inquisitiveness leads her to spy through a keyhole on her naked cousin, Joe. In her excitement, she loses her balance and falls into Joe's room. As Ashbee relates: "The contemplation of her cousin's nude manliness has so far disposed her, that very little coaxing on his part is sufficient to induce her to submit to his embraces, and make him master of her virginity."[13] It was Tilly's detailed description of her ensuing defloration by her cousin that Whiting chose to include in Hobbes' indictment:

> Joe, who had drawn me by the legs to the very edge of the bed across which he had laid me, had the precaution, for some special reasons of his own, to place a pillow beneath the critical pass to be stormed, so that at the first push with which he sought with steady force to send the stiff in-driven wedge home to its ultimate destination, I could feel its turbulent head lodged fairly enough within the magic circle and driving furiously onward along the central route, till I felt it hitch suddenly against the narrowed inlet which refused him further passage toward the interior.

In reproducing a woman's blow-by-blow account of her first experience of sexual penetration, the indictment further underscored the emerging connection between female erotic subjectivity and obscenity.

The last extract belonged to another apparently lost pornographic text, *The Amorous History and Adventures of Raymond De B— and Father Andouillard, Detailing Some Curious Histories, and Disclosing the Pastimes of a Convent, with Some Remarks on the Use and Advantages of Flagellation.* On the basis of its title, one can assume that this work belonged to a body of explicit anti-Catholic pornography that circulated widely in Europe during the eighteenth century and well into the first half of the nineteenth.[14] The title's reference to flagellation is noteworthy because explicit literature on whipping and sadomasochism rarely appeared in obscenity indictments in antebellum New York or in the catalogues of New York's leading erotica dealers, even though it was quite popular in English pornography circles of the day.[15] The relative rarity of such books in the New York market may mean that corporal punishment had less resonance as an erotic motif for consumers in New York than in England. In any event, the excerpt chosen by the district attorney, copied out in meticulously neat handwriting, did not touch on flagellation. Instead, it graphically described a sexual encounter between a young man, a girl, and an older woman, including the woman's "longing" to engage in fellatio.

The Hobbes indictment concluded by noting that the "most gross and filthy scenes of lewdness and obscenity" from *Memoirs of the Life and Adventures of the Celebrated Courtesan Mademoiselle Celestine of Paris* were "not fit or proper to be used, named or mentioned in any language, or in any court of Justice." The same reticence, which reflected a strategy that would become increasingly common in the coming years, marked the district attorney's treatment of Hobbes's editions of *The Curtain Drawn Up; or, The Education of Laura; The Lustful Turk;* and *The Auto-Biography of a Footman.*[16]

Though the Hobbes bill declined to offer an example from *The Curtain Drawn Up,* accompanying indictments against a print shop owner and a bookstand operator who sold the book helpfully include three allegedly obscene selections from the edition produced by Hobbes.[17] This work, which remained a staple of American erotica catalogues throughout the nineteenth century, was an asserted English translation of a lascivious, libertine classic of the French Enlightenment attributed to Mirabeau, *Le Rideau levé; ou, L'Education de Laure.*[18] Like many of the other allegedly obscene texts, it was narrated by a female protagonist. Two of the quoted passages emphasized the heroine's preoccupation with sex and her eager erotic spectatorship. This item from her diary, for instance, alluded to female masturbation and described her obsessive observation of male genitalia:

> Arrived at home. I failed not to profit by the knowledge I had acquired through Isabella and, like her, procured myself each day the most delicious sensations of pleasure, and frequently my heated imagination urged me to double the dose. I thought of nothing but a man, and I never saw one without fixing my eyes upon that part which I knew contained the idol of my desires, and which the very idea of filled me with a fire that was insupportable.

The indictments also copied out this scene, in which she spies on a man she regards as her father having sex with his mistress:

> The next day my father, who was only dressed in his night gown, took Lucette, who was also as lightly clad, into his room. He took great care to fasten the door, and also to place the curtain right, but thanks to my invention I had guarded against these obstacles. They had hardly been gone two minutes when my impatience led me to the door and I lifted gently the corner of the curtain. I saw Lucette, her breasts entirely bare, which my father held in his hands, at the same time covering them with kisses. This lasted not long, for tormented with desire, he soon took off petticoats, stays, shift; in short, everything was thrown aside.

According to the indictments, the Hobbes version of *The Curtain Drawn Up* supplemented incestuous voyeurism of this sort with numerous prints of men and women engaged in various acts of copulation.[19]

Another 1842 indictment against a second early publisher of obscene books in New York, Henry R. Robinson, named the identical nine books that Hobbes was charged with selling. It also included the same three excerpts from *Memoirs of a Woman of Pleasure* that were quoted in the Hobbes bill. The eight other titles were summarily alleged to contain "divers wicked, false, feigned, impious, impure, bawdy, and obscene matters wherein are represented the most gross and filthy scenes of lewdness and obscenity."[20]

The repetition in the cases against the two publishers suggests that the titles in question may have constituted a discrete corpus of books that New York authorities at the beginning of the 1840s considered obscene. Turning to obscenity prosecutions in the 1850s, we see that five of the books named in the earlier cases—*Memoirs of a Woman of Pleasure, The Curtain Drawn Up, The Lustful Turk, The Confessions of a Voluptuous Young Lady of High Rank,* and *Memoirs of the Life and Adventures of the Celebrated Mademoiselle Celestine of Paris*—also appear in indictments for this decade, a testament to both their perennial popularity and their continuing status as forbidden books.[21] Other titles, such as *The Life and Adventures of Silas Shovewell* and *The Secret Habits of the Female Sex,* first surface in indictments during the 1850s; that they thereafter recur multiple times suggests that they were recent additions to publishers' lists but soon entered the canon of condemned works. Moreover, although several New York publishers began to experiment in the mid-1850s with selling erotic stories composed by American authors, both records of obscenity prosecutions and catalogues of publishers from this decade indicate that European imports continued to dominate the market for fancy print.[22]

During this second decade of obscenity prosecution, district attorneys routinely declined to include in their indictments specific passages considered to be obscene, out of an ostentatious concern with protecting the modesty of the court's records. Though the 1850s indictments are therefore less revealing, one can infer that sexual narrations by women continued to trigger classification of certain works as obscene. For instance, the title of one 1850s text prosecuted for obscenity, *Mary Ann Temple: Being an Authentic and Romantic History of an Amorous and Lively Girl; of Rare Beauty, and Strong Natural Love of Pleasure!* conveys the leitmotif of female passion. This work was unusual in that it seems to have been of American rather than European authorship. It was also distinctive in appearing in a relatively cheap, yellow-covered edition, for twenty-five cents.[23] Even without the explicit engravings that often accompanied more expensive, bound erotica, *Mary Ann Temple*'s first-person rendition of a girl's sexual awakening made it vulnerable to an obscenity charge. In the novel's opening pages, the eponymous heroine boldly confesses her love of naughty reading. Although she was born in Boston to respectable parents, she admits that as a girl she liked nothing better than "to get up in the attic with a forbidden novel" or to saunter through the streets attracting the admiration and catcalls of saucy young men. She also describes her avid study as a fourteen-year-old of a "book of a peculiar character" lent to her by a friend, "whose opportunities for the study of comparative anatomy had been much more extensive" than hers and who makes Mary Ann promise not to show it to anyone. When she realizes that the book contains plates of "scene[s] which often [take] place in married life; but which young ladies are supposed to be wholly ignorant of," she "devour[s] all its contents and examine[s] its pictures thoroughly." Her sexual curiosity is so powerful that the book, hidden under her pillow, invades her subconscious and stimulates lascivious dreams at night.[24]

By the 1850s, the ban on overt representation of female sexuality sometimes applied regardless of the erotic content of the publication. The repeated prosecution of sellers of *The Secret Habits of the Female Sex* is a prime case in point. Allegedly written by a French physician, Dr. Jean Dubois, *The Secret Habits of the Female Sex* was often marketed by erotica dealers as a vehicle for sexual stimulation. The complete title of this unusual work conveys a more accurate sense of its contents: *The Secret Habits of the Female Sex: Letters Addressed to a Mother on the Evils of Solitude, and Its Seductive Temptations to Young Girls, the Premature Victims of a Pernicious Passion, with All Its Frightful Consequences: Deformity of Mind and Body, Destruction of Beauty, and Entailing Disease and Death; but from Which, by Attention to the Timely Warnings Here Given, the Devotee May Be Saved, and Become an Ornament to Society, a Virtuous Wife, and a Refulgent Mother!* As its full name suggests, *Secret Habits* was actually an extremely dour, if sensationalized, tract on the perils of female masturbation. Of "all the causes of disease," it announced, "there was none more fruitful than that secret vice to which the name of onanism, or self-pollution, has been given. Among young females, more particularly, does this vice exist to an alarming extent."[25] Nonetheless, the book's allusions to the mysterious sexual practices of women, its French author, and accompanying illustrations of nubile female nudes probably misled men into buying it for the purpose of sexual excitement or satisfying their curiosity about female sexuality. By calling attention to the erotic explorations of insatiable girls and young women, *The Secret Habits of the Female Sex*, even though it dwelled on the morbid consequences of those practices, also ran directly afoul of the emerging legal taboo against articulations of female desire.

Fancy publications portraying sex and nudity or featuring female passion and pleasure were not the only forms of sexual discourse

3.1 Frontispiece, Jean Dubois, M. D., The Secret Habits of the Female Sex *(New York, 1848).*

COURTESY OF THE KINSEY INSTITUTE FOR RESEARCH IN SEX, GENDER, AND REPRODUCTION.

THE

SECRET HABITS

OF

THE FEMALE SEX;

LETTERS ADDRESSED TO A MOTHER ON THE EVILS OF SOLITUDE, AND ITS SEDUCTIVE TEMPTATIONS TO YOUNG GIRLS, THE PREMATURE

VICTIMS OF A PERNICIOUS PASSION,

WITH ALL ITS FRIGHTFUL CONSEQUENCES:

DEFORMITY OF MIND AND BODY, DESTRUCTION OF BEAUTY,

AND ENTAILING DISEASE AND DEATH;

BUT FROM WHICH, BY ATTENTION TO THE TIMELY WARNINGS HERE GIVEN, THE DEVOTEE MAY BE SAVED, AND BECOME AN ORNAMENT TO SOCIETY, A VIRTUOUS WIFE, AND A REFULGENT MOTHER!

This Work should be read by all classes; while it forcibly describes the Misery attendant upon Solitude, it prescribes a Medical Treatment and regimen which has never failed of success.

From the French of Jean Dubois, M. D.

NEW-YORK:

SOLD BY THE BOOKSELLERS GENERALLY.

1848.

3.2 Title page, Jean Dubois, M. D., The Secret Habits of the Female Sex *(New York, 1848).*

COURTESY OF THE KINSEY INSTITUTE FOR RESEARCH IN SEX, GENDER, AND REPRODUCTION.

produced by antebellum publishers. In any reconstruction of the meaning of obscenity, it is instructive to consider not only what kinds of sexual representations triggered prosecutions, but also what kinds did not.

Recall that publishers of the second generation of flash crime papers, starting with the *National Police Gazette*, successfully crafted ways to market sexually themed writing without inciting obscenity charges, despite repeated condemnations of such journals by custodians of traditional morality. The explosion of American sensational fiction in the 1840s and 1850s provides another revealing guide to the boundaries of obscenity in antebellum New York.[26] This genre originally derived from European "city mystery" novels and British "penny dreadfuls."[27] The American version, often called yellow-jacket literature, recounted "tales of criminal underworlds, urban squalor, and elite luxury and decadence."[28] (The phrase "yellow jacket" referred to the garish yellow wrappers used to attract buyers for these early paperbacks, though publishers issued them in bright blue, green, and orange covers as well.[29]) The most risqué examples also specialized in horrifically detailed depictions of violence and torture, combined with euphemistic, titillating references to sexual license.[30] The erotic scenes, while elliptical in their descriptions, nonetheless raised highly provocative themes. The sexual practices alluded to in sensational fiction included "incest, sadomasochism, homosexuality, group sex, miscegenation, child sex, [and] mass orgies."[31] Because of its obsession with the dark secrets and sexual excesses of life in the big city, this literature has appropriately been described as "American porno-gothic."[32]

Significantly, the leading publishers of American porno-gothic novels were often the very same men who published the expensive fancy books that typically provoked prosecution for obscenity. Frequently using a separate imprint to distinguish the genres, they typically marketed this relatively safe category of indecent literature as "racy" reading. Unlike bound fancy books, which sold for two dollars or more, racy novels were usually issued as slim, paper-covered pamphlets that cost only a quarter. A representative advertisement for "Rich, Rare, and Racy Reading" in 1857, for instance, listed numerous paperback sensational novels for twenty-five cents.[33] Because of their low cost, racy pamphlets were accessible to a much broader segment of the population than fancy books were. Less than a hundred pages long, small enough to fit in a pants pocket, and illustrated only with a few rough woodcuts, the pamphlets were intended to be read quickly and probably disposed of with similar dispatch.[34]

George Thompson, a native New Yorker, wrote much of the most sexually scandalous and violent sensational fiction published in New York in the late 1840s and the 1850s. While living in Boston and New York during his twenties and early thirties, Thompson was part of a rambunctious, bohemian subculture of writers, reporters, actors, and theater impresarios who made their living from popular entertainment.[35] In this setting, he churned out lurid blends of graphic violence and euphemistic sex with titillating titles like *The Ladies' Garter* (c. 1851), *The Gay Girls of New York* (1854), and *The Bridal Chamber, and Its Mysteries* (1856). Henry Spencer Ashbee, the leading nineteenth-century bibliographer of erotic and semierotic literature, estimated that Thompson had written nearly a hundred books. References to more than sixty of these exist today, in addition to more than twenty-five novels in their entirety.[36] During his most productive years, Thompson maintained close professional ties with at least three men known for publishing or dealing in pornography, penning stories for George Akarman's sexually explicit periodical, *Venus' Miscellany*, and editing two semierotic newspapers, Thomas Ormsby's *Weekly Whip* and Prescott Harris's *Broadway Belle*.

Although Thompson sometimes wrote about other locales, the

chief inspiration for his stories came from the "mysteries and miseries" of New York. Adopting the tongue-in-cheek moniker Greenhorn to suggest the innocence of the author confronting the mysterious and dangerous ways of the city, Thompson opened his 1850 novel *Jack Harold* with an evocative description of rampant sexual license in Gotham. New York was a "mighty metropolis that lies brooding upon the waters like a slumbering giant; in commerce, a monster—in vice, a hell—in splendor, almost equal to the fabled Oriental cities of the East—and in licentiousness, a rival of gay, voluptuous Paris." Never known for his modesty, he also inserted an epigraph from Byron's *Don Juan:*

> I mean to show things as they really are,
> Not as they *ought* to be; for I avow
> That till we see what's what in fact, we're far
> From much improvement.[37]

Significantly, he omitted the first line of Byron's stanza: "But now I'm going to be immoral."[38] Unlike Byron, Thompson passed off his tale of the criminal Jack Harold as "a story with a moral," a cautionary tale that revealed "the awful effects of crime, the consequences of vice, the power of beauty, the seductive influences of voluptuousness, the blighting results of passion, and the mysteries of city life."[39]

In what he described as his "own peculiar style," Thompson's chief device for showing "things as they really are" was the inversion of conventional sources of mid-nineteenth-century moral and social authority.[40] In blatant mockery of those who envisioned the city as an orderly, well-governed society, Thompson's novels presented the metropolis as deeply corrupt, carnivalesque, and terrifying. It was a world where ministers were always licentious and immoral, middle-class women were always faithless and lecherous, and judges were always lawless and unjust.[41]

Sex and violence, often linked together, were Thompson's signature vehicles for expressing these themes of disorder and darkness. As his leading biographers have asserted, his works are "filled with gore, sex, and perversity to such a degree that Thompson can be identified as the most shockingly sensational" American author of his period.[42] Characters in his novels experience brutal whippings, violent rapes, disfigurement by acid, cannibalism, and other forms of torture, presented in chillingly graphic detail.

In sharp contrast to the expansive attention that he lavished on acts of violence and horror, Thompson wrote coyly and allusively about sex, substituting naughty winks to the reader for his otherwise ample powers of observation. In a representative passage from one his most popular novels, *City Crimes,* Thompson related an incestuous sexual triangle comprising a lecherous mother, her equally wanton daughter, and a ship captain whom they have seduced: "And clasping both ladies around the waists, he kissed them alternately, again and again. That night was one of guilty rapture to all the parties; but the particulars must be supplied by the reader's own imagination."[43] In *The Delights of Love; or, The Lady Libertine,* he again called on the imagination of his audience to fill in "the particulars" when contemplating the union of the widowed heroine, Julia Hamilton, and a man whose "vigorous thighs" have attracted her attention: "After indulging in every imaginable luxury, [they] fell asleep in each other's arms, and their intermingled breath wafted their souls to the rosy realms of golden dream-land."[44]

The preoccupation of mid-nineteenth-century American sensational fiction with sexual transgression, violence, and crime often led reformers to condemn it as immoral and dangerous.[45] They were especially concerned about the dangers such books presented for young working-class readers. Shopgirls and mechanics seemed particularly susceptible to the charms of cheap literature, in the eyes of these self-appointed custodians of morality, though reformers acknowledged that the well-off sometimes succumbed to temptation as well. An anonymous 1855 book by a Chicago doctor, *The Confessions and Experience of a Novel Reader*, was emblematic of growing concern over the allegedly destructive influence of racy novels. "If, I say, any one has any doubts as to the fearfully rapid increase of this public poison—a demoralizing literature, the real 'Pandora's box of evil passions'—the floodgate, from beneath whose slimy jaws runs a stream of pollution, sending forth its pestilential branches to one great ocean of immorality, let such an one take a trip with me through the length and breadth of our land." According to the author, the very survival of the nation depended on the suppression of literature of this sort. Otherwise, it threatened to "subvert the purity of our Republican Institutions" and incite "elements of revolution" that "will crush us in the might and magnitude of our fancied security."[46]

Writing in a similar vein, a New York representative of the American Tract Society took devout readers to "the door of Satan's workshop." There, they could see an indecent publishing operation in full swing, where Satan's literary minions—"authors, compositors, printers, engravers, publishers, booksellers, venders, by myriads"—were "all busy and indefatigable" in concocting an "awful laboratory of mental and moral poison." What additional revelations could possibly be needed, he wondered, to convince authorities to suppress the nation's dangerously "unprincipled press"? In his impassioned view, the "plagues of Egypt were tolerable" by comparison with the "loathsome swarms of literary vermin" who were invading the country's dwellings and seeking to "'corrupt the land,' to deprave the hearts, and ruin the souls of our citizens."[47]

Foreshadowing the late nineteenth-century campaigns of Anthony Comstock against "Vampire Literature," yet another guardian of morality mourned the growing prevalence of what he viewed as "satanic literature." It was not enough for greedy publishers to "descend into the sewers of French demoralization, and gather up for American homes the worst literary abominations of the old world." Now they had hired "native anonymous scribblers" to write "flimsy trashy" pamphlets. Even worse, these indigenous "moral monstrosities" circulated much more widely than expensive European erotica: "Got up in cheap form, rendered attractive by meretricious engravings and exaggerated titles, these pernicious books are thrust into almost every accessible place, and are infecting to the core a large portion of the youth of the country."[48]

Despite widespread criticism of this type, the distinctive fusion of graphic violence and sexual allusion in racy pulp fiction failed to arouse the wrath of legal authorities in New York. Throughout the antebellum period, obscenity prosecutions targeted only sex, not violence, even when writers and publishers outdid themselves in offering the most gruesome and eroticized representations of violence that their imaginations could invent.

In his groundbreaking work *Beneath the American Renaissance,* David Reynolds has argued that the indirectness that characterized sexual expression in even the most shocking examples of sensational literature may have stemmed from "deep-seated guilt" about sexual desire and the "residual repressiveness of the Puritan conscience." This guilt, he writes, "engendered a notably furtive quality in erotic expression, as seen in . . . the prevalent use of euphemisms like 'snowy globes.'" One is indeed struck when reading these texts by the wide disparity between the vivid, detailed presentation of violence and the allusive, elliptical presentation of sex and the human body. An understanding of the legal culture of antebellum New York makes clear, however, that the "odd combination of furtive sexuality and unbridled violence" that Reynolds rightly detects in much of the popular fiction of the 1840s and '50s, rather than expressing puritanical guilt, instead reflected the strategic maneuvering of individuals working in the field of erotic entertainment.[49]

For writers and their publishers, a crucial feature of the late antebellum legal climate was the existence of legal bans on certain kinds of sexual representations, especially those in explicit form. For this reason, even though racy novels were not subject to prosecution, the genre of racy prose was strongly shaped by the law of obscenity. Indeed, it is no accident that at the same time that obscenity was emerging as a new category of morals regulation, New York publishers of fancy books also began to produce provocative novels that alluded to sex without directly describing it.[50]

Authors and publishers who operated within this climate quickly learned to negotiate the law of obscenity to their advantage. In his monumental work *History of Prostitution* (1858), the health reformer and physician William Sanger blamed licentious literature for driving men to brothels and fueling the spread of prostitution.[51] The chief culprit was not fancy books, which after all were expensive and relatively scarce, but the widespread dissemination of "cheap pamphlets" that hinted at sexual disclosure but stopped short of "absolute obscenity." Sanger singled out one unnamed novelist as especially dangerous. Like George Thompson, this sly author wrote "in a strain eminently calculated to excite the passions, but so carefully guarded as to avoid absolute obscenity, and embellishe[d] his works with wood-cuts which approach lasciviousness as nearly as possible without being indictable."[52]

Thompson was especially skilled at invoking the law of obscenity to invest his tales with an aura of forbidden excitement. One of his favorite stylistic devices was to draw attention to a sexual scene and then abruptly "draw the curtain" or "draw the veil." A typical scene from *The Delights of Love* illustrates this strategy, in which Thompson also uses asterisks to elide illicit material. "'Be my Adonis!' murmured the lady libertine, as she pantingly sank into the arms of the eager youth, who whispered, as he pressed her yielding form to his wildly throbbing heart—'I am yours, my Venus!'**** It is a great pity, we know, and the reader may blame us for it; but we are here reluctantly compelled to drop the curtain."[53] Thompson often attributed such restraint to a desire to avoid censure by authorities and, implicitly, legal censorship. In a characteristic passage from another novel, he begins to describe a dinner party served by naked adolescents that turns into an orgy between the teenagers and the adult guests, a scene he claims has actually taken place in New York. Just as the sexual action takes off, Thompson pulls back: "Our ready pen longs—yea, longs to glide off into the most delicious *details*. . . but Society, like a grim and harsh pedagogue, flourishes its rattan of Censure above our devoted pate, and talks of 'morality,' and 'propriety.'"[54]

Thompson's calculated omission of explicit sexual acts only intensified the prurience of his plots and invested the point at which he "drew the veil" with an added frisson. At the same time, the omissions helped fetishize the perceived boundary between the obscene and the nonobscene, as evidenced by the prolonged leering at partially clothed women, exposed cleavages, and the like, that runs throughout his work.

Through such strategies, sensational novelists like Thompson were able to profit from the distinction between merely suggestive or racy works that "excite[d] the passions" by flirting with obscenity and those works, to use Sanger's words, of "absolute obscenity" that were frequent targets of indictment. At a basic level, authors of racy pamphlets employed literary indirection because doing so spared their publishers (who paid them their living) from the threat of prosecution.[55] But producers of such texts more than made up for what they could not show when it came to sex with exceedingly graphic, stomach-churning portrayals of violence, which metropolitan authorities did not censor as obscene.

Deference to the obscenity taboo also offered the benefit of heightening the public's interest in sexual themes and enhancing the appeal of sensational novels that approached but did not cross the legal threshold for obscenity. At the same time, by inscribing in their writing the prohibition on overt representations of sex, racy authors invited violation of that ban in illegal fancy books produced by the same men who marketed racy paperbacks. To aid this process, characters in sensational fiction often referred to the existence of more explicit, forbidden sexual print. In George Thompson's *Mysteries of Bond Street; or, The Seraglios of Upper Tendom* (1857), for example, a cruel seducer installs the innocent heroine in a brothel. Thompson points out that the house has a library that contains copies of *Fanny Hill, The Lustful Turk, Betty Ireland,* and other "detestable volumes." Similarly, in *The Ladies' Garter; or, The Platonic Marriage,* the female protagonist, whose elderly husband has imprisoned her in an attic, "beguiled my time by reading several delicious (but forbidden) French novels, by a certain free-and-easy author whose name cannot with strict propriety be pronounced by female lips." Likewise, in *City Crimes,* the femme fatale Julia Franklin is caught "feasting her impure imagination" on engravings of "an obscene character, consisting principally of nude male figures."[56]

By encouraging the production of borderline or semierotic publications, the obscenity taboo dramatically increased the sheer *volume* of sexual discourse that was commercially available in the city before the war. To give just one example, the *New York Tribune* reported that during a raid on one pornographer's establishment in 1857, the police found "several dozens of volumes of the most obscene and filthy stuff that ever disgraced language, with illustrations to match" but by contrast uncovered "several thousand specimens of yellow-covered literature." The same publisher estimated at only one in twenty the ratio between the fancy books he published that were "in opposition to law" and his "humbler pamphlets" of racy fiction that circulated freely.[57]

Racy novels also multiplied the *types* of sexual practices that were represented in antebellum culture. At their tamest, racy books reworked and re-presented the once scandalous subjects of the original flash press—prostitution, sex crimes, the misdeeds of the rich and powerful—but made them more acceptable by adding the veneer of fiction. A novel about prostitution like Thompson's *Gay Girls of New York*, for instance, revisited the turf first trodden by the flash editors but now took the legal, more legitimate form of a literary treatment. At other times, sensational novels pushed beyond the limits of the flash weeklies, often thematizing subjects like incest, sadomasochism, and mass orgies, which were understood as far more transgressive than prostitution. While skirting around the description of actual sexual acts, racy novels nevertheless reflected sexual possibilities at least as provocative as those described in the books that prosecutors typically regarded as obscene. And the novels did so in a relatively inexpensive medium that was increasingly available to a mass audience.[58]

The interdiction of obscene speech, then, did little to enforce decency or improve the morals of metropolitan readers. Rather than stamp out licentious writing, obscenity prohibitions encouraged the creation of a huge body of risqué literature that publicized a myriad of non-normative sexual desires and practices.

A second major category of popular writing that touched on sexual matters but largely escaped indictment for obscenity in antebellum New York (although not later on) consisted of quasi-medical guides, ostensibly designed for married people or "those about to marry," concerning human anatomy, sexual technique, reproduction, contraception, and abortion. Many of the best-selling titles, such as Frederick Hollick's *Marriage Guide* and Thomas Low Nichols's *Esoteric Anthropology*, were published in New York and circulated freely there.[59] The increasing volume and explicitness of books on reproductive control and sexual anatomy that became available to lay audiences after 1850 helped create a publishing boom for commercial self-help literature.[60] Thinly veiled advertisements for contraceptive devices and abortionists in popular newspapers and mail circulars were also common.[61]

Like sensational fiction, physiological discussions of contraception and abortion were frequently denounced by moral reformers. On the whole, although a few publishers of books on reproductive control were recognized as reputable, the business "was neither openly accepted nor respectable."[62] Nonetheless, there is no record in antebellum New York of any successful prosecution specifically directed at a seller of literature on contraception or abortion. On one unusual occasion in 1847 a freethinker and publisher named Charles Lohman was indicted for selling an allegedly obscene book, *The Married Woman's Private Medical Companion*.[63] This tract, published by Lohman just a few months before under the alias A. M. Mauriceau, contained plainly marked sections offering advice on the "prevention of pregnancy" and providing information on methods of abortion.[64] But Lohman was not just any author. He was the husband of the notorious "Madame Restell" (Caroline Ann Trow), who had emigrated to New York from England in 1832. Once in the city, Madame Restell established a lucrative abortion practice that catered to New York gentry. With a lavish lifestyle that included daily rides up and down Broadway in a regal, four-horse-drawn carriage, she became a symbol of the decadence of the city's aristocratic elite. As such, she repeatedly drew the ire of self-proclaimed populists like the *National Police Gazette*'s George Wilkes and his old boss, the labor advocate Mike Walsh.[65]

Even under these circumstances, Lohman's arrest and subsequent grand jury indictment were highly unorthodox. Up to that time, New York officials had declined to prosecute publishers of medical advice literature and marital guides containing information on reproductive control, including abortion. But the indictment papers in the Lohman case make clear that it was the defendant's association with Restell, who had been indicted for the third time the week before on a felony charge of manslaughter and a misdemeanor charge of "procuring miscarriage," that had prompted his prosecution.[66] A private party had written to the Democratic district attorney John McKeon to bring *The Married Woman's Private Medical Companion* to his attention and had emphasized the author's connection to Restell: "This book contains about 160 pages and its sole object is the advertising of Madame Restell's pills under the name of M. De Someaux's Preventive to Conception." Fuming that "This Lohman boast[ed] of having sold over twenty five thousand of these books in less than three months" and alleging that he advertised both his book and Restell's abortion practice extensively in newspapers throughout the country, the complaint implored the district attorney to take action against the "immense . . . dealings of this couple in wholesale murder."[67]

McKeon was highly receptive to this plea. He was then in the midst of prosecuting Restell under a recent New York law that criminalized as second-degree manslaughter abortions causing the death of a woman or of a fetus after quickening. Indeed, McKeon would make his name in office primarily through a series of sensational trials against this abortionist to the elite. Shortly after receiving the letter, he had Lohman arrested and arraigned. The celebrated criminal defense attorney James Topham Brady, who earlier in the decade had represented the editors of the *Sunday Flash* and was engaged in defending Madame Restell, served as Lohman's counsel. Lohman entered a plea of not guilty and was released on bail.[68]

The subsequent indictment included two passages from *The Married Woman's Private Medical Companion* as evidence of its obscenity. The first excerpt alluded to the only two birth control methods purportedly available to women: forced miscarriage (that is, abortion) or the prevention of conception altogether by using De Someaux's pills. In touting the second remedy, Lohman appealed directly to women by highlighting the idea of female control, a critical issue in an era when popular contraceptive strategies such as withdrawal relied almost entirely on the man's cooperation and willpower: "Miscarriage, although attended with but little danger when skillfully effected and properly conducted, can only be considered as an alternative, only a choice of evils. But thanks to the indefatigable researches of the learned and humane M. De Someaux . . . pregnancy can be prevented. By this discovery *every woman can have in her own power the means of prevention.*" A second excerpt addressed a different audience: fathers worried that their unmarried daughters might be impregnated. Rather than subjecting their female offspring to inevitable "ruin" and themselves to "despair," would it not be far more charitable if fathers allowed their daughters to take De Someaux's pills? "I appeal to any father trembling for the reputation of his child

. . . whether a preventive which shall save her from a situation which would soon disclose all to the world would not be an act of mercy, of charity, of philanthropy—whether it might not save him from despair, and her from ruin?" Whereas "fastidious conformists" might object, truly compassionate men would acknowledge the superiority of contraceptive pills.[69]

Despite the anomaly of the indictment, New York criminal authorities subsequently acted in a fashion that was consistent with their customary tolerance for quasi-medical texts on reproductive control and abortion, by declining to bring Lohman to trial.[70] Nor did Lohman's brush with an obscenity prosecution impede ongoing sales of *The Married Woman's Private Medical Companion,* which went through numerous editions between 1847 and 1860. "Fastidious conformists" apparently were no match for the steady demand for information about contraception and abortion.[71] Moreover, Lohman's work continued to be advertised openly in New York for two decades. As one would expect, it was a staple of the back pages of second-generation flash weeklies, as evidenced by this 1855 notice from the *Atlas* promoting the twentieth edition of the book: "The Married Woman's Private Medical Companion by Dr. A. M. Mauriceau, Professor of Diseases of Women, Twentieth Edition, Price, $1.00. 'THIS WORK IS INTENDED ESPECIALLY FOR THE MARRIED, or those contemplating marriage, as it discloses important secrets, which should be known to them particularly.'"[72] But advertisements for Lohman's book also appeared in respectable mainstream papers.[73]

It should be noted that before the Civil War other locales showed less tolerance for literature on reproductive control. In Massachusetts, in the same year that Lohman was indicted in New York, a doctor named Walter Scott Tarbox was convicted of distributing allegedly obscene circulars to households in Boston advertising an early version of the diaphragm. The Supreme Judicial Court overturned his conviction on a technicality, but it did not reject the link between contraception and obscenity.[74]

In Philadelphia the health reformer Frederick Hollick was also indicted for obscenity in 1846 for selling a collection of his popular lectures on health, sex, reproduction, and anatomy. This book, *The Origin of Life: A Popular Treatise on the Philosophy and Physiology of Reproduction in Plants and Animals, including the Details of Human Generation with a Full Description of the Male and Female Organs,* had first been published in New York in 1845. A second indictment accused Hollick of circulating "lewd pictures: the colorful anatomical plates that boosted book sales." A third obscenity charge stemmed from his use on the lecture circuit of life-size, papier-mâché "anatomical models" of naked women, imported from Paris.[75] As Hollick described these nude models in his preface to *The Origin of Life:* "The conviction that they are natural is, at first, so strong, that many have even *fainted away* at a first view, from the impression that they were viewing a real body!"[76]

Though the philosophy propounded by Hollick attracted a significant middle-class following, his ideas were as controversial as the titillating visual aids in his lectures and books. Among other things, he emphasized the importance of sexual pleasure for married couples and the right of both women and men to control their own bodies.[77] He offered advice on contraception and even advertised condoms. He also promoted the use of aphrodisiacs like tea, coffee, and marijuana to improve sexual performance and enjoyment.[78]

At the Philadelphia trial, Hollick's counsel defended him as a popular physician, and his works as medical and scientific knowledge. The judge hearing the case disagreed. He stated that "he had examined the volume, and was of opinion that it was an improper publication, and entirely different from the scientific works adopted as class books by medical students."[79] Classifying *The Origin of Life* as obscenity rather than science, he also asserted that the reformer's status as an "irregular" physician and his lack of licensed medical credentials prevented him from speaking on subjects of sex and anatomy.[80] The trial had to be postponed when the prosecution could not produce a witness to prove that Hollick had disseminated his work in Philadelphia. Even so, the court required him to post a thousand dollars as security that he would not sell *The Origin of Life* locally, pending continuation of the trial. It also warned that if his lectures "contain[ed] language as low and obscene as some that is found in his book he had better suspend them for the present."[81]

Yet Hollick was ultimately able to turn this prosecution for obscenity to his advantage. He skipped out on his bond and moved to the more hospitable publishing climate of New York, where he resumed his lecturing and publishing ventures without legal interference. In a new edition of *The Origin of Life* published in 1846 Hollick proclaimed: "I am happy to state, that, during this persecution, my practice has been more extensive than before, and that it is still on the increase." Announcing his intent to distribute his books even more widely, he boasted: "I am now preparing to resume my lectures, at the proper season, and I have also written and published some new scientific works—for the million!"[82] In 1850 he published a second book, *The Marriage Guide*. Thanks in large part to the publicity generated by the Philadelphia trial, it was also a resounding commercial success.[83] In an afterword, Hollick characterized that prosecution as "an absurd and bungling attempt" that "not only failed, most completely," but also "increased the popularity of both books and lectures by a hundredfold, while the would-be monopolists of knowledge became truly pitiable objects of public scorn and contempt."[84] Like his earlier work, *The Marriage Guide* contained frank treatments of sexual anatomy, offered explicit advice about sex, and showed a flair for the sensational. Listed among its chapter headings were "The Vagina," "The Penis," "Proper Time for Sexual Indulgence," and "Singular Case of Female Hermaphrodism." It included numerous illustrations, with captions such as "View of the Organs with the Clitoris Hanging Down in its Natural Position, When Not Erect." It also contained nine pages on the "prevention of conception." Nonetheless, New York officials did not interfere with its sale.[85]

This forbearance demonstrates the relatively free commerce enjoyed by the city's publishers and booksellers to promote quasi-scientific works on health reform, sexual physiology, and reproductive advice, including those considered highly provocative and even obscene in other jurisdictions. At the same time, sex manuals that struck New York officials as designed for sexual arousal rather than edification about sexual physiology could cross over the line into illicit obscenity. Two sex guides that purported to offer advice to married couples but were sold by men who were heavily involved in the erotic print trade fell into this group: *Mysteries of Women . . . Containing Advice to Husbands and Wives regarding the Means of Making the Marriage Bed, the Throne of Venus' Joys* and *The Marriage Bed, or Wedding Secrets Revealed by the Torch of Hymen*. In addition, *The Secret Habits of the Female Sex*, a work by a purported physician that dwelled on female masturbation and included pictures of shapely nude women, triggered multiple obscenity charges in New York County.[86]

A final category of controversial writing that escaped prosecution for obscenity in antebellum New York consisted of literary works that contained erotic allusions. An instructive example is Walt Whitman's *Leaves of Grass*, first published in New York in 1855. Many critics charged that Whitman's frank treatment of sexual desire was highly indecent, and some went so far as to urge criminal prosecution for obscenity. A review in the New York journal *Criterion*, for instance, concluded: "Thus, then, we leave this gathering of muck to the laws which, certainly, if they fulfill their intent, must have power to suppress such gross obscenity." Similarly, an 1856 review of *Leaves of Grass* in *Frank Leslie's Illustrated Newspaper* carped: "We shall not aid in extending the sale of this intensely vulgar, nay, absolutely beastly book, by telling our readers where it may be purchased." Suppression was the only appropriate response: "The only review we shall attempt of it, will be to thus publicly call the attention of the grand jury to a matter that needs presentment by them."[87]

Earlier in the same decade, conservative commentators, hurling similar charges at Nathaniel Hawthorne's *Scarlet Letter*, had attacked it as an immoral book that encouraged sexual license.[88] Cultural arbiters opposed to the "licensed libertinism of our established literature" also denounced Byron's *Don Juan* and Rousseau's *Confessions*.[89] Despite these criticisms, New York authorities consistently declined to censor artistic works issued by relatively highbrow publishers, even when they offended mainstream moral sensibilities.[90] Such restraint caused the *National Police Gazette* to allege the existence of a double standard for reputable publishers of libidinous poetry and clandestine purveyors of "coarser books": "The strictly moral may go further than they have yet gone, and seize upon certain editions of modern poetry, and confiscate them for immorality—an immorality that exceeds in its pernicious effects anything that the coarser books, surreptitiously sold on street corners and up sheltering alleys, contain."[91]

Municipal officials in antebellum New York thus came to define obscenity in relatively circumscribed terms. Although in theory legal doctrine empowered them to punish any speech that had a tendency to corrupt public morality, in practice they demonstrated a significant level of tolerance for many titillating products of the city's popular print culture. These included semiscientific books on sexual physiology and reproductive control like Hollick's *Marriage Guide* and George Thompson's sexually suggestive, graphically violent urban melodramas, which deliberately skirted the line between illicit obscenity and racy sensationalism. At the same time, antebellum publishers understood that whenever they sold fancy publications that openly depicted sex or nudity in a nonscientific context, especially in a way that violated bourgeois conventions about the purity of respectable women, they invited indictment for obscenity.

Chapter 4

The Publishers

The founders of New York's obscene book trade, despite the disreputable and often criminal status of their business, in many ways typified the era of the self-made man. Like many of their colleagues in the mainstream publishing industry, they had imbibed the period's heady atmosphere of economic enterprise and get-up-and-go. To be sure, they developed a greater tolerance for police raids, confiscation of property, public shaming, and imprisonment than their rivals in more legitimate fields of publishing. Nonetheless, manufacturers of erotic print displayed a keen appetite for profit, a bold capacity for risk taking, and remarkable resilience and versatility in the face of adversity. These traits, together with an aptitude for guile and deception, enabled a close-knit network of wily entrepreneurs to build a lucrative pornography industry, even in the midst of a legal culture that criminalized critical parts of their enterprise.

A pivotal event in the emergence of erotic publishing on American soil was the enactment in 1842 of a U.S. law banning the importation of "indecent and obscene" pictures. Attributing the nation's supply of licentious illustrations to foreign sources, Congress outlawed the importation of "all indecent and obscene prints, paintings, lithographs, engravings, and transparencies." It also authorized customs officials to seize such articles and to bring court proceedings for their destruction. It is unclear what inspired Congress to adopt this novel prohibition, as there is no record of any debate on the subject.[1] The law most likely rested on an assumption that domestic production of erotic images was not yet a major issue in the United States. It probably also reflected a desire to place the blame for commerce in obscenity on purportedly corrupt, decadent Europe, and particularly France, rather than the supposedly virtuous new republic. Whatever the motivation behind the law, its passage made the purchase of European erotica more difficult than before. Sneaking a single volume with obscene images or a single erotic engraving through customs in order to copy and publish it domestically may still have been possible after 1842. It was far less practical to import illustrated erotic works on a wholesale basis, however.

Customs inspectors stationed in the port of New York were quick to enforce the new provision. In the first published case involving the ban in 1843, *United States v. Three Cases of Toys*, a federal court upheld the decision of New York customs officials to confiscate nine German snuffboxes containing indecent pictures under their covers, which were apparently hidden in three crates of toys.[2] Two years later, a customs inspector in New York seized copies of several art books destined for a private collector. One of the condemned works was *Herculaneum et Pompeii*, an illustrated guide by two French scholars to archaeological discoveries unearthed in southern Italy, which depicted erotic wall drawings, figurines, and sculptures from ancient Rome.[3] The Philadelphia bookseller who had ordered the confiscated books argued that they "would never be made public but remain in the private collection of the antiquarian." Federal Judge Samuel Betts, evidently unimpressed by this defense, ordered that the works be destroyed. It was an interesting choice for the first nationally sanctioned book burning, given the status of the seized books as choice, scholarly texts. In 1847 the king of Prussia, presumably unaware of the book's prior ignominious reception in New York, formally presented an elegant copy of *Herculaneum et Pompeii* as a gift to New York State.[4]

While New York customs inspectors were using the new law to block the importation of high-end art objects, New York publishers were already involved in domestic production of lewd books and pictures. In August 1842, shortly after the barrage of indictments against the editors of flash weeklies for obscene libel, a major series of arrests and police raids exposed the operations of two large manufacturers of erotic print, as well as a number of smaller, street-level vendors. The arrests came about when Alderman Clarkson Crolius, Jr., a wealthy Whig representative of the Sixth Ward, caught a boy named Edward Scofield in the act of offering "obscene books and prints" for sale in his ward. Scofield told Crolius that he and other youths had obtained the items to sell to tourists in hotels around the city from bookstands and bookstalls throughout lower Manhattan. Probably in exchange for avoiding prosecution, the youngster provided two affidavits indicating that he regularly obtained obscene literature from men like Cornelius Ryan, who kept a bookstand on Wall Street near the Custom House, in the heart of the city's financial and government district.[5]

What were the books? European standards like *The Confessions of a Voluptuous Young Lady of High Rank*, *The Lustful Turk*, *The Curtain Drawn Up*, and *Memoirs of a Woman of Pleasure*, usually illustrated with "indecent plates" and woodcuts, which Ryan kept in a tin box under his stand.[6] Ryan's subsequent indictment on a separate charge of "Obscene Prints" indicated that he also sold fancy standalone prints showing men and women "with their private parts" exposed and in the "act of carnal copulation." One of them, titled "Do You Like This Sort of Thing, Eh?" depicted a naked woman in an "obscene, impudent, and indecent posture." Another aimed at bawdy religious humor by portraying a man and woman having intercourse, accompanied by the caption, "The Wedding Night. Beloved Ruth shall we go to sleep or how? Why Obediah if the spirits moveth I think we *had better how first* and go to sleep afterward." An affidavit in a related case indicated that a middleman like Ryan could purchase ten erotic lithographs that were probably similar to these from their producers for $3.50, equal to about $75 today.[7]

Scofield testified that he had bought the same books he obtained from Ryan from vendors at four other bookstalls scattered along the docks on South Street. He also disclosed that he had asked another boy to procure a copy of *The Curtain Drawn Up* from a bookstore at the corner of Nassau and Ann streets that belonged to Charles P. Huestis. Huestis was an engraver and publisher of a range of literary genres that included an illustrated almanac of murders, an etiquette guide, songsters, and children's books. The location of his store suggests that the Nassau Street area had already become a center of New York's erotic print trade in the early 1840s. Soon afterward, the police arrested all five of the sidewalk booksellers named in Scofield's affidavit, seized a large quantity of books, prints, and papers found in their possession, and deposited the seized items in the city prison. After searching the premises of the shop run by Huestis, the police also apprehended him. Interrogations of Huestis and William Bradley, one of the bookstand operators, in turn led the municipal authorities to the witnesses' two main suppliers, the principals who had manufactured the confiscated goods.[8]

The first to be arrested was Henry R. Robinson, the renowned publisher of lithographs who owned a large, bustling establishment at 52

Courtlandt Street, a few blocks southwest of the intersection of Nassau and Ann. As mentioned earlier, Robinson, a passionate Whig, was especially well known for publishing scathing caricatures of Democratic politicians. Perhaps to give the appearance of bipartisanship, both Clarkson Crolius, the Whig alderman, and George Matsell, a Democratic police court justice (and later police chief and *National Police Gazette* publisher), accompanied three police officers during a raid on Robinson's store. The *Herald* floridly reported that, upon their arrival, "such a scene was presented to the eyes of modest men as would cause a blush to gleam from the face of brass." They found a huge cache of erotica in a variety of formats, ranging from engravings, etchings, paintings, lithographic sketches, and prints to pamphlets and books "of all sizes and shapes, with every possible characteristic of obscenity and lewdness that could be presented to the eyes or ears." On the spot, the police confiscated "several thousand Prints and Books all of an obscene nature," allegedly valued at nearly twenty thousand dollars. Robinson was arrested and held on two thousand dollars' bail, twice as much as that set for the smaller vendors who had been arraigned earlier. Even so, he quickly posted bail and was released pending action by the district attorney and the grand jury.[9]

In September 1842, the grand jury for New York County returned a battery of indictments against Robinson and the other men arrested in August, all on charges of purveying "obscene books." Robinson's indictment, drafted by district attorney James Whiting, described him as "a person of a wicked and depraved mind and disposition." It further accused him of acting with the intent to "corrupt the morals of all the citizens of the State of New York and to debauch, poison, and infect the minds of all the Youth of this State, and to bring them into a state of wickedness, lewdness, debauchery, and brutality." His specific crime consisted of publishing "certain wicked, nasty, filthy,

4.1 Henry R. Robinson, "Lithographer, Publisher and Caricaturist," trade card depicting Robinson's storefront at 52 Courtlandt Street.

COURTESY OF THE AMERICAN ANTIQUARIAN SOCIETY.

bawdy, and obscene" libels, "to the high displeasure of Almighty God, to the scandal and reproach of the Christian Religion, in contempt of the People of the State of New York and their laws, to the great offence of all Civil Governments, to the evil and pernicious example of all others, and against the peace of the People of the State of New York and their dignity." Each of the other indictments repeated this language. Like the original Bonfanti and McLelland indictments for selling obscene books in 1824, these indictments tracked the English common-law form for an obscene libel charge provided in Joseph Chitty's *Practical Treatise on the Criminal Law.* First published in London in 1816, this practice guide on criminal law, which had been issued in several American editions by 1842, would have been readily available to Whiting.[10]

Just as the legal charges against Robinson relied on English precedent, so the books named in his indictment came from English sources. They included a number of volumes that had circulated in London's erotic print trade for many years, such as *Memoirs of a Woman of Pleasure*, *The Curtain Drawn Up*, and *The Confessions of a Voluptuous Young Lady of High Rank*. One title, however, was of strikingly recent vintage: *The Auto-Biography of a Footman*. This work had been serialized the very same year in a London erotic journal called *The Exquisite* that was published by William Dugdale, the leading English-language pornographer of the mid-nineteenth century. The rapid arrival of this serialized narrative in New York underscores the importance of the London–New York pornography connection, and the Dugdale–New York link in particular. Throughout the antebellum era, New York sex publishers paid extremely close attention to the latest developments in the transatlantic erotica trade. They were especially tied into happenings involving Dugdale, who turned out vast quantities of pornography before he died in a London prison in 1868 while serving a sentence for publishing obscene books.[11]

Indeed, it is quite likely that Robinson and other pornographers in antebellum New York generated the bulk of their inventory by pirating content from Dugdale's extensive catalogue of erotica and creating their own stereotype plates for the stolen works in New York. Stereotyping, a process invented in England, had come to the United States around 1811 and flourished among New York printers. It allowed metal plates to be created from lead molds taken from set type. Using the plates, publishers could print books in small runs, to meet existing demand, and easily reprint additional books from the plates when the need arose. (Looking ahead, ownership of physical plates was one reason nineteenth-century pornographers were more likely to articulate their rights in terms of physical property than of intellectual property or free speech.) The possibility of renting stereotype plates also encouraged cooperation and joint ventures among publishers and supplied a steady source of income for the owners.[12]

Robinson was charged with selling libidinous lithographs—a genre that was evidently his specialty—in addition to obscene books. One witness stated that Robinson had offered to sell "twenty obscene filthy and indecent prints, representing men and women in attitudes and situations of great and scandalous indecency lewdness and obscenity, and representing men and women with their private parts in most indecent postures and attitudes and representing men and women in the act of carnal copulation in various attitudes and postures." The indictment described three prints in particular. The first employed racist sexual imagery to mock antislavery activists. It was said to depict "a standing member of the Abolition Society, giving an example of practical amalgamation" by showing a Quaker man "in an obscene, impudent and indecent posture with a negro woman." The titles of the two others, "Victoria, Studying Her Comfort" and "Queen Victoria and Her Page in Attendance," presumably employed sexual representations to ridicule the reigning British monarch.[13] Although these illustrations were originally attached as exhibits, it is difficult to identify them with any certainty because they no longer survive in the court files. Given the prominence of royalty as subject matter, however, it is likely that Robinson's bawdy prints, like his lewd books, had been copied from British originals.

Robinson's case was called for trial at the Court of General Sessions in January 1843. His first instinct seems to have been evasion, for he skipped out on his court date. Two months later, though, he was forced to surrender when his sureties delivered him to the authorities, and he was committed to the Tombs.[14] Democratic-leaning papers delighted in Robinson's public embarrassment and incarceration. A jubilant *Brooklyn Eagle* gloated over the spectacle of a spokesperson for the Whig party, which was closely associated with moral reform and decency, being arrested for publishing and selling obscenity: "Ah! has it come to this? The great 'whig' caricaturist of the late administration . . . the idolized of the *decency* party . . . is this distinguished gentleman, we say, really indicted for 'publishing and vending obscene prints, books, &c.,' and, worse than all, has he been surrendered by his bail? Verily the 'way of the transgressor is hard.'"[15] At the same time, it became clear that Robinson's September 1842 indictment did little to halt sales of obscenity by the "idolized of the *decency* party." An affidavit attached to his case file after he was turned over to the authorities points out that Robinson sold "some eight or ten obscene prints" to another publisher, named James Craft, in December of the same year. According to Craft's affidavit, Robinson did take one precaution. Though he still offered a "very large quantity" of obscene prints for sale, he kept them "in a small room partitioned off for that purpose." Even so, the open spaces of Robinson's emporium hardly represented a model of propriety. Many other pictures, which Craft described as only slightly "less obscene," were still "publicly exposed in his principal store room where persons were continually passing in and out."[16]

In spite of Robinson's reputation as a "great manufacturer" of obscenity and the strong evidence of his recidivism, the minutes of the Court of General Sessions show no further proceedings in his case, an indication that he avoided conviction. Then again, he hardly got away scot-free, having suffered the loss of the thousands of obscene prints and books confiscated by the police, personal humiliation at the hands of the Democratic press, and a brief imprisonment after being turned in by his bail.[17]

It is unclear whether these unwelcome experiences convinced Robinson to forego further manufacture and sale of obscene publications in the years between 1843 and his death in 1850. It is plain, though, that erotic materials, including Robinson's specialty of sexually explicit lithographs, continued to be sold in New York. An 1843 article in a flash paper, the *New York Sporting Whip*, highlighted the ready availability of obscene pictures. While making a show of withholding specific addresses, it pointed readers to the places where they could find such items: "Those exciters of impure passions—those horrible evidences of the prurient state of French Society—richly colored and beautifully engraved prints, representing the connection of the sexes in all varieties, may be found in nearly every small book and print shop of New York. One on Nassau street, we speak of in particular."[18]

In addition to obtaining lewd pictures from bookstores and print shops in the vicinity of Nassau Street, residents and visitors could buy them from street-level bookstalls or from peddlers in a range of public spaces: markets, wharves, street corners, railway depots, and hotel lobbies throughout the city. Vendors of sexual images certainly did not operate with impunity, however. In 1848 two men named Adam Hartman and Charles Lee were arrested for hawking "in a public manner" more than twenty prints showing men and women in an "impudent and indecent posture." Indicted and convicted, Hartman and Lee were sentenced to thirty days each in prison.[19]

Rather than motivating peddlers to abandon the sale of improper prints, the risk of arrest and incarceration encouraged various shenanigans, often quite comic, to evade the prying eyes of the police. One blasphemous ploy involved disguising erotic prints as moral reform literature. In 1850, an officer caught one Michael Sullivan in the act of selling obscene pictures, books, and brothel guides in the streets. The policeman confiscated a copy of a book whose cover and title page announced that it was a sermon on the evils of covetousness published by the American Tract Society. (One of the many strange juxtapositions of Nassau Street was the Tract Society's location at 150 Nassau, in the thick of the city's erotica zone.) In actuality,

4.2 Hand-colored erotic print, c. 1850. This was one of five graphic, hand-colored pictures confiscated during an 1850 arrest for selling obscene prints in the city.

COURTESY OF THE AMERICAN ANTIQUARIAN SOCIETY.

the "sermon" contained leaves from *The Confessions of a Voluptuous Young Lady of High Rank*. It also included three explicit prints that presumably would not have pleased supporters of the society. One represented only "the lower portion of a female's body—legs, thighs, buttocks, and private parts, in a most lascivious and indecent attitude"; a second depicted "a male and female in the act of having sexual intercourse"; and a third showed "a male and female with their private parts exposed about to have sexual intercourse together."[20] The deception worked in reverse as well, when newsboys used the bait-and-switch technique to attract customers with sexually explicit illustrations, only to pawn prim religious tracts off on the unsuspecting buyers at inflated prices.[21]

What did pictures of this sort look like? An 1850 case against another huckster who cheekily sold erotic prints concealed between the pages of ostensibly proper books offers a rare glimpse of the kind of explicit sexual images that customers could purchase on the streets of mid-nineteenth-century New York. Each of the five surviving prints is hand-colored, with the sexual organs highlighted in red and pink. In two of the pictures, including one shown in Figure 4.2, a masturbating woman intently watches a man and woman during intercourse. In a third, four androgynous figures, entirely naked except for their knee-high stockings, have sex while flagellating and masturbating one another. In a fourth, a couple copulates in the courtyard of an opulent palace. In the fifth, a fancily dressed woman whips a man who is bound to a sumptuous divan, his pants drawn down to his knees to expose his bare buttocks to her lash.[22]

The second manufacturer of obscene publications implicated in the August 1842 investigation instigated by Alderman Crolius was Richard Hobbes, a publisher whose printing office was in East Chester, a town in Westchester County just north of the city. Whereas Robinson specialized in lubricious prints, Hobbes was the source, according to the *Herald*, of "nearly all the obscene and infamous books that flood the city." Although he produced obscene books on a large scale and had made an "immense fortune in the business," he, like Robinson, was outwardly a man of respectable reputation. At the time of his arrest, several sources noted, he was an active member of his local church.[23]

Under arrest, the publisher and engraver Charles Huestis cooperated with the police by swearing out an affidavit against Hobbes, testimony that provides valuable clues about the workings of the erotic book trade in early 1840s New York. Perhaps as an exculpatory move,

Huestis insisted that he did not advertise or market such books directly to customers, but instead relied solely on word of mouth. As he explained, customers in the know placed orders with him for specific titles. He relayed their requests to Hobbes, who produced the volumes in East Chester. Hobbes then filled the orders from his inventory and sent them to Huestis for distribution. In exchange, Huestis received a percentage of the sale price from Hobbes. Attached to Huestis's affidavit was a list of the books that Hobbes supplied in this way. All were of European provenance: *Night Thoughts, Rochester* (presumably bawdy poems by the Earl of Rochester), *The Curtain Drawn Up, The Cabinet Unlocked, The Confessions of a Voluptuous Young Lady of High Rank, The Lustful Turk, Betty Ireland,* and *Flash Songs.*[24]

According to newspaper reports, Hobbes received a tip that allowed him to remove all the objectionable books from his printing office before the police arrived in Westchester. As a result, he was spared the large-scale confiscation of property that Robinson experienced. Hobbes at first eluded capture, too, but the police apprehended him by the next morning. In September 1843 district attorney Whiting indicted the publisher, along with Robinson, Huestis, and the five bookstall operators. When his case was called for trial in January 1843, Hobbes, like most of the other defendants, failed to appear.[25]

Two days later, however, Hobbes suffered the indignity, just as Robinson did a few months later, of having his surety, the printer William Applegate (who also worked with the editors of the *Sunday Flash*), surrender him in open court. The publisher entered a plea of not guilty and was committed to jail pending trial. William Price, who represented the publisher, was a seasoned criminal defense lawyer who had recently served as counsel for one of the minor flash editors and was also defending several of the bookstand operators indicted along with Hobbes. Price had a reputation for being a nasty but effective advocate. A week later, Hobbes changed his plea to guilty. This strategy initially seemed to backfire, when the court imposed a prison sentence of sixty days. But Price was able to negotiate a commutation on the grounds that his client had provided assistance of an undisclosed nature to the police. In the end, Hobbes's penalty amounted to a modest fifty-dollar fine. This apparent travesty of justice led the scandal-mongering *New York Herald* to demand that the "hoary headed debauchee" be indicted again in Westchester.[26]

The keeper of the bookstand near the Customs House, Cornelius Ryan, was not as fortunate. He appeared for trial on two obscenity charges the same day that Hobbes was tried. The Court of General Sessions dismissed Ryan's indictment for selling obscene books, evidently in exchange for his guilty plea on a separate indictment for obscene prints. The court then sentenced him to thirty days in jail. Two other bookstand operators forfeited their recognizances rather than appear for trial. Other than the initial indictments, the minutes of the Court of General Sessions contain no indication of further proceedings against the three remaining booksellers, including Charles Huestis. As a result, the only recorded convictions from the first municipal crackdown on vendors of obscene books and prints were a thirty-day prison sentence for Ryan, whom the papers described as a poor man who could not afford to pay a fine, and a fifty-dollar fine against the well-off publisher, Hobbes.[27]

It is telling that none of the eight defendants indicted in 1842 chose to exercise their right to a trial by jury. Most simply forfeited their bail by failing to show up for trial; those few who were forced to appear by their sureties swiftly entered guilty pleas. One consequence was that none of the publishers or vendors who were caught up in the city's first wave of sexual censorship made any effort to defend in a court of law their right to produce or sell sexual representations.

Like Henry Robinson, Richard Hobbes does not appear in any court records after 1843. As a consequence, it is difficult to assess whether his involvement in New York's obscene book trade continued after that point. But it is clear that a new player was already standing in the wings, a publisher who would soon eclipse both Robinson and Hobbes as a producer of fancy print. Writing in 1877, Englishman Henry Spencer Ashbee looked back on the progress of the United States in turning out indecent books during the course of the century. "America, as in other branches of industry," he observed, "has made of late years great progress in the production of books, and not the least in those of an improper character." For Ashbee, who wrote three pseudonymous bibliographies of erotica that were privately printed in London between 1877 and 1885, the mid-1840s appeared to be a watershed for the United States, primarily because of the efforts of a legendary publisher named William Haines. Before 1846, Ashbee asserted, "the Americans produced nothing, but merely imported such books; when an Irishman, W. Haines, began to publish, and soon became a rich man."[28]

In truth, Ashbee's assertion that Americans "produced nothing" in the way of books of an "improper character" until precisely 1846 was somewhat inaccurate. Court records of obscenity cases establish that at least two New York publishers, Hobbes and Robinson, were engaged in the manufacturing and marketing of sexually explicit works by the early 1840s. Despite the faulty chronology, however, Ashbee correctly identified the leading role that publisher William Haines played in building the nineteenth-century American pornography industry.[29]

When the famous smut hunter Anthony Comstock began to investigate New York's erotic print trade in the early 1870s, he discovered that Haines was the largest manufacturer of obscene books in the United States.[30] Likewise, Gustav Lening's 1873 exposé, *The Dark Side of New York Life,* highlighted Haines's critical contributions to the creation of American erotica:

> Until 1846 the importations from England and France sufficed to supply the American market with these disgraceful publications. This importation, however, was such a risky thing that the number of obscene books was necessarily very small, and the prices very high. Obscene books and pictures were therefore until then very rare. But the taste for them had already been developed, and the demand, in spite of the high price, was considerably greater than the supply. This induced an Irishman, who had until then imported obscene books, to try the publication of these works. The name of this man, W. Haines, deserves to be held up to public disgrace forevermore, in the annals of our Republic, as the first man who naturalized obscene literature in our country. He began on a small scale, but he thoroughly understood his business, and was soon a rich man.

As Lening noted, the 1842 federal ban on importing obscene prints, by making importation "such a risky thing" and driving up prices, had the counterproductive effect of fueling domestic production and thereby "naturalizing" obscene literature in the United States.[31]

According to Comstock, Haines was "an Irish surgeon of marked ability and skill, and a graduate of one of the English universities." Despite his skills, he was a "foul-minded and licentious man," who allegedly was forced to leave England "after his marriage to a certain nobleman's daughter, because of having been untrue to his marriage vows." After immigrating to New York in 1840, he quickly took up publishing and selling the "most obscene and indecent books." In this endeavor, he was aided by his second wife, Mary E. Haines, an American who was considerably younger. Account books seized by Comstock showed that Haines entered the business in 1842, the same year in which the federal law banning the importation of obscene illustrations went into effect, when he was approximately thirty-eight years old.[32]

Initially, like his colleagues in New York's early erotic print trade, Haines probably obtained his inventory from pirated versions of European pornography published by William Dugdale. By relying on material copied from English sources, Haines spared himself the usual publishing tasks of developing content and negotiating with authors. If Comstock is correct, Haines's contribution to the production of American erotica later extended to authorship of a number of pornographic texts.[33] Even though he was spared the necessity of commissioning writers, Haines's role as publisher still required him to choose which books to produce, and to finance and coordinate the processes of setting text onto stereotype plates, creating illustrations, printing the text, stitching the printed sheets together, binding the pages into books, and marketing and distributing the final products.[34] In addition, he sometimes furnished materials to other publishers of lewd books, supplying paper to George Akarman for one.[35]

By the end of the decade, Haines had established himself as the nation's largest and most notorious publisher of erotic print, a vocation he tirelessly pursued, aided by his wife, for nearly thirty years. Before his death in 1872 he was said to have published at least 320 books "of the most obscene character, which have all had an extensive circulation, and have paid exceedingly well."[36] Despite the pivotal role he played in launching the American pornography trade, no publication bearing Haines's imprint has survived. As a result, his career is especially difficult for historians and bibliographers to reconstruct.[37] Fortunately, evidence from three New York obscenity prosecutions involving Haines, in 1846, 1849, and 1853, as well as a fateful encounter with Comstock in 1872, shed some light on the enigmatic publisher, his business practices, and his responses to legal prohibitions on the sale of obscene literature.

In July 1846, when the grand jury for New York County presented a bill against Haines, he became the third publisher to face an obscenity indictment in the city. The charges stemmed from a complaint by a police officer who had observed Haines in the act of peddling obscene books and prints. The subsequent indictment, drafted by the new Democratic district attorney, John McKeon, charged Haines with selling *The Curtain Drawn Up; or, The Education of Laura*, the same fancy book that Henry Robinson and Richard Hobbes had been prosecuted for selling four years before. Like the earlier versions, Haines's edition of *The Curtain Drawn Up* was said to be illustrated with an "obscene print representing a man and woman naked and uncovered in an obscene, impudent and indecent posture." In addition, the indictment charged Haines with selling a separate picture titled "Belshazzar's Feast—Festia de Balthazar," which portrayed "divers men and women, in obscene impudent and indecent postures" and was evidently based on the orgy scene referred to in the biblical Book of Daniel. Significantly, the police officer's complaint specified that Haines had offered these items for sale "in a certain open and public market."[38]

Haines went to trial shortly after the indictment, but there was no press coverage of the proceedings. Instead, a brief notice appeared in the *National Police Gazette* and other tabloids providing the title of the illicit book and print in question and reporting Haines's conviction. In what must have been a shock to the publisher, considering the lenient treatment of Hobbes and Robinson just a few years earlier, he was sentenced to three months in the Tombs.[39]

After serving his prison term, Haines took steps to conduct his business in a more secretive manner. He reportedly assumed an alias, Piggot.[40] Like other antebellum suppliers of pornography, he worked through agents when possible, making use of street peddlers and newsboys to distribute illicit erotica to customers. One such peddler may well have been young Edward Scofield, the youth whose arrest had precipitated the city's first crackdown on pornography dealers in 1842.[41] In 1847 an officer apprehended Scofield for selling English erotic standards like *Memoirs of a Woman of Pleasure* and *The Lustful Turk*, along with a local directory of brothels, *List of All the Gay Houses and Ladies of Pleasure in the City of New York*, in the vestibule of the Astor House hotel on Broadway, across the street from City Hall Park.[42] According to the affidavit of the arresting officer, Scofield was selling *Fanny Hill* for two dollars. Under the circumstances, it is no surprise that he chose the Astor House, then the most fashionable hotel in New York and a meeting place for dandies and upper-class loungers, to peddle his wares. Because of the high price of his offerings, they were likely to have been beyond the reach of most working people, considering that even skilled white male workers earned only about a dollar a day and faced frequent intervals of unemployment.[43]

Back in 1842, Scofield had escaped indictment by providing evidence to the police about his suppliers, although even then he was held in jail several months, until his mother could drum up the money to post a bond guaranteeing his return as a material witness.[44] This time, the grand jury indicted him on a misdemeanor charge for selling obscene books. Only one work was named in the indictment, *Memoirs of a Woman of Pleasure*, one of the same books he had been

4.3 Lounging at the Astor House hotel. Nicolino Calyo, The Astor House Reading Room, *watercolor, c. 1840, Mrs. Elon Hooker Acquisition Fund, 41.3.*

MUSEUM OF THE CITY OF NEW YORK.

arrested for hawking five years before. The latest version, like its 1842 predecessor, was allegedly illustrated with explicit "bawdy and obscene prints . . . representing and exhibiting men and women in the act of carnal copulation, in various attitudes and postures." For his crime, Scofield was tried, convicted, and sentenced to six months in prison, the heaviest penalty imposed for an obscenity offense in antebellum New York.[45]

Even farming out sales of erotic books to street peddlers like Scofield did not spare Haines a second arrest in 1849, when one of his agents was nabbed by the police and disclosed the publisher as his source. As the *National Police Gazette* reported, Haines had been arrested for selling unidentified "obscene books to a young man named

James Morrison. Morrison had been arrested before Haynes, for offering the books for sale, and to save himself said that he had purchased the books from Haynes to sell again." The item further identified Haines as the "manufacturer" of the forbidden books.[46] Significantly, however, no indictment for Haines or his alias, Piggot, appears in the district attorney's files or the minutes of the Court of General Sessions for 1849. Later evidence suggests the possibility that Haines avoided criminal penalties by paying off law enforcement officials, a practice he would perfect during his long and prolific career as a pornographic entrepreneur.

During the next decade, Haines took additional precautions to circumvent prosecution for obscenity, though they did not spare him a third arrest in 1853. It came about when a police officer apprehended a man who stated that he had purchased "indecent and grossly immoral books prints and publications" from the bookstore of one Albert Gazeley. Relying on this evidence, the officer secured a warrant to search Gazeley's shop, where he found and seized a large quantity of erotic books and pictures. The district attorney, N. Bowditch Blunt, then obtained an indictment from the grand jury charging Gazeley with selling a "certain lewd, wicked and scandalous book or pamphlet having an obscene print representing a woman naked and uncovered in an obscene, impudent and indecent posture."[47]

The illustrated obscene book was identified as *The Confessions of a Voluptuous Young Lady of High Rank Illustrated by Numerous Elegant Engravings,* an English work that had been a favorite offering of New York pornographers for more than a decade.[48] Following the language of indictments from the 1840s (in turn drawn from English treatises), Gazeley was accused of selling this book with the intent to "debauch and corrupt" the morals of youths and "divers other citizens of the State of New York" and "to raise and create in their minds inordinate and lustful desires." Yet the minutes of the Court of General Sessions show no proceedings in his case after the initial indictment, an indication that authorities declined to pursue his prosecution.

In Gazeley's case, it is possible that the district attorney dropped the matter in exchange for his cooperation.[49] Just as Charles Huestis had tipped off the police to publisher Richard Hobbes back in 1842, Gazeley led detectives to another mother lode by identifying Haines as the supplier of all the various lewd publications he sold at his store. Haines, of course, was no stranger to obscenity prosecutions, having spent three months in the Tombs following his conviction in 1846. In the earlier case, however, he had been arrested for peddling erotic wares in an open marketplace.[50]

By this time in 1853, Haines had taken steps to separate himself from both the production and the distribution of obscene books. He no longer sold forbidden works directly to customers but instead distributed them through local bookstores like Gazeley's, as well as similar shops outside the city. In addition, as an increasingly sophisticated publisher, he outsourced some aspects of the production process for his works to independent agents. A printer named John McLoughlin, for instance, confessed that he did the printing for Haines, running off popular English titles like *Fanny Hill*, *The Curtain Drawn Up*, and *La Rose d'Amour* at his shop from the stereotype plates that Haines provided. The text that McLoughlin produced bore no trace of Haines's involvement and contained a number of red herrings as to the identity of the publisher. According to court records, the copies of *Memoirs of a Woman of Pleasure* and *La Rose d'Amour* seized by the police at the premises of McLoughlin and Gazeley falsely listed London as the place of publication. *La Rose d'Amour* showed the publisher as "Strokeall & Company, Ten inches up red lane, Maidenhead, Sportsman's Square." This was the same fictitious imprint used by London pornographer William Dugdale. (Capitalizing on the common association of erotic license with France, the title page of *La Rose d'Amour*, a novel about a Frenchman who constructs an Ottoman harem for himself at a château in Brittany, also falsely asserted that the text had been translated from the "French of Rosseau.")[51]

A rare surviving copy of another work seized from McLoughlin's shop, *The Life and Adventures of Cicily Martin*, allegedly published in New York by a firm called Sinclair & Bagley in 1846, has been preserved in the archives of the American Antiquarian Society. The narrative relates the sexual adventures of a New York courtesan in the 1840s. The extant copy also contains five explicit engravings. Although it is uncertain whether this volume is the same as the one published by Haines, it is clear that the identity of the publisher on the title page was fabricated. No firm by the name of Sinclair & Bagley is recorded in the city directories for the period. Moreover, publishers' circulars and other evidence suggest that *Cicily Martin* was first published in the 1850s, not 1846.[52] Given McLoughlin's admission that he printed this title for Haines in 1853 and Haines's practice of using specious imprints, the possibility exists that Haines was responsible for publishing the surviving volume. If so, it represents the only known copy of a Haines publication still in existence.

Despite Gazeley's clear testimony that Haines had been deeply involved in the "business of producing and circulating . . . obscene books, plates, papers and prints for several years," the subsequent bill of indictment failed to pin responsibility on him for the city's burgeoning commerce in lascivious books. Instead, it modestly charged Haines with only one offense, "obscene book nuisance," for selling *The Confessions of a Voluptuous Lady of High Rank* to Gazeley.[53] Moreover, although a bench warrant was issued for his arrest at the time of the indictment, the minute book for the Court of General Sessions shows that authorities took no further action against him. To

THE

LIFE AND ADVENTURES

OF

CICILY MARTIN.

NARRATIVE OF FACT.

WRITTEN BY HERSELF.

NEW YORK:
SINCLAIR AND BAGLEY.

1846.

4.4 Title page, The Life and Adventures of Cicily Martin *(New York, 1846[?]).*

COURTESY OF THE AMERICAN ANTIQUARIAN SOCIETY.

4.5 Distribution outlets for William Haines. The shop where Albert Gazeley sold Haines's books was located on William Street, near the corner of Frankfort, one block east of Nassau. William Perris, plate 6, hand-colored lithograph (New York, 1857).

THE LIONEL PINCUS AND PRINCESS FIRYAL MAP DIVISION, THE NEW YORK PUBLIC LIBRARY, ASTOR, LENOX AND TILDEN FOUNDATIONS.

judge by later developments, it is likely that the publisher was able to evade further penalties by paying bribes. Indeed, a newspaper exposé of the obscene book trade published in 1871 estimated that Haines had spent over twenty thousand dollars on kickbacks over the preceding decade. In addition, Haines's wife Mary complained to Comstock in 1872 that her husband would have left her independently wealthy had it not been for the constant necessity of bribing law enforcement officers.[54]

Looking ahead, we see that Haines and other publishers of his ilk became even more vigilant about disguising their connection to the production and sale of obscene books in subsequent years. By the time of his 1872 run-in with Comstock, Haines had organized his business in such a way that the printing, binding, and storing of his inventory were carried out by discrete entities, coordinated from afar by the publisher. In a further effort to avoid detection, he made sure that each element of the production process was conducted in a distinct geographic location and even in separate jurisdictions. Through a web of independent contractors and associates, he arranged for texts to be printed in Brooklyn, bound in Manhattan, and warehoused across the Hudson River in Jersey City, New Jersey. He employed a special courier, used only by publishers of obscene books, to transport his commodities from point to point during production. For extra insulation, he relied on a designated middleman to coordinate the marketing and distribution of finished products to consumers.[55] Together with his ability to pay hefty bribes, these behind-the-scenes machinations helped keep the mysterious publisher out of jail, and at the helm of a lucrative pornography franchise, for the remainder of his illustrious career.

In the early 1850s, another New York publisher of Irish descent, Frederic A. Brady, joined Haines as a critical player in the mid-nineteenth-century pornography trade. Under his own name, Brady published adventure novels and melodramatic sensational fiction by George Thompson and others. He also produced a series of what he called "negro farces," part of the minstrelsy genre that was popular among white working-class audiences in the 1850s.[56] Under the sham impress of "Henry S. G. Smith & Co." or "H. S. G. Smith & Co.," he carried on a sub rosa trade in texts that placed him at risk of prosecution for obscenity. As the *New York Times* asserted in describing Brady's establishment, "the obscene department . . . trades under the style of SMITH & Co., while the legitimate business, if any, is carried on under the style of BRADY."[57] The New York publisher may have adopted the Smith alias in an attempt to exploit the goodwill of the leading English pornographer of the day, William Dugdale, who often used the pseudonym Henry Smith. Or perhaps he intended it as an admiring homage to Dugdale's oeuvre. In any event, Brady did not always observe the strict division between trade names for obscene and nonobscene works noted in the *Times*. On several occasions, he shamelessly passed off texts as more erotically charged than they actually were, by using the imprint for Smith & Co. rather than Brady.[58]

According to an interview with a credit agent in 1859, Brady took up book publishing in 1852 or 1853. Within a few years, under the guise of Henry S. G. Smith & Co., he was responsible for a substantial catalogue of erotic books. Among the titles published under the Smith imprint in 1855 were *Mysteries of Women . . . Containing Advice to Husbands and Wives Regarding the Means of Making the Marriage Bed, the Throne of Venus' Joys; The Secret Habits of the Female Sex; The Musical Student; The History of a Rake; Adventures of a Bed-stead; Julia; or, Where Is the Woman That Wouldn't; Venus in the Closet; Intrigues of Three Days; Memoirs of an Old Man of Twenty-Five; The Intrigues and Secret Amours of Napoleon; Memoirs of a Woman of Pleasure; or, The Singular and Surprising Adventures of Thermidore and Rosette;* and *Memoirs of a Man of Pleasure; or, The Amorous Intrigues and Adventures of Sir Charles Manly.*[59]

In compiling his famous bibliography of erotica, Ashbee examined a copy of the last cited work, which Dugdale originally published in 1827 and Brady reprinted in a relatively cheap edition, priced at fifty cents, in 1855. According to Ashbee, the H. S. G. Smith edition of *Memoirs of a Man of Pleasure* related the "amatory adventures" of its hero, Sir Charles Manly. As Ashbee described the plot, Sir Charles's passion for women arose unusually early, when his pregnant mother, Louisa, transmitted her own lust for a pretty female bedmate to Sir Charles while carrying him in the womb. The bibliographer quoted a passage from the book describing how Louisa, while her husband was away from home, "made a young lady, a kinswoman of hers, her bed-fellow." "This lady was young and frolicsome, and one night, when undressed for going to bed," she played "some wanton tricks to make Louisa laugh." In the process, Louisa "discovered a certain promontory" of her companion "more naturally coveted by a man than by a woman." "Casting her eyes on that seldom seen spot," she suddenly became "seized with an unaccountable desire to taste it." Though "she endeavoured to check the thought as soon as conceived," her efforts were futile; "the more she strove to banish the unnatural idea, the more it haunted her imagination." Though Ashbee apparently found this portion of the narrative amusing, he dismissed the three woodcuts in the H. S. G. Smith production as "wretchedly done." Overall, he sniffed, the "style is poor, and it cannot be looked upon as a composition of anything but inferior order."[60]

As a comparatively new publisher of sexual texts, Brady proved to be an industrious and reliable businessman. Summing up his financial history during the 1850s, a credit reporter for R. G. Dun & Co. opined that his "business has been rather a profitable one for a few years past—and it is thought, he has made money—Has paid his bills very promptly and been in fair credit. Always apparently flush with means sufficient for his bus[iness]."[61]

But Brady's economic success came at a cost. In 1855 the connection of Henry S. G. Smith & Co. to obscenity attracted the attention of police officials. That year, on the heels of a well-publicized campaign by Mayor Fernando Wood to clean up the city by arresting street prostitutes, law enforcement officials made a brief show of suppressing another moral nuisance, peddling of obscene publications on the street. This use of the city's public spaces was a constant source of irritation to middle- and upper-class pedestrians, who viewed such peddling as a chronic nuisance and insult, especially to women of the "respectable classes." A typical complaint in the *New York Times* charged, "Lazy scapegraces who make a business of hawking about obscene publications, and indecent pictures . . . haunt every hotel, railroad depot and steamboat landing, and thrust their disgusting wares on all that come in their way." It was futile "to tell them you don't want to buy: they will not only exhibit to you the nastiest daubs they have but go on to explain them into the bargain . . . even though you be accompanied by ladies." Lacking all restraint, some scamps "frequently expose those things to the ladies themselves."[62]

On the lookout for affronts of this kind, members of the mayor's police arrested three young men for hawking obscene books that contained "lewd, indecent and filthy pictures" along the docks on the west side of lower Manhattan. An officer said that he had caught one suspect in the act of selling a "filthy" illustrated work called *Mysteries of Women . . . Containing Advice to Husbands and Wives Regarding the Means of Making the Marriage Bed, the Throne of Venus' Joys*. This volume, attributed to "Henry S. G. Smith & Co.," included advertisements for ten additional books produced by the same firm.

The other youths were charged with selling yet another book published by Smith & Co., the antimasturbation tract *The Secret Habits of the Female Sex.* The edition issued by Smith claimed to be "illustrated with four beautiful colored engravings."[63]

The prosecutions of the three peddlers failed to keep either them or Henry S. G. Smith's brand of smut off the streets, however. On the same day they were indicted, each young man pleaded guilty, received a suspended sentence, and was set free to ply his trade again. (Indeed, the police reapprehended one of them, described as "an Irishman, 21 years of age, a peddler who can neither read nor write," for the exact same offense in 1858.) At the time the defendants were discharged, authorities took no action against their supplier, whose true identity may still have been unknown.[64]

Two years later, in September 1857, law enforcement officials finally tracked down Brady himself when a street peddler who had been detained by the police led them to his Ann Street address. Earlier that month, the city's daily papers had rushed to print the salacious details of a raid that took place a few blocks away on the publishing establishment of one of Brady's most notorious colleagues, George Akarman.[65] In recounting the most recent arrest and the seizure of cartloads of obscene books, the *Times* attempted to shock followers of the earlier scandal by asserting that in Brady's case the "works and prints found are said to far exceed in immorality and tendency to vice anything found in AKARMAN'S premises."[66]

In response to such press, Brady (borrowing a strategy recently employed by Akarman) wrote to the editor of the *Herald* to deny any connection with obscenity. He insisted that the "books taken by the police . . . are commonly sold by dealers in cheap publications throughout the United States."[67] With this statement, Brady sought to portray himself as a legitimate publisher of racy pamphlets, rather than the kind of fancy, sexually explicit texts that were generally condemned as obscene in New York courts. In fact, unlike Robinson, Hobbes, and Haines before him, Brady seems to have specialized in relatively cheap, paper-covered, often unillustrated editions of sexually explicit works. Perhaps his appeal succeeded, at least temporarily, because the district attorney did not pursue his prosecution. Although his books were confiscated and his case was referred to the grand jury, Brady managed to escape indictment.

But the prolific publisher was soon back in the police blotter. His troubles began in a typical way, when an officer of the mayor's squad arrested three men for peddling obscene books and prints in early 1858. One told the police he obtained the items from two sources—William Haines and Brady—and that Brady kept a "room for the sale of obscene or indecent books at number 12 Ann street . . . first floor at the head of the stairs." Another stated that Brady was "in the habit of making daily sales of such books to persons in this city, and supplying orders therefor from the country."[68] On the basis of this evidence, the new mayor, Daniel Tiemann, issued a warrant authorizing the police to search Brady's business at 12 Ann Street, a few steps to the east of P. T. Barnum's American Museum at the corner of Broadway and Ann. A second dramatic police raid led to Brady's arrest and the seizure of his entire stock of books. At his arraignment, the publisher again appealed to industry custom and questioned how all the confiscated books could be obscene when most were "openly sold by all the trade." Recorder George Barnard, who presided over the Court of General Sessions, seemed unimpressed with Brady's efforts to classify his inventory as a manifestation of everyday popular culture rather than as illicit commodities. Setting bail at a steep five thousand dollars, Barnard boasted that he "intended to break up this business, and would send every one convicted of being engaged in it to the Penitentiary."[69]

Unable to secure bail, Brady was forced to remain in prison awaiting indictment. A Dun credit agent filed an informative report on the publisher during this time, capturing both the financial rewards of Brady's line of work and the high personal and economic risks that constantly confronted entrepreneurs in his field. While describing his business in general as "rather . . . profitable," the report alluded to Brady's legal problems by noting that the publisher had "lately experienced . . . reverses, from which he may find it difficult to extricate himself, without incurring a heavy penalty." It then provided the unpleasant details: "He was arrested by the police for selling obscene books, and being unable to procure 5,000 in bail, he was incarcerated in the Tombs, where he now is, awaiting the action of the 'Grand Jury' and his stock (of books &c.) seized."[70]

Nearly three weeks later, the Democratic district attorney Peter B. Sweeny and the grand jury for New York County presented two indictments against Brady. The first charged him with selling three obscene publications from a range of genres: *The Secret Habits of the Female Sex*, a sex guide entitled *The Marriage Bed; or, Wedding Secrets Revealed by the Torch of Hymen*, and an erotic novel, *Mary Ann Temple*.[71] The second accused him of possessing three additional obscene works, which he kept "secreted" at his store: an English-language edition of an eighteenth-century French pornographic novel *(The Life and Adventures of Silas Shovewell)*, a New York brothel directory *(Guide to the Harem)*, and a colored print of a copulating couple that the police had discovered while executing the search warrant.[72]

A month later, Brady had secured his release by posting bail. In a telling illustration of the class dynamics at work in the criminal process, the minute book for the Court of General Sessions shows that authorities imprisoned Brady's street peddlers for over a month because they were too impoverished to provide security for their appearance at trial as material witnesses.[73] Meanwhile, Brady's prosecution was never pursued. Despite Recorder Barnard's boast about breaking up the trade and sending all the participants to jail, the minutes document no further proceedings in the case of Brady himself. Although he served time in prison while trying to raise money for bail, Brady apparently managed to avoid conviction, or even trial, on his two obscenity indictments. A later newspaper article on police corruption hinted that he may have solicited the services of a notorious local gambler and thief, Marcus Cicero Stanley, to pay bribes on his (Brady's) behalf.[74]

In September 1859 Brady, by now a widower with children to care for, assured credit reporters that he had bounced back from his arrest, imprisonment, and indictment and had reestablished his good financial standing:

> Sept 30/59. (His statement.) Has been in bus 6 or 7 yrs & is w[orth] 30000 $, some of it being left him by relatives in Ireland. Besides this 30000 $ he md investments in [property] some time ago in the name of his wife for the benefit of herself & children. She is now dead & the children will h[a]v[e] the whole benefit. He owes 6 or 7000 $ & has abt the same amt due to him.

Despite these solid economic credentials, the credit agent felt compelled to modify the representation Brady made of himself as a conscientious businessman and father by noting his continuing sales of obscene publications: "We learn from others that his char[aracter] does not st[an]d well on a/c of his connection with the sale of obscene books for which he was arrested + imprisoned some time ago." Nonetheless, the entry stated that Brady was thought to hold substantial assets and "can buy all he wants on gd terms. He has a gd stk of Books & does a f[ai]r bus."[75]

In 1863 Brady, by then located at 24 Ann Street, sold his premises to an up-and-coming associate in New York pornography circles, twenty-six-year-old Jeremiah H. Farrell, for five thousand dollars. Included in the sale were copies of printed books and some of the stereotype plates owned by Brady. Among the items Farrell acquired were books with the short titles *Secret Habits, Wedding Secrets, Cloister*, and *Old Man*. The first two designated works that had been the subject of Brady's 1858 indictments: *The Secret Habits of the Female Sex* and *The Marriage Bed; or, Wedding Secrets Revealed by the Torch of Hymen*. The remaining titles probably referred to *Venus in the Cloister* and *Memoirs of an Old Man of Twenty-Five*, erotic texts published by Brady in the 1850s.[76]

Throughout the 1860s, Brady continued to provide financial information to agents for R. G. Dun, in order to demonstrate his creditworthiness. Though he may have been winding down his business, he also continued to publish illicit books. In 1867 a credit reporter took note of Brady's ongoing connections to erotica: "Above does bus in obscene books but has good cr[edit] + making money." A final entry reported his death in 1870. Coming two years before Anthony Comstock began his investigation of New York's obscene book trade, Brady's timely death spared the entrepreneur the hostile encounters with Comstock experienced by the other major erotica producers of the mid-nineteenth century, namely, Haines, Farrell, and Akarman.[77]

In the early 1850s, two men, Thomas Ormsby and George Akarman, became partners in a small publishing house known as Akarman and Ormsby. They seem to have offered popular adventure novels and city mysteries about the horrors and scandals of metropolitan life. One of three publications that have survived from their firm is an urban melodrama by the popular New York writer Ned Buntline (E. Z. C. Judson) called *Mysteries and Miseries of New Orleans*, which they published in 1851.[78] For unknown reasons, Akarman and Ormsby dissolved their partnership after a short time, but they stayed in the same publishing circles and followed similar career trajectories, both men soon venturing into the sale of obscene books.

In 1855 the detention of a street peddler led to the arrest of Ormsby at his bookstore on Fulton Street, near its intersection with Nassau. When a policeman searched the premises, he seized a number of forbidden works. In addition to the ubiquitous *Memoirs of a Woman of Pleasure* and *The Curtain Drawn Up,* he confiscated two more-recent additions to the city's roster of obscene books, *The Life and Adventures of Silas Shovewell* and *The Voluptuary; or, Woman's Witchery, a Romance of Passion.*[79] At the time of the arrest, Ormsby was engaged in a variety of enterprises related to the field of indecent literature. In addition to selling obscene books from his store, he had just put out, under the alias Gillen & Co., a new flash paper called the *Weekly Whip.* He was also the publisher of at least one brothel directory, *Guide to the Harem; or, Turkish Palaces of the Empire City,* as well as a large inventory of racy novels, mostly written by the New Yorker George Thompson but falsely attributed to French author Charles Paul de Kock.[80]

Once again, no conviction was forthcoming. In years to come, Ormsby continued to turn up in both court and publishing records in connection with obscene publications. In March 1856 a court officer testified that he bought a copy of *Memoirs of a Woman of Pleasure* from Ormsby's store, now located at 100 Nassau Street. While there, he "saw several other obscene works" of the same type. Ormsby agreed to sell him twenty-four such works for twelve dollars per dozen. The officer arrested him on the spot. After this latest arrest, Ormbsy's former partner, the publisher George Akarman, who was then on the verge of launching the nation's first sexually explicit periodical, came to his aid by paying his five-hundred-dollar bail.[81]

Ormsby's name resurfaced in 1858, when he was arrested a third time. The ensuing indictment charged him with selling obscene books, under the sham trade name Gillen & Co., and offering catalogues of such books, each of which contained an indecent print to tempt recipients.[82]

Even this third arrest for obscenity did not chasten Ormsby, who remained an active player in New York's smut trade until his death in 1865.[83] A mail-order circular from the early 1860s for "Thomas Ormsby's Commission Bureau" advertised his willingness to procure "fancy goods" for "parties living in inland towns, or those wishing any articles that can only be procured in New York City." His prior run-ins with the New York police led him to be circumspect about specific titles and to avoid describing the items he could procure. Yet rural men familiar with New York's sporting culture, perhaps from a business trip, would certainly have understood "fancy goods" and "articles that can only be procured in New York City" as referring to the availability of erotic books, sex toys, and contraceptives. In addition, one of the titles he advertised, *The Marriage Bed; or, Wedding Secrets Revealed by the Torch of Hymen*, had been named in one of Brady's 1858 indictments for obscenity.[84]

A revealing credit report filed on Ormsby in 1864 paints a picture of a book dealer and occasional publisher who was economically successful but socially marginal. In general, the Dun agents describe the men who fueled the erotic print trade in mid-nineteenth-century New York as shrewd, energetic businessmen—high praise in the credit lexicon. They often had backgrounds in skilled labor in fields such as binding and printing, possessed moderate amounts of capital, and displayed strong entrepreneurial ambitions.[85] At the same time, credit records make clear that mainstream publishers considered their activities disreputable and did not accept such men as colleagues. The Dun report for Ormsby fits this pattern exactly. Listing his occupation as "Books," the entry praised him as "a smart active fellow." It also noted that he "makes more than a living" at his trade. However, it added that he was "not of the chastest cha[racter]." It concluded that he had "no st[an]d[in]g with the regular book trade who do not know him + he is not entitled to a bus cr[edit]."[86] On the other hand, Ormsby may not have needed credit from the "regular book trade," as he probably could rely on other participants in New York's growing network of pornographic publishers, such as George Akarman, to supply credit, pay bail when needed, or make other financial arrangements.

What inspired men like Robinson, Hobbes, Haines, Brady, and Ormsby to develop a specialty in obscene books and persist in the trade despite the legal risks? In answering this question, it is useful to compare the motivations of New York pornographers with those of their principal source, London publisher William Dugdale. As both a labor radical and a sexual libertine, Dugdale espoused fiercely egalitarian, republican politics. This mixture of political and sexual nonconformity led him to produce editions of Voltaire and Paine and political tracts advocating land redistribution, Chartism, and the abolition of workhouses, alongside a large body of pornography.[87] In combining sex and politics, Dugdale followed in the footsteps of Enlightenment-era intellectuals in England and France, who frequently deployed the shock of sex to subvert the authority of the established church, the royal monarchy, and a hereditary aristocracy. One eighteenth-century revolutionary thinker whose work migrated to nineteenth-century New York was the Comte de Mirabeau, who wrote *The Curtain Drawn Up*. As the historian Robert Darnton has observed, "It no longer seems so puzzling that Mirabeau, the embodiment of the spirit of 1789, should have written the rawest pornography and the boldest political tracts of the previous decade. Liberty and libertinism appear to be linked, and we can find affinities among all the best-sellers in the clandestine catalogues."[88]

In sharp contrast, there is little to suggest that the leading publishers of erotic texts in antebellum New York were motivated by anything other than the desire for commercial profit. As a result, works such as *The Curtain Drawn Up* and *Memoirs of a Woman of Pleasure,* which had a subversive, egalitarian edge in a European context, lost their revolutionary charge when they were republished in the United States. Even the anti-authoritarian editors of the original flash weeklies, several of whom had close ties to working-class radicals in the Democratic Party, printed sexually titillating gossip and erotic exposés less as a political critique of social inequality than as a tool to extract blackmail from victims.

A corollary of the largely apolitical outlook of early New York pornographers was that few participants in the obscene print trade challenged the legitimacy of moral censorship in any direct way. For the most part, the individual publishers described here and their broad network of associates—printers, binders, lithographers, engravers, bookstore and print shop owners, bookstand operators, and street peddlers—reacted to obscenity prosecutions by failing to show up at their arraignment, or forfeiting their bail when they failed to appear for trial, or quickly pleading guilty to the charges against them.

But the law of obscenity was far from irrelevant in their lives. On the contrary, these individuals understood that obscenity prohibitions posed substantial risks to both their liberty and their property. On a visceral, personal level, the law posed grave dangers, including incarceration, for all the participants in the lewd print trade, particularly those at the bottom end of the supply chain. They were responsible for distributing erotic works to consumers and were the most likely to suffer imprisonment. On an economic level, prohibitions on obscenity also presented a considerable hazard. The loss of income could be devastating for poor families of street peddlers who were jailed for obscenity. Publishers, who had the greatest investment at stake, faced a risk of a different kind. If raided, they could lose thousands of printed books, engravings, and lithographs, as well as valuable stereotype plates to provide additional print runs, lithographic stones, and copperplates and steel plates to produce new illustrations. Frederic Brady, for example, experienced two raids on his premises, confiscations of his large inventory, and imprisonment for a time.

Despite these painful run-ins with the law, men like Brady did not abandon the obscene book trade. Instead, the more highly capitalized participants continually strategized about ways to operate more unobtrusively and minimize the possibility of detection. Henry Spencer Ashbee, a keen observer of the transatlantic pornography scene, noted the pervasive use of subterfuge among authors, publishers, and sellers of erotic books in their efforts to escape prosecution. "The author writes, for the most part, anonymously, or under an assumed name . . . To discover these authors is frequently impossible." In addition, the "publisher generally affixes a false impress with an incorrect date; and the title is not unfrequently worded so as to mislead with regard to the real contents of the book." Dealers in obscene works—men willing to risk the constant threat of prison for the promise of high profits—were just as difficult to track down. "To trace the booksellers who have set the law at defiance, who have sometimes made large profits, and at others succeeded at only getting into prison, is a pursuit equally interesting, but quite as difficult."[89]

Ashbee's observations certainly ring true for the New York pornography milieu, where falsehood and deception abounded. Publishers who dared to "set the law at defiance" commonly adopted aliases and published under false imprints. They routinely fabricated the dates, places of publication, and even titles of the works they issued. They employed middlemen whenever possible, to distance themselves from the point of sale. For extra protection, a major producer like Haines took the precaution of assigning to independent contractors operating out of separate locations the tasks of printing, binding, and storing works that authorities regarded as obscene. In addition, almost all pornographers understood the necessity of keeping an ample supply of cash on hand to bribe snooping police officers, politicians, and judges.

Along with the risks, however, prohibitions on obscenity furnished the potential for lucrative profits. At the outset, the 1842 ban on importing obscene pictures encouraged American manufacturing of erotica and created an opening that audacious, resourceful publishers like Haines were quick to recognize. Obscenity prosecutions also generated a steady stream of publicity that transmitted knowledge about erotic publications and aroused interest in them. Publishers and dealers in obscene materials, rather than passively accept the strictures of the law, focused on ways to manipulate the rules to serve their own ends. One strategy was to produce a voluminous body of racy pamphlet novels that carefully skirted the obscene and substituted explicit violence for forbidden sex. At the same time, savvy New York pornographers looked for other ways to exploit the commercial possibilities created by law—both "positive" laws promoting capitalist expansion and "negative" laws banning the sale of obscene publications.[90]

Chapter 5
Venus in the Mail

The career of one of New York's most enterprising and innovative publishers, George Akarman, reveals in unusual depth how obscenity prohibitions not only threatened sex publishers with imprisonment and loss of property, but also sustained and inspired their trade. In the early 1870s Anthony Comstock identified Akarman as the second-largest publisher of obscene material in the United States, after William Haines. Together with Haines and a third publisher, Jeremiah Farrell, he was responsible for generating a huge supply of obscene publications in the United States, enough to meet the demand of four thousand dealers and countless individual consumers spread across the country.[1] To understand the dominance Akarman exercised in Comstock's day, however, it is necessary to go back nearly two decades—to his groundbreaking role in transforming New York's local trade in obscene literature into an extensive national market before the Civil War.

Owing to the clandestine nature of Akarman's occupation, he left few deliberate traces of his life and business dealings for others to uncover. Early on, however, he granted an interview to a credit reporter from R. G. Dun & Co. that provides valuable insights into his background, as well as into the highly volatile nature of publishing ventures in antebellum America. The interview took place in 1852, at a time when he had temporarily absented himself from the publishing business and had not yet become deeply involved in illicit publications. Akarman told the Dun agent that he originally hailed from New Hampshire but had moved to Boston as a young man to learn bookbinding. Entrepreneurial and ambitious from an early age, he soon left Boston for New York, where he struck out on his own in the binding trade. Apparently he did well as a solo proprietor, accumulating three thousand dollars of capital. After a time, he sold his business, moved to Cincinnati, and began publishing "cheap publications" with the firm of Burgess & Akarman. One of the works they issued in 1848 survives, A. W. Franklin's statistical compendium, *American Cottage Library; or, Useful Facts, Figures, and Hints, for Everybody.*[2]

But the fledgling publisher failed to earn money in the Midwest, and he returned to New York sometime in the late 1840s. At first, he resumed bookbinding. Then he reentered the "cheap publications" business with a partner, Thomas Ormsby, in a firm known as Akarman and Ormsby, located at 102 Nassau Street, at the junction of Nassau and Ann. Though it is not clear whether this partnership involved the production of erotic books, Ormsby would soon become a prominent purveyor of fancy literature, whose activities triggered multiple arrests for obscenity.[3]

For unexplained reasons, Akarman sold his share of the partnership with Ormsby in 1851. He then started a new venture with several other men, also in "cheap publications," called Garrett & Co., a precursor of Dick & Fitzgerald, a famous nineteenth-century publisher of popular adventures and romances. A separate credit entry for Garrett & Co. from the same time period favorably concluded that all its principals were "v indus enterpris men, hard working & deemd wort[hy] of a reason[able] cr[edit], say $500." Though the Dun reporter was not certain about the amount of capital in the firm, he noted that it was reputed to be worth $8,000.[4] In July 1852 the enterprising Akarman left Garrett & Co., again selling his interest in the partnership for a profit. Flush with capital from previous ventures, he agreed to lend money to some wine merchants. As he explained to the Dun reporter, he had been drawn into the liquor trade when they defaulted and he was forced to take possession of their stock. At the time, he estimated his net worth at $10,000.[5]

Akarman's 1852 interview resulted in a glowing financial review. "We learn that he is a smart shrewd bus man, vy atten[tive] + indus, + an excellent financier," the entry noted. "Has been prompt in meeting his engagemts + is said to have made money. He seems easy in his finances, + is always ready to share a note."[6] A mere four months later, however, the tone of the Dun report shifted markedly. Akarman had sold his stock of liquors and had somehow sullied his good standing: "His actions of late h[a]v[e] not been looked upon vy favorably + those who formerly had a gd opinion of him th[in]k otherwise." The February 1853 entry concluded: "His associations are bad. Shd be dealt with cautiously." The final note on Akarman, recorded eight months later, in October 1853, stated that he was no longer in the city directory or at his former office and was thought to be out of business.[7]

Though Akarman's credit evaluations end in 1853 and suggest he had fallen on hard times, his withdrawal from the business world was in fact short-lived, if it took place at all.[8] The final Dun report did not reveal details of his bad conduct or "bad associations," but later accounts of Akarman's activities disclose that he had begun to produce and market large quantities of obscene books and other forms of sexual entertainment by the early 1850s.[9]

Undoubtedly, by the middle of the decade, Akarman had amassed enough capital to create his own little empire of commercial vice. To provide a front for his various enterprises, he falsely claimed to operate a business under his own name that he amusingly called Akarman's Self-Applying French Hair Dye. But for his more risqué product lines, he followed the practice of the industry by adopting aliases. Posing as a publisher named James Ramerio, he sold lurid paperback novels by sensational writers like George Thompson, advertising these as "racy" books. Posing as an importer mischievously named Jean Rosseau, he sold much more expensive editions of sexually explicit texts, often containing graphic illustrations, which he advertised as "fancy" books. As Rosseau, he also dealt in condoms and sex toys. As one Dr. Ashwell, Akarman sold an assortment of pills and powders that he claimed could be used as aphrodisiacs or abortifacients.[10]

No sloth, in 1856 Akarman also launched the nation's first fancy periodical, the "weekly journal of wit, love and humor" that he called *Venus' Miscellany*.[11] Far more sexually explicit than any newspaper or journal previously published in New York, this publication also presents a fascinating point of entry into the origins of American pornography. Among other things, it provides an intriguing perspective on the mid-nineteenth-century male sexual imagination, a perspective that challenges much of the received wisdom about the history of pornography. In particular, the paper's eroticization of female autonomy and its positive portrayals of sexually independent women call into question interpretations that identify female subordination as the central convention of Victorian erotic writing.[12]

From his office at 14 Frankfort Street, just southeast of City Hall and a few doors down from the powerful Democratic political organization located at the intersection of Nassau and Frankfort, Tammany Hall, Akarman oversaw the production of *Venus' Miscellany*. Each issue featured four pages of bawdy pictures, advertisements, jokes, poetry, short stories, and letters to the editor. The cover and back pages were dominated by excerpts from serialized romances written in a titillating, sexually allusive style that was typical of the racy literature of the day. The ten extant issues included two complete stories, "Inez de Castro" by "Julia Gaylove" and "The Amorous Adventures of Lola Montes" by "Eugene de Orsay," a pseudonym for racy novelist George Thompson, who was a regular contributor. Both tales played with fantasies about ethnicity and sexuality by recounting the erotic adventures of passionate, lustful Spanish heroines. The paper also ran installments of Thompson's *Mysteries of Bond Street* and *Loves of Cleopatra.*

The first page of each issue carried a picture illustrating a scene from the featured serial. While obviously intended to be sexually stimulating to readers, they are rather modest by today's standards. A common image depicted a female character in a state of partial dishabille, with her "snowy globes" (to use the parlance of the time) fully exposed and the bottom of her dress raised above her knees to display her thighs, a highly eroticized body part in an era of long dresses. One such engraving presented a shapely woman asleep on a bed, dreaming of a "tall, manly" lover, with her dress conveniently unfastened to reveal her "burning, swelling" bosom, "quivering with intense desire." A similar picture (Figure 5.1) portrayed a scene from Thompson's "Amorous Adventures of Lola Montes" in which a "vigorous sailor-boy" fondles the bared breasts of the fiery female protagonist. Another popular strategy for revealing the female body involved representations of women bathing, singly or in groups. A typical illustration in this genre, captioned "Donna Inez—The Wanton Bather," showed a voluptuous female naked in a pond, her hips and breasts revealed, awaiting her lover.[13]

The two inner pages contained material that was even more salacious. Advertising for companies selling fancy books, contraceptives,

5.1 "Lola and Young Stanhope in the Cable Tier," Venus' Miscellany, *June 20, 1857, 1.*

COURTESY OF THE RARE BOOKS DIVISION, DEPARTMENT OF RARE BOOKS AND SPECIAL COLLECTIONS, PRINCETON UNIVERSITY LIBRARY.

and aphrodisiacs filled the second page. When Akarman's financial records were seized in the fall of 1857, it became apparent that he actually owned most of the companies listed there. Akarman contributed to the vibrant business in contraceptives in the second half of the nineteenth century in the guise of "French importer" Jean Rosseau, who offered "Cundums, Cundums, Cundums" for sale.[14] Rosseau explained this product's substantial benefits: "This great invention is to prevent conception in females, and has been a long time in general use by the French. Its being a cap, or thin transparent skin, that entirely covers a part of the man, and prevents an emission from entering the female, at the same time detracts nothing from the pleasures; and, in fact is, the only safe thing to be relied on." Rosseau also ran promotions along these lines: "Fancy, Fancy, Fancy, Fancy. French Transparent Cards, French Prints, Fancy Books, Advantage Cards, etc. by the single pack, dozen, or gross." One of Rosseau's bound fancy books, *The Adventures and Intrigues of the Duke of Buckingham, Charles the Second and Earl of Rochester, with All Their Amorous Exploits during the 'Merry Monarch's' Reign*, came with ten "colored Fancy engravings."[15] This volume, priced at two dollars, was one of four titles later named in Akarman's indictment for obscene libel. Although it has not survived, we can speculate from evidence contained in other arrests for obscene prints in the 1850s that the "fancy engravings" it included were quite explicit.[16]

Under the heading "Rich, Rare and Racy Reading," Akarman customarily advertised a selection of inexpensive publications at a cost of a quarter or fifty cents each. Of more than thirty books regularly included in this section, a substantial portion can be attributed to George Thompson.[17] Supplementing Thompson's fiction, Akarman's "Racy Reading" list contained several works about the licentious ways of European nobles and monarchs, such as *Chevalier De Faublas; or, Debauchery of the Old Nobility of France* and *Merry Wives of London; Being a Picture of Licentiousness of the Court.*

In addition, the second page of *Venus' Miscellany* offered aphrodisiacs, more contraceptives, and abortion pills for sale by mail order from a Dr. J. C. Norton. The doctor's "Love Nectar," priced at five dollars a bottle, promised to impart to "the sickly wife . . . that degree of vital force necessary to the crowning joy and great object of matrimony. To the debilitated husband it gives the nervous and muscular energy which characterizes manhood . . . Ladies of delicate constitutions, subject to those derangements peculiar to the feeble of their sex, will obtain immediate relief from its use." His "celebrated preventive" was promoted as an "enviable secret" for married couples "who do not wish to increase their families," while his "periodical

To Book Pedlars and Dealers in

CHEAP PUBLICATIONS.

RICH, RARE AND RACY READING. Your attention is called to the following Cheap Publications, just now issuing monthly in uniform covers, handsomely illustrated with colored engravings, and said to be the most saleable works ever published. Pedlars will do well to send on their orders direct to us as we are the publishers, consequently can sell them at less rates than those that purchase of us, to sell again; we have one price and no agents, the largest profits can be realized in this business, should any one feel disposed to engage in it, and with but very little outlay. As for instance by purchasing ten dollars worth of books at our rates, you can clear fifteen dollars profit for yourselves. In sending orders, please Register your letters containing money or we will not hold ourselves responsible.

Title	Price
The Mysteries of Bond Street; or, the Seraglios of Upper Tendom.	25
The Amorous Adventures of Lola Montes.	25
Adventures of a Sofa; or, Drawing-room Intrigues	25
Marie de Clairville; or, The Confessions of a Boarding School Miss	25
The Amorous, Intrigues and Adventures of Aaron Burr	25
La Tour De Nesle; or, The Amours of Margurite of Burgundy	50
Flora Montgomery	25
The Bridal Chamber and its Mysteries	25
Anna Mowbray; or, Tales of the Harem	25
The Amours of a Quaker; or, The Voluptuary	50
The Loves of Byron, his various Intrigues with Celebrated Women	50
Merry Wives of London; being a Picture of Licentiousness of the Court	50
The Chevalier; a thrilling tale of Love and Passion	50
The Gay Deceiver; or, Man's Perfidy and Woman's Frailty	25
Dissipation; or, Crime and its Consequences	25
Julia King; or, The Follies of a Beautiful Courtezan	25
The Irish Widow; or, The Last of the Ghosts	25
Harriet Wilson; or, Memoirs of a Woman of Pleasure	25
Madeline, the Avenger; or, Seduction and its Consequences	25
Paul the Profligate; or, Paris as it is	25
Adventures of a Country Girl; or, Gay Scenes in my Life	25
Simon the Radical; or, The Adventures of a Bonnet Rouge	25
Amelia Moreton; or, Life at a Fashionable Watering Place	25
The Countess; or, My Intrigues with the Bloods	25
Venus in Boston, an exciting Tale of City Life	25
The Adventures of a Libertine	25
Evil Genius; or, The Spy of the Police	25
Sharps and Flats; or, The Perils of City Life	25
The Lame Devil; or, Asmodeus in Boston	25
Demon of Gold; or, The Miser's Daughter	25
Kate Montrose; or, The Maniac's Daughter	25
Aristotle, Illustrated	25
Complete Masterpiece	50
The Wedding Night; or, Advice to Timid Bridegrooms; plain, 5 plates	25
" " colored, 5 plates	37
Secret Passion, colored	37
" " plain	25

Address all orders to JAMES RAMERIO, Publisher, New York.

N. B.—Copies sent by mail, free of postage.

5.2 George Akarman's racy book list. "Rich, Rare, And Racy Reading," Venus' Miscellany, *May 16, 1857, 2.*

COURTESY OF THE RARE BOOKS DIVISION, DEPARTMENT OF RARE BOOKS AND SPECIAL COLLECTIONS, PRINCETON UNIVERSITY LIBRARY.

pills" were available for "unhealthy and delicate females who have neglected to use [Norton's] preventive, and whose strength will not permit child-bearing."[18]

The inner pages also contained an assortment of short stories from contributors with fanciful pen names like "Lucy Druidress," "Pole," and "Nastycus," along with a smattering of bawdy puns and smutty jokes about national politics. One asked: "Why is Ex-President Pierce like the privates of a man? Because he went in *Hard* and came out *Soft*." Another involved Mormon polygamy, then a subject of considerable national anxiety: "Much has been said latterly about the oppression of the Mormons. But Brigham Young cannot be said to rule with a rod of iron, as he emphatically enforces his commands by a pole of flesh! It is *hard*, no doubt, but not fatal."[19]

By far the most sexually explicit fare in *Venus' Miscellany* appeared in the form of a regular column on page three, "Correspondence," which reproduced letters from female readers boasting of their sexual daring.[20] It was certainly no accident that Akarman chose to link erotic arousal with culturally and legally transgressive themes. As Sigmund Freud declared early in the twentieth century: "Some obstacle is necessary to swell the tide of the libido to its height; and at all periods of history, wherever natural barriers in the way of satisfaction have not sufficed, mankind has erected conventional ones to be able to enjoy love."[21] Later in the century, Georges Bataille argued that the pleasure of pornography depends on an accompanying prohibition that it appears to transgress and thereby "completes."[22] More recently, such theorists as Michel Foucault and Judith Butler have explored the "productive and multiple possibilities of the law," to reveal the ways in which ostensible instruments of "repression" and "prohibition" have instead publicized sex, promoted sexual discourse, and created the conditions for new forms of desire.[23] As Foucault famously reinterpreted Freud's theory of sexual repression, "What is involved is the production of sexuality rather than the repression of sex."[24]

Obscenity prohibitions played a similar role in the creation of antebellum print culture. As we have seen, early obscenity prosecutions singled out expressions of female passion and pleasure for special condemnation. In the process, they helped to make literature that drew attention to the sexual autonomy of women seem especially forbidden and thrilling. Akarman sought to exploit this dynamic to the hilt, in crafting his "Dear Venus" column in a way that deliberately highlighted female desire and even control over sex.

Within American publishing circles, Akarman's attention to female erotic aggression was not entirely unprecedented. Sensational novels in particular also featured sexually voracious women. But these works generally portrayed such characters as dangerous and monstrous.[25] In contrast, *Venus' Miscellany* depicted sexually assertive women in a much more sympathetic and appealing light. Moreover, unlike most female characters in sensational fiction, the women who populated the pages of *Venus' Miscellany* were never depicted as prostitutes. Instead, they were valorized as autonomous subjects who engaged in sex for their own amusement and pleasure. To be sure, the paper carried occasional testimonies from male readers boasting of their sexual conquests of young virgins. But it more frequently offered audacious sexual confessions by supposedly real women, including a number of married women. Though one strongly suspects that Akarman was the author of these confessions, his emphasis on first-person female narrations of erotic desire and his affirmation of women's right to sexual satisfaction are bracing, nonetheless.

A series of letters Akarman printed between two women in 1857 is emblematic of his special interest in representing the sexual curiosity and boldness of middle-class American wives. In these, he cleverly combined a classic pornographic device dating back to Aretino's sixteenth-century *Ragionamenti,* involving a dialogue between two courtesans, with a more modern, democratic device inviting participation by "average" female readers. In one letter, "Maria C." reveals that her "husband has a peculiar taste which he desires me to gratify." The "peculiar taste" is having his wife tell him whether she has ever been "naughty" with other men. Maria relates that, while reading a racy novel together one night (George Thompson's *Amours of*

Marguerite of Burgundy, which Akarman serialized in early numbers of *Venus' Miscellany* and advertised in book form in the same issue in which Maria C.'s letter appeared), her husband suddenly urges her to tell him whether she had "enjoyed the delights of love" before their marriage. When she confesses to one affair, he responds enthusiastically. As she recounts: "Presently disrobing me, he smothered me with kisses on every part of my person, and declared it was the most delightful moment he had ever enjoyed with me, nor did he withdraw from the ardor of his embrace till he had three times subdued himself in my arms, all the time whispering the delight he felt and urging me to tell him all about it." But should she gratify her husband's voyeuristic desires by confessing her dalliances *since* their marriage? Confused, she solicits advice not from the male editor but from other *female* readers. "If you publish this perhaps some of your readers whose husbands have the same kind of desire, will be able to answer even better than you."[26]

In answer to Maria's request, the very next issue brings a response from a married woman, one whose husband is "kind enough" to bring home *Venus' Miscellany* to her each week. Predictably, this woman wholeheartedly endorses Maria's disclosures to her husband and encourages her adultery. "Be assured," she counsels, "that the greater *pleasurist* your husband finds you, the more he will love you, and the oftener he will take you to his arms."[27]

Maria's correspondent confesses to being an avid pleasurist herself, putting a libidinous twist on the bohemian free love movement of the 1850s, which supported sexual relationships rooted in "passional attraction" rather than the law of marriage.[28] "My husband and I," she relates, "found out the first night, the true secret of Love. The consequence is, that we are both *pleasurists.* He enjoys whom he pleases. Perhaps I sometimes wander myself." One of the pleasures she describes is that she and her husband, primed by reading the latest issue of *Venus' Miscellany*, pursue a *ménage à trois* with their female neighbor, Martha, every Saturday night. "Satisfied myself," the writer explains, "I turn my back." As she blithely puts it: "Why be jealous and wicked?"

Two months later, Maria writes to inform the editor that she has followed her correspondent's advice about using stories of her sexual adventures to excite her husband. As a result, "now we enjoy one continued stream of happiness, heightened to the highest degree by pleasurable conversation, and in the height of ecstasy by softly whispered confessions." Manifesting a new emphasis on the pleasures of reading, Maria and her husband also arouse each other by perusing *Venus' Miscellany*. As she compliments the editor: "The spicy tales, anecdotes, and correspondence contained in your excellent sheet, bring ten thousand thrills of delight to your readers, and increase the mutual pleasure tenfold."[29]

But Maria takes her correspondent's advice about "pleasurism" to heart as well, by beginning a torrid relationship with *her* married female neighbor, "Mrs. S." Indeed, she reports that she and Mrs. S. "have enjoyed each other's society twenty times since I last wrote to you." When Maria confesses the lesbian affair to her husband, he is not angered in the slightest; on the contrary, the revelation throws him into another "ecstasy of delight." Given his taste for voyeurism, he of course declares "he must be a witness of the scene." Generously, Maria agrees that he can watch, by "peeping through a hole he had made in the door," while she and her neighbor make love. She also provides readers with a description of her mutual oral sex with Mrs. S., including a moment that presumably pleased male readers by having the spying husband take his wife's place in this act: "At length, as we had before arranged, I had her in such a position, her back to the door, and our heads and tails somehow so mixed that we were laying *[sic]* at reverse ends, when my husband crept softly in and assisted me in completing the pleasure, without for the moment her becoming aware of it." Clearly, these letters were designed both to parody the free love movement and to titillate male audiences with depictions of women making love, a continuing staple of twenty-first century male fantasy.[30]

Were women like Maria simply creations of the male editor's imagination? In all likelihood, this type of correspondence was the work of Akarman's hand. He obviously believed there was a demand among male readers for stories that eroticized female agency and male passivity in the sexual sphere. By inverting cultural norms of passivity and "passionlessness" for middle-class wives and defying legal prohibitions on depictions of erotic knowledge and assertiveness among women, stories like Maria's provided Akarman's customers with a delicious thrill of transgression.[31]

At the same time, it is certainly possible that some American women derived satisfaction from reading *Venus' Miscellany*—perhaps, as many of its scenarios suggested, with their husbands or suitors. Several daily papers expressed horror over the apparent appeal of Akarman's publications to women. The *New York Times* reported in 1857, "It is a disgraceful fact, that out of 3,300 subscribers" to *Venus' Miscellany*, "nearly one half were females." The same article asserted that Akarman hired women to manufacture obscene books, employing them "in stitching the sheets of the works and in coloring the plates." In an era when female laborers were often hired to bind books together and to hand-color illustrations, this last claim was plausible.[32] Perhaps most scandalous was the charge that female writers helped to create the stories in *Venus' Miscellany:* "Contributions to the literary content of the paper, in many cases written by females, and of the most obscene description, were also found."[33] While the *Times* probably exaggerated women's role in order to shock readers, other evidence supports the assertion that some women of this era actively participated in the production and consumption of pornography. Mary Haines, the wife of the most successful nineteenth-century pornographer, William Haines, assisted him throughout his lengthy and prolific career. In the 1860s the spouse of William Simpson, one of New York's largest distributors of pornography, was said to specialize in marketing erotic literature to shop girls. Indeed, when Comstock began his crusade against obscenity in New York shortly after the Civil War, he insisted that females, particularly schoolgirls and young women, were among the most avid consumers of obscene books and prints.[34]

Moreover, it is worth emphasizing that female "passionlessness" was an ideological prescription of the bourgeoisie, not a social reality.[35] We can surmise that numerous nineteenth-century women read sexual advice literature and manuals on contraception.[36] In addition, we know that some middle- and upper-class women sought out doctors and spas that offered sexual massages and clitoral hydrotherapy treatments in the mid-nineteenth century.[37] George Thompson salaciously alluded to this practice in his novel *New-York Life: The Mysteries of Upper Tendom Revealed* (1849). He described a particular doctor who developed a flourishing medical practice by conducting examinations "*per vaginam*" and administering "daily fingerings" to various well-to-do New York matrons, who were "doctored for no other reason than a liking for the medicine."[38]

Less prurient sources also attributed an unnatural sexual curiosity to otherwise "respectable" women, especially young women. In 1859 Erastus Dow Palmer's *White Captive* was displayed at the William Schaus gallery on Broadway, the city's most fashionable thoroughfare. The sculpture depicted a naked pioneer girl who had been kidnapped by Indians, stripped of her clothes, and had her hands tied behind her back. The sadomasochistic eroticism of the statue was emphasized by its presentation: it was displayed on a rotating pedestal and "illuminated by gaslight filtered through a tinted shield that lent its marble surface a realistic fleshlike tone."[39] Nearly three thousand people of both sexes reportedly visited the gallery in the first two weeks. A scandalized editorial in the *New York Times* expressed particular shock at the number of young women flocking to the exhibition room, which had become a "convenient lounging and flirtation place": "We have all of us in the persons of our mothers, wives, or children, learned to attach a certain sanctity to the female form, which makes us instinctively shrink with pain when we see young girls hanging on the arms of leisurely-looking men, eye glass in hand, surveying the 'White Captive' from every point, coolly making their criticisms, or warmly expressing their admiration."[40] In the same period a small but visible band of adventuresome middle-class women also appalled the *Times* editors by openly attending meetings that discussed free love and the perils of marriage and monogamy.[41]

Finally, the stories in *Venus' Miscellany*, by publicizing sexual intimacy between women, might well have encouraged women who desired women to engage in subversive readings of the content.[42] In an 1854 work on physiology, *Esoteric Anthropology*, the health reformer, free love advocate, and former flash newspaper editor Thomas Low Nichols remarked on the "not unfrequent" occurrence of "Sapphic love." As he described this love, it was a "passion of females for each other, and their mutual gratification of each other's desires."[43] Whereas Nichols categorized such passion as a "perversion," the columns of *Venus' Miscellany* may have presented female readers with a more positive context in which to fantasize about sapphic sex.

In all probability, when newspaper reporters claimed that half the subscribers to *Venus' Miscellany* were women, their motives were largely sensational. Even so, the shock value of attributing a desire for sexual stimulation to women may also have conveyed an unsettling truth—that female readers *could* use the *Miscellany*'s tales of independent women, its depictions of sapphic passion, and its affirmation of women's right to sexual pleasure to forge erotic fantasies of their own.

As a pioneer in sexual explicitness and in provocative tales about sexually assertive American women, Akarman was constantly confronted with and responsive to the threat of arrest and imprisonment. Because he operated in a zone of criminalized speech, he devoted particularly close attention to crafting strategies to avoid prosecution. Indeed, the pages of *Venus' Miscellany* make plain that Akarman spent a lot of time thinking about obscenity law. Yet the risks he faced did not lead him to mend his ways, cease selling obscene publications, and take up an honorable calling. Instead, they prompted him to improvise ways to guide his various business ventures through the maze of legal restrictions that confronted him.[44]

Early on, Akarman seized on the idea of using the mails as the best solution to the legal problems he faced. Akarman, like most American citizens before the Civil War, conceived of morals regulation, including obscenity prosecutions, as a function of local, or at most state, governance. He accordingly devised his strategy to take advantage of the local focus of morals prosecutions. By distributing his products through the U.S. mail, Akarman sought to deprive local governments, especially New York City officials, of the legal power to regulate a business that he hoped would become exclusively an interstate, mail-order trade in obscene publications. In an effort to escape the jurisdiction of authorities in New York, he even decided to refrain from marketing his most illicit publications within the city. In doing so, he gave up the profits he could have made from over-the-counter sales in New York bookstores, print shops, and news depots and from face-to-face sales in hotel lobbies, on street corners, and at other well-established urban sites for transactions involving obscene literature.

As Akarman explained his strategy in 1857, he chose to market his fancy products, including *Venus' Miscellany*, only by mail order to "'gentlemen' at a distance."[45] This practice led to some amusing results, such as when the *New York Herald*, upon discovering that no New York residents figured on the list of subscribers to *Venus' Miscellany*, wrote a lengthy article congratulating Gothamites for having higher standards of morality than inhabitants of more provincial towns like Boston or of the rural hinterland. (The *Herald*, a vitriolic opponent of all progressive reform, predictably went on to blame the popularity of lewd literature in the countryside on the infiltration of woman's rights advocates, socialists, and free lovers.)[46]

Akarman's legal maneuvers went beyond his move to forsake the local metropolitan market. He further instructed his out-of-town customers to shun *their* local news depots, bookshops, and street peddlers and instead to place orders exclusively through the mail. So convinced was Akarman of the superior safety of the mail that he even announced his intention to stop selling *Venus' Miscellany* on newsstands altogether once the number of subscribers had reached 10,000. As he told readers in an early issue, he was determined to place the paper "entirely into a subscription circulation, which will insure it to those who want it, and keep it from those who do not want it."[47]

To induce customers to alter their buying habits, he promised that he could offer much more explicit sex if the *Miscellany* became a mail-order, subscription-only paper. As he put it, exclusive reliance on subscriptions would allow the paper to print "every delicacy we [are] pleased to serve" and to publish stories "which we could not publish while our paper circulated where it now does." In anticipation of a subscription-only paper, he commissioned a story of the most "voluptuous grandeur . . . that could ever possibly be conceived" from one of his female authors, "Julia Gaylove." Unfortunately for Akarman, readers failed to do their part by subscribing in sufficient numbers. His continued reliance on street sales all over the country forced him to tone down the voluptuousness of the promised story by instructing the "fair authoress to rewrite, and modulate her production to suit the present state, and tide of the *Miscellany*."[48]

In future issues, Akarman continued to chide out-of-town readers for purchasing *Venus' Miscellany* from retail agents rather than through the mails. He argued that public purchases drove up the cost of the paper, made it more difficult to obtain, and increased police harassment. "We are besieged with letters every day from every City in the Union." Readers, he claimed, grumbled: "They cannot get the paper without paying from ten to twenty-five cents a copy for it; and in other places they cannot get it at all, and again that they are watched when they go to buy it."[49] Akarman printed a letter from two women in Philadelphia reporting that the legal authorities there had "even declared war against the little boys" by arresting street peddlers of the *Miscellany*. As in other cities, the police action had the effect of increasing the price of the paper and contracting the supply, so that "*Venus* has not been attainable even at a considerable premium."[50] The *New York Tribune* pointed to a similar dynamic, though it overstated the exclusivity of the mail as the mode of distribution. Because the "sheet was not publicly sold, and was only to be obtained by addressing a letter" with money to a post office box, the "difficulty of obtaining the paper increased the demand for it." Newsboys who were clever enough to procure the hard-to-find issues from a mail-order source were then able to peddle them at inflated prices.[51] In Akarman's mind, the solution was simple. "To all these complaints we answer" by "advising all to send their money to us and get your paper direct by mail at first cost."[52]

Though Akarman yearned to sidestep the constraints of local regulation, he sometimes stopped to challenge the heavy-handed tactics of municipal authorities. In a sarcastic editorial, "Boston Morality," for instance, he complained about repeated police harassment of the *Miscellany*'s agents in Boston, and briefly adverted to interference by the state with the freedom of his readers to consume the literature of their choice. "We understand that the ferocious officers of the Police in that moral city have made another demonstration against some of our agents," Akarman fumed. He also related that a "gentleman . . . a first class citizen of Charlestown" had been stopped in the street by the police, "and the contents of his pockets demanded." When a copy of *Venus' Miscellany* turned up, the man was arrested. Living in a city where only sellers, not consumers, of obscenity were punished, Akarman was clearly taken aback by this violation of personal rights, exclaiming: "Verily, this is a free country!" Significantly, however, he did not complain about state interference with his own right to freedom of the press. Instead, he tried to defend current issues of the *Miscellany* from charges of obscenity, asserting, "There is nothing in the character of the paper, as it now is, that the law can take offence at." The qualification "as it now is" represented another veiled plea for readers to subscribe to a new version of the paper, in which he could safely publish uncensored material that even he acknowledged would be obscene under local law.[53]

The next issue described further trouble with municipal authorities, this time in Philadelphia. Akarman again denounced "meddling" police officers and judges who interfered with the circulation of his paper. In this editorial, however, he eschewed libertarian arguments and instead resorted to a blackmail scheme. He offered his readers a one-hundred-dollar reward for intelligence concerning the "movements," "private character," and "little pecadilloes" of police and judicial authorities in Philadelphia and Baltimore.[54] Of course, even Akarman's preferred mode of delivery, mail-order circulation, had its flaws. Early on, he chided local postmasters who confiscated *Venus' Miscellany* not for purposes of censorship, but for personal gratification. "Now, if these same postmasters *who rifle the mails,* will allow us their names, we will send them our paper gratis, provided they will let those belonging to subscribers alone." Akarman added a threat for good measure: "Don't let us hear any more complaints."[55]

Still, the sticky fingers of postal workers seemed a small price to pay for the remarkable benefits of the mail. In an 1857 exposé of Akarman's business methods, the *New York Herald* reported that he "transacted an extensive business, almost exclusively through the Post Office." Conveniently, the New York post office (Fig 5.3) was located on Nassau Street between Cedar and Liberty, about seven blocks from Akarman's Frankfort Street office. According to the *Herald,* Akarman visited the post office, which was housed in a former church, three times a day. He "regularly received over fifty letters at a time, which contained orders for his vile sheet and other indecent publications, accompanied by postage stamps and bills to the amount demanded for them." Perhaps most alarming was the purported breadth of the audience he was able to reach using the mail: "These orders were given by young men and women, residents of nearly every town and village of the Union."[56]

By the time he launched *Venus' Miscellany,* then, Akarman was well aware of the risks and burdens that obscenity law posed for business ventures like his. To reduce these dangers, he published *Venus' Miscellany* and many of his other offerings under aliases. He kept plenty of cash on hand to bribe local authorities who threatened him with arrest and incarceration. And he dreamed of escaping obscenity regulation altogether, by creating a subscription-only paper that would travel surreptitiously through the interstate mail.

Akarman's groundbreaking attempt to evade obscenity prosecution by forgoing local, street-level commerce in fancy publications like *Venus' Miscellany* altered not only his methods of distribution but also his editing of the paper. In his view, the success of his deci-

5.3 The New York Post Office on Nassau Street, which Akarman frequented. North Interior View of the New York Post Office *(1845).*

COURTESY OF THE LIBRARY OF CONGRESS.

sion to operate by mail turned on his ability to build a new audience for erotic journalism that was both national in scope and bourgeois in orientation. His intent to create an interstate, middle-class vehicle for erotica can best be appreciated by comparing the style of *Venus' Miscellany* with that of the first breed of sexually themed periodicals produced in New York, the flash weeklies of the early 1840s.

One fundamental difference was a shift in editorial tone. The original flash papers addressed a specific metropolitan audience, or at most a regional one. On the assumption that readers were familiar with the exuberant New York sporting scene, these papers offered frequent reviews of local entertainment, along with detailed information about the location, employees, and cleanliness of various brothels in the city. *Venus' Miscellany*, by contrast, reached out to a more homogenous, national community. It rarely mentioned New Yorkers or New York locales. Indeed, Akarman edited the paper in such a way as to remove its association with any particular urban provenance and to position it within a hazier, more universal setting. His chief strategy for achieving the desired transcontinental reach was to print raunchy letters to the editor from randy readers in small towns and cities across the United States.

Venus' Miscellany also substituted generic sexual humor and fictional tales for salacious local gossip. Whereas flash editors took delight in exposing sexual transgressions among the city's financial, religious, and political elite, as well as among the men about town and brothel madams of their own milieu, Akarman rarely mentioned actual individuals. Instead, he relied on correspondence from purported readers to supply verisimilitude. In the process, he both broadened his potential audience and reduced the risk that any offended parties would seek to have him indicted for obscene libel, as had often happened to his predecessors in the flash press.

Whereas the flash papers were deliberately lowbrow, vulgar, and brash in their appeal, Akarman projected an audience of more refined and unobtrusive readers. This change was at least in part a product of his legal strategy to market *Venus' Miscellany* to out-of-town purchasers of sufficient wealth and sophistication to arrange for mail-order subscriptions. His ideal customers were those who wished their copies of *Venus' Miscellany* to arrive in their post office boxes, concealed in discreet paper wrappers, rather than be "thrust in the[ir] face" in the public streets.[57]

One of Akarman's most ingenious tactics for reaching a more upscale audience was to construct a new domestic setting for erotic fantasies. Very deliberately, he moved sex out of the street and out of the brothel, which had been the principal subjects of the flash press, and into the recently idealized middle-class home. For it was precisely in this period that the bourgeoisie transformed the traditional household into a "home," a new term that came to signify "a pillar of civilization, an incubator of morals and family affections, a critical alternative to the harsh and competitive world of trade and politics." Many of the fictional encounters in *Venus' Miscellany* took place in this recently created haven of safety and affection. In this way, Akarman cleverly appealed to budding middle-class tastes by appropriating the accoutrements of bourgeois life to stoke the sexual fantasies of his intended customers. Of course, the prevailing ideology of domesticity celebrated the home not only as a source of security and order, but also as the particular locus of women's moral power, piety, and virtue.[58] Akarman's association of this sphere with female sexual license thus made the *Miscellany* especially transgressive and, as Akarman presumably hoped, all the more exciting to his anticipated audience.

Another remarkable aspect of Akarman's aspirations for a national, middle-class readership was the success of his marketing and editorial strategies. Admittedly, it is difficult to ascertain the actual audience for *Venus' Miscellany* with any precision. Akarman claimed that the paper had a national circulation of forty-nine thousand readers, a figure that was probably inflated. In September 1857 the *New York Herald* estimated his subscription list at seven thousand and growing, on the basis of evidence that one thousand customers had been added in the months of May and June alone.[59] Regardless of the true number of subscribers, newspaper investigations of Akarman's publishing enterprise confirm the broad geographic reach of the *Miscellany*. They reported subscribers in rural locales like Williamsport, Pennsylvania; Bergen, New York; Kensington, Connecticut; and Lane Station, Illinois; small cities like Lexington, Utica, and Wilmington; and major urban centers like Philadelphia and Boston—virtually everywhere except Akarman's principal place of business in New York City. Moreover, the publisher could take pride in charges that *Venus' Miscellany* appealed to an elite clientele. With its characteristic flair for the sensational and hyperbolic, the *New York Herald* declared that "the persons who buy these things are the leading men of the country—preachers, teachers and guides of the people; members of the national Congress; lights of the pulpit, the bench and the bar; thunderers upon the political rostrum; presidents of councils and caucuses and conventions; directors of banks and insurance offices."[60]

For nearly a year, Akarman's strategy of marketing *Venus' Miscellany* outside the city and encouraging distribution by mail spared him from detection, or at least from arrest. In August 1857, however, the publisher and his journal became the target of a major police investigation. Unlike with other prosecutions of sex publishers in 1850s New York, which were often triggered by street sales of pornography, Akarman's troubles began when the parents of a young man from out of state who had received one of his mail-order catalogues complained to New York officials. In response, the police began to monitor Akarman's post office boxes. By September, the daily press reported that "the Editor of a vile sheet entitled the *Venus' Miscellany*" had been arrested at the Nassau Street post office while picking up a batch of mail addressed to "Jean Rosseau," "James Ramerio," and "Dr. Ashwell." After being arraigned before the police court, where bail was set at one thousand dollars, Akarman was committed to the city jail. His bail was soon paid by a news agency, Ross & Tousey, which also served as the agent for the flash crime tabloid the *National Police Gazette*.[61]

From that point on, all the daily papers gave prominent coverage to minute details of the Akarman affair. He was tried and convicted before the Court of Special Sessions, which handled minor criminal offenses, and received a fifty-dollar fine. The presiding judge justified the lenient treatment by saying that he had "consulted with the District Attorney . . . and c[o]me to the conclusion that the imposition of a nominal fine would subserve the ends of justice, and felt confident that the defendant would turn his attention to some virtuous employment." This statement suggests that Akarman had promised Tammany district attorney A. Oakey Hall that he would plead guilty and desist from publishing *Venus' Miscellany* if Hall would recommend that the publisher get away with just a fine. Other observers suggested that bribery was at work. In any event, Hall agreed to the plea but warned Akarman that he would seek an indictment in the Court of General Sessions, which was reserved for more serious crimes, if Akarman continued production.[62]

Disgusted that he had received no more than a slap on the wrist, the editors of the *New York Tribune* dismissed the criminal proceedings against Akarman as a farce. Two days after the fine was levied, the dailies revealed that Akarman had speedily resumed publication of "the obscene journal called *Venus' Miscellany*." According to the *Herald*, as "soon as he was liberated, he hastened to his headquarters in Frankfort street, and applied himself with increased diligence to the nefarious traffic which had been temporarily impeded by his incarceration." The article referred ominously to the specter of judicial corruption: "It is said that he has often boasted that he had money enough to buy up all the Justices in the city." Whether or not bribery played a role in the lightness of his initial sentence, Akarman's cheeky defiance of the law soon prompted renewed efforts on the part of the police. After obtaining a search warrant from the city judge, on September 15, 1857, six officers invaded the shop where *Venus' Miscellany* was printed. Accompanying them were journalists from the daily press, who had been invited to witness the raid.[63]

As the next day's papers excitedly reported, the police first discovered a pressman and two assistants, who had already printed about thirty-five hundred copies, engaged in striking off the regular edition. From there, officers proceeded to Akarman's office, where *Venus' Miscellany* was folded and his books were stitched together and bound. In the first room, they found "several thousand specimens of yellow-covered literature." Forcible entry into a second, larger room, where printed sheets were assembled into pamphlets, revealed additional specimens of racy paperbacks. But the search yielded more shocking evidence when the police uncovered Akarman's cache of fancy books, reportedly consisting of "several dozens of volumes of the most obscene and filthy stuff that ever disgraced language, with illustrations to match." Another article indicated that these volumes were filled with "immoral stories and obscene pictures, were bound in gold leaf, in attractive style, and calculated to sell at enormously high prices." The officers also found a large copperplate, used to create an engraving that Akarman sent as a bonus to customers who agreed to subscribe to *Venus' Miscellany* by mail.[64]

In addition to all the "obscene and filthy stuff," police confiscated Akarman's subscription book and account ledger. The authorities must have allowed journalists to examine these records, because the next day's papers recited detailed information about the financial structure of his business. They reported his annual revenue at a hefty $60,000, equivalent to more than $1.3 million today, with estimated profits of $12,000 for the year, equal to about $265,000 today. Along with the income he derived from selling indecent publications, Akarman earned money by selling and lending stereotype plates to obscene book publishers in other cities, including Boston and New Orleans. Accounting documents further revealed that Akarman relied on a network of colleagues and independent contractors to supply essential materials and services related to his publishing enterprise. The pornographer William Haines, for instance, supplied him with paper. Bills for printing, engraving, and stereotyping services were also found on his premises, as were receipts from the *National Police Gazette* reflecting payments for advertising.[65]

Perhaps alerted by friendly parties within the police, Akarman escaped before the raid, though two of his assistants were arrested. Soon thereafter, the grand jury for the Court of General Sessions indicted him for obscene libel.[66] The bill charged him with publishing four obscene books, all of European origin: *Memoirs of a Woman of Pleasure, Memoirs of the Life and Voluptuous Adventures of the Celebrated Mademoiselle Celestine of Paris, The Life and Adventures of Silas Shovewell,* and *The Adventures and Intrigues of the Duke of Buckingham, Charles the Second and the Earl of Rochester.* All the named texts appear to have been expensive bound volumes. As mentioned earlier, Akarman, under the pseudonym Jean Rosseau, advertised *The Adventures and Intrigues of the Duke of Buckingham, Charles the Second and the Earl of Rochester* as a "fancy, fancy" publication "got up in bound book form" at the high cost of two dollars.[67] Moreover, three of the four titles, *Memoirs of a Woman of Pleasure, Memoirs of the . . . Celebrated Mademoiselle Celestine,* and *The Life and Adventures of Silas Shovewell,* had been named in several prior obscenity indictments in New York County. Attentive as he was to legal developments, Akarman was well aware that New York officials regarded these books as illicit.[68]

From the moment of his first arrest until he was indicted, the daily papers in New York denounced Akarman and his publications as "vile," "wicked," and "depraved." In a characteristic passage, the *Herald* congratulated the police on "stopp[ing] up one of the vilest fountains of disgusting filth that ever polluted even the city of New York."[69] Though clearly offended by this treatment, Akarman, like the other publishers who faced obscenity charges in the 1850s, did not choose to defend himself in a courtroom. Instead, perhaps relocating his business for a while to neighboring New Jersey, he skipped town to avoid a trial.

But Akarman was far from passive in the face of his indictment and his vilification by the press. While hiding from the police, he wrote a bold letter to James Gordon Bennett at the *New York Herald*, the nation's largest-circulation newspaper, protesting his "persecution."[70] In part, he took this step to assure his Southern customers that the police had only seized his subscription book for the North and that their names would not be disclosed. Submitting in lawyerly fashion that "there are two sides to all such questions," he also used it as an occasion to defend himself in the court of public opinion against the charges of obscenity. This letter, together with editorials he wrote for *Venus' Miscellany* before his indictment, offers rare insights into the legal and political consciousness of a mid-nineteenth-century American pornographer.

Significantly, Akarman never made the argument that might seem obvious to us today—that he had a constitutionally protected right to freedom of speech or of the press. Challenging the constitutionality of prohibitions against obscenity on the grounds of free speech was not among the range of legal defenses or public relations strategies that he perceived to be available to him.[71] Rather, he mobilized other ideas about vested rights that circulated in the 1850s as a defense against excessive state power, particularly the right to property. In this sense, as in others, he was strongly shaped by the legal culture of his day.

In his letter to Bennett, Akarman implicitly raised an early version of a substantive due process defense, based on an individual right to property under the New York constitution. Specifically, he attempted to exploit the recent winning argument by liquor dealers in *Wynehamer v. People* (1856), a case that challenged New York's 1855 Prohibition statute as depriving them of private property without due process of law. The liquor merchants had relied on Article 1, Section 6, of the state constitution: "No person shall be . . . deprived of life, liberty, or property, without due process of law; nor shall private property be taken for public use, without just compensation." In striking down the statute, the New York Court of Appeals articulated a forceful defense of individual property rights, describing them as superior to the state's desire to protect public welfare: "In a government like ours, theories of public good or public necessity may be so plausible, or even so truthful, as to command popular majorities. But whether truthful or plausible merely, and by whatever numbers they are assented to, there are some *absolute private rights beyond their reach, and among these the constitution places the right of property.*" As a result, state officials could not "annihilate the value" of property in liquor that was previously considered to be legal, even when they did so for the legitimate governmental purpose of preventing "intemperance, pauperism, and crime."[72]

Similarly, Akarman argued that New York City authorities violated *his* right to property by confiscating publications that legal officials had not previously condemned as obscene. In his view, his publishing enterprise fell into two by now familiar branches. One category consisted of a large quantity of "humble," racy pamphlets that municipal authorities had traditionally tolerated. Another, much smaller and more expensive category consisted of "a few dozen of what are called 'fancy books,'" which he grudgingly acknowledged to be "in opposition to law."

Akarman went on to protest that "stock similar to nineteen-twentieths of that seized, and now recommended to be burnt, has been sold openly for the last twenty years in this city." He expected municipal authorities to recognize the customary distinction between the obscene and the merely indecent and to respect his property rights in racy publications that approached, but did not cross the line into, illegal obscenity. (At the same time, he may have accepted and even welcomed a narrow prohibition on obscenity, which invested his fancy offerings with an aura of illicit excitement, so long as he could find loopholes that allowed him to operate within the interstices of the law.) In Akarman's opinion, the police had clearly overstepped their authority by confiscating both his racy pamphlets and every other "movable thing, including (if the expression is not obscene) several bundles of virgin white paper, clothing and other articles which could not be condemned." While still on the lam, he even hired a well-known criminal defense lawyer, Charles Spencer, to file an action to recover the nonobscene property wrongfully seized by the police, though there is no evidence that this gambit succeeded.[73] Instead, the ruthless and arbitrary conduct of police officials with regard to his property made clear to the publisher that they would not be satisfied until they had achieved the complete "taking and destruction of Akarman."

Akarman also pointed to the interstate nature of his business in illicit fancy books, arguing that mail-order transactions in such literature should be immune from prosecution in the courts of New York County. He explained, "None of those books which are condemned by the laws [of New York] have ever been sold or distributed by me in this city." Tapping into traditional concepts of federalism and local sovereignty, Akarman portrayed obscenity law, like the regulation of morals in general, as a function of local government. To circumvent obscenity prosecutions in New York, he had deliberately reserved his fancy books exclusively for "mail orders from 'gentlemen' at a distance, who might otherwise have been compelled to send their money to London or Paris, where are less virtue and civilization (?) than are claimed for our righteous City." Because he sold books "condemned by the law" only to people in other states and localities, he insisted he had done nothing to corrupt the morals of New York's populace.

In contrast to his vigilant efforts to protect New York residents from immoral literature, Akarman claimed, the New York police had worked to *increase* the city's supply of obscene publications. During the raid on his premises, they allowed "crowds of boys from the streets" to roam about his establishment taking "the humbler pamphlets," and "almost every man who left the premises had a small parcel of 'bound books' snuggly tucked under his arms (perhaps for Sunday reading)." As a result of police misconduct, not his own, there would be "no cause to complain that New-York does not have its share of 'fancy reading' hereafter until the stock is exhausted."

Akarman concluded his letter by complaining that municipal authorities had unfairly singled him out for punishment. Any perceptive and honest person could see that New York was a burgeoning metropolis in which both suppliers and consumers of off-color entertainment were omnipresent.[74] Again drawing on the legal and political controversy swirling around the state's power to prohibit the sale of alcohol, he likened his business to selling liquor—an occupation he had briefly taken up a few years before. According to Akarman, most people regarded trade in sexually stimulating publications, like the sale of alcohol, as not only pervasive but generally harmless. As a legitimate form of commerce that delivered desired commodities to customers, he implied, neither business represented an appropriate target of criminal prosecution.

Though he continued to be vilified in the press and could not prevent the loss of nearly his entire inventory, Akarman managed to elude further fines or incarceration. The minutes of the Court of General Sessions show no additional proceedings in his case after the indictment. Given that no issues of *Venus' Miscellany* after 1857 have survived, it is possible that this prosecution convinced him to discontinue production of the paper. He certainly kept a lower profile. Before the indictment, he had been listed in the city directory as a publisher at 14 Frankfort Street, the address the police raided. Thereafter, his name ceased to appear in the directory.

Clearly, however, Akarman did not forsake the pornography industry, or his New York headquarters, for very long. Comstock's investigation determined that he had pursued the business of publishing obscene books in New York City continuously for more than two decades. Moreover, despite several legal wrangles and occasional confiscations of his stock, the savvy publisher succeeded in avoiding imprisonment throughout his remarkable career. Indeed, for the next fifteen years, he continued to profit from supplying pornography to the national, middle-class audience that his *Venus' Miscellany*, aided by the facilities of the U.S. mail, had helped create.[75]

Chapter 6

The Triumph of Pornography

With the coming of the Civil War, many Northern businesses failed. Wartime disruptions and the cessation of trade with the South created legions of "bankrupts of '61." In contrast, New York's mail-order trade in sexually arousing literature burgeoned. Thanks to the innovative vision of publishers like George Akarman, the U.S. mail became the vehicle of choice for advertising and distributing a vast range of erotic books, prints, and newspapers to consumers even before the war began. By the start of the decade, New York dealers were placing advertisements in nationally circulated New York sporting papers that solicited customers with thinly veiled euphemisms for pornographic books and articles that could be sent through the mail. As Thomas Ormsby, who was arrested for obscenity three times in the 1850s, coyly asked readers of the *New York Clipper* in early 1861: "Do you wish anything from New York? If you do, you can have any book . . . sent to your address, post paid, by remitting the price in cash or stamps." Looking to extend markets for fancy goods throughout the nation and counting on potential clients to read between the lines, Ormsby guaranteed, "You can have any article you wish that cannot be obtained in the city or town where you reside."[1]

With the onset of war, pornography dealers leaped at the chance to capitalize on the military conflict by marketing indecent publications to soldiers stationed in Union camps. Ever the opportunists, such businessmen recognized that many fighting men, encamped for long periods of time and faced with the constant threat of death and disease, felt a desperate need for diversion. Given a quasi-captive audience eager for pleasure or distraction of any kind, New York dealers responded by filling the back pages of the city's flash papers with advertisements for mail-order erotica.

In a typical issue from 1862, the classified section of the *New York Clipper*, which routinely offered baseball equipment, boxing memorabilia, playing cards, implements for billiards, and cures for gonorrhea, also contained seven notices for an assortment of "Rich and Racy" books, "Books on Love," "Gay Books for Gay Boys," and "Sporting and Fancy Articles." Readers could procure these items through the mail by writing in for a free catalogue or, if they knew the title they wanted, sending payment in money or postage stamps. Jeremiah Farrell, a publisher whom Comstock later identified as one of the principal traffickers in obscene literature in the 1860s, ran an ad for "BOOKS! BOOKS!! BOOKS!!! SPORTING ARTICLES, CARDS AND PRINTS . . . All Books, Sporting and Fancy Articles you may see advertised, will be furnished to order. Catalogues sent on application." Some advertisers tried to lure readers into paying for their catalogues by packaging them with cheap offerings of bawdy prints and sketches. A New York firm, Edgar, Murphy & Co., boasted that it had "THE BIGGEST THING OUT." It instructed customers to "send twenty-five cents, and procure our Great Bijou Package, containing Sketches, Songs, and a Rich Plate, which alone is worth three times the money, together with our Catalogue of Gay Books for Gay Boys."[2]

The long duration of the war provided numerous opportunities for aspiring erotica entrepreneurs to turn a profit. Between 1862 and 1864, for instance, the number of firms regularly placing mail-order advertisements for pornography in the *New York Clipper* tripled. A representative issue from 1864 listed twenty sources for books and photographs variously described as "rich and spicy," "rich, rare, and racy," and "rare and fancy," along with "mysterious articles for sporting men." Many establishments boasted of their rising popularity and prosperity. In one ad a firm named W. H. Lindsay & Co. proclaimed that "IMMENSE NUMBERS OF SPORTS In all parts of the Union favor this Reliable Establishment with their Patronage, expressing every manifestation of delight at the BEAUTIFUL, RACY, LUSCIOUS AND ORIGINAL BOOKS, PRINTS, CARDS AND SPORTING ARTICLES OF EVERY DESCRIPTION which they continue to receive from us." As a result of widespread demand, this company declared that it was "now in the full tide of prosperity."[3]

Reading indecent publications soon became a favorite pastime among Union troops, even for devout Christians. Early in the conflict, one Christian soldier reported that "in our company, and in fact throughout the whole regiment, are young men who are professors of religion, scarcely through their probation" who "have taken to reading flimsy publications, obscene books, and the worst species of yellow-covered literature."[4] The primary culprits, everyone agreed, were publishers and dealers operating out of New York. Another pious soldier wrote to the *New York Times* in 1863 demanding that the U.S. government take action to block the mail-order trade in obscene publications. As the institution in charge of both the army and the post office, it bore the blame "for the existence of such an immense plague" and therefore had the duty to eradicate it.[5]

The next year, a captain in the Illinois infantry made a similar appeal for national intervention. Taking his case to the top, he urged President Lincoln to issue an order prohibiting the advertisement and circulation of obscene publications in the army, which he asserted were "continually distributed in large numbers," along with "medical papers advertising books and medicines for the treatment of private diseases." To prove his point, he enclosed a mail-order circular marketing "New Pictures for Bachelors." The captain felt obliged to explain his appeal to national authorities, indeed the President himself, rather than authorities in New York, where the circulars originated: "I at first intended to send this circular to proper officials in New York City, but fearing that negligence or complicity might fail to bring parties to justice, I concluded to do differently." Moreover, as "no police measures have been established in the army to checkmate and suppress the operations of those villains in N.Y.," he decided to bypass military channels and write to Lincoln directly.[6]

The predilection of Union soldiers for sexually arousing reading was not the only factor driving the expansion of New York's mail-order erotica trade in the 1860s. Another lay in technological improvements in intercontinental transportation and postal distribution. Of particular importance was the institution of mail delivery by rail in the early 1860s. The adoption of railway mail service allowed mail to be picked up by rail, sorted en route in specialized mail cars (Fig. 6.1), and deposited at rail stops in different spots around the country. Railway mail service had the great advantage of increasing the speed of mail delivery while further reducing its costs.[7]

In addition, the advent of photography marked the birth of an astonishing new medium of sexual representation. Erotic photographs provided a unique kind of visceral, direct satisfaction for viewers, by

***6.1** Exterior and interior views of a railway mail car.*

COURTESY OF THE LIBRARY OF CONGRESS.

conveying an immediacy that cheap yellow-covered novels and flash crime papers could not. Because erotic photographs often sold for a quarter or less, they were much more accessible than fancy books with explicit engravings. Even illiterate consumers and poor people who could not afford to purchase photographs themselves might experience such items by seeing them on display in a shop, being peddled on a street corner, or tucked into the knapsack of a fellow soldier.

Although the daguerreotype had been invented in Paris more than two decades before, erotic photographs did not enter the U.S. economy on a large scale until the 1860s, when nude photography produced by French sources—the undoubted "leaders in the visual porn market"—began flooding foreign markets.[8] This transformation can be attributed in part to the introduction of two phenomenally popular new forms of photography, also invented in Paris, which were far less expensive and more commercially viable than the daguerreotype: the *carte de visite* and the stereoscopic view. *Cartes de visite* were small-format pictures, usually studio portraits, which often portrayed actresses or other celebrities. Underground *cartes de visite* represented a range of indecent images, from the relatively tame (academic studies of female nudes ostensibly intended for use by artists, mass-produced actress cards "often exposing large areas of bosom and calf") to the overtly pornographic (depictions of women masturbating, men and women engaged in sexual intercourse).[9] Stereoscopic views, first unveiled in 1857, produced a three-dimensional effect when users looked at prints through a special instrument called a stereoscope or stereoscopic box. Stereoscopic pictures, with their ability to convey lifelike multidimensional figures, were a common vehicle for visual pornography, such as images revealing female genitals or men and women engaged in sex.[10]

Cartes de visite and stereoscopic views were also more durable and portable than the earlier daguerreotypes, features that allowed them to be easily shipped through the mail. A collection of advertisements in a New York sporting paper from 1863 demonstrates the growing importance for New York erotica dealers of both *cartes de visite* and stereoscopic views. A typical item read, "JUST IMPORTED FROM PARIS. Carte de visites from Life, very rich, price 25 cents" and gave a New York post office box for orders. One anonymous proprietor, who also listed only a New York post office box, promised "NEW BOOKS! NEW BOOKS!--STEREOSCOPIC VIEWS, CARTES DE

VISITE, Sporting Goods, Books, Cards, Prints, &c. Send for a circular." Another offered "ELEGANT, BEAUTIFUL, FANTASTICAL, PLAIN, Painted, or Armorus [*sic*]. Enclose 15 cents and one stamp, and state which kind of Photograph I shall send you." A vendor named H. Poncia advertised knives containing "microscopic pictures, taken from French models" for four dollars, five hundred selections of *cartes de visite* for twenty-five cents each, and two hundred different stereoscopic views, for between seventy-five cents and two dollars each, "all sent by mail."[11]

Paradoxically, it was the threat of morals prosecutions in France that provoked the sudden deluge of photographic pornography in the United States in the early 1860s. By exporting erotic pictures for sale abroad, as opposed to selling them at home, Parisian producers were able to evade prosecution for obscenity. "When images were directly shipped overseas," notes an historian of Parisian photography, "the censors (and the police) often looked the other way." As a result, France earned a "growing reputation as a source of 'dirty pictures.'"[12] In this respect, interdictions on obscenity in Paris during the 1860s created a situation similar to that produced by common-law prohibitions in New York in the 1850s. In both settings, municipal surveillance failed to persuade purveyors of sexual materials to abandon their trade. Instead, the threat of prosecution inspired such entrepreneurs to shift their distribution networks away from local customers and toward more widely dispersed markets that were national or (in the case of Parisian photographers) even international in scope.

Another catalyst for the expansion of the Civil War–era pornography industry was a new emphasis on erotic novels that were written by American, rather than European, authors. It represented a watershed of sorts that all the books classified as obscene in New York indictments in the 1860s were created by Americans. In June 1865, for instance, a bookseller named James Hanley was indicted in the New

York Court of General Sessions for selling a book called *The Beautiful Creole of Havana*. Priced at $2.50, it was one of a series of homegrown pornographic novels packaged as "'Venus' Library;' Or Tales of Illicit Love." A publisher's prospectus for this series emphasized the unique provenance of the novels and described them as "New and Original Works, which are got up in a style never before attempted in this country." Each contained 180 pages; all may have been written by the same author and made their first appearance during the Civil War. Two of the titles, *Confessions of a Washington Belle* and *Adventures of Anna P—; or, The Belle of New York*, highlighted their American settings. The table of contents for *The Beautiful Creole of Havana* also listed such chapters as "New England Village" and "Beautiful New York Girl."[13]

To be sure, New York authors had been churning out city mysteries and crime novels set in American metropolitan contexts since the 1840s. But these were cheap, sensational paperbacks, written in a sexually titillating rather than explicit style and illustrated at most with a few sexually suggestive, clumsily executed woodcuts. What was new about Venus' Library was the graphic carnal content and superior production quality of the novels, traits that previously had been confined to American reprints of classic European texts like *Memoirs of a Woman of Pleasure* and *The Curtain Drawn Up*. The high cost of the copy of *The Beautiful Creole of Havana* sold by James Hanley in 1865 registers its status as a fancy book, almost certainly published in a cloth-bound edition with explicit, colored steel engravings. A New York dealer named C. S. Wood also conveyed the stylishness of the text and illustrations in the Venus' Library collection in this 1864 notice: "Rich and Spicy—Just Published, Five New Books Entirely Original. And surpassing all other previous works of the kind ever issued in richness of description—abounding in the most piquant amatory scenes, vividly delineated by a master hand. They are handsomely bound in cloth, with fine illustrations." Wood further alluded to the graphic nature of these novels by assuring customers that their mail-order purchases would be "neatly and securely sealed."[14]

The one surviving text in the Venus' Library series, a bound copy of *The Libertine Enchantress; or, The Adventures of Lucinda Hartley*, was published in 1863.[15] Following in the footsteps of Akarman's *Venus' Miscellany, The Libertine Enchantress* inverted established gender norms by championing female erotic subjectivity. Written in the first person, the novel recounted the sexual awakening of the heroine, a teenage orphan and heiress named Lucinda Hartley. In one early scene, after witnessing a beautiful young woman and man having sex, Lucinda rushes to her room to examine her body, with the aid of a looking glass:

> I put down my clothes in haste, ran into the other room, and, having obtained the glass, in a great flutter of spirits (for I was now very much interested) I threw myself upon my bed, pulled up my clothes, opened my legs, and placed the glass between them. In this way I could see the inside surface of my thighs reflected in the glass, as well as the whole length of the crevice. On each side of the crevice rose a ridge of spongy flesh, which had a very voluptuous appearance; then, in the upper part of the opening, there was a projection, like the end of a small tongue. The whole apparatus interested me so much that I surveyed it a long time as it appeared in the mirror.[16]

Much of the proceeding plot unfolds as a celebration of female voyeurism. Numerous scenes are devoted to Lucinda's eager, detailed observations of a multitude of chance sexual encounters, in which she admires both women's and men's bodies and both female and male pleasure.

Yet another critical innovation in the 1860s pornography market was the production of sexually explicit writing, again by Americans, in the form of cheap pamphlets. One stimulus for this development was the increasing dominance of the Fourdrinier paper-making machine. First introduced in the United States in the 1820s, this device cut the cost of paper in half by 1860, thereby fueling the proliferation of "dime novels." Falling prices and intense competition for readers among publishers of cheap books also contributed to the heightened sexual explicitness of pamphlet literature. In particular, pornography dealers began to offer a series called Cupid's Own Library (Fig. 6.3). Described as a "great treat for lovers of the fancy," it contained twelve yellow-covered paperbacks that sold for between twenty-five cents and a dollar, with many priced at only a quarter. The reference to Cupid was intended to signify not only the erotic nature of the pamphlets, but also their diminutive size and brevity in comparison to the large-format, heavily illustrated books in the Venus' Library series. Among the works in Cupid's Own Library were *Love Scrapes; or, Gay Times in a Boarding House* by "Miss Carrie L.O.V.E. Cox," *The Secret Services and Duties of Major Lovit* by "Nick L. Ass," and *Sports with Venus; or, The Way to Do It.*[17]

The first offering in the series, *Amours of a Modest Man,* narrated the adventures of a shy, unmarried man in a New York boardinghouse. Though this work no longer exists, Henry Spencer Ashbee's nineteenth-century bibliography provides a helpful précis of the plot. The main characters were the "modest" bachelor and a pretty, sexually aggressive Southern widow named Mrs. Jane Sweet, who was also a boarder. One day, the frisky Mrs. Sweet "invites the bashful Mr. Bachelor into her room, closes the window blind, and fairly forces him to enjoy her." During their frolics, they are spied upon by Mary, an Irish maid, who peers through a keyhole. To persuade Mary not to disclose the affair, the ingenious widow proposes a ménage à trois between herself, Mr. Bachelor, and the servant. Mary of course accepts the offer, leading to an orgy "in which tribadism and sodomy are practiced." Ashbee summed up the story's happy conclusion in this way: "Finding his strength unequal to the task of satisfying both women, Bachelor desires to get away from one of them, Mary, and to enjoy a short repose. Mrs. Sweet leaves for her native town, Richmond, Virginia, where our hero follows, and weds her, and—her fortune, which is immense."[18]

Ashbee then declared that the novel displayed "bad" printing, contained "two obscene illustrations," and possessed "no literary merit whatsoever." Obviously unimpressed by the Cupid's Own Library collection, he curtly dismissed it as a "series of trashy publications." That said, is not hard to imagine that many Union soldiers and other Northerners might have taken pleasure in fantasizing about sexual unions between a Northern man and a wealthy Southern belle, notwithstanding the inferior print quality and literary shortcomings that offended Ashbee.[19]

Only one selection in the Cupid's Own Library series survives in its entirety, and it is held in the archives of the Kinsey Institute in Bloomington, Indiana. This sixty-four-page pamphlet, called *The Love Feast; or, A Bride's Experience: A Poem in Six Nights,* further testifies to the development of sexually graphic text in low-quality, ephemeral formats. The title page (Fig. 6.2) facetiously asserted that it was printed by the Associated Female Press at "Blind Alley, Coney-hatch, Maidenhead" in 1865. The book was published in tiny, three by four inch dimensions that would fit easily in a pants pocket, in a small hiding place, under a pillow, or even in the folds of a skirt. It usually sold for between fifty cents and a dollar, far less than fancy bound offerings of new American erotica like *The Beautiful Creole of Havana* or standard works of European pornography like *The Curtain Drawn Up.*[20] Nonetheless, it supplied exceedingly raunchy, graphic content. Purporting to relate the experience of a young couple's honeymoon from the bride's point of view, it begins with her anticipation of marital consummation:

> I tremble with a new delight,
> Anticipate the joys of night,
> And long yet fear, and hope yet dread
> My husband's advent to my bed.
> He comes! He comes! Be still my heart,
> And you, you little amorous part,
> Why do you throb, and burn, and pant,
> And want, not knowing what you want? . . .
> He's in the room, he's by my side, . . .
> His dressing gown is cast aside,
> And bulging out in front is spied
> A prick of such enormous size,
> Can never go between my thighs.

The descriptions become even more explicit as the bride and groom hone their lovemaking skills over the next six uninterrupted days and nights of their "love feast."[21]

Through erotic photographs and paperbacks like *The Love Feast,* sexually explicit writing and images became available to a much broader range of American consumers than in the past. High-quality, graphically illustrated books remained expensive and inaccessible to most working-class purchasers. Yet average men and women might have the ability to obtain vividly sexual *cartes de visite* for a quarter

THE LOVE FEAST;

OR,

A BRIDE'S EXPERIENCE.

A POEM IN SIX NIGHTS,

BY PHILOCOMUS.

"Cunnus virumque cano."—*Virgil.*

PRINTED BY THE ASSOCIATED FEMALE PRESS,
BLIND ALLEY, CONEYHATCH, MAIDENHEAD.

1865.

6.2 Title page, Philocomus, The Love Feast; or, A Bride's Experience, *1865.*

COURTESY OF THE KINSEY INSTITUTE FOR RESEARCH IN SEX, GENDER, AND REPRODUCTION.

or flagrantly carnal pamphlets for fifty cents each. As a result, the Civil War era brought about a significant democratization and expansion of the potential audience for pornographic materials.

A final factor behind the dramatic expansion of the erotica trade in the 1860s was the growing popularity of mail-order birth control

5

FANNY HILL.

THE MAN OF PLEASURE'S TEXT BOOK.

Large size containing 24 magnificent Colored Engravings—which for beauty of design cannot be surpassed—by the first French Artists—which alone are worth the price of the book. In fact, it is *the* Fancy Book, having never been surpassed in the splendor of its illustrations, or the style in which it is written. It is handsomely printed and bound, and is as large as three of the $2 books. To all who want a Great Book, we would say, get this and you will not be disappointed. Price $5.

CUPID'S OWN LIBRARY.

New genuine Fancy Books that "speak right out loud," handsomely illustrated, commanding the unqualified admiration of every one reading them.

No. 1—Amours of a Modest Man. By a Bachelor. 25 cents.
2—Love on the Loose. . . . . 25 "
3—Red Staff: or the Mysterious Lover. . . 25 "
4—Bed Larks: or, How to Do It. . . 25 "
5—Sports with Venus: or, The Way to Do It. . 25 "
6—Scenes in a Nunnery. Very plain words. 25 "
7—Secret Services and Duties of Major Lovit. By Nick L. Ass . . . . . 50 "
8—Love Scrapes: or Gay Times in a Boarding House By Miss Carrie L. O. V. E. Cox. . . 50 "
9—Love in a Maze: or, Battles of Venus. . 50 "
10—Rakish Rhymer: or, Fancy Man's own Songster. 50 "
11—Royal Amours: or, The Loves, Intrigues and Amours of Charles II. A Stunner. . . $1.00
12—The Bride's Experience. A Poetic rhapsody—very hot. $1.00

[NEW SONGS.]

VENUS SONGSTER.

Number One, Two and Three Now Ready.

Containing a choice collection of New Flash Songs never before published, set to popular and familiar tunes, together with Spicy Stories, Jokes, Conundrums, &c. Price 30 cents each; or the three (all different) for 75 cents.

Guide for Pleasure Seekers: or Fancy Directory.

Containing a List and Description of the principal Houses of Pleasure in all the principal Cities throughout the country. Price 50 cents

THE GREAT SEDUCTION CASE.

The Great Seduction Case of LITTLEQUIM *vs.* BRANDYCONE! with the Judge's summing up and charge, also verdict of Jury—A most outrageous pamphlet The richest specimen of "legal lore"(!) extant. Price 15 cents.

***6.3** Erotica circular, "Grand Fancy Bijou Catalogue of the Sporting Man's Emporium," 1870.*

COURTESY OF THE AMERICAN ANTIQUARIAN SOCIETY.

products. Well-established medical and drug supply firms, dry goods dealers, rubber manufacturers, druggists, and physicians often sold contraceptives through the mail in this period. These included "condoms, douching syringes and solutions, vaginal sponges, diaphragms, and cervical caps." Mail-order circulars promoting contraceptives even targeted women directly. The Congregationalist minister John Todd described how birth control dealers in the 1860s sent their catalogues to brides whose marriages had been announced in the newspaper: "There is scarcely a young lady in New England—and probably it is so throughout the land—whose marriage can be announced in the paper without her being insulted within a week by receiving through the mail a printed circular, offering information and instrumentalities, and all needed facilities, by which the laws of heaven in regard to the increase of the human family may be thwarted." This early form of direct-mail marketing demonstrates how extensive the commerce in reproductive control had become by the 1860s, thanks to a combination of aggressive entrepreneurship, widely distributed newspapers, and the medium of the U.S. mail.[22]

One of the most famous mail-order contraceptive dealers of the 1860s was the popular "eclectic" physician Edward Bliss Foote, who published his first medical guide for lay readers, geared especially toward married couples, in 1858. A great commercial success, *Medical Common Sense* was reissued in several 1860s editions. In the 1864 version, for instance, Foote included a section on "Prevention of Conception" in a chapter captioned "Essays for Married People Only." At the end of the book, he advertised four forms of birth control, each of which could be purchased through his mail-order house. Two were designed for use by husbands: "membraneous envelopes" (condoms made out of fish membranes, for five dollars a dozen) and "apex envelopes" (rubber condoms that covered the tip of the penis, for three dollars a dozen). Two were designed for use by wives: "electro-magnetic preventive machines" (devices that delivered electric currents to women, "in consequences of which the womb is too greatly excited electrically to retain the seed of the male," for fifteen dollars each) and the enormously popular "womb veil" (Foote's version of a cervical cap or diaphragm, for six dollars each).[23]

Physicians, druggists, and rubber vendors were not the only businessmen to recognize the commercial appeal of contraceptives to nineteenth-century consumers. Perceiving a connection between sexually stimulating literature and reproductive control, purveyors of erotica moved to diversify their offerings to include a variety of contraceptive information and devices early on. Recall that in the 1850s George Akarman supplemented his offerings of fancy literature with frequent advertisements for a French invention that he called the cundum and for a "celebrated preventive" for married couples "who did not wish to increase their families." By the 1860s, the mail-order trade among pornographers in products designed to limit reproduction had become even more open and widespread. Another major sex publisher, Jeremiah Farrell, routinely placed newspaper advertisements linking the sale of contraceptives with the sale of sexually arousing publications. A typical Farrell notice in the *New York Clipper* beckoned readers to "send for a mammoth package, containing Four Fancy Articles; price twenty-five cents. Also, Rubber Goods for Gentlemen's Use." New York dealer David Gomperts used the *Sunday Mercury* to promote both "Rich and Rare Books and Carte de Visite, from life, for gentlemen" and "French Safes for gentlemen to prevent disease and generation." Likewise, a mail-order circular seized by the New York police in 1869, in addition to a cornucopia of fancy books and pictures, advertised "French Caps to prevent Generation." Another contemporaneous erotica catalogue advertised womb veils for women, which could be "used by the female without danger of detection by the male," and three different kinds of condoms, which were imported from Brussels and Paris and made from either the "fine transparent skin of an animal" or vulcanized rubber.[24]

As New York pornographers actively employed the mails to extend markets for their products throughout the Union, the primary legal challenge they faced at home shifted from avoiding obscenity prosecution to negotiating a deeply corrupt municipal law enforcement system. The 1860s have long been regarded as one of the most violent, politically dishonest, and vice-ridden decades in New York City's history. The carnage and terror inflicted during the deadly draft riots of 1863, the crookedness of Tweed Ring politicians, and the proliferation of licentious dance halls, brothels, and concert saloons have all contributed to the lore of the sin- and crime-filled sixties. Numerous popular guidebooks of the period, such as Matthew Hale Smith's *Sunshine and Shadow in New York*, dwelled on descriptions of New York's "gay life" and its sexual underworld. These guides left a literary testament to the city's dual role as a media capital and a center of sexual license.[25]

The years immediately following the Civil War have taken on a particularly lurid cast, prompting one later chronicler of the New York underworld, Herbert Asbury, to characterize them as the time "when New York was really wicked." It was then that the city "entered upon an unparalleled era of wickedness; so demoralized were the police by political chicanery and by widespread corruption within their ranks that they were unable to enforce even a semblance of respect for the law." As morals regulation receded, police extortion and brazen immorality took its place: "dives, dance halls, and houses of ill-fame" all "operated without molestation so long as the owners paid the assessments imposed by their political overlords."[26] The rampant corruption of elected municipal officials and their minions, particularly those charged with law enforcement, provided a powerful rallying cry for civic reformers and Republican opponents of Tammany Hall for the rest of the nineteenth century.[27]

The political culture of urban New York during the Civil War and the early Reconstruction era can also be seen in a more positive light, however. In many ways, the city government displayed populist, egalitarian qualities. Whereas Republicans controlled the state legislature and national politics for much of the 1860s, Democrats dominated municipal-level politics in New York. Within the city, the Democratic Party became closely identified with a working-class, largely Irish-American constituency. The political machine of Tammany Hall exemplified this metropolitan style of politics, which rejected any assumption that the plebeian classes would defer to the rule of social and economic elites. Instead, professional politicians with strong ties to working-class communities, tenements, and saloons strove to cultivate the support of a mass electorate of white male voters. By contrast, the Republican organization tended to reflect the perspective of prosperous and often evangelically inclined industrialists, merchants, and professionals.[28]

Two aspects of New York party politics in the 1860s shaped evolving attitudes toward obscenity regulation. First, the Democratic and Republican Parties repeatedly clashed over the use of criminal law to enforce morality. The opposition of the Democratic Party to state involvement in matters of religion and morality rested on a longstanding Jeffersonian aversion to an intrusive, moralizing state and a commitment to personal liberty. It also tapped into a strong tradition of anticlericalism and free thought. Similarly, the Federalist and Whig predecessors of the Republican Party had long shown a propensity for morals regulation and support for state intervention in the moral reformation of society. The Second Great Awakening only deepened the commitment of Yankee Protestant politicians to rooting out licentiousness and selfishness. By the 1850s, battles between Democrats and Whigs / Republicans raged in the state legislature and in the streets of New York over the prohibition of alcohol.

These divisions hardened in the 1860s. Many prominent Tammany Hall politicos of this era seemed to flaunt their connections to the world of gambling, drinking, and prostitution, a cultural milieu that was anathema to genteel Republican reformers. In turn, municipal Democrats often portrayed Republican legislative initiatives like prohibition laws and even bans on Sunday drinking as elitist Protestant plots to impose homogeneous evangelical values on a diverse, secular metropolis.[29]

Democrats and Republicans also differed sharply on the question of local autonomy for New York City and the benefits of centralized government. By the Civil War, the Democratic Party had become closely associated with the cause of municipal home rule. Again, this was not an entirely new development. Political leaders of the Jeffersonian persuasion had long harbored a suspicion of strong central government. Following in this tradition, municipal Democrats of the 1850s and '60s vigorously opposed the state legislature's efforts to replace police and health departments controlled by the mayor or the common council with state-run commissions, which were often controlled by Republicans.[30]

The evils of centralization and the virtues of localism were key campaign themes of the New York Democratic Party in the Civil War era. The party platform in 1865 urged a return to the "old-fashioned, time-honored regard for the relations and rights of the States and the Federal Government," and cautioned that "the centralization of power in this State, no less than in the Union, is fatal to the harmony of our political system."[31] The popular Democratic organ the *New York World* made a similar plea for limited government. It yearned for the "old Democratic doctrine . . . to permit the town to do nothing which the school district could not as well do; the county nothing which the town could do; the State nothing which the county or city could do; and the federal government nothing the State could as completely and safely accomplish."[32] In the coming years, this defense of localism and municipal home rule, like opposition to government-mandated moral reform, would manifest itself in conflict over new forms of state and national obscenity regulation.

One sign of Tammany's dominance of municipal government was that morals prosecutions virtually disappeared from the Court of General Sessions, the city's main criminal tribunal. The central, indeed almost exclusive, concern of the district attorney's office during the Civil War and its aftermath became the protection of individuals and their property, rather than public order or morality. The indictment records are overwhelmingly dominated by crimes against property, such as larceny, burglary, embezzlement, and forgery. The records also evidence a sharp rise in the number of prosecutions for violent crimes: assaults, riots, mayhem, and homicides, often carried out with handguns, which were becoming increasingly common.

In contrast, indictments for all morals offenses, including obscenity, assumed even less importance than they had in the antebellum era. During the Civil War, prosecutions for obscenity were especially infrequent. In 1862, A. Oakey Hall, a Tammany Hall Democrat, was elected to a second stint as district attorney, an office he held until 1868. During his tenure, the grand jury for the Court of General Sessions presented only two indictments for obscenity. Indeed, the grand jury returned only six obscenity indictments for the entire period from 1860 to 1870. This figure represented a much smaller number of prosecutions than in any similar interval during the two preceding decades.[33] Furthermore, the few individuals who were indicted appear to have evaded any kind of trial or to have been discharged without significant punishment after pleading guilty. Of the six indictments in the records of the Court of General Sessions, five show no evidence of any further proceeding after indictment; they were evidently pigeonholed by the district attorney. In the one other case, the defendant pleaded guilty and was discharged with a small fine. According to the *New York Times*, the sentencing judge in that case told "the prisoner that for reasons known only to himself and the District Attorney, and which nobody else had any right to know, he had concluded to be thus lenient in his sentence." In an era when the Democratic machine and Tammany Hall controlled many judicial elections and corruption reached unprecedented levels, this outcome may well have reflected collusion on the part of the court, the district attorney, and the defendant.[34]

Obscenity prosecutions in 1860s New York provide a strong counterpoint to historical narratives that portray enforcement of public morality as a central, consistent concern of nineteenth-century governance.[35] Jurisprudence of the period, it is true, continued to exhibit a preoccupation with protection of public order and public morality. In categorizing the chief goals of criminal law, the 1865 edition of Joel Bishop's influential treatise *Commentaries on the Criminal Law* characteristically placed "Protection to Individuals" behind six categories of a public nature: (1) "Protection to the Government"; (2) "Protection to the Public Health"; (3) "Protection to the Public Morals, Religion, and Education"; (4) "Protection to the Public Wealth and to Population"; (5) "Protection to the Public Convenience and Safety"; and (6) "Protection to the Public Order and Tranquility."[36] Bishop's formulation of the primary objectives of criminal law, however, bore little resemblance to the operation of the criminal justice system in Civil War era New York.

One might argue that law enforcement in New York County diverged from the vision of criminal law expressed in legal treatises only because corrupt municipal officials abdicated their responsibility to maintain public order and morality. Certainly, bribery and corruption were endemic elements of the relationship between municipal law enforcement and the commercial vice trade. The city's newspapers teemed with articles detailing the close connections between the operators of brothels, gambling "hells," and lottery shops, on the one hand, and policemen, politicians, and criminal court judges on the other.[37] Similarly, several publishers and vendors of pornography, some even publicly boasting of their extensive political influence, admitted to paying protection money to government agents. And the amounts in question were far from trivial. In an 1871 article on the obscene book trade, it was estimated that William Haines had paid over twenty thousand dollars in bribes during the preceding decade.[38]

There were also less sinister reasons for the weakness of municipal morals enforcement, though. On a cultural level, Democratic politicians did not regard the vices that Republican moral reformers commonly railed against—gambling, drinking, violating the Sabbath, reading racy novels, perusing flash papers—as crimes against morality so much as harmless entertainment. District Attorney A. Oakey Hall, for instance, famously refused to enforce state liquor laws requiring saloons to close on Sunday. In addition, Democratic leaders firmly rejected the ideological model of a coercive Christian state embodied in Republican moral reform and the traditional fusion of law, orthodox morality, and Protestantism.[39] In other words, the legal and political culture of 1860s New York City manifested both pervasive corruption *and* principled opposition to Republican moral ideology. In both ways, that culture gave the lie to juristic claims that the main function of criminal law was the maintenance of an orderly, virtuous, well-regulated society.

Disturbed by the permissive stance of municipal officials, Protestant evangelical activists began lobbying the state legislature to enact laws banning commerce in salacious entertainment. The New York City chapter of the Young Men's Christian Association (YMCA) was the organization that was most active on this front. Founded in 1852, it gave voice to the desire of successful Republican industrialists and financiers to suppress what they saw as distasteful aspects of the same capitalist markets that had made many of them extraordinarily prosperous.[40] Purity reformers had long sought to transform the moral conditions of city life, but the YMCA was an especially aggressive, efficient proponent of using law to shape morality and enforce public order.

In 1866 the YMCA resolved to make a special push for statewide legislation to expand and systematize common-law prosecutions against obscene publications. To build a case for this new exercise of the state's police power to protect public morality, the association also commissioned a study of vice among young men in the city. The subsequent report, "A Memorandum respecting New-York as a Field for Moral and Christian Effort among Young Men; Its Present Neglected Condition; and The Fitness of the New-York Young Men's Christian Association as a Principal Agency for Its Due Cultivation," laid the foundation for the YMCA's pitch to the legislature for the state's first antiobscenity statute. Two aspects of this report are particularly noteworthy, for they foreshadow styles and traits that Anthony Comstock and the New York Society for the Suppression of Vice would perfect in the coming decades.[41]

The authors of the study demonstrated an unusual penchant for systematically observing, classifying, and cataloguing the world of vice. The memorandum carefully delineated seven demoralizing influences on men under forty years of age: (1) billiard saloons, (2) theaters, (3) gambling "hells," (4) porterhouses and barrooms, (5) concert saloons, (6) houses of prostitution and assignation, and (7) obscene books and papers. In an appeal to rational, scientific argument, the authors also presented statistics from the census, tax records, licensing receipts, and police reports. When possible, the study identified the number of participants in each category of vice and calculated the revenue that each generated. Though the social goals of the YMCA were conservative, its use of statistical evidence (like its resort to regulation and state intervention to solve social problems) prefigured strategies more commonly associated with Progressive reformers at the turn of the twentieth century.

The report also introduced a scorched-earth strategy for attacking the trade in obscene publications. Evangelical reformers were aware that criminal authorities in New York had long tolerated trashy, titillating literature, whether in the form of flash tabloid newspapers or violent, semierotic pamphlet novels, so long as the publishers steered clear of direct depictions of sex. Now Christian activists became determined to erase the customary distinction between racy, suggestive print and fancy, graphic obscenity. The YMCA study strongly criticized municipal officials for allowing "vile weekly newspapers" and cheap "licentious books, each one illustrated by one or two cuts, at prices ranging from thirty-five to sixty cents," to be displayed openly at newsstands. Such publications, the authors insisted, were just as harmful as the more expensive, explicit bound books that were "illustrated with the most obscene cuts . . . at prices ranging from one to six dollars."

In seeking to suppress "vile weekly newspapers" and low-cost sensational novels, the YMCA faced a formidable challenge, given the enormous appeal of these print forms. In one of the numerous guides to the "sins of the city" published in the 1860s, Junius Henri Browne described the prominence of "flaming," "flashy" weeklies in newsstands along Broadway, the city's leading thoroughfare. "The newsdealer knows how to arrange his supplies. A single glance takes in the contents of his stand. The more flashy his literature, the greater its display," observed Browne. "The regular issues—*Herald, Tribune, Times, World, Sun,* and the rest—are folded modestly in a corner; so are the *Nation, Round-Table, Independent, Ledger, Harper's, Frank Leslie's,* and the better class of weeklies." The dealer calculated that his customers craved more indecent fare, however. "The *Day's Doings, Clipper, Sunday News, Mercury* and *Police Gazette* are flamingly arrayed, with their sensational contents revealed."[42]

The weekly Sunday papers were particularly licentious and wanton. "The Sunday papers, such as the *Mercury, News* and *Police Gazette,* are sensation journals of a curious sort, to which a murder is a benison, and an intrigue a godsend," wrote Browne. "They deal with what the dailies will not mention, or print in brief, enlarging with keen relish and elaborate pruriency upon details that delicacy would eschew. They reprint all the sensational facts and gossip they can find in the country press, or exhume from the licentious haunts of the City." Despite the unsavory qualities of these Sunday papers, Browne declared that they were "widely read, of course" and "for the most part, profitable." By far the worst of this class were the "*Police Gazette* and the publications devoted to prize-fighting, criminal news and flash intelligence." These were "abominably written, and illustrated with hideous cuts." Nonetheless, they were "read with avidity" by sporting blades and the flash men who populated the city's red-light districts around Greene, Mercer, Water, and Houston Streets.[43]

Browne assumed that the principal audience for flash weeklies consisted of members of the "depraved classes," men who were more readily drawn to the "sensual," "cheap," "lowbrow," and "hideous." Customers betrayed their individual weaknesses and predilections through their physiognomy. An observer "might tell from the appearance of the purchaser what paper he wanted . . . You can see each one's particular need in his face." A customer with a "crimson, sensual face is searching for the *Day's Doings* and its cheap sensations." Another with a "low brow and hard, cruel eye [is] in quest of the *Clipper*." And "that dull, heavy fellow will have nothing but the *Police Gazette* and its hideous array of revolting crimes." Browne conceded, however, that even the well-to-do and refined sometimes succumbed to the temptations of the Sunday papers: "The better class of the community do not read them, unless they happen to contain something extraordinarily racy and wanton, when curiosity overcomes the scruples of conscience and the dictates of decorum."[44]

Moral reformers charged that indecent newspapers were especially dangerous because they whetted readers' appetite for the stronger, fancier fare that they promoted through advertising. In another tour guide to the metropolitan underworld, *The Dark Side of New York Life*, Gustav Lening substantiated this charge, asserting that flash weeklies, as a cultural phenomenon, "fully deserve the epithet of obscene." As a strict legal matter, he acknowledged, "they very wisely keep within the line which the law has laid down." Instead of talking about sex directly, they "confine themselves to hinting, by pictures and by reading, what they would so very gladly express openly." The legal distinction between hinting at sex and expressing it openly did little, in Lening's view, to restrain sexual license. Rather, the circumspection of flash papers served only to "excite the imagination of their readers, and prepare them for the much spicier reading of the obscene books" that were advertised in their back pages.[45]

Despite frequent charges by middle-class moralists that flash papers and racy, yellow-covered novels were indecent and obscene, YMCA activists did not have an easy time pushing the sweeping anti-obscenity legislation they desired through the state legislature. Although the initial bill sailed through the Senate, it stalled in the assembly in both 1866 and 1867. Introduced again in 1868, the proposed legislation aimed to prohibit the sale, advertisement, or manufacture of "any obscene and indecent book, pamphlet, paper, drawing, lithograph, engraving, daguerreotype, photograph, stereoscopic picture, model, cast, instrument, or article of indecent or immoral use." It also set out to ban the sale or advertising of any "article or medicine for the prevention of conception or procuring of abortion."

Through this bill, the YMCA and its supporters sought to systematize and expand in critical ways the types of commerce that could be prosecuted as obscene. Capitalizing on the concurrent lobbying by licensed doctors against abortion, the bill broadened the scope of common-law prohibitions against obscenity by classifying the sale of devices and medicines for contraception and abortion as obscene.[46] This equation of obscenity with instruments for birth control and abortion went against nearly three decades of law enforcement practice in New York City, which had exempted such articles, as well as publications advertising them, from prosecution. Moreover, YMCA activists hoped that the proposed ban on publishing advertisements for obscene literature, photographs, and materials would strike a major blow at the profitability of flash weeklies. While steering clear of obscene representations, most of the city's Sunday papers, and even some reputable newspapers, regularly ran advertisements for fancy books, articles for preventing conception, and abortifacients. Under the terms of the bill, publishers who accepted such ads would now be redefined as criminal actors. Convictions could be punished by imprisonment for up to one year or a fine of up to a thousand dollars for each offense. To motivate citizen complaints, one-third of any fine was to be paid to the informer supplying the evidence for the conviction.[47]

Another section of the bill authorized magistrates to issue warrants directing police officers to search for "obscene and indecent" materials and, following a summary determination by the magistrate of their obscene character, to destroy the items seized. This was a vital element of the law in the eyes of proponents. In dispensing with the usual due-process requirements, such as a full opportunity for the accused to present evidence, the law vested in government officials the power to inflict substantial economic damage on purveyors of obscenity, by demolishing large quantities of their property.[48]

Patrick Keady, a Democratic assemblyman from Brooklyn and one of the state's most important trade union leaders, spearheaded the opposition to the bill.[49] Objections centered on two items, one classifying newspapers that merely carried ads for indecent publications or immoral devices as criminally obscene and another granting magistrates summary powers to seize and destroy objectionable periodicals without a trial. In the view of Democrats in the legislature, these provisions constituted an infringement of freedom of the press inspired by radical Republicanism and religious fanaticism. The sensational, pro-Democrat *Sunday Mercury*, schooled in fighting Republican efforts to expand state power by banning Sunday drinking and shutting down concert saloons, promoted the Democratic resistance. An editorial portrayed the bill as an example of "Radical despotism" that would both violate a publisher's civil right to due process and destroy the liberty of the press. The anti-advertising and summary confiscation provisions, the editors charged, would empower "any magistrate or any policeman . . . [who] finds a paper with an advertisement in it that he thinks is not sufficiently refined for his pure imagination—[to] seize the same and transmit specimens of it to the District-Attorney's office, and forthwith destroy the remainder thereof." Petty government agents, "in other words," could "destroy the entire edition of the paper . . . without complaint or process of law." The editorial ominously warned that the proposed obscenity legislation could also lead to a sweeping scheme of political censorship, in which allegations of obscenity could serve as a pretext for suppressing popular Democratic periodicals that disagreed with the

Radical Republican agenda. If the legislature granted summary powers to Republican officials to destroy newspapers they regarded as obscene, it "would be to give Radical despotism a machinery for crushing out opposition, surpassing any thing it has applied in the South."[50]

Keady's opposition must have garnered significant support from Democrats, because the language granting summary powers to magistrates was deleted from the amended version submitted to the Senate. The revised bill stated that obscene materials could be destroyed only following trial and conviction of the publisher or seller. Otherwise, the provisions remained the same.[51]

Even with the requested amendment, downstate assemblymen continued to object to the legislation. Most of the dissenters evidently feared going on record against it, however. Instead, some expressed their displeasure by failing to show up for the final vote; others went along with the measure. With only two Democrats voting against the bill, it passed by the lopsided count of 82 to 2, a margin that masked the substantial opposition.[52] Later the same day, New York City Democrats caucused in an effort to maneuver reconsideration of the bill. During the evening session, they formally moved for a new vote. But even Keady's assertion that the law was really "a blow at the Democratic press" failed to carry the day.[53] The tally fell largely along party lines, with all the Republican members of the assembly voting to defeat reconsideration.[54] On April 24 the state Senate passed the Act for the Suppression of the Trade in and Circulation of Obscene Literature, Illustrations, Advertisements and Articles of Indecent or Immoral Use . . . (Obscene Literature Act), as amended by the assembly, by a vote of 20 to 3. Among the three dissenters was prominent New York City Democrat William (Boss) Tweed.[55]

Republican newspapers lost no time in charging Democrats with encouraging sexual license. The *New York Tribune,* the leading Radical Republican newspaper, gleefully assailed them as the "Obscene Democracy." Turning Keady's defense of freedom of the press against his party, the *Tribune* proclaimed that "suppression of obscene, immoral, and disgusting literature would strike out of existence half the Democratic journals in the country." Attempting to stigmatize the Democrats as the party of indecent entertainment and obscene literature, the article declared that "next to the prohibition of liquor-selling" the law against obscenity "would be the hardest blow that could be given to the party."[56] Democratic voters allegedly had a particular fondness for "those yellow-covered books . . . that are hawked around railway stations, hotels, and grog-shops by low-browed, sinister looking members of the party." Referring to racy novels and flash Sunday weeklies, the *Tribune* jeered: "This stuff is peculiarly relished and patronized by Democrats. It is a manifestation of their idea of liberty of the press. As the grog-shop is the Democratic nursery, so these bawdy publications are their fairy stories."[57]

This partisan skirmish provided an early demonstration of the political capital to be gained by sponsoring laws against obscenity. At the same time, even some Republicans criticized the YMCA's political campaign against indecent literature as overzealous and misguided. While the antiobscenity bill was making its way through the assembly, the *New York Times,* which spoke for what it regarded as the pragmatic, moderate wing of the Republican Party, expressed pointed skepticism about the heavy-handed use of coercive state laws to dictate morality. It printed an editorial chiding moral reformers for their efforts to suppress "unwholesome" reading through laws against obscenity. "In Boston and Philadelphia, as well as in our own City, there is just now an outcry against what is called 'obscene' literature—a strong style of expression which seems to convey more than is probably meant." The *Times* acknowledged that a great deal of popular literature was "certainly light and flashy, unwholesome and perhaps indelicate." Nonetheless—in what would turn out to be an unwarranted display of optimism—it asserted that "we must do the people the justice to think that real obscenity could have no great attractions for them, and that no publisher would invest his money in it."[58]

According to the *Times*, the market for "flashy, unwholesome" literature and other forms of sexually titillating entertainment was also too dynamic to be reined in by the law. Remarking on the "growing love of reading among all sorts of people," the paper asserted: "They must have something to read, even if it is not in the best taste." The *Times* drew an analogy between racy literature and then-fashionable plays featuring female dancers clad in form-revealing costumes and diaphanous tights that called attention to their seemingly bare legs. Even "educated citizens are thronging to those pleasant but improper spectacles of the 'Black Crook' and the 'White Fawn'; and what can be done?" One thing was clear—criminal sanctions were not only useless but counterproductive: "Prohibition and penalty can do no good. They failed in the Garden of Eden." Eschewing censorship, the *Times* reasoned that the only true remedy for the appeal of impure literature was an increase in the circulation of moral literature, especially in settings like free reading rooms and public libraries that were open to all. In the editors' view, the unimpeded forces of free trade and consumer distaste for "real obscenity" would do a better job of rooting out indecency than a strategy of "prohibition and penalty," which would only whet the public's appetite for the forbidden fruit.[59]

Though disappointed that summary powers to confiscate and destroy obscene literature had been removed from the final draft of the Obscene Literature Act, the YMCA quickly embraced the new law. It authorized three members to act as detectives in investigating violations and in 1871 created its first Committee on Obscene Literature, later renamed the Committee for the Suppression of Vice. This committee would be spun off in 1873 as an independent charitable corporation run by Anthony Comstock, known as the New York Society for the Suppression of Vice.[60]

Fittingly, the first indictment under the new statute prominently featured the YMCA. Prosecution records from 1869 show that Riley Bricke, a director of the association and a member of its Committee on Obscene Literature, received a copy of a catalogue for lewd books from one James S. Dexter. Given that Dexter frequently advertised his Sportsman's Emporium in the *New York Clipper*, Bricke probably sent in a three-cent stamp, as directed by the ad, in exchange for his "great circular." Bricke then showed up in person at Dexter's place of business, where Dexter, an alias for a twenty-eight-year-old Irish immigrant named Thomas O'Connor, showed him six "obscene and indecent" books.[61]

From these Bricke selected two volumes, paid three dollars for them, and departed. The first was an English harem novella, *La Rose d'Amour; or, The Adventures of a Gentleman in Search of Pleasure. Translated from the French of Rosseau. By Lola Montez, Countess of Landsfelt*, one of approximately a dozen editions of European pornography that American erotica dealers regularly stocked in that era. The second came from the Venus' Library collection of recent American pornography: *Life and Amours of the Beautiful, Gay and Dashing Kate Percival. The Belle of the Delaware Written by Herself—Voluptuous, Exciting, Amorous and Delighting. Illustrated by Twelve Elegant Steel-Plate Engravings Designed for the Text.* According to Bricke's affidavit, the text of these books contained a "description of demoralizing, sensual, indecent and thoroughly infamous and revolting scenes of sexual excesses" as well as "obscene engravings of the most vulgar, degrading, and disgusting character." Both were listed in the Sportsman's Emporium catalogue at the highest price, $2.25, whereas other titles in the catalogue sold for only twenty-five cents. According to O'Connor's circular, both works also contained colored illustrations.[62] Although no copies of either *La Rose d'Amour* or *Kate Percival* have survived from the Civil War era, an extant 1870 circular for erotica touted *Kate Percival* as "one of the richest volumes ever offered to an amatory community" with twelve "of the most exquisite and exciting illustrations (steel engravings) ever designed." As it instructed: "Every reader of fancy literature who would like to have a good long talk with beautiful KATE, the Belle of Delaware, '*nude,*' should lose no time in securing this book." The colored steel engravings, along with the size of the book, its binding, and the quality of paper used, probably accounted for the high price O'Connor charged for *Kate Percival.* By comparison, his twenty-five-cent offerings were probably printed on cheap paper, bound in paper wrappers, and illustrated (if at all) with a few crude black-and-white woodcuts.[63]

Bricke next approached District Attorney Samuel Garvin, a Tammany Democrat, and demanded that he prosecute O'Connor. Garvin passed Bricke along to a police justice, together with a short letter stating that Bricke wished to file a complaint. The letter provided a citation to the new Obscene Literature Act and asked the police court to take whatever action it deemed proper. Bricke swore out an affidavit describing his visit to O'Connor's store and urging his arrest. He also sought a warrant to seize all "obscene and indecent books, papers, and articles found in possession of said Dexter." The next day, the police raided O'Connor's shop, with Bricke tagging along to identify the culprit, whom they arrested. They also confiscated two items as evidence, O'Connor's latest mail-order catalogue and a letter from a disgruntled customer in Nebraska complaining that O'Connor had taken his money but had not mailed his copy of *Love Scrapes; or, Gay*

Times in a Boarding House. At the subsequent arraignment, a police justice set bail in the amount of $2,500. District Attorney Garvin, again at Bricke's urging, presented the case to the grand jury for the Court of General Sessions, which returned an indictment for selling an unnamed obscene book and printing an obscene circular.[64]

Despite this initial success, frustration lay in store for Bricke and his colleagues at the YMCA. Although O'Connor elected to plead guilty to the offense, the indictment records indicate that his sentence was suspended and that he was discharged without punishment. This setback would be the first of many that moral reformers would experience in prosecuting obscenity cases in New York County courts.

The next month, the grand jury presented its second indictment under the Obscene Literature Act against one of the city's leading distributors of pornography, David J. Gomperts, who was also known as the Black Doctor. Throughout the 1860s, Gomperts had openly advertised his wares in lowbrow flash weeklies like the *New York Clipper* and the *Sunday Mercury*. A typical advertisement from 1867 announced "Rich and Rare Books and Cartes de Visite, from life, for gentlemen" as well as "French Safes for gentlemen to prevent disease and generation" and "all kinds of Sporting Fancy Goods." At the time of his arrest, Gomperts was fifty-eight years old and a self-described "book agent." The bill of indictment charged him with selling unspecified obscene books at his Nassau Street store, printing obscene circulars, and distributing handbills stating how such books could be purchased. Gomperts apparently supplied newsboys and bookstand proprietors as well, for his arrest was precipitated by the testimony of a bookstand operator that he regularly obtained obscene books (all from the Cupid's Own Library series of cheap American paperbacks) from Gomperts. Two weeks later the grand jury returned a second indictment. This bill charged Gomperts with offering two of the same volumes advertised by Thomas O'Connor: *The Life and Amours of the Beautiful, Gay and Dashing Kate Percival: The Belle of the Delaware* and *The Secret Service and Duties of Major Lovit.* The first was part of the upscale Venus' Library collection of bound fancy books, and the second was a pamphlet from the Cupid's Own Library series.[65]

Though the court records do not show the outcome of the two indictments, an 1873 exposé of the trade in obscene literature reveals that the book agent was released without penalty. "Gomperts, to the astonishment of all respectable citizens, was discharged and in a short time was again at his old business—more secretly, but on a much larger scale," it reported. Bribery was allegedly to blame: "Fortunately for him, but unfortunately for public morality and justice, Gomperts had already become rich in his disgraceful business, and money is the best lawyer." Thus, in a turn of events that infuriated moral reformers, neither of the first two indictments brought under the Obscene Literature Act resulted in punishment of the offender.[66]

At the same time as the YMCA's Committee on Obscene Literature was working to enforce New York's new antiobscenity statute, a young purity activist was operating on a separate but parallel track. Born on March 7, 1844, Anthony Comstock was a model of rural Christian propriety. Raised on a farm in New Canaan, Connecticut, he was reared as a strict Congregationalist. In 1863, not yet twenty years old, he left home to join the Union Army, to replace a brother who had been killed on the first day of fighting at Gettysburg. While serving in the army, rather than falling prey to the "flimsy publications, obscene books, and the worst species of yellow-covered literature" that pervaded Union camps, he occupied his free time leading Bible classes among the troops.[67]

Discharged at the end of the war, Comstock took the first employment offered him, as a clerk and bookkeeper in a New Haven grocery store. But he had greater ambitions. "The life that most attracted the country boy," reveals his authorized biographer, "was that of the successful New York City dry-goods merchant; his dream was to become the proprietor and director of a big establishment of his own." Fortune smiled on the penniless clerk when a banker he had met previously offered him five dollars to move to New York to try to make his mark. Seizing the opportunity, Comstock purchased a ticket and arrived at City Hall in 1867, with $3.45 left to his name. Having rented a room in a boarding house for two dollars a week, he secured employment at a wholesale dry goods house called J. B. Spellman and Sons. He began as a stock clerk at a weekly salary of five dollars but was soon promoted to a sales position. By 1871 he had obtained an even better-paying sales job in the notions department of a new dry goods and general merchandise establishment on Broadway—Cochran, McLean and Company.[68]

Within a year of his arrival in the city, however, Comstock had started down a different path, on a crusade that would consume him for the rest of his life. His first step was to undertake an obscenity prosecution against a book dealer named Charles Conroy in 1868. The intensely pious salesman, then twenty-four, became convinced that Conroy was responsible for selling lewd books to a friend of Comstock's that incited his lust, with the result that the friend contracted a fatal venereal disease from a brothel. Acting as a "volunteer detective and complainant," the young Christian activist purchased one of Conroy's offerings, filed a complaint with the police court, and secured Conroy's arrest under the Obscene Literature Act. To Comstock's dismay, Conroy, like his fellow erotica dealers Thomas O'Connor and David Gomperts, received a suspended sentence and was soon back in business.[69]

The next year, Comstock was again frustrated in his attempts to have the Obscene Literature Act enforced. Still working on his own, he filed a complaint against another bookseller, named William Simpson, who was also responsible, Comstock believed, for contaminating the minds and bodies of young people. He explained that several of his fellow dry goods clerks had "got in the habit of using & reading" Simpson's books and had become "runners for whorehouses" as a result.[70] Since 1860 Simpson and his wife had run the Great American Book, Stationery and Novelty Head-Quarters on Centre Street, near the Tombs prison and the site of today's state and federal courthouses. They advertised books, newspapers, joke cards, "Franco-American transparent playing cards," stationery, sheet music, and a variety of other items. In an effort to attract youths to their store, they also sold athletic goods, including a large assortment of baseball equipment.[71]

According to Comstock, the couple's real specialty was providing "obscene books and pictures" to youngsters. For a dime apiece, the husband loaned "the grossest kind of obscene books, to wit Fanny Hill, Lustful Turk, Silas Shovewell, and the like" to young men and boys for a week, while his wife loaned the same to shop girls. Thanks to this informal lending library, youths familiar with the Simpsons' variety store had access not only to the cheap flash newspapers and dime novels that were sold at every newsstand, but also to hard-core, explicit books that they otherwise could never have afforded.[72] A few years later, a *New York Times* reporter provided a vivid description of the Simpsons' "filthy depot." A "motley crowd of idlers, composed chiefly of the youth of both sexes" congregated outside the store. The chief attraction was a "number of vulgar and indecent photographs and stereoscopic views in a case at the door, together with a display of books and pictures of a similar character in the window." Inside the establishment, one wall held a small library of obscene books, and lewd pictures hung from the ceiling.[73]

Unbeknownst to Comstock, Simpson and his wife also conducted a more extensive business through the mail. Their offerings included an assortment of racy sensational fiction, sexually explicit erotica, illustrated marriage and medical guides, fancy photographs, and (in what would prove to be Simpson's downfall) small joke cards containing scatological poems and ribald drawings.[74] According to one source, Simpson was one of the "principal fountains that supply the various dealers [in obscene books] throughout the United States, at wholesale."[75] Eventually, Comstock would turn his attention to Simpson's mail-order activities and would achieve a stunning victory in federal court at Simpson's expense.[76] At this point in 1869, however, Comstock was concerned only with Simpson's local, over-the-counter sales. On the basis of his complaint, Simpson was arrested and brought before the Court of Special Sessions, which was reserved for minor criminal cases and nonjury trials. The pornography dealer, who had close political connections to Tammany Hall, confidently pleaded guilty and received a small fine, which he paid on the spot. He subsequently boasted that his landlord, a Tweed Ring school commissioner named Timothy Brennan, had gotten him off because Simpson paid double the going rate in rent.[77]

In 1871 Comstock made a second futile attempt to bring Simpson to justice. On visiting his stationery shop to secure evidence for another prosecution, the "volunteer detective" committed a rookie mistake. He told a police officer outside the store about his mission and asked the officer to wait there until he was called in to make an arrest. While Comstock perused a price list for fancy books, the policeman entered the shop and tipped off Simpson's clerk to his purported customer's true purpose, thus foiling Comstock's plan to apprehend the owner.[78]

These early forays into putting New York's obscenity law to work left Comstock bitterly disappointed. But not for long. Like the publishers and dealers who had thus far been his nemesis, the antismut activist had a flair for turning defeat into opportunity.

Chapter 7

The Comstock Act

In the aftermath of the Civil War, the success of dealers and publishers of erotic print in building a national market for their products brought about new demands for censorship and prompted critical transformations in methods of regulating obscenity. Most significantly, the focus of enforcement activity moved dramatically upward from the local to the state to the national level. A major beneficiary of these regulatory innovations was the up-and-coming anti-obscenity activist Anthony Comstock.

In 1872, furious that the erotica dealer William Simpson had escaped arrest, Comstock filed a complaint against the policeman he accused of helping Simpson get away, and had the officer dismissed from the force. This step generated his first taste of publicity, an attack on his practices in the flash periodical the *Sunday Mercury*. Long antagonistic toward both private moral reform and state regulation of morals, the paper charged Comstock with ulterior motives. The editors implied that he targeted men like Simpson who had close ties to Tammany Hall, while ignoring other, more culpable dealers who blatantly violated state law. As Comstock recalled, the paper jeered: "If I was the Christian man I professed to be, I could find plenty of these men in Ann and Nassau street and elsewhere."[1]

"Profiting by this hint," the energetic dry goods salesman took up the challenge. Even at this early date, Comstock displayed both media awareness and a talent for self-promotion by asking the *New York Tribune* to assign a reporter to join him on an exploratory mission to the turf identified by the *Sunday Mercury*. On a chilly Saturday in March 1872, Comstock revisited the site, accompanied not only by the *Tribune* reporter but also by a ward police captain who apparently sympathized with his growing obsession with the damage done by erotic publications.[2]

At the time, Comstock still had no official standing in either a governmental or an organizational sense. It was not until the following year, 1873, that he would become both a special agent of the U.S. Post Office, charged with investigating violations of federal antiobscenity law, and the secretary and chief agent of a new organization, chartered by the state legislature, to promote purity: the New York Society for the Suppression of Vice. In March 1872, though, he was just a zealous private citizen working on his own to ensure enforcement of a morals law—New York's Obscene Literature Act—that he felt local criminal justice officials had been remiss in implementing.

When the smut hunter, the reporter, and the policeman journeyed to the heart of the city's trade in erotica, their first stop was the shop of Patrick Bannon at 16 Ann Street. A search of the store yielded an allegedly obscene circular entitled "Women's Rights Convention," which one can surmise was a bawdy satire on the woman's rights movement. The police captain seized a thousand copies of the circular and arrested Bannon's brother-in-law and eleven-year-old son, who were working in the store. When the police dropped obscenity charges against the boy, Comstock objected that "political influence [had] saved him" and that "he ought to have been punished."[3]

The trio next approached the neighboring store of William and Charles Brooks at 19 Ann Street. Comstock later learned that the brothers' real last name was Barkley and that they had recently purchased their shop from George Akarman, who was in the process of winding down his business. At Brooks's shop Comstock bought a copy of a classic fancy book of English origin, *The Confessions of a Voluptuous Young Lady of High Rank*, which had been circulating in New York pornography circles for three decades. He also spotted an edition of another European classic, *The Festival of Love; or, Revels at the Fount of Venus,* classified in a contemporaneous erotica circular as one of twelve "standard works of the voluptuary."[4] On the basis of evidence supplied by Comstock, the captain arrested both Barkleys and confiscated about two thousand obscene circulars, a hundred obscene photographs, a hundred obscene books, and a large supply of "rubber goods."[5]

Finally, the group visited the nearby shop of James McDermott at 75 Nassau Street, described by Comstock as a claustrophobic ten-by-four-foot room. While there, he bought a third European work—*La Rose d'Amour*—and spied a copy of a fourth—*The Curtain Drawn Up*—on display. The captain arrested twenty-six-year-old McDermott and a thirteen-year-old sales clerk, Thomas Ward; Comstock's notes, exhibiting his familiarity with street slang, described the boy as the "cats-paw of McDermott." Treating Ward with somewhat more sympathy than Bannon's son, Comstock grudgingly acknowledged: "As he was only a boy, he was discharged, inasmuch as we had the principal." While there, the police seized approximately five hundred stereoscopic views and photographs, thirty books, a thousand circulars, one steel engraved plate, and a batch of microscopic pictures for watches.[6]

The subsequent state prosecutions against McDermott and the Barkleys brought Comstock his first real satisfaction in the county courts. Fortunately for him, the three men had been caught selling explicit erotic works, the kind of hard-core fancy books that New York law enforcement officials and publishing circles had considered obscene for many years. William and Charles Barkley were charged with violating state obscenity law for selling *The Confessions of a Voluptuous Young Lady of High Rank* and possessing a copy of *The Festival of Love* with intent to sell it. To represent them, the defendants chose New York's most flamboyant criminal defense lawyer of the 1870s, William F. Howe. Howe was the lead partner in Howe & Hummell, a law firm already legendary for its liberal use of bribes to obtain favorable outcomes for clients. The Barkleys pleaded guilty, perhaps expecting that their lawyer's reputation for behind-the-scenes machinations would lead to their getting off with a slap on the wrist. But the Court of General Sessions responded with unusual harshness. The owner, William, was sentenced to one year on Blackwell's Island and a five-hundred-dollar fine. His brother, Charles, received three months. McDermott, who was indicted for selling *La Rose d'Amour* to Comstock and also for possessing *The Curtain Drawn Up*, experienced a similar fate. Having elected a bench trial in the Court of Special Sessions, he was convicted and sentenced to one year in prison and a two-hundred-dollar fine.[7]

In the future, Comstock would meet with much less success in the county courts, especially when he ventured beyond cases involving explicit European erotica and into prosecution of more ambiguous, borderline material. As is evident from repeated gripes in his arrest notes and the Annual Reports of the Society for the Suppression of Vice, hundreds of indictments in the Court of General Sessions were pigeonholed by the district attorney and never brought to trial. In 1872, his arrest ledger asserts that political influence or bribery tainted seventeen out of thirty-two county-level obscenity cases. By 1877, although forty-five individuals were arrested through the society's efforts and thirty-nine were indicted in the Court of General Sessions, the district attorney's office brought not a single one to trial. On the infrequent occasions when obscenity cases were tried, petit juries often refused to convict defendants, even when Comstock considered the evidence against them overwhelming.[8]

Despite the clear-cut victories stemming from his investigations of the Barkleys and McDermott in March 1872, the increasingly savvy religious activist remained in a state of agitation. On the basis of evidence gleaned from these cases, he surmised that over-the-counter retail sales of obscene publications by shop owners like the Barkleys and McDermott and their clerks represented only the most visible stratum in an extensive metropolitan business. Digging deeper, he discovered that a small cadre of publishers in New York had generated nearly all the obscene works circulating in the city. Over the following months, Comstock ascertained that there were exactly 144 "bad books" in existence, which he categorized by price. "Of the bad books there are *thirty-five* different varieties of the more expensive class, which are sold at prices ranging from $1 to $6," he asserted. "Of the cheap books, sold for 25 to 50 cents, there are *one hundred and nine* varieties." (In his 1883 book *Traps for the Young* he recalculated the total number of obscene books in existence in 1872 at 165 rather than 144.) He soon concluded that just three individuals were responsible for publishing all but two of these "bad books." Two of them—William Haines (assisted by his wife, Mary Haines) and George Akarman—we have met several times before. The third was a younger publisher named Jeremiah H. Farrell, who had followed in the footsteps of Frederic Brady (aka H. S. G. Smith) after having purchased some of Brady's stereotyped plates in 1863. Brady was no longer on the scene in 1872, having died in 1870.[9]

Though still employed as a dry goods salesman, Comstock committed himself to suppressing the city's pornography trade by forcing Haines, Akarman, and Farrell "to give up, and get out of the business" of obscene literature. In the end, the only one he instigated criminal charges against was Farrell. It was probably no coincidence that Farrell was the sole publisher who kept a storefront and even ran newspaper ads inviting customers to examine his stock in person; he was thus the most vulnerable to arrest. As for Haines and Akarman, Comstock negotiated the purchase of their equipment and inventory with donations from sympathetic patrons of the YMCA and the American Tract Society.[10]

The event that most likely triggered Comstock's investigations of the top three publishers and soon united him with the YMCA was the March 1872 arrest of James McDermott. During the search of McDermott's premises, Comstock learned that the Nassau street bookseller was a "confidential man" for Haines and was keeping one of the publisher's steel engraved plates at his store. Shortly after McDermott's arrest and the discovery of evidence linking him to Haines, another obscenity dealer who worked for Haines, Edward M. Grandin, supposedly told the publisher that Comstock was after him and that the "damn fool won't look at money." According to Comstock, Grandin was a "shrewd villain." He acted as Haines's "confidential middleman," taking orders from customers and coordinating the shipment of deliveries, in order to insulate the publisher from the point of sale. In Comstock's account, the shock of Grandin's message led to Haines's death that same night.[11]

A few days later, Comstock received word that the publisher's wife, Mary Haines, was willing to sell his inventory of books and stereotype plates. It is unclear how this offer was communicated to him or how they arrived at the bargain basement price of $450. (She told Comstock that Grandin had offered her $3,000 for the same goods.)

That the dry goods salesman was able to obtain these items at such a steep discount suggests either that he was a sharp negotiator or that Mary Haines, with her husband so recently deceased, was in a desperate state.[12]

Because Comstock still needed money to close the deal, he was prompted to seek out an organization for funding. Perhaps he had discovered that the YMCA had been conducting its own surveillance of the erotic book trade. Or perhaps he simply hoped the association would be interested in suppressing the sale of anti-Christian publications to young men. In any event, on March 23, 1872, he wrote to YMCA secretary Robert McBurney pleading for financial aid: "Now Sir, my private resources are exhausted. I have borne the costs thus far myself. I have a family to support, and I appeal directly to your Association for whatever may be necessary to complete this work." The new head of the association, Morris Jesup, noticed Comstock's appeal. In addition to being a wealthy banker, Jesup was a prominent philanthropist, an organizer of the United States Christian Commission, and the president of both the American Sunday School Union and the New York Mission and Tract Society. He agreed to send $600, including $150 for Comstock's own use. The extra money may have been intended for personal legal expenses, for Comstock had written: "I am now threatened by W. F. Howe [the] Tombs shyster, with imprisonment in Ludlow st Jail, on a Civil Suit unless I desist from this work. He is counsel for most of these parties." Although there is no record that a civil case (presumably for false arrest) was ever filed, William Howe's reputation for ferocious defense of his clients' interests made a counterattack on Comstock a distinct possibility.[13]

With Jesup's donation Comstock purchased twenty-four cases of stereotype plates that Haines had used to print approximately twenty different obscene books, nearly two hundred steel plates and copperplates that he used to produce illustrations, and the publisher's remaining inventory of thousands of volumes of books. Altogether, Comstock valued the worth of the property at between thirty thousand and forty thousand dollars. Before he could take possession of the haul, however, Mary Haines apparently changed her mind. She stationed a covered express wagon behind her house in Brooklyn, ready to pull away with crates of Haines's stereotype plates. Sensing that something was afoot, Comstock rushed to Brooklyn, dramatically intercepted the wagon, and drove it to the YMCA office, where he unloaded the contents. In early April 1872 he helped to destroy all the plates he had obtained from Haines with acid at a laboratory of the Polytechnic Institute of Brooklyn.[14]

Despite threats from his targets and from lawyers like Howe, Comstock was relentless. Not content with simply destroying Haines's plates, he set out to track down everyone who had been working for the publisher. The ensuing investigation led him to a network of widely dispersed photographers, printers, binders, and couriers. He first secured the arrest of a twenty-two-year-old photographer named Adolph Beer (or possibly Beery), who had been creating photographs from bookplates provided by Edward Grandin. The subject of the Beer indictment was a print entitled "The Church Tithe," one of fifty negative plates seized by the police at Beer's Bowery shop. In the tradition of European anticlerical pornography, it depicted a clergyman having sex with one of his female parishioners. Beer, who was represented by William Howe, pleaded guilty and was sentenced to six months on Blackwell's Island.[15]

Comstock next located the binder that Haines had used at the end of his career—a man named John Ulm, who had received a dime from Haines for each book he bound. In an effort to keep the business going after her husband's death, Mary Haines had stored a large quantity of printed pages and some surviving stereotype plates with Ulm—after pretending to sell them all to Comstock. But

Comstock arrived at Ulm's place a few days too late. When the wily Mary learned that her opponent had discovered Ulm's identity, she had Ulm transfer the inventory to another binder. Though Ulm was not arrested, he must have told Comstock the address of the new binder, a man named Riehl. By this time, production had become increasingly stealthy and desperate; Riehl was hiding the letterpress under his bed and working on it at night in his apartment. Shortly thereafter, Comstock and the police raided Riehl's tenement. Riehl was not arrested, but they seized nearly two hundred thousand obscene pictures and half a ton of printed text. In reporting on this case, Comstock took all the credit for the results: "This stock was seized by Comstock April 1872 in Riehl's place 5th floor of a tenement house, under his bed."[16]

Comstock also discovered a delivery company used by Haines and other pornographic publishers called Snowden's Express, located across the Hudson River in Jersey City, New Jersey. According to Comstock, the publishers had employed Snowden's to transport stereotype plates, prints, text, and other materials to various agents during the production process and to store the finished products in Jersey City. The manufacturers had also used the firm to convey packages to reputable courier companies, which reportedly refused to work directly with known publishers of obscene books, for safe distribution to out-of-town dealers and individual customers. In his notes, Comstock stated that he had forced Snowden to leave the business, an achievement crowned by the courier's death a few months later.[17]

Meanwhile, the antismut crusader began to negotiate the purchase of the stock and equipment of the second leading publisher of pornography after Haines, George Akarman. By Comstock's count, Akarman "published about 22 to 25 years Ob[scene] Books, and manufactured 'French Transparent Cards.' Printed from 18 to 24 different books." Comstock first approached Thomas Timpson, the superintendent of a major news agency on Nassau Street, about his connections with Akarman in late April 1872. Comstock had discovered that Timpson had been serving as Akarman's financial backer for years, an investment that was said to have netted him forty thousand dollars in profits. According to their arrangement, Timpson supplied the publisher's production costs up front and received principal and interest in the form of obscene books at a steeply discounted price. He then sold the books through his news agency, the National News Company. He also employed one of Akarman's five children. Most shocking to Comstock, an ardent Congregationalist, was that Timpson dared to serve as a trustee of a local Congregational church. In confronting the newsdealer, Comstock threatened him with public exposure unless he persuaded Akarman to surrender his inventory. As Comstock reported their conversation: "At first [Timpson] denied knowing him. Afterward was very anxious to write to him & have him turn over all his stock to be destroyed . . . For fear of exposure he caused Ackerman [*sic*] to deliver up stock."[18]

Thanks to Timpson's powers of persuasion and to funds from a supporter of moral reform who was willing to purchase Akarman's property, the publisher agreed to meet with Comstock two days later. In what must have been a surreal scene, Akarman, dressed as an Episcopal priest, agreed to hand over the remainder of his inventory and equipment in exchange for a payment from a patron of the American Tract Society. Comstock's authorized biographer attributed Akarman's clerical garb to an unbalanced mind, the pathetic result of too many years of being harassed and blackmailed by the police. Yet the costume was also strangely fitting. If nothing else, the existence of laws against obscenity had ensured that masquerade and deception were integral aspects of the New York pornography trade. Akarman, having operated under a variety of fake imprints, false business fronts, and aliases for more than twenty years, was especially adept at disguise. One can also imagine that the publisher, undoubtedly familiar with the tradition of bawdy anticlerical literature dating back to Rabelais and Boccaccio, relished the chance to mock the moral sanctimony and Christian rectitude of his self-righteous young adversary. In any event, the receipt of compensation must have brought some solace to Akarman, by allowing him to interpret the transaction as a sale of legitimate property rather than a seizure of illicit contraband, a point that had been of particular importance to him since the 1850s.[19]

Even after the sale of his Ann Street store to William Barkley the year before, the vestiges of Akarman's life's work made for a remarkable haul. Over a period of three days in early May, he delivered nearly six thousand obscene playing cards, half a ton of printed sheets for binding into obscene books, more than a hundred steel plates and copperplates, and four thousand obscene pictures to Comstock in person at the headquarters of the American Tract Society at 150 Nassau Street, the future site of the New York Society for the Suppression of Vice. Although Comstock did not disclose what amount of money Akarman received in return, he later valued the worth of the property at sixteen thousand dollars. Perhaps the publisher agreed to a low price because he had already started disengaging from the business. Or perhaps he was ill; Comstock's entry for Akarman states that he died the following year, in May 1873. Though Comstock later implied that he had contributed to the demise of all three leading publishers by "worrying them to death," no other evidence links Akarman's death to Comstock's investigation.[20]

During the same time period, the self-appointed hunter of vice pursued the city's third major publisher of erotica, Jeremiah Farrell. Farrell, then thirty-five, had a significant history of unsavory business practices, though not as extensive as that of Haines or Akarman. Fairly early in his career, in 1864, a credit reporter who interviewed

Farrell for R. G. Dun & Co. commended him as a "smart active bus man, d[oin]g a success[ful] bus, buys + sells for cash, asks little cr[edit] w fully 15,000$ + adding to his worth, correct + hon[es]t in his dealings, prompt in his paymts, cr gd." In 1867 the reporter again gave him high marks for creditworthiness, but now added a low rating for morality. He observed, Farrell "pays his way but is a man of bad char[acter]. He is a publisher of obscene books in which he manages to do a good bus." By January 1871 even the financial assessment of Farrell had darkened. "Bad man, bad business, bad habits, bad character," concluded a January entry. "Not recommended." A July 1871 entry was similarly negative: "Dealer in obscene periodicals. Intemperate + unworthy of credit. Not safe to trust overnight."[21]

Comstock's own investigation determined that Farrell had been in the business of publishing obscene books for sixteen years, even longer than the Dun report indicated. Remarkably, he had managed to escape arrest during that whole length of time, a feat his antagonist attributed to his ability to pay blackmail.[22] In all, Comstock asserted that Farrell published 109 different books that he considered obscene—exactly the number of cheap "bad books" that Comstock had found in existence when he wrote a report summarizing the work of the YMCA Committee for the Suppression of Vice in 1872 and 1873. This was a much greater number of "bad books" than he attributed to Haines or Akarman, who were said to be responsible for around twenty works each. The disparity suggests that Farrell's forte was mass-market pamphlet literature, whereas Haines and Akarman specialized in graphically illustrated fancy books designed for a more upmarket clientele. As Comstock's authorized biographer succinctly concluded, Farrell's books "differed from the others [that is, those of Haines and Akarman] in that they contained no pictures."[23]

On April 8, 1872, Comstock entered Farrell's store on Ann Street and purchased a book called *The Adventures of a French Bedstead,*

Containing Many Singular and Interesting Amorous Tales and Narratives. This work derived from a story that had been serialized in *The Rambler's Magazine* of London in 1784 and then issued in book form by William Dugdale in 1840. Farrell probably purchased the stereotyped plates for this work from Frederic Brady, given that Brady had offered his own pamphlet version back in the 1850s under his Henry S. G. Smith & Co. imprint. After visiting Farrell's store, Comstock filed a complaint with a police magistrate describing his purchase. The magistrate referred the complaint to the district attorney, who promptly obtained an indictment against Farrell for "publishing and selling obscene books."[24]

Before Comstock could have Farrell arrested, however, the publisher allegedly received a tip from police officers to whom he had been paying protection money: "Jerry, [we] have a warrant for you. If you don't want to be taken get out of the way." Although Farrell decamped, he died of unknown causes shortly thereafter, on May 11, 1872. Nonetheless, when Comstock revisited Farrell's bookstore later that month, he found clerks still "carrying on [Farrell's] business for his wife." He filed another complaint, and the clerks were arrested. Their statements first led Comstock to Thomas Holman, a printer in Yonkers, who had been hired to do Farrell's printing in 1868 after a New York City printer found it too risky to continue the work in the wake of the new Obscene Literature Act. According to Comstock, Holman was outwardly pious. A "prominent church man," he even warded off suspicion about the kind of books he produced by distributing free religious tracts in his front office. (Evidently, it was not uncommon for individuals engaged in the obscene print trade to pose as religious publishers, to avoid detection.)[25]

On May 28 police arrested Holman and searched his back office, where they seized six tons of Farrell's stereotype plates, used for printing lewd books. At the time of the raid, the printer had the pages for nearly fifty thousand volumes on hand. Remarkably, invoices showed that Holman had run off more than one hundred forty thousand copies of obscene books for Farrell in the preceding four years.[26] The same day, the police also arrested two New York City bookbinders and paper suppliers, a man named Charles Darrow and his son Joseph, who operated a successful bindery near City Hall. The Darrows had provided the paper to Holman and then bound the resulting sheets into books. Comstock's arrest ledger noted with disgust that the Darrow firm was "counted as highly respectable" and employed about forty "young girls" in binding books, a common occupation for female laborers in that era. The police also seized a ton of books and printed sheets, including the pages for more than eight thousand books that had just been printed by Holman.[27] The next day, Comstock visited the store of Arthur Brown, a lithographer employed by Farrell. He convinced the police to seize thirty-three engraved steel plates and allow him to destroy forty stones used to create lithographs. For unspecified reasons, Brown was not arrested.[28]

At first, things seemed to go Comstock's way. His testimony led a grand jury to indict the printer Holman and the two bookbinders, Charles and Joseph Darrow, for violating state obscenity law; however, his plan was thwarted when the district attorney's office repeatedly adjourned their cases in the Court of General Sessions. These "cases have all been fixed up by Dist. Atty. + . . . pigeon-holed," he observed bitterly. "Evidence in each case most positive."[29]

During the spring of 1872, Comstock also targeted a fourth publisher, Louis Beer. Beer's production, consisting of only two unspecified books, was evidently less extensive than that of William and Mary Haines, Akarman, or Farrell. But the antipornography crusader claimed to have forced Beer out of business as well. Perhaps the publisher gave up his stock in exchange for avoiding arrest. Or perhaps, like Haines and Akarman, he received payments from moral reformers as an inducement for quitting the business. Unfortunately, Comstock's entry for Beer does not supply any details. It simply records: "Published 2 Ob[scene] Books. Destroyed Plates." But it does contain one additional claim, giving Beer credit for an innovation in American erotic entrepreneurship: "First introduced 'Dildoes' in America." An 1870 circular for fancy books, photographs, and sex toys explained the purpose of this invention, which it described as an "Artificial Penis" that could be purchased for six dollars. "This instrument is manufactured of white rubber, and is a wonderful fac simile of the natural penis of man." The ad also took a jab at the woman's rights movement, then vigorously pursuing suffrage for women: "For reserved females it is a happy and harmless substitute for the natural 'Champion of Woman's Rights.'"[30]

When Comstock finally met with leaders of the YMCA in May 1872, he was able to regale them with his accomplishments in arresting the Nassau and Ann Street booksellers and in obtaining stereotyped plates, photographs, lithographic stones, books, and other property from major pornographic publishers like Haines, Akarman, and Farrell. Alluding to Thomas Timpson's financial support of Akarman and Thomas Holman's printing for Farrell, Comstock also startled his audience by revealing that "persons high in official position and honored in the Church" had "made fortunes by backing men who manufactured and sold these things." In recognition of his work, the YMCA's Committee on Obscene Literature informally retained Comstock as one of its investigators and awarded him a respectable salary of a hundred dollars a month.[31] He continued in the role of private detective for the YMCA for the next year, initiating scores of obscenity cases, including a controversial prosecution of the charismatic woman's rights leader Victoria Woodhull for publishing allegedly obscene articles in her feminist periodical, *Woodhull & Claflin's Weekly*.[32]

Wary of the negative publicity that Comstock's aggressive tactics were provoking, YMCA leaders decided in 1873 to create a separate organization dedicated to the enforcement of laws against obscenity. On May 16 the New York legislature approved a charter for the new organization, the New York Society for the Suppression of Vice. Significantly, the charter included a provision requiring the New York City police force to assist the society's agents in pursuing violations of state and federal laws against the circulation of obscene literature.[33] The close ties between the YMCA and the Society for the Suppression of Vice were manifest in the new society's list of incorporators. Among the seventeen men who founded the organization were all eight members of the former YMCA Committee for the Suppression of Vice.[34] In addition to tapping a host of prestigious YMCA leaders, the society attracted a large number of supporters from New York City's upper and upper-middle classes. Future contributors consisted principally of merchants, bankers, manufacturers, doctors, lawyers, and other members of the social and economic elite.[35] At its first organizational meeting on November 28, 1873, Comstock was named secretary and chief special agent, a position he held until his death in 1915.[36] For forty years, his role as the secretary of the Society for the Suppression of Vice gave him valuable access to the social prestige, political connections, and economic resources of some of New York's most prominent citizens.

Although Comstock focused his early smut-fighting efforts on the city's retail pornography trade in lower Manhattan, he soon realized that commerce in obscenity was far from a purely local affair. The greatest danger, he saw, did not lie in over-the-counter transactions in dingy Nassau and Ann Street bookstores. As he described his discovery, "In 1872, when I undertook the great and all-important work of suppressing by legal process this hydra-headed monster, what did I find?" Among other things, he found a "systemized business," which was responsible for "flooding the land through the mails." "*The mail of the United States is the great thoroughfare of communication leading up into all our homes, schools and colleges,*" he declared. "*It is the most powerful agent, to assist this nefarious business,* because it *goes everywhere* and is *secret.*"[37] After grasping the extent of the problem, he quickly concluded that the state law he initially set out to enforce was inadequate to the task of attacking the New York erotica trade and the principal source of its profits: interstate, mail-order traffic in obscenity.

Even though Comstock himself was initially naive about the transcontinental reach of this business, others were not so blind. Indeed, by the end of the Civil War, New York dealers' exploitation of the mails to market sexual publications triggered a significant new development in the regulation of obscenity. In early 1865, Postmaster General William Dennison advised the Senate's Post Office Committee that "our mails are made the vehicle for the conveyance of great numbers and quantities of obscene books and pictures." As he reported, these were sent not only to the U.S. Army, but "here and there and everywhere," becoming a "very great evil." He accordingly asked the committee to present a measure drafted by the Post Office Department that would prohibit the mailing of obscene material by federal law. Specifically, the measure would authorize criminal prosecution for mailing "an obscene book, pamphlet, picture, print, or other publication, knowing the same to be of a vulgar and indecent character." If convicted, individuals faced fines of up to five hundred dollars, imprisonment for up to one year, or both. In more controversial sections, the bill also provided that "no obscene book, pamphlet, picture, print, or other publication of a vulgar and indecent character, shall be admitted into the mails of the United States." And it granted postmasters the power to seize and destroy all obscene publications "deposited in or received at any post office, or discovered in the mails."[38]

To be sure, the proposed law was not the first federal measure directed at obscenity. Congress had inserted a provision in the Tariff Act of 1842 banning the importation of obscene prints, permitting customs officials to seize such items, and authorizing federal agents to petition a federal court for their destruction.[39] But the new measure represented the first congressional effort to regulate obscenity within the nation's borders. Almost immediately, the idea that postal officials should be empowered to censor the mail to root out obscenity struck some members of the Senate as dangerous and possibly unconstitutional. Their objections centered not on what modern readers might anticipate—apprehension about interference with freedom of speech or freedom of the press—but rather on concerns that such a law would violate personal privacy. The Senate debate focused in particular on the provisions stating that no obscene publication should "be admitted into the mails" and allowing postmasters to seize and destroy obscene publications "discovered in the mails."[40]

The Vermont senator Jacob Collamer, who was the chairman of the Post Office Committee and a former postmaster general, began by introducing the bill with a less than ringing endorsement. He pointed out, "It may be liable to some objection," and added that he himself was "not perhaps satisfied with it." Senator Reverdy Johnson of Maryland, an old-line Democrat who generally opposed the centralizing tendencies of the Lincoln administration, promptly took advantage of the opening to challenge the measure. If obscene publications were sent in sealed envelopes, he inquired, "how does the postmaster know what they are?" Collamer replied that the publications in question were "always sent open at one end" and therefore the law would not "require the breaking of seals." But he thought he knew what Johnson was getting at; alluding to proposals in the 1830s for a national law banning antislavery literature from the mail, Collamer said: "I take it the objection would be mainly that [the proposed bill] might be made a precedent for undertaking to give [the postmaster] a sort of censorship over the mails and allow him to discard matter which was not satisfactory, politically, to some party—like throwing out the abolition papers that used to be talked about." Conceding that the bill as drafted raised the risk of political censorship, he offered to delete both the provision declaring that no obscene materials "shall be admitted into the mails" and the provision authorizing postmasters to confiscate and destroy obscene materials "discovered in the mails."[41]

It soon became clear, however, that Johnson's real concern was not the threat of political censorship. Rather, it was the need to preserve sealed first-class mail from government intrusion. At the time, mailable matter was divided into three categories: first class (all correspondence); second class (newspapers, journals, and other printed matter "regularly issued at stated periods"); and third class (books, pamphlets, "occasional publications," maps, and photographs). Johnson presciently predicted that though it was "true that most of the printed matter" was "sent without being covered or sealed up," once the law was changed and criminal penalties loomed, "those who send this species of publications [would] no doubt soon begin to seal them." Then, he continued, "the postmaster, whenever he suspects that the envelope contains anything which is obnoxious to objection, will break the seal." Following Senator Collamer's suggestion, Johnson moved to strike the objectionable provisions on the ground that "it would be establishing a very bad precedent to give authority to postmasters to take anything out of the mail." This motion would have left in place only the criminal prohibition on mailing obscenity.[42]

In Johnson's view, the harm done by postal inspectors' rifling through sealed letters would be far greater than the harm from pornographers' manipulation of the postal service to secure surreptitious delivery of their goods. Thirteen years later, the U.S. Supreme Court affirmed Johnson's priorities in *Ex parte Jackson,* an important case challenging the constitutionality of legislation banning lottery advertisements from the mail. Writing for the Court, Justice Stephen Field recognized a critical distinction between sealed first-class mail, which was "intended to be kept free from inspection," and other printed matter (second- and third-class mail), which was "purposely left in a condition to be examined." Although *Ex parte Jackson* found no conflict between the statute banning lottery advertisements in the mail (and, by extension, legislation against obscenity in the mail) and the First Amendment, it emphasized that such laws could not interfere with the sanctity of sealed mail. "No law of Congress can place in the hands of officials connected with the postal service any authority to invade the secrecy of letters and such sealed packages in the mail," Field declared. As a result, "all regulations adopted as to mail matter of this kind must be in subordination to the great principle embodied in the fourth amendment of the Constitution." He further defended individual privacy interests by confirming that sealed items deposited in the mail were "as fully guarded from examination . . . as if they were retained by the parties forwarding them in their own domiciles."[43]

In an effort to save one of the anti-obscenity provisions challenged in the 1865 Senate debates, John Sherman of Ohio suggested another compromise. Postmasters would be allowed to exclude mail they suspected of being obscene so long as they did not break any seals. In proposing this resolution, he pointed his finger directly at publishers and dealers from New York. According to Sherman, they were so confident in their ability to distribute obscenity safely through the mail that they did not even bother to hide their identity: "We are well aware that many of these publications are sent all over the country from the city of New York with the names of the parties sending them on the backs, so that the postmasters without opening the mail matter may know that it is offensive matter, indecent and improper to be carried in the public mails." As a result, "the legislative prohibition against carrying such matter when it is known to the postmasters should be left." To clarify that postmasters were not authorized to break seals, the Senate passed a motion deleting the provision allowing postal officials to seize and destroy all obscene publications "discovered in the mails." Apparently satisfied by the assurance that first-class mail would remain sacrosanct, Senator Johnson withdrew his objections and the amended bill passed the Senate and later the House easily. Abraham Lincoln signed it into law on March 3, 1865.[44]

The new federal legislation did little to stem the nation's burgeoning mail-order pornography trade, however. As Senator Johnson had predicted in the floor debates on the 1865 law, purveyors of erotic print, pictures, and merchandise responded to the new regulatory regime by becoming more guarded in their use of the mails. Even before Congress took action, some vendors had begun to assure clients that their orders could be shipped in sealed envelopes to ensure privacy. After 1865, erotica dealers focused their attention on devising ways to elude detection by postal officials and other government agents. They prepared circulars, for instance, in which each item was carefully numbered to ensure secrecy; customers were instructed to order only by the number rather than by the title of books or the name of products.[45] In addition, dealers began to offer clients a menu of choices for delivering their orders, ranked by degree of safety and assurance of delivery.

A set of four brightly colored advertisements from approximately 1870, each captioned "Private Circular, for Gentlemen Only" and offering "Genuine Fancy Books!" with "Elegantly Colored Plates," nude photographs, dildos, and condoms, vividly illustrates these strategies. The vendor in question might have been the enterprising George Akarman, the creator of *Venus' Miscellany*. Circular no. 2 carried a large ad in bright blue ink for a new collection of stories excerpted from *Venus' Miscellany* called *The Roue's Pocket Companion; or, Gems from Venus' Miscellany*, listed for two dollars. It was billed as "the most beautifully written and elegantly illustrated 'fancy and amorous' work that has ever appeared in this country." A contemporaneous catalogue from another dealer praised this volume as "a selection of choice Witty Stories and Jokes of a rich character, from the original 'Venus Miscellany,' interspersed with some of the finest amorous poetry—a collection from the best wits and Free Love writers of the age." Circular no. 1 (Fig. 7.1) featured "French Transparent Playing Cards," one of Akarman's specialties. These were described as the "finest article in the FANCY STYLE that has ever been produced—they can be played with the same as a common card by persons unacquainted with them—and by holding them to the light you have 52 BEAUTIFULLY COLORED FANCY PICTURES." Other clues pointing to Akarman's possible involvement are the circulars' emphasis on an exclusive audience of "gentlemen" and their repetition of "fancy" as a code word for literature narrated by sexually adventurous women. For instance, one "fancy book," *Love-A-La-Mode; or, The Amorous Confessions of Marguerite Moncreiffe*, was described as the "life of a rambling and voluptuous young lady, who lost her virginity in pursuit of pleasure, written by herself, and splendidly illustrated with ten beautiful fancy pictures, designed and engraved expressly for this book." Moreover, just as Akarman had done in 1857,

PRIVATE CIRCULAR, FOR GENTLEMEN ONLY.

GENUINE FANCY BOOKS!

BEAUTIFULLY PRINTED! ELEGANTLY COLORED PLATES! HANDSOMELY BOUND!

Every work named on this Circular is printed from new type, on *fine paper*, handsomely illustrated with BEAUTIFUL COLORED PLATES, and richly bound in cloth. They can be sent either by *Mail or Express*, with perfect safety, and done up in such a manner as to defy detection.

Persons ordering can rest assured that their orders will be promptly and faithfully attended to.

EVERY WORK NAMED IS EXACTLY AS REPRESENTED.

FANNY HILL, Her Life and Amours, 10 colored plates, . . $2 00
ROSE DE AMOUR, The French Courtesan, 10 colored plates, . . 2 00
LUSTFUL TURK, or Love in the Harem, 10 colored plates, . . 2 00
TWO COUSINS, Their Confessions, 10 colored plates, . . 2 00
SILAS SHOVEWELL, His Amours with the Nuns, 10 colored plates, ... 2 00
CURTAIN DRAWN UP, or The Education of Laura, 10 colored plates, ... 2 00

VOLUPTUOUS CONFESSIONS IN BED, 5 colored plates, . . $1 00
MADAME CELESTINE, Her Intrigues, 5 colored plates, . . 1 00
CICILY MARTIN, The Woman of Pleasure, 5 colored plates, . . 1 00
CABINET OF VENUS UNLOCKED, 5 colored plates, . . 1 00
FLASH AND FRISKY SONGSTER, 5 colored plates, . . 1 00

FANNY HILL

LARGEST SIZE, 24 COLORED PLATES—THE LARGEST WORK EVER PRINTED OF THE KIND—IT IS A SPLENDID VOLUME, ... $5 00

FRENCH TRANSPARENT PLAYING CARDS. The finest article in the FANCY STYLE that has ever been produced—they can be played with the same as a common card by persons unacquainted with them—and by holding them to the light you have 52 BEAUTIFULLY COLORED FANCY PICTURES, Price $2 00

FRENCH "SAFES," OR "CONDOMS," *Warranted.*—The *only certain Preventive against Disease or Pregnancy.* Manufactured from fine transparent India Rubber—they cover the *Penis* entire, and increase the pleasures. Price, single, 50 cts., one dozen $3 00

PRINTS OF VARIOUS SIZES, ... From 50 cts. to $2 00 each.

TOBACCO BOXES, Double covers, illustrated, Price $3 00

CIGAR CASES, 10 illustrations, secret drawer, ... 3 00

☞ Recollect, none of the above can be had at our office in New York. All orders must be sent by mail, and they will receive early and prompt attention, and the articles ordered forwarded to their destination, in the most compact, reliable and expeditious manner.

7.1 *Erotica circular, "Private Circular, for Gentlemen Only," c. 1870.*

COURTESY OF THE AMERICAN ANTIQUARIAN SOCIETY.

the "for gentlemen only" vendor refused to sell obscene materials locally. He instructed readers: "Recollect, none of the above can be had at our office in New York."[46]

Regardless of the dealer's identity, security was clearly a critical concern. Circular no. 2 stated that two newly issued books, *The Roue's Pocket Companion* and *The Festival of Love*, could be mailed to any part of the United States or Canada on receipt of payment, of two and three dollars, respectively. Though it promised that the books would be "packed in such a manner as to defy detection," it nonetheless encouraged customers to take additional precautions. In particular, by sending fifty-four cents extra to cover first-class postage, purchasers could receive their books folded "as a letter, sealed close from observation." (Note that one new erotic genre—nude photographs—was especially easy to mail in first-class envelopes.)[47]

Alternatively, the circular offered purchasers the option of avoiding the U.S. mail altogether by having their fancy books sent by private express, a method that was even "more certain and safe." New York erotica dealer Thomas O'Connor similarly touted the safety of express companies in his 1869 catalogue, assuring customers that "fancy goods," such as a heavily illustrated edition of *Fanny Hill*, could be "forwarded by Mail or Express with perfect safety, so as to defy detection." Testimonials of this sort in all likelihood provided a powerful benefit to the express industry, which was then competing with the Post Office to transport letters, periodicals, and books. Though the use of private couriers was costlier than regular mail delivery, their operation outside the scope of federal obscenity law made them attractive conduits for erotic materials after 1865. Indeed, Congress did not include a provision banning obscenity from interstate commerce (and thereby outlawing the shipment of obscene materials by express companies rather than by mail) until 1897.[48]

The "for gentlemen only" circulars further informed customers that even some types of merchandise could be sent disguised as correspondence in the first-class mail. Although the postal service did not accept parcels until the early twentieth century, buyers were instructed that certain articles could be folded and mailed in sealed first-class envelopes, just like fancy books. Among these was a pocket-sized stereoscope for viewing pictures "depicting the most ravishing scenes, and all photographed from life—male and female, together and separate, in the most amorous positions." Customers could purchase one folding stereoscope with twenty-four pictures for fifteen dollars, "sent by mail, sealed as a letter." The dealer in question could also ship by correspondence class, protected by a seal, sex toys designed to enhance female enjoyment of sexual intercourse. Circular no. 3, for instance, promised that "the French tickler; or, ladies' delight," which it described as a rubber ring for the penis that gave the "most exquisite pleasure to both sexes," could be packaged in a sealed first-class envelope.[49]

A competitor of the "for gentleman only" dealer implemented even more rigorous methods to escape detection after Congress instituted the ban on obscene material in the mails. In 1870 the Grand Fancy Bijou Catalogue of the Sporting Man's Emporium announced a "change of system" whereby "after this, all Fancy Goods [would] be sent by EXPRESS, and in *no other way*." As the catalogue explained, "goods will be done up so as to render it impossible to detect their contents, and express agents know nothing of the nature of the goods." Some customers, the sellers acknowledged, would have to travel to retrieve their packages, given that express depots were not as ubiquitous as post offices: "Where parties have no express office in their own town, they will inform us of the nearest one to them, and the goods will be sent there, and a duplicate express receipt will be forwarded by mail to their own residence, so that they can present it at express office and receive their goods." Nonetheless, such inconveniences were necessary to ensure delivery. The only books that the Sporting Man's Emporium was willing to ship in the mail were two works that were unlikely to trigger suspicion because they purported to be medical guides rather than erotica: *The Book of Nature* and *The Magic Wand and Medical Guide.* The company also agreed to mail condoms, presumably because federal officials had not yet banned contraceptives from the mail in 1870.[50]

As the "for gentlemen only" circulars and the Grand Fancy Bijou Catalogue demonstrate, the advent of national legislation against obscenity in the mail did not persuade erotica dealers to abandon their business ventures. Rather, they responded by conceiving new strategies to elude censorious officials. In this respect, the circulars illuminate the ongoing dialogue between purveyors of erotica and the various legal regimes designed to suppress them, demonstrating yet another way in which the law of obscenity and commerce in pornography had become intimately intertwined.

By the winter of 1873, Comstock's meticulous investigation of New York's erotic print trade had at last opened his eyes to the vast economic and geographic scope of the industry. It had also convinced him that the existing legal framework for regulating obscenity had failed to check interstate commerce in obscene literature. To meet the unprecedented challenges of a nationwide mail-order market, the leaders of the New York City chapter of the YMCA agreed to dispatch their enthusiastic young agent, still only twenty-eight years old, to Washington to lobby for new legislation.

With this legislative mission in mind, and for the edification of interested congressmen, Comstock brought along an eye-popping array of fancy books and photographs, contraceptives, abortifacients, and sex toys that he had uncovered during the past year. He used these items to set up exhibits on the floor of the House and in the vice president's office in the Senate that were designed to showcase the shocking specimens of obscenity he had discovered being sent through the mail. His diary records that all the legislators who viewed his display were "very much excited" by it and enthusiastically offered him their support. He also carried a draft of a new bill that was intended to strengthen and extend the existing federal ban on mailing obscene materials. Before submitting it to supporters in Congress, he received vital advice on revising the proposed law from a sitting U.S. Supreme Court justice, William Strong, who was an ardent proponent of evangelical causes.[51]

In lobbying for expanded legislation, Comstock was especially eager to convey to congressmen and other federal officials that commerce in obscene publications was no longer a small-scale, marginal enterprise. Rather, thanks to the efficiency of the U.S. Postal Service, it had become a massive, interstate business. He was also determined to demonstrate that existing local, state, and national laws had proved incapable of suppressing mail-order traffic in obscenity. Through his exhibits and his discussions with members of Congress, Comstock showed that canny New York pornographers, using a web of aliases, coded newspaper advertisements, and the secrecy of first-class correspondence, had continued to flood the mails with indecent texts and images, despite the prohibitions in place.

During the preceding year, for instance, tawdry illustrated newspapers like *The Days' Doings*, which was published by the New York newspaper mogul Frank Leslie, ran dozens of easily decoded advertisements for erotic merchandise in each issue. A typical notice from one C. L. Taylor in Brooklyn announced: "Books! Books!! Books!!! PHOTOGRAPHS and SPORTING GOODS, rich and unique! Sample Superb Stereoscopic view, 75 cts. Specimen of French Photo, highly colored . . . Send a 3 cent stamp for new circular." Mail-order dealers who chose to operate more cautiously, such as those who had

7.2 Frontispiece, Anthony Comstock, Frauds Exposed; or, How the People are Deceived and Robbed, and Youth Corrupted *(New York, 1880), showing the centrality of the New York Post Office to the U.S. obscene book trade.*

COURTESY OF THE AMERICAN ANTIQUARIAN SOCIETY.

significant property at risk of confiscation, were also able to drum up business through presorted customer lists. Copies of such lists, containing the names and addresses of thousands of persons who were likely to purchase sexually explicit matter, were regularly shared or sold among vendors of erotica. In this way, dealers could solicit preidentified customers throughout the country with mail-order circulars, all without attracting attention by placing public notices in newspapers.[52]

Armed with his startling collection of physical evidence and detailed accounts of the untrammeled flow of pornography through the mail, Comstock obtained exactly the results he wanted in Washington. On March 3, 1873, his advocacy was rewarded when Congress passed the Act for the Suppression of Trade in, and Circulation of,

Obscene Literature and Articles of Immoral Use, which soon became known as the Comstock Act. Unlike the 1865 proposal to exclude obscene material from the mail, the Comstock Act generated minimal debate and encountered little opposition in Congress. It banned a long list of printed publications and immoral articles. Specifically, the act declared, "No obscene, lewd, or lascivious book, pamphlet, picture, paper, print, or other publication of an indecent character, or any article or thing designed or intended for the prevention of conception or procuring of abortion, nor any article or thing intended or adapted for any indecent or immoral use or nature, nor any written or printed card, circular, book, pamphlet, advertisement or notice of any kind giving information, directly or indirectly, where, or how, or of whom, or by what means either of the things before mentioned may be obtained or made . . . shall be carried in the mail." President Ulysses S. Grant signed the bill into law the next day, just before his second inauguration.[53]

The Comstock Act represented an important victory for moral reformers from the YMCA and elsewhere on a number of fronts. One of the most significant changes from prior federal law was the introduction of a new prohibition on mailing articles "for the prevention of conception or procuring of abortion." In justifying this addition, Comstock and his allies relied on recent legislation in the state of New York. There, YMCA activists had persuaded the legislature to include a similarly worded prohibition on the distribution of articles designed to promote abortion or prevent conception in the Obscene Literature Act of 1868.[54] In lobbying Congress, Comstock was able to draw a close association between the mail-order sale of sexually arousing publications and the mail-order sale of devices for reproductive control. He pointed out that men such as George Akarman and Jeremiah Farrell, who had been distributing large volumes of sexually explicit literature through the mail for almost two decades, also offered mail-order "cundums," "rubber goods for ladies," and various powders alleged to induce miscarriages. Even a glance at the classified pages of *The Days' Doings* for the year preceding Comstock's visit to Washington would have confirmed the overlapping identities of dealers in pornography and purveyors of contraceptives. Throughout 1872, for instance, a New York vendor known as Professor Rogers regularly advertised mail-order offerings of "Rich and Rare PHOTOGRAPHS" and "Rare Illustrated Books . . . with Beautiful Pictures" side by side with "ladies' and gents' rubber goods."[55]

In addition, proponents of classifying devices for contraception and abortion as illicit obscenity were aided by the fact that public opposition to both practices was fairly uncontroversial in the 1870s. Indeed, commentators espousing a range of political perspectives expressed hostility toward reproductive control, which they viewed as unnatural, immoral, and harmful.[56] This outward consensus made it relatively easy for national lawmakers to defer to the precedent New York had set, as well as the urging of prominent industrialists and financiers associated with the YMCA.[57] (That said, despite public protests against contraception, it is clear that large numbers of Americans privately embraced the use of birth control—and would continue to do so even after its criminalization. Similarly, women who felt they needed to terminate their pregnancies continued to seek abortions in the last quarter of the nineteenth century, despite the illegality of procedures and devices for abortion.[58])

The Comstock Act also added obscene newspapers, which the 1865 law did not cover, to the list of illicit publications. In addition, the new legislation instituted a ban on mailing advertisements for obscene literature and immoral articles. The Comstock Act also imposed heightened penalties for each offense: imprisonment at hard labor for a minimum of one year and a maximum of ten years, or fines from a minimum of one hundred dollars to a maximum of five thousand, or both, in the discretion of the court. It gave U.S. marshals explicit power to search for and confiscate obscene materials pursuant to court orders and to seek their destruction in separate condemnation proceedings. And it outlawed the manufacture and sale of obscene literature and articles in the District of Columbia, over which Congress had direct jurisdiction.[59]

With the benefit of historical hindsight, the most momentous aspect of the Comstock Act may have been the separate administrative appointment of Anthony Comstock as special agent of the post office in charge of enforcing the new law.[60] Under the 1865 statute banning obscenity from the mail, overburdened postal inspectors rarely pursued criminal activity; between 1865 and 1872 the post office initiated only seven prosecutions for obscenity.[61] But all this changed when Comstock received his commission. From the outset, he astutely insisted that he receive no government pay for the special agent position, for he sensed that "if a salary was attached to the office, there would be a constant scramble for it among politicians for their friends." His hunch paid off: he was reappointed virtually uncontested, year after year. As postal inspector, Comstock vowed to use all available means to attack the mail-order trade in obscenity—now defined to include a vast range of merchandise, including contraceptive devices—as aggressively as possible. Over the next seven years Comstock alone initiated more than one hundred federal obscenity cases, which stood in contrast to the scarcity of prosecutions before his appointment. Along with tremendous energy and moral passion, he brought an agile legal mind and cunning strategic instincts to the task.[62]

Even before receiving his postal commission, Comstock devised a plan to collect incriminating evidence against mail-order purveyors of sexual materials. He first scoured lowbrow flash newspapers that catered to sporting men and looked for advertisements that might signal a connection to lewd publications. His early biographers, Heywood Broun and Margaret Leech, who had access to Comstock's diary (it has since been destroyed), described how he clipped items from *The Days' Doings* to find potential targets: "Both the illustrations and the advertising gave offense, the latter being especially rich in notices of fancy books and pictures, of gambling materials, swindling schemes and contraceptive articles. Anthony had a small pocket notebook in which he posted clippings of the objectionable advertisements."[63]

Rather than reject pornographers' resort to duplicity and masquerade as a distasteful emblem of their morally degraded character, Comstock enthusiastically, even gleefully, mimicked their methods. A favorite technique, one that he would perfect over the years, involved the use of decoy letters. In these, he would pose as a potential customer and write, using a false name and assuming a fake identity, to vendors he suspected of selling illicit materials. He justified this trickery by pointing to the devious character of the erotica trade: "The *insidious nature* of the traffic is one of its most dangerous features. It seeks darkness, it practices concealment, it lives only by deception."[64] In essence, by copying the methods of erotica dealers and turning their strategies against them, Comstock resolved to undermine their ability to evade existing laws against obscenity through secrecy and deceit.

Thus, pornographers first turned to the mails to avoid local prosecutions; Comstock turned to the mails to place orders and collect evidence for federal prosecutions. Pornographers used aliases to avoid detection by him; he used aliases to avoid detection by them. Pornographers set up fake postal addresses; he set up fake postal addresses. In the process, he clearly became enthralled with the cloak-and-dagger nature of these pursuits. He took delight in signing his decoy letters with smart-alecky names like Harry Ketchem or Ketcham & Co., which conveyed thinly veiled boasts about his prowess as a sleuth and law enforcer.[65]

In the cat-and-mouse games that unfolded between Comstock and the various individuals who made their living from the trade in obscenity, decoy letters were an especially effective ploy. Because the letters Comstock received in response to his inquiries were addressed to the aliases he had invented, he asserted that he was justified in opening them even if it meant breaking a seal without a court order. In this way, the decoy tactic enabled him to infiltrate the network of New York erotica dealers who had successfully used sealed first-class mail to escape detection in the past.

In relying on decoy letters, Comstock also strove to neutralize potentially significant political and constitutional objections to his efforts to suppress obscenity in the mail while acting as an agent of the U.S. government. Far from being the unsophisticated rube he is often portrayed as, Comstock was intensely cognizant of the legal and constitutional issues raised by his line of work and took shrewd steps to address them. As he tried to assure supporters of the New York Society for the Suppression of Vice: "This Society and its Agent regard the inviolability of the mails as essential to the preservation of our free institutions, and have neither the wish nor the power to interfere with them."[66] In a series of books and articles that spelled out precise legal arguments, Comstock went out of his way to appear sensitive to individual privacy concerns and to defend the legality of his investigative practices.[67] In his 1883 work, *Traps for the Young*, he seized on Justice Field's solicitude for the sanctity of sealed mail in *Ex parte Jackson* as a validation of his detective methods. He underscored Field's statement that although "regulations excluding matter from the mail cannot be enforced in a way which would require or permit an examination into letters or sealed packages subject to letter postage, without warrant issued upon oath or affirmation," they could be enforced *"upon competent evidence of their violation obtained in other ways, as from the parties receiving the letters or packages."* As Comstock confidently concluded: "Thus the Supreme Court of the United States approves and sanctions the very method which has been pursued by the writer from the very beginning."[68]

One of Comstock's earliest federal cases, a prosecution involving the New York erotica dealer Henry Camp, neatly exemplifies his resourceful investigative techniques.[69] In July 1872 Comstock spotted an advertisement in *The Days' Doings* from H. Cameron & Co. in New York City offering "beautiful and rare photographs" and a catalogue. He then wrote two letters in which he posed as customers named John Beardsley of Bedford, Ohio, and George Nicoll of Norwalk, Connecticut. Pretending to be a fan of fancy goods, he requested the company's catalogue and some of the "rare" photographs, enclosing payment and providing a false mailing address. Once the orders were filled, Comstock convinced a New York postal official to intercept the envelopes. (After Comstock became an inspector of the post office, he could seize such letters on his own.)

Although Cameron & Co. enclosed Comstock's orders in sealed envelopes, the strategy offered no protection. On the grounds that the correspondence was addressed to him (or rather, his aliases), Comstock broke the seals of the letters. With the material he received in hand, he filed a complaint with a U.S. commissioner for the Southern District of New York and obtained an arrest warrant against the principal of the firm. When Comstock and two U.S. marshals executed the warrant, they learned that the vendor in question, like Comstock, was using an alias; Cameron & Co. turned out to be a sixty-year-old man named Henry Camp. In a further effort to escape detection, Camp had been receiving his mail at a location separate from his place of business; he had also persuaded the letter carrier on his route to work in collusion with him. These precautions, however, proved no match for Comstock and the marshals. When they followed Camp back to his business after he had picked up his mail, they found and confiscated "about 50 letters containing obscene books, ready to mail and about 30 letters just received by mail."

The U.S. attorney for the Southern District of New York subsequently indicted Camp on three counts of "depositing obscene publications in the U.S. mail." On each count, the unspecified obscenity was said to be "too indecent" to be set forth in the indictment. Unlike the courts in New York County, where Comstock often experienced frustration and defeat, the federal forum delivered satisfaction. Camp pleaded guilty, and U.S. Circuit Court Judge Charles Benedict sentenced him to one year in prison and a five-hundred-dollar fine.

Comstock was particularly proud of another early investigation that he directed against a longtime nemesis, the wily and incorrigible New York erotica dealer William Simpson. After failing to shut down Simpson's operations through arrests under state law, Comstock tried using a series of decoy letters in which he posed as a Canadian pornographer named Harry Ketchem. With this ruse, he succeeded in enticing Simpson into mailing him a batch of cards containing smutty jokes. In a stunning victory for Comstock, this evidence eventually led to Simpson's indictment in federal court and conviction in 1874 under the newly enacted Comstock Act. At Comstock's urging, Judge Benedict sentenced the recidivist pornographer to an unusually harsh five-thousand-dollar fine and ten years at hard labor in a federal penitentiary.[70]

In the following years, despite a steady stream of criticism that his methods involved unacceptable deception and entrapment, Comstock employed similarly crafty procedures in hundreds of cases involving mail-order pornography. In these endeavors he received substantial support from sympathetic officials at the Justice Department, especially federal marshals and U.S. attorneys for the Southern District of

New York, who worked closely with him in gathering evidence and mounting prosecutions. Whereas elected district attorneys in New York County frequently let obscenity prosecutions languish after the indictment stage, appointed federal prosecutors regularly brought cases to trial. In addition to the support Comstock received from national law enforcement officials, the relatively rural composition of federal juries probably contributed to his success in the federal forum. The Southern District of New York, for instance, comprised not only urban Manhattan but also Westchester, Dutchess, Ulster, Sullivan, Putnam, and Orange counties, which were heavily rural and aligned with the Republican Party. It also became fairly routine for federal judges to sentence convicted defendants to prison terms of a year or more.[71]

Historians, legal scholars, and other commentators have long debated the causes of the Comstock Act and the ensuing national crusade against obscenity in the mail. To many, the law seems to have appeared out of nowhere, unleashing a sudden new cultural obsession with enforcing sexual purity and restricting indecent speech with puritanical zeal. Yet a longer view of the Comstock Act, one that interprets it within the context of the nineteenth century as a whole, makes clear that the late nineteenth-century offensive against obscenity in the mail was many years in the making. In essence, the 1873 law and Comstock's subsequent rise to power had their origins in the ability of erotica dealers to exploit the limitations of federalism and local sovereignty over nearly two decades of interstate marketing activity. The success of those dealers created an anxiety among moral reformers and national legislators alike about the capacity of the traditional regulatory order—which treated the power to police morality as the quintessential prerogative of states and localities—to deal with a world that had been transformed by national markets and national communications systems. By investing federal officials with sweeping new authority to enforce morality, the Comstock Act seemed to rescue lawmakers (and in the eyes of some observers, the nation itself) from the regulatory and cultural crisis that New York pornographers had precipitated.[72]

Chapter 8

New Frontiers

In the last quarter of the nineteenth century, rigorous enforcement of local, state, and national obscenity laws sharply increased the legal risks and penalties that participants in the erotica trade confronted. Producers and sellers of sexual publications in the Gilded Age felt the pressure of the law bear down on them much more heavily than in the experience of any of their pre–Civil War forerunners. By 1900 the New York Society for the Suppression of Vice could proudly report the conviction and sentencing of hundreds of individuals for obscenity-related crimes.[1]

A glance at the society's annual reports, which meticulously counted, weighed, and catalogued every obscene item confiscated by its agents, makes plain that the Comstock Act and various state-level "little Comstock Acts" also resulted in the seizure and destruction of a staggering amount of erotic material. (One incidental byproduct of the society's thoroughness is that today, even in archival collections, erotic works from the nineteenth-century United States are exceedingly scarce.) Taking stock of a quarter century of work, the 1900 annual report provided this formidable tally: "Books and Sheet Stock seized and destroyed—78,608 lbs; Obscene Pictures and Photos [seized and destroyed]—877,412; Negative Plates for making Obscene Photos [seized and destroyed]—8,495; Engraved Steel and Copper Plates [seized and destroyed]—425; Stereotype Plates for Printing Books, etc. [seized and destroyed]—28,050 lbs; Indecent Playing Cards destroyed—6,436; Circulars, Catalogues, Songs, Poems, etc. [destroyed]—1,672,050."[2]

Even the aggressive prosecutions carried out by Anthony Comstock fell far short of obliterating commerce in erotica, however. As is attested by the arrest ledgers of the Society for the Suppression of Vice, case files of federal and county criminal courts, and records of investigations by the U.S. Post Office Department, the market for sexually arousing literature and images persisted in late nineteenth-century America. Rather than eliminate such commerce, heightened regulation redefined and reshaped the business of selling sex.

In the early going, Comstock's success at driving Haines, Akarman, and Farrell out of the industry had the immediate effect of creating opportunities for a new guard of gutsy small-scale entrepreneurs who sought to fill the vacuum left by their departure. Despite the immense new energy devoted to suppressing obscene print—or, according to some perceptions, because of it—demand for erotic material seemed to be on the rise. Even the Society for the Suppression of Vice was forced to acknowledge the heightened allure of prohibited obscenity. As its annual report for 1875 revealed, "the natural thirst for forbidden knowledge" was motivating new consumers, especially young people, to seek out sexual publications as never before. Though "literature most destructive to the morals of readers" was "no new thing," the report noted, "within a few years the evil has so increased as to strike thoughtful and observant minds with amazement." Agents of the society made sure that the personal and economic costs of supplying the growing demand for "forbidden knowledge" would be heavy. A big payoff, however, awaited those who were audacious and shrewd enough to assume the risk. Manufacturers of erotic literature and other sexual merchandise, if they went undetected, could expect profit margins between 300 and 500 percent, by comparison with the relatively small profits of 10 to 20 percent earned by legitimate publishers.[3]

The combination of the contraction in supply caused by the exit of the old-line publishers, the growth in consumer demand, and the prospect of heady profits induced a number of existing participants to jump at the chance to become producers. Some of these individuals were already established in erotic print circles, such as a bookseller named Charles Meackey, who was investigated by Comstock in August 1872. According to Comstock, Meackey was a "church member, Sunday school teacher (a class of young ladies), a Mason or Odd Fellow, and yet one of the lowest wretches known in the business." For several years before, he had been in the business of marketing erotic literature under his alias, American Publishing Co. In 1870 he ran an ad under the caption "Books That Are Books" in *Days' Doings* that listed numerous libidinous paperbacks at thirty-five cents apiece, including *Racy Yarns*, *Marriage Bed*, *Wedding Night*, *Habits of the Female Sex*, *Gems of Love*, and *Love's Festival*, along with the invitation: "So wake up, boys." By the time of his arrest, however, he had gone beyond distributing reprints of existing titles and had ventured into creating new works. As Comstock recorded, when U.S. marshals went to seize Meackey's stock, they also confiscated "1 manuscript for ob[scene] book + 10 sketches to illustrate same."[4]

Despite Meackey's federal arrest, conviction, and one-year prison sentence, others took up where he left off. In 1873 Comstock brought charges against a forty-year-old New Yorker named David Shaw for writing an erotic poem titled *Love's Young Dream, Being a Voluptuous Interpretation of the Initiatory Love Lessons of Lucy and William—Superbly Illustrated.* The indictment included a manuscript of the poem, which had not yet been typeset, as an exhibit.[5] Complete with drawings, *Love's Young Dream* depicted a young couple's sexual experimentation before their marriage, focusing on Lucy's transition from initial chastity and sexual reticence to bold sexual enthusiasm. It turned out that Shaw worked for James Bryan, a dealer in quack medicines, who aspired to publish new erotic works. Toward that end he probably commissioned *Love's Young Dream* from Shaw; a few months later, Bryan himself was arrested for mailing obscene books. When Comstock entered Bryan's place of business, he discovered a huge cache of allegedly obscene reading material: approximately twenty-five thousand pamphlets and three hundred books.[6]

Still other recruits to the New York erotica trade had a more marginal economic status and more limited means. In contrast to the full-time professional publishers of the mid-nineteenth century, many later entrants took up manufacturing lewd publications as a daring sideline. In 1874 the police arrested two men who had previously operated a bookstand for newspapers and secondhand books and had just begun to put out their own pornography. Comstock noted, "These men were about publishing a series of obscene books, when they were arrested. Their stock was secreted in the rear of the liquor saloon corner Broadway & Fulton st, which ran through Ann st basement."[7] The next year, a twenty-six-year-old Irish printer named Edward Murray was indicted for printing an obscene one-page poem in a basement saloon. He charged one dollar for a hundred sheets. Apparently not intimidated by the incipient evangelical war on obscenity, the author cheekily titled the poem "Programme of the Young Men's Christian Association." The first two stanzas called out:

> O, Jimmy, come fuck me, I'm dying for skin,
> You know how we tried, but it wouldn't go in!

And I never had it but twice in my life—
And to get it, dear Jim, would pay any price,

Now, Jimmy, come over to-night after nine,
And the old folks will be fast asleep by that time;
Now don't disappoint me, for I feel so forlorn—
And eat some raw oysters to get a 'hard-on.'[8]

In 1876 Comstock caught a printer named Stephen Schall, an eighteen-year-old employee of a paper bag manufacturer, running off three hundred copies of a second short poem of an a llegedly obscene nature. It also consisted of a single-page sheet, captioned "Parody on Excelsior." A comic take on Henry Wadsworth Longfellow's "Excelsior," it opened this way:

The shades of night were falling fast,
As t'wixt her thighs John Thomas passed
To her this was no new device,
She only murmured "OH HOW NICE"
Up Higher.

My shirt tail flapped, my tool beneath
Flashed like a falchion in its sheath:
And on the midnight air, there rang
The accents of her silvery tongue,
Up Higher.

According to Comstock, Schall and a partner had just sold seventy copies of the poem to a nearby lager beer saloon.[9]

Cases like these suggest that the demise of the well-capitalized publishers from the 1850s and 1860s attracted men at lower levels of the book and novelty trade, such as job printers, bookstand operators, photographers, and secondhand book dealers, to move into writing, manufacturing, and distributing pornography. But these neophytes clearly operated with far less capital and produced goods in much smaller formats and in lower quantities than the old-guard publishers. Moving away from bound fancy books, erotica producers in the Comstock era focused instead on more ephemeral commodities that were lighter and easier to conceal. Instead of classic works such as *Memoirs of a Woman of Pleasure* or *The Curtain Drawn Up*, they offered photographs, playing cards, songs, postcards, and poems.[10]

In 1878 the Fourth Annual Report of the Society for the Suppression of Vice substantiated this trend. Unlike in earlier years, the table of "stock confiscated" showed no seizures of the kinds of valuable materials prized by the major pornographer-publishers of the past: stereotype plates, steel plates and copperplates, or lithographic stones. "It is satisfactory to observe," stated the report, "that within the past year no one has dared to put any great amount of capital into merchandise of this description." For this reason, such "large seizures among the dealers, as formerly, [could] no longer be expected." At the annual meeting, Comstock similarly boasted that when he had "commenced operations he found 161 books, 'large bound volumes,' that were published in this country." During the previous year, however, "only three small pamphlets had been found."[11]

In its report on its work during 1883 the society again remarked on the absence of significant capital investment among producers of fancy goods: "Where there were manufactories of obscene publications and criminal articles, they no longer exist." Rather than discovering huge quantities of materials "as formerly in a single place, now we find the business confined principally to some o'erventuresome scoundrel, who runs the risk of a small lot, for the sake of raising a little money." Still, the organization was able to inform supporters that it had destroyed more than eleven thousand obscene pictures that year.[12]

In some cases, the hope of "raising a little money" even led poor women to run the risk of commissioning and distributing erotica, such as photographs of nude women or copulating couples. In the 1870s and 1880s, respectable employment for working-class women typically yielded paltry and inadequate wages. Women working in the garment industry, for instance, earned between six and twelve dollars a week.[13] The money that could be made from selling erotic goods, such as cheaply and quickly produced nude photographs, may have made smut peddling appealing to women with few economic alternatives, especially in times of personal or financial distress. To be sure, female laborers had long worked behind the scenes for major producers like Akarman and Farrell by hand-coloring engravings or binding books. Selling pornography outright was far more dangerous, however, particularly in the Comstock era. Perhaps female dealers hoped their sex would shield them from scrutiny or spare them from prosecution if they were caught. Such expectations may have panned out on occasion for some women, but others were not so fortunate.

In a particularly poignant New York obscenity trial in 1884, a thirty-five-year-old German woman named Elena Del Varto testified that an undercover operative of the Society for the Suppression of Vice, Joseph Britton, had pressured her into obtaining obscene pictures for him. She told the court that Britton presented himself as a wealthy sporting man who sought "red hot photographs" to share with members of his patrician men's social club, the Union League. As she stated, he announced at their first meeting, "I am a queer fellow, do you see what a man I am. I have got money. I never go out without three or four hundred dollars. I am very fond of antiquities,

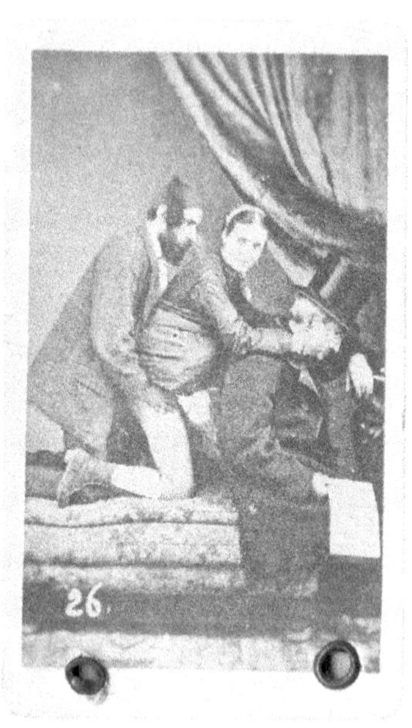

8.1 Front of a photographic exhibit in People v. Elena Del Varto, *New York County Court of General Sessions, 1884.*

COURTESY OF THE NEW YORK CITY MUNICIPAL ARCHIVES.

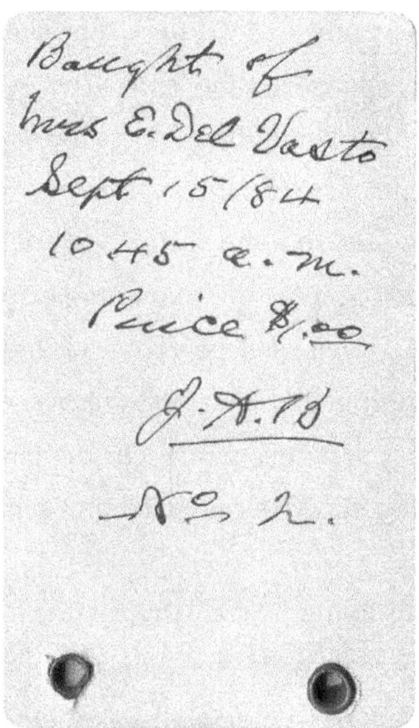

8.2 Back of the same photographic exhibit in People v. Elena Del Varto, *New York County Court of General Sessions, 1884. The initials J. A. B. refer to Joseph A. Britton, Anthony Comstock's chief deputy at the New York Society for the Suppression of Vice.*

COURTESY OF THE NEW YORK CITY MUNICIPAL ARCHIVES.

prints, and lithographs." Knowing that she was destitute and in frail health, he told her "wanted to befriend [her] and help [her] to an honest living." He then promised that if she found a photographer to reproduce two hundred fancy images, he would reward her by setting up a bathhouse for men that she would be able to run. According to Del Varto, a recent widow who had immigrated to New York three years earlier, she succumbed to Britton's repeated badgering only in the hope that the proposed bathhouse venture would enable her to support herself and her young daughter. Working with a photographer, she agreed to procure sexually explicit pictures for the agent of the society, including the one shown in Figure 8.1. In several of the black and white photographs, the sexual organs were hand-painted in reddish pink ink. Despite her poverty, poor health, and insistence that Britton had manipulated and deceived her, Del Varto's plea for acquittal or clemency was unavailing. On the basis of Britton's and Comstock's testimony, she was convicted and sentenced to one year in prison.[14]

While the core pornography trade fragmented among small-scale, often fly-by-night producers of cheap, insubstantial items, a coterie of New York booksellers who catered to an elite clientele realized that stronger prohibitions on obscenity had created attractive opportunities for profit. By making erotic books increasingly scarce and dangerous to own, the Comstock Act also made them extremely enticing to bibliophiles. To exploit this demand, upscale publishers and dealers such as J. W. Bouton and David G. Francis in New York began to offer special "rare books," usually imported from Europe, that depicted a variety of sex acts, phalluses, and flagellation scenes for well-to-do American connoisseurs. As a rule, these volumes were quite expensive, printed on high-quality paper, and ornately bound. Other euphemisms for pornography that appeared in the catalogues of fashionable bookstores and print shops were "curiosa," "facetiae," and "privately printed editions." The same dealers commonly included grandiose claims that they served only a highly refined, exclusive audience of book lovers, scholars, physicians, lawyers, and other professionals, who supposedly desired such texts solely for their educational value.[15]

In an effort to evade prosecution for obscenity, sellers of such works often described their sexual subject matter as a form of scientific, scholarly exploration. In typical fashion, Henry Spencer Ashbee praised an illustrated edition of *Ancient Symbol Worship: Influence of the Phallic Idea in the Religions of Antiquity*, published by Bouton in New York in 1874, as "written in a scientific spirit . . . for the purpose of arriving at truth." He added that the volume "is clearly printed on excellent paper, and does credit to its enterprising American publisher."[16]

In addition, highbrow erotic books were frequently disguised as "anthropological" studies of "aberrant" sexual behaviors or sexual "perversions." Much of this literature was produced by a group of English aesthetes known as the London Anthropological Society, who enthusiastically embraced sexual transgression and debauchery. Bouton's inventory included several erotic texts that were designed to appeal to the anthropologically inclined, such as two privately printed works by John Davenport, *Aphrodisiacs and Anti-Aphrodisiacs* and his six-volume *Curiositates Eroticae Physiologiae; or, Tabooed Subjects Freely Treated. In Six Essays, viz.: 1. Generation. 2. Chastity and Modesty. 3. Marriage. 4. Circumcision. 5. Eunuchism. 6. Hermaphrodism, and Followed by a Closing Essay on Death.*[17]

Bouton's holdings also gave an unusual prominence to English flagellation literature, a genre that had not played a major role in the market for antebellum erotica. He imported hundreds of copies, for instance, of an allegedly ethnographic treatise on flagellation that had been issued by John Camden Hotten, London's leading publisher of pornography in the 1860s and early 1870s, entitled *Exhibition of Female Flagellants in the Modest & Incontinent World.* Its provocative subtitle, *Facts That a Number of Ladies Take a Secret Pleasure in Whipping Their Own, and Children Committed to Their Care, and That Their Passion for Exercising and Feeling the Pleasure of a Birch-Rod, from Objects of Their Choice, of Both Sexes, Is to the Full as Predominant, as That of Mankind,* conveyed more of its true function. In addition, Bouton advertised a seven-volume collection of "Rare Tracts on Flagellation" for thirty-five dollars that contained most of the major English texts, including *Exhibition of Female Flagellants, A Treatise of the Use of Flogging in Venereal Affairs,* and *Sublime of Flagellation: In Letters from Lady Termagant Flaybum to Lady Harriet Tickletail.* (Despite the collection's large size, Ashbee found it deficient in at least one respect: "It is always the woman who wields the rod, never the man," he complained. "This, to say the least of it, is entirely one sided; for there can be no doubt that men have as strong a predilection for whipping girls (and even boys) as for being whipped themselves.")[18]

Bouton filled out his inventory of high-end, imported erotica with Mirabeau's *The Curtain Drawn Up* in the original French, Boccaccio's *Decameron* in Italian and French, Swinburne's *Poems and Ballads,* and libertine poetry by the Earl of Rochester. He also offered a "very scarce" illustrated edition in French of the Marquis de Sade's *Justine* for the steep sum of fifty dollars. David Francis carried selections of libidinous literature that were similar to Bouton's, under the heading "Facetiae." Francis's catalogue for September 1874, for instance, offered *The Romance of Chastisement; or, Revelations of the School and Bedroom.* The June 1875 catalogue advertised *The Sublime of Flagellation, Exhibition of Female Flagellants,* and a new English edition of the *Decameron* with "ten very free illustrations," all published in London.[19]

By the end of the century, purveyors of luxury erotica were also smuggling pornographic novels in from Paris, where London's erotic book publishers had moved to escape successive waves of obscenity prosecution by English authorities. One of the most graphic volumes to make its way across the Atlantic was an incest novel, *The Romance of Lust* (1879). Such works were prized by American collectors and commanded high prices. An anonymous U.S. bookseller's catalogue from the turn of the century offered an edition of *The Romance of Lust*, bound in Moroccan leather with a gilt top, for $65, the equivalent of more than $1,500 today. To enhance the book's appeal, the seller asserted, "Perhaps not more than twenty copies are now in existence." The same circular included what was touted as the first English translation of Sade's *Justine*, offered in a paperback edition for the relatively low cost of $25. It also advertised a complete set of Ashbee's three-volume, privately printed bibliography of what it described as "curious and uncommon books" for a hefty $150.[20]

Although limited circulation to a clientele of patrician aesthetes offered a degree of safety, it did not render Gilded Age book dealers immune to prosecution where explicit sexual images were involved. In 1880 Comstock and his chief deputy, Joseph Britton, raided the establishment of J. Sabin's Sons at 64 Nassau Street, which was operated by the sons of the renowned bibliographer Joseph Sabin. While in the store, the society agents seized 390 pictures and 25 books. Subsequently, both William Sabin, twenty-nine, and Robert Sabin, twenty-one, were indicted under state law for possessing a stash of nearly 100 explicit engravings. The bill of indictment attached a number of the confiscated prints, which depicted dramatic, vivid scenes of sexual intercourse, orgies, and erotic flagellation. In one exhibit, a standing, half-dressed man actively engaged in copulation with a woman lying on the edge of a bed reaches out to strike a cat that has clawed his naked buttocks. In another, two women whip a third woman's unclothed posterior with a bundle of sticks. The Sabin brothers were also charged with selling an obscene book called *The Merry Muses,* probably a version of *The Merry Muses of Caledonia,* a collection of bawdy drinking songs and verse attributed to Robert Burns. The notorious British pornographer John Camden Hotten had recently reissued the original work in a revised, more graphic edition, under the abbreviated title *The Merry Muses.*[21]

It is unclear whether the elder Sabin, who had retired from the rare-book business the year before to work on his epic fourteen-volume bibliography of books about the United States *(Dictionary of Books Relating to America, from Its Discovery to the Present Time),* was aware of his children's sideline. At least some patrons of the family business, which included wealthy collectors like J. P. Morgan, must have known they could obtain flagrantly pornographic publications from the sons, because Comstock stated that he had received numerous complaints about the Sabin store. His arrest ledger contains the notation: "In this place rich men's sons supply themselves with most obscene and filthy matter. Many complaints had been received and at last they were arrested. One book they sold was without exception the very worst I ever saw. It had a parody of 'Rock of Ages.' Most damnable."[22]

Following their arrest, Sabin's sons retained the law firm of Phelps & Spooner, which was able to obtain successive adjournments of their trial date. Despite Comstock's view that the defendants sold some of the most obscene materials he had ever seen, their counsel, presumably in an effort to have the prosecution dropped, sought to "plead respectability as an excuse and defense." This strategy failed to persuade Comstock, and the lawyers never had a chance to test it before a jury. Instead, when William's case was finally called at the end of 1880, he chose to forfeit his $2,500 bail rather than stand trial. Comstock's notes state that William was rumored to have escaped to Europe, where his father had extensive connections in the book trade from his numerous business trips. Thereafter, no further proceedings took place in the cases against either William or Robert Sabin. Moreover, the sons' brush with obscenity prosecution in 1880 evidently failed to sully the reputation of the father as a distinguished bibliophile. When Joseph Sabin died the next year, a lengthy, highly laudatory obituary on him appeared in the *New York Times*.[23]

A similar case involving booksellers to the elite who doubled as erotica dealers unfolded in 1887. The court file in this case is especially revealing about the investigative methods used by agents of the Society for the Suppression of Vice. It shows that Joseph Britton and another of the society's operatives, George E. Oram, visited a store specializing in rare books, located on Barclay Street in lower Manhattan, to inquire about the availability of erotica. It is unclear whether the society had received complaints about the establishment or whether the nationality alone of the proprietor, a Frenchman named George Maas, had aroused suspicion. In any event, Oram swore out an affidavit stating that Britton had asked an eighteen-year-old clerk at the shop, Rudolph Geering, if he had a copy of *Fanny Hill* to sell. Geering allegedly replied, "Yes, I have Fanny Hill with illustrations, the finest in the country, but I want $200 for it."[24]

Britton, most likely put off by the exorbitant price (about forty-five hundred dollars in today's money), quickly switched gears and inquired whether Geering had any photographs. According to Oram's affidavit, the clerk answered that he had "photographs from life and right in the act just the things you want." But such items were not kept in the store, presumably because it was too risky to keep blatantly obscene materials on site. What Geering could offer then and there were "copies of pictures . . . of nude women, in various postures" for fifty cents each. These were probably imported photographs of oil paintings exhibited at the Paris Salon that featured voluptuous female nudes. At the time, many art galleries and book dealers in the city were selling such items as substitutes for illicit photographs of actual naked women. In the same time period, enterprising booksellers were also offering abridged editions of bawdy classics like the *Decameron*—edited in a way that highlighted the carnal scenes—as "substitutes for suppressed books." As the Society for the Suppression of Vice reported: "These works, heretofore carefully concealed from public view, and kept by booksellers only to meet what some consider the legitimate demand of the student, or gentleman's library, are now advertised and sold by certain parties as 'rich, rare, and racy' books, 'amorous adventures,' 'spicy descriptions,' 'love intrigues on the sly,' etc."[25]

Britton chose two of Geering's photos, paid a dollar for them, and left. A short time later, he paid a second visit to Maas's shop. This time, Geering, obviously unaware of Britton's true identity, pointed to an associate and said, "A friend of mine here makes a specialty of erotic works, and will do business with you." To deflect suspicion, Britton slyly asked, "That is all right; but how do I know he is not a detective?" The friend in question, who introduced himself under the alias J. Archie, was actually Achille Verdalle, a representative of a nearby publisher, antiquarian bookseller, and exclusive art dealer named E. F. Bonaventure. According to Britton, Verdalle assured him, "You need not be afraid of me." The dealer then "pulled out a package wrapped up in white tissue paper, partially opened it and showed . . . a number of unmounted photographs of the most obscene character." To establish his credibility, Verdalle explained, "You see I am in the business." He added, "I sell to some of the best people in New York." When Britton prompted, "Sell what?" the dealer offered one of his profession's standard euphemisms for pornography: "Fascetious [*sic*] works" (Facetiae).[26]

Voicing his own concern for safety, Verdalle refused to transact business with Britton at his own store because of "trouble with Comstock." Instead, he insisted on going to his purported customer's office. Britton agreed, giving the dealer an address and telling him to come within half an hour. When he arrived, Britton again brought up *Fanny Hill*: "I understood the gentleman over in Barclay street [i.e., Rudolph Geering] to say that he had a copy of Fanny Hill with illustrations for which he wanted two hundred dollars." Verdalle laughed and said, "He has not got it, I have it, but not with me." Britton then asked Verdalle what he had brought. The dealer drew out a package of graphic photographs similar to those he had shown Britton at the store. He refused to sell any unless Britton agreed to buy the whole dozen, presumably because only a significant sale justified the legal risk he was taking. He set the price at twelve dollars, but Britton, a hard bargainer, persuaded him to accept ten dollars instead. Perusing his purchases in Verdalle's presence, Britton pursued his advantage: "I see one of the women in the picture is using a dilldo [*sic*]; do you sell them?" Verdalle replied that he did. "I have just got rid of three, and in two weeks will have some more and will be glad to sell to you." Sizing up Britton as a potential repeat customer, Verdalle asked, "Do you read French?" When Britton said no, Verdalle expressed disappointment: "I wish you did as I could sell you some very fine books, much better than 'Fanny Hill.'"[27]

On the basis of Oram's and Britton's testimony, Verdalle and Geering were both indicted for violating New York's Obscene Literature Act. Although Verdalle's affiliation with a reputable, upscale book dealer and publisher did not save him from arrest, his connections nonetheless proved valuable. He and Geering both pleaded guilty and received small fines. Class privilege thus did not guarantee elite booksellers who obtained pornography for rich men protection from prosecution, but it could shield them from the harsh prison sentences that were often doled out to more economically vulnerable defendants.[28]

By the late 1880s Comstock's pursuit of prosecutions against dealers of high-end, "aesthetic" forms of erotica increasingly risked prompting unfavorable publicity and charges of philistinism. In 1887 Comstock sparked a public relations debacle when he made the controversial decision to arrest the owner of an exclusive art gallery on Fifth Avenue, the Knoedler Gallery, for selling photographs of Parisian Salon paintings. In a pretrial ruling in the case, a judge in New York County held that thirty-five out of thirty-seven photographs confiscated by Comstock were not obscene. Afterward, Knoedler and his assistant pleaded guilty, and each was fined fifty dollars—clearly intended as a slap on the wrist.[29]

A similar setback occurred in 1894. On behalf of the Society for the Suppression of Vice, Comstock objected to a bankruptcy receiver's proposed sale of certain assets of an insolvent publishing firm, Worthington Company, that consisted of elegantly bound, "choice editions" of a number of erotic classics. Included among the company's holdings were Payne's translation of *The Arabian Nights,* Fielding's *Tom Jones,* Ovid's *Art of Love,* Boccaccio's *Decameron,* Rousseau's *Confessions,* the *Heptameron, Tales from the Arabic, Aladdin,* and the collected works of Rabelais. Comstock urged the court to order that the works be committed to flames because they constituted illicit obscenity. In the first use of the word "pornography" to appear in an American legal opinion, the judge hearing the case responded by drawing a pointed distinction between "high" art and "low" pornography that would become a staple of twentieth-century debates about obscenity. As the court stated, it was "very difficult to see upon what theory these world-renowned classics can be regarded as specimens of that *pornographic literature* which it is the office of the Society for the Suppression of Vice to suppress." The court's ruling emphasized the refined character of the imagined purchasers, as well as the elegant quality of the books themselves. "They rank with the higher literature, and would not be bought nor appreciated by the class of people from whom unclean publications ought to be withheld." In a stinging rebuke, the judge chided Comstock that to burn such "rare and costly" editions would amount to a "wanton destruction of property." With this formulation, Comstock was rendered not puritanical but "wanton" as a result of his crude overreaching.[30]

While erudite metropolitan booksellers stealthily procured limited-edition erotica for wealthy collectors, former dealers in mail-order pornography schemed about ways to defeat Comstock's offensive against obscenity in the mail. Some ingenious entrepreneurs tried to dodge the Comstock Act's prohibition on printed obscenity by using a stylograph, a type of mechanical pen, to reproduce the text of full-length lewd books. This invention allowed multiple copies of sexually explicit works to be copied in cursive rather than printed in type, so that the material in question did not appear to be a "publication." In 1888 an outraged U.S. senator railed against this latest subterfuge by smut dealers. "They succeeded in evading the law. The present law did not reach the case of written publications; it only applied to print. These scoundrels went to work and used the new stylographic process, frequently used by public men now, giving a fac-simile imitation of your letter and your signature." Their sneakiness was almost too much for the senator to bear. "They took these awful publications, which I shall not name here, and stylographed them from one end to the other and put them in the mail, and they are being sent forth all over the country to young people. Sir, there is no crime in the calendar, not even murder, that is worse than this."[31]

In a more comprehensive strategy to circumvent the Comstock

Act, interstate pornography dealers also altered their methods of distribution. Most notably, the vehicle of choice for disseminating sexually arousing print shifted from the U.S. mail to the private express company. Fortunately for erotica dealers, Congress, still uncertain of the scope of its authority over interstate commerce, did not act until 1897 to prohibit the circulation of obscene publications via express couriers and other common carriers. Thus, just as 1850s pornographers like George Akarman had seized on the U.S. Postal Service as a means of escaping local obscenity prohibitions, so Gilded Age pornographers, perceiving another regulatory loophole, flocked to express companies as a solution to national regulation of the mail.[32]

In the quarter century between the passage of the Comstock Act in 1873 and congressional prohibition of interstate commerce in obscenity in 1897, commercial couriers became a popular instrument for transcontinental transmission of sexual materials. Indeed, unregulated private express companies may have offered erotica dealers (and their customers) even greater safety and discretion than the U.S. mail formerly had. A representative late nineteenth-century circular from a Chicago dealer encapsulated the benefits of commercial couriers. Addressed to "GENTS AND SPORTS," it touted "a set of twelve, full-length Cabinet Photographs of *nude females . . . everything revealed, nature as plain as day.*" The circular emphasized, "We positively cannot send these photos by mail, we send *only by express.*" Patronage of this sort undoubtedly provided a significant boost to the profitability of the express industry as it competed with the post office to transport packages across the country.[33] Promoters of another purportedly immoral form of commerce banned from the mail—lotteries—adopted the same strategy. Following an 1892 decision by the U.S. Supreme Court affirming the constitutionality of a federal law excluding lottery materials from the mail, an assistant attorney general for the post office observed that express companies simply increased their lottery business "in the direct ratio of the decrease of that business through the mails."[34]

Like their antebellum predecessors, late nineteenth-century erotica dealers resisted obscenity laws primarily through strategies of evasion, subterfuge, and bribery. When those tactics failed, purveyors of erotica followed the model of their forerunners by rarely pursuing constitutional defenses to their prosecutions. In particular, there is no evidence that they ever sought to challenge their arrests on the grounds of free speech. In this respect, it is interesting to compare erotica dealers with another group of publishers and booksellers that Comstock vigorously prosecuted for obscenity and often lumped together with pornographers: social reformers advocating free love, birth control, and sex education. These individuals developed sophisticated legal strategies that ranged from technical challenges to their indictments to sweeping, innovative claims contesting the constitutionality of the Comstock Act.

In high-profile court cases and self-published political tracts, sex radicals voiced a number of important constitutional arguments. They boldly asserted that federal obscenity legislation infringed on the First Amendment guarantee of freedom of speech and freedom of the press. They contended that postal inspectors' use of decoy letters to get at the contents of sealed, first-class mail constituted unreasonable searches and seizures in violation of the Fourth Amendment. Opponents of the Comstock Act also protested that national morals regulation ran afoul of the Tenth Amendment by usurping the traditional prerogative of states to police morality. And reformers insisted that prohibitions on obscenity were unconstitutionally vague.

In 1878, birth control proponent Edward Bliss Foote and other "libertarian radicals" even formed a special organization, the National Defense Association. Largely bankrolled by Foote, the association litigated cases on behalf of individuals prosecuted under the Comstock Act and mounted numerous constitutional challenges to obscenity regulation in the last two decades of the century.[35]

It was Comstock's position that people who espoused free thought, sex education, contraception, and free love were all, as he called them, smut dealers. As a result, Comstock argued, distinctions between social reformers and pornographers were entirely specious. In his second book, *Traps for the Young*, he disparaged the strident "shouts" of "Liberals" and "infidels" about freedom and liberty as simply a pretext for their desire to peddle smut.[36] But sex radicals and freethinkers, who were just as adamant about drawing a line between their allegedly legitimate speech and the allegedly unacceptable speech of erotica dealers, often went out of their way to convey their strong disdain for commerce in sexually arousing materials. In other words, they defended their own unorthodox speech in part by condemning and marginalizing the expression of those with even less social capital. In the process, social reformers made clear that purveyors of commercial erotica were not welcome in the emerging civil liberties movement. Edward Bliss Foote, for instance, supported state prosecution of obscenity, so long as the crime was clearly defined to single out crass commercial publications designed for sexual excitement. The free love advocate Ezra Heywood likewise criticized the proliferation of lewd books and pictures as "alarming" and harmful.[37]

In contrast to sex radicals, pornographers typically relied on craftiness and stealth, not constitutional advocacy, to protect their interests. For Gilded Age erotica dealers, the goal was not to confront obscenity law, but to devise strategies that would enable them to make an end run around it. Rather than honing free speech challenges to the ban on indecent literature from the mail, pornographers chose to move their distribution business from the U.S. Postal Service to private courier companies. Indeed, in urging repeal of the Comstock Act, libertarian radicals were fond of pointing out that it was ineffectual in suppressing traffic in lubricious literature and other lust-exciting merchandise, given that the "forbidden articles can still be sent everywhere by express."[38]

When efforts to circumvent existing regulations failed, smut merchants continued to rely extensively on bribery to escape arrest, especially for violations of state law. If bribery did not succeed, they might flee the jurisdiction and forfeit their security rather than stand trial, as William Sabin did in 1880. In other cases, defendants with social and political influence might enter guilty pleas with the expectation that their connections would broker them a light sentence, as Achille Verdalle did in 1887. In still other cases, defendants might plead guilty and offer extenuating personal and family circumstances in the hope of mitigating punishment.[39] On many occasions, however, pornography dealers admitted guilt and stoically accepted the standard penalty—one year at hard labor in federal cases and a month to a year of imprisonment in state cases—as the painful cost of pursuing a profitable but highly risky business.

Despite the absence of constitutional advocacy, there is little evidence that purveyors of erotica internalized the moral reformers' portrayal of their trade as a sinister and villainous enterprise, tantamount to the poisoning of innocent youth. On the contrary, dealers in sexual materials actively subverted the power of legal prohibitions by repeatedly defying the law, even though they exposed themselves to lengthy prison sentences and stiff fines as a result. Pornographers also thwarted the objectives of obscenity statutes by formulating strategies of evasion that allowed them to operate covertly in the interstices of the law.[40]

In addition, many individuals arrested for disseminating salacious publications did fight their prosecutions, though not on constitutional grounds. Frequently, their lawyers pursued a technical defense in the hope of having the indictment thrown out of court. One tack was to argue that the specific goods a defendant sold did not fall within the scope of the relevant statute. The lawyer for the young printer Stephen Schall, for instance, contended that the one-page poem Schall had published, "Parody on Excelsior," did not constitute a "pamphlet" within the meaning of New York's Obscene Literature Act. Although the presiding judge rejected the lawyer's interpretation of the statutory language and Schall was convicted, the jury recommended clemency. In response, the court sentenced the printer to two months in prison and to remain confined until he paid a one-hundred-dollar fine.[41]

Another common strategy was to charge Comstock and his associates with perjury. Because agents of the Society for the Suppression of Vice were almost always the chief prosecution witnesses (and often the only ones) at obscenity trials, defense counsel regularly attacked the veracity of their testimony. After all, if their credibility could be called into question, juries might be persuaded to acquit. Typically, this tactic focused on claims that overzealousness led Comstock or his deputies to exaggerate or even falsify critical pieces of evidence. In Elena Del Varto's 1884 trial, for instance, she testified that Britton and Comstock planted dozens of obscene photographs in her home, far more than the handful she admitted having in her possession. In a number of other prosecutions, defendants went so far as to accuse Comstock of blackmail, asserting that he trumped up the charges against them in order to extort hush money.[42]

One of the more compelling courtroom defenses employed by alleged pornographers involved arguments that they had been entrapped into committing their offenses. In mail-order prosecutions brought in federal court, defense counsel often argued that Comstock's use of decoy letters from fictitious customers who masqueraded as devotees of fancy books and photographs was improperly deceptive and coercive. In actions under state law, defendants also maintained that Comstock and his network of undercover agents had lured them into violating the law. Evidence concerning the manipulative and heavy-handed investigative techniques used by antivice agents almost never persuaded judges to dismiss prosecutions, but obscenity defendants continued to press such strategies in court. In the early 1890s, a Saint Louis photographer named William Grimm pursued an entrapment defense all the way to the U.S. Supreme Court. Grimm had answered a fictitious letter from a salesman (in fact, U.S. Postal Inspector R. W. McAffee, the leader of a Western antivice society) asking for fancy photographs. Siding with the prosecution, the Supreme Court rejected Grimm's defense and explicitly approved the use of decoy letters and undercover investigations by government agents in connection with enforcement of the Comstock Act.[43]

Nonetheless, descriptions of the ways in which undercover investigators deceived suspects and induced them to sell sexual material, while rarely compelling to judges, may sometimes have convinced juries to recommend clemency or to acquit defendants altogether. In the face of rising suspicion, representatives of the New York Society for the Suppression of Vice were frequently forced to justify their investigative procedures before the court of public opinion. In their defense, they insisted that duplicity was an essential tactic in light of the entrenched skulduggery of pornography dealers. The "necessity of 'fighting the devil with his own weapons,'" they claimed, trumped "whatever doubt or moral objection overhangs the practice of decoy letters and kindred devices of the volunteer detective." Antivice society agents also cast their techniques as modern innovations that were designed to compensate for the antiquated, often corrupt practices of law enforcement officials, especially at the local level. One source summed up the society's justifications: "The ways of policemen seem slow, and those of District Attorneys devious, in comparison with the activity of agents of a 'society.'"[44]

Still, many observers were unconvinced that it was acceptable to use the "devil's own weapons" to fight crime. In 1881 an "anti-spy" bill was introduced in the New York legislature to make evidence obtained by "volunteer detectives [who] . . . make it a practice to go part of the way with offenders toward the commission of a crime, in the expectation of collecting evidence to convict and punish them" inadmissible in court. Although the proposed law failed to pass, it succeeded in inviting scrutiny of the intrusive and often unsavory methods that antivice societies mobilized to capture offenders. Even the *New York Times*, hardly a defender of the obscene book trade, agreed that it would be desirable for the legislature to develop clear ground rules governing permissible undercover operations. Such guidelines would have the salutary effect of restraining antivice agents from employing abusive techniques while collecting evidence and "decoying offenders," including the use of decoy letters to entrap "old offenders."[45]

Perhaps the most striking transformation wrought in the New York pornography industry by Anthony Comstock and the Comstock Act was the displacement of the metropolis from its decades-long role as the nation's smut capital. With the demise of the Haines-Akarman-

Farrell triumvirate in the early 1870s and the establishment of the headquarters of the Society for the Suppression of Vice at 150 Nassau Street—in what had been the thick of the city's pornography trade—the production and distribution of sexually explicit materials split off in a variety of directions. After Comstock's arrival on the scene, it was no longer possible to walk into a storefront like William Simpson's or Jeremiah Farrell's in downtown Manhattan and find erotic pictures dangling from the ceiling or fancy books displayed on shelves behind the counter. Nor was it possible to obtain an elaborate catalogue for sexually explicit novels, nude photographs, sex toys, and condoms simply by perusing the back pages of a New York flash paper and ordering the desired goods through the mail. To be sure, some producers and distributors of erotica found ways to persevere in late nineteenth-century New York. But the few that remained operated in a much more limited and clandestine manner.

The difficulties of pursuing a business in bawdy books and pictures within New York City nonetheless opened up opportunities for resourceful erotica entrepreneurs elsewhere in the country. In the Gilded Age, the manufacture and dissemination of pornography was more likely to take place in far-flung cities like Philadelphia, Saint Louis, Chicago, and San Francisco, or in small towns across America, than on Nassau or Ann Street in New York.[46]

In the context of late nineteenth-century New York, it is especially revealing to compare publishers of pornography with another group engaged in the business of promoting illicit sex—brothel proprietors. In the final decades of the century, the New York legislature passed a number of measures designed to stamp out prostitution in the metropolis. Instead of curtailing the sex trade, however, these laws seemed to encourage its growth. In large part, prostitution persisted in the face of stricter legislation because municipal officials chose to foster commercial sex as part of the city's prosperous black-market economy. Rather than enforce prohibitions on brothels and other forms of prostitution, ward politicians saw a chance to profit from the continued operation of such businesses. More than a few policemen and politicians routinely extorted hefty payments from owners of assignation houses, concert saloons, brothels, and other places where the exchange of sex for money flourished. Proprietors who played along received police protection, while those who resisted learned that an inconvenient police raid or arrest lurked just around the corner. In this way, Gilded Age laws aimed at safeguarding public morality and curbing prostitution, like earlier legal actions designed to suppress the obscene book business, had the effect of fueling the urban vice economy rather than dampening it.[47]

In the closing years of the century, the close ties between metropolitan prostitution and municipal politics grew even stronger. In the 1890s, large-scale syndicates arose that brought together brothel proprietors, real estate agents, ward politicians, police captains, and other individuals who had an investment in prostitution rings. These syndicates helped structure the nominally illicit economy of prostitution. Among other things, they facilitated the payment of protection money to city officials in exchange for staying in business, settled disputes among syndicate members, and fronted costs for legal fees as needed.[48]

Producers of erotica lacked the economic and political clout that investors in prostitution syndicates possessed at the end of the century. Without major publishers such as George Akarman or William Haines on the scene, those who remained were unable to rally municipal politicians, ward precinct officers, and other individuals who were in a position to profit from the erotic print trade. In addition, Gilded Age erotica dealers faced a critical legal threat that brothel proprietors did not. Because of Comstock's ability to initiate federal prosecution against any dealer who attempted to send sexual material through the mail, Tammany politicians generally lacked the ability to protect even politically well-connected individuals from punishment on obscenity charges brought in federal court. As a result, purveyors of sexual books and pictures in the city found themselves increasingly isolated and marginalized.

Given these harsh realities, New Yorkers who sought to make money from lewd publications faced stark challenges by the turn of the twentieth century. Savvy entrepreneurs in the city's sexual pleasure industry, however, soon discovered alternative ways of arousing and satisfying the public's appetite for sexual titillation and transgression. In addition to supplying venues for prostitution, early twentieth-century sex merchants came to offer consumers a wide array of risqué dance halls, burlesque theaters, and motion picture palaces that featured erotic entertainment. Each new form of commercial sexual culture in turn generated new rounds of concern and rising agitation over what seemed to be an endless expansion of obscenity in the city.[49]

While Comstock and John Sumner, who succeeded Comstock as secretary of the Society for the Suppression of Vice in 1915, worked tirelessly to enforce laws against obscenity, Gotham remained the nation's premier showcase for sexual commerce well into the twentieth century. With the passage of time, even the erotic book business made a striking comeback. Although the vibrant trade in fancy books that had been concentrated in and around Nassau Street never revived, the city witnessed a major resurgence of erotic publishing in the 1920s and 1930s. With distribution outlets no longer confined to a handful of blocks south of City Hall, inquiring consumers could find salacious publications in an assortment of locales, ranging from secondhand book marts on Fourth Avenue and low-rent magazine shops around Times Square to upscale Fifth Avenue bookstores.[50] In this twentieth-century incarnation as a capital of erotic entertainment, the city continued to offer a vivid example of the ways in which obscenity prohibitions promoted, as much as suppressed, the proliferation of sexual representations.

Appendix

Notes

Acknowledgments

Index

Appendix

Titles of Books Named in New York Obscenity Indictments, 1840–1860

The Adventures and Intrigues of the Duke of Buckingham, Charles the Second and the Earl of Rochester

The Amorous History and Adventures of Raymond De B— and Father Andouillard, Detailing Some Curious Histories and Disclosing the Pastimes of a Convent, with Some Remarks on the Use and Advantages of Flagellation

The Amorous Songster or Jovial Companion Being an Entire New and Choice Collection of Modern Songs Distinguished for Taste, Humour, Mirth and Merriment

The Auto-Biography of a Footman

The Cabinet of Venus Unlocked in a Series of Dialogues between Louisa Lovestone and Mariana Greedy, Two Cyprians! of the Most Accomplished Talent in the Science of Practical Love

The Confessions of a Voluptuous Young Lady of High Rank

The Curtain Drawn Up; or, The Education of Laura

The Directory; or, Pocket Companion Containing a List of All the Gay Houses and Ladies of Pleasures in the City of New York

How to Raise Love

The Life and Adventures of Silas Shovewell

The Lustful Turk

Note: Titles are listed in alphabetical order.

The Marriage Bed; or, Wedding Secrets Revealed by the Torch of Hymen
The Married Woman's Private Medical Companion
Mary Ann Temple
Memoirs of the Life and Voluptuous Adventures of the Celebrated Courtesan Mademoiselle Celestine of Paris Written by Herself
Memoirs of a Woman of Pleasure
Mysteries of Women; or, Guide to the [illegible], Containing Advice to Husbands and Wives, as Regarding the Means of Making the Marriage Bed, the Throne of Venus' Joys
La Rose d'Amour
The Secret Habits of the Female Sex
The Voluptuary; or, Woman's Witchery, A Romance of Passion

Notes

Introduction

1. *People v. Thomas Ormsby and John Atcherson* [*sic*], Feb. 23, 1855 (District Attorney Indictment Papers, New York County Court of General Sessions); Junius Henri Browne, *The Great Metropolis: A Mirror of New York* (Hartford, Conn., 1869), 381, 387–388; Helen Lefkowitz Horowitz, *Rereading Sex: Battles over Sexual Knowledge and Suppression in Nineteenth-Century America* (New York, 2002), 244–248; Lynda Nead, *Victorian Babylon: People, Streets and Images in Nineteenth-Century London* (New Haven, Conn., 2000), 161–189. Except where otherwise noted, all references to prosecutions in New York City refer to the manuscript District Attorney Indictment Papers for the New York County Court of General Sessions, which are held at the New York City Municipal Archives and Record Center in New York, New York [hereafter Indictment Papers, CGS].

2. *People v. Thomas Ormsby and John Atcherson*, Feb. 23, 1855 (Indictment Papers, CGS); Edward K. Spann, *The New Metropolis: New York City, 1840–1857* (New York, 1981), 368–369; Grand Fancy Bijou Catalogue of the Sporting Man's Emporium for 1870, 4.

3. "Law Intelligence," *New York Times*, Feb. 24, 1855, 3; Spann, *The New Metropolis*, 37–38; *People v. Thomas Ormsby and John Atcherson*, Feb. 23, 1855 (Indictment Papers, CGS), with attached letter of May or Wood.

4. "Obscene Books," *New York Atlas*, Feb. 18, 1855, 2.

5. *New York Clipper*, Feb. 1, 1862, 336.

6. On the importance of the distinction between liberty and license in nineteenth-century America, see Norman Rosenberg, *Protecting The Best Men: An Interpretive History of the Law of Libel* (Chapel Hill, N.C., 1986); and Sarah

Barringer Gordon, "Blasphemy and the Law of Religious Liberty in Nineteenth-Century America," *American Quarterly* 52 (2000): 682–720.

7. Francis Wharton, *A Treatise on the Criminal Law of the United States* (Philadelphia, 1855), 841; Thomas M. Cooley, *A Treatise on the Constitutional Limitations Which Rest upon the Legislative Power of the States of the American Union* (Boston, 1868), 596.

8. In his influential work *The People's Welfare* William Novak does just this, arguing that enforcement of public morality "remained a primary objective of criminal, municipal, and police regulation and a crucial obligation of local and state governments" throughout the nineteenth century. William J. Novak, *The People's Welfare: Law and Regulation in Nineteenth-Century America* (Chapel Hill, N.C., 1996), 151. For a similar perspective, see Herbert Hovenkamp, "Law and Morals in Classical Legal Thought," *Iowa Law Review* 82 (1997): 1427–1465. For an extended discussion of the historiographical foundations of *Licentious Gotham*, see Donna I. Dennis, "Obscenity Law and the Conditions of Freedom in the Nineteenth-Century United States," *Law and Social Inquiry* 27 (2002): 369–399.

9. Act for the Suppression of Trade in, and Circulation of, Obscene Literature and Articles of Immoral Use, 17 *Statutes at Large* 598 (1873).

10. Spann, *The New Metropolis*, 313. On New York's dominance of the publishing industry and its role as a national communications center, see Ronald Zboray, *A Fictive People: Antebellum Economic Development and the American Reading Public* (New York, 1993), 12; and Allan R. Pred, *Urban Growth and the Circulation of Information: The United States System of Cities, 1790–1840* (Cambridge, Mass., 1973).

11. A brief note about terminology is in order. Although "obscenity" was a widely used term in nineteenth-century America, "pornography" was not. Indeed, "pornography" did not appear in any version of Noah Webster's *American Dictionary of the English Language*, the leading American dictionary throughout the century, from its first edition in 1828 through 1860. When the term was first included in 1864, it was narrowly defined as "licentious painting employed to decorate the walls of rooms sacred to bacchanalian orgies, examples of which exist in Pompeii." Entry "pornography," in Noah Porter, ed., *An American Dictionary of the English Language* (Springfield, Mass., 1864), 1013. Only in the early twentieth century did *Webster's* begin to treat "pornography" in a broader sense, as a term encompassing literature as well as painting, though the dictionary continued to emphasize ancient history and lascivious frescoes. Entry "pornography," in *Webster's Revised Unabridged Dictionary* (Springfield, Mass., 1913), 1115 (defining "pornography" as "licentious painting or literature; especially, the painting anciently employed to decorate the walls of rooms devoted to bacchanalian orgies"). Nonetheless, as this book makes clear, a market for erotic

pictures and literature flourished in the nineteenth-century United States, even before the Civil War. I often refer to such representations by the code word that publishers and dealers who specialized in them developed, in other words, "fancy." In addition, however, I sometimes use the term "pornography" as an analytical category. In this context, "pornography" refers to literary or visual representations that presented sexual behavior or sexual organs in overt form and in a way that intentionally violated the moral, cultural, and legal taboos of the day.

1. "Beware of Print and Fancy Goods Stores"

1. New-York Magdalen Society, *The Magdalen Report: First Annual Report of the Executive Committee of the New-York Magdalen Society* (New York, 1831). My understanding of McDowall has been shaped by Paul S. Boyer, *Urban Masses and Moral Order in America, 1820–1920* (Cambridge, Mass., 1978), 18–21; David S. Reynolds, *Beneath the American Renaissance: The Subversive Imagination in the Age of Emerson and Melville* (New York, 1988), 62–64; Marilynn Wood Hill, *Their Sisters' Keepers: Prostitution in New York City, 1830–1870* (Berkeley, Calif., 1993), 17–21, 27; Helen Lefkowitz Horowitz, *Rereading Sex: Battles over Sexual Knowledge and Suppression in Nineteenth-Century America* (New York, 2002), 145–151; and Carroll Smith-Rosenberg, "Beauty, the Beast, and the Militant Woman: A Case Study in Sex Roles and Social Stress in Jacksonian America," in *Disorderly Conduct: Visions of Gender in Victorian America* (New York, 1985), 110–118.

2. *McDowall's Journal* II (September 1834), 70–71.

3. *New York Evening Post*, July 25, 1833, 2; minutes of the Court of General Sessions for New York County, held at the New York City Municipal Archives and Record Center in New York, New York [hereafter CGS Minutes], Mar. 14, 1834, 42.

4. For a representative later attack on *McDowall's Journal*, see "Another Exposé—M'Dowall and the Infidels," *New York Herald*, Jan. 14, 1836, 2. On McDowall's final years, see Boyer, *Urban Masses and Moral Order*, 20; and Hill, *Their Sisters' Keepers, 21.*

5. Reynolds, *Beneath the American Renaissance*, 87.

6. Laurence Sterne, *A Sentimental Journey through France and Italy* (New York, 1795); John Tebbel, *The Creation of an Industry, 1630–1865*, vol. 1, *A History of Book Publishing in the United States* (New York, 1972), 151; Elizabeth Haven Hawley, "American Publishers of Indecent Books, 1840–1890" (Ph.D. diss., Georgia Institute of Technology, 2005), 213–215.

7. Peter Wagner, "Introduction," in John Cleland, *Fanny Hill; or, Memoirs of a Woman of Pleasure*, ed. Peter Wagner (New York, 1985), 7–11 (hereafter Wagner, Introduction to *Fanny Hill*).

8. On the fusion of sexual explicitness and anti-authoritarian politics in eighteenth-century European pornography, see especially Robert Darnton, *The Literary Underground of the Old Regime* (Cambridge, Mass., 1982); Darnton, *The Forbidden Bestsellers of Pre-Revolutionary France* (New York, 1995); and Lynn Hunt, "The Invention of Pornography: Obscenity and the Origins of Modernity, 1500–1800," in *The Invention of Pornography: Obscenity and the Origins of Modernity, 1500–1800*, ed. Lynn Hunt (New York, 1993).

9. Lisa Z. Sigel, *Governing Pleasures: Pornography and Social Change in England, 1815–1914* (New Brunswick, N.J., 2002), 31–32.

10. Wagner, Introduction to *Fanny Hill*, 17.

11. Bradford K. Mudge, *The Whore's Story: Women, Pornography, and the British Novel, 1684–1830* (New York, 2000), 199.

12. Cleland's original also famously included a description of anal intercourse between two men, but this scene was excised from most nineteenth-century editions. Sigel, *Governing Pleasures*, 31.

13. *People v. Joseph Bonfanti*, June 9, 1824 (Indictment Papers, CGS).

14. Ibid. On the creation of illustrated editions of *Memoirs of a Woman of Pleasure*, see Wagner, Introduction to *Fanny Hill*, 15. For the 2007 value of 1824 dollars, see Inflation Calculator at http://www.westegg.com/inflation/infl.cg.

15. On Thomas and Whipple, see Horowitz, *Rereading Sex*, 34–35. On the Vermont printing, see M. A. McCorison, "Two Unrecorded American Printings of 'Fanny Hill,'" *Vermont History* 40 (1972): 64–66 (emphasis in the original); M. A. McCorison, "Memoirs of a Woman of Pleasure or Fanny Hill in New England," *American Book Collector* 1 (1980): 29–30. On the Holmes case, see *Commonwealth v. Holmes*, 17 Mass. 335 (1821). On Howe, see undated typescript, Cleland, BDSDS 1810, at the American Antiquarian Society. On the three Boston men, see *New-York Gazette and General Advertiser*, May 11, 1820, 2. On McLelland, see *People v. Joseph McLelland*, June 9, 1824 (Indictment Papers, CGS); and *Longworth's American Almanac, New-York Register, City Directory* (New York, 1824), 283.

16. "Modesty," *New York Daily Advertiser*, Feb. 9, 1833, 2; CGS Minutes, June 10, 1834, 194, and June 14, 1834, 213; "Indecent Prints," *New York Daily Advertiser*, June 27, 1835, 2.

17. Peter C. Welsh, "Henry R. Robinson: Printmaker to the Whig Party," *New York History* 53 (1972): 25–53.

18. Patricia Cline Cohen, *The Murder of Helen Jewett: The Life and Death of a Prostitute in Nineteenth-Century New York* (New York, 1998), 305; Horowitz, *Rereading Sex*, 216–218; *People v. Henry R. Robinson*, Sept. 28, 1842 (Indictment Papers, CGS).

19. Philip Howell, "Sex and the City of Bachelors: Sporting Guidebooks and

Urban Knowledge in Nineteenth-Century Britain and America," *Ecumene: A Journal of Environment, Culture, Meaning* 8 (2001): 20–50.

20. A Butt Ender, *Prostitution Exposed; Or, A Moral Reform Directory, Laying Bare the Lives, Histories, Residences, Seductions &c. of the Most Celebrated Courtezans and Ladies of Pleasure of the City of New York* (New York: Published for Public Convenience, 1839). On its novelty, see Timothy Gilfoyle, *City of Eros: New York City, Prostitution, and the Commercialization of Sex, 1790–1920* (New York, 1992), 131.

21. "A Political Scene in the Police Court," *New York Daily Express,* Apr. 16, 1839, 2 (portraying Democratic mayoral victory as the end of the "*moral* power of a Whig City government" and a triumph for rough and violent forces: "the Indomitables, the Butt-Enders and the Point-Enders").

22. "Effects of Butt-Endism," *New York Daily Express,* Apr. 20, 1839, 2.

23. "Democratic Celebration," *New York Evening Post,* Apr. 19, 1839 (announcing meeting of delegates from the Indomitables [and] Butt Enders, signed by Wooldridge). Patricia Cline Cohen also identifies "Butt Ender" as a reference to a company of firemen. Cohen, *The Murder of Helen Jewett,* 424, n. 28.

24. On the rise of sexual purity activism by evangelical women in the 1830s New York, see Smith-Rosenberg, "Beauty, the Beast, and the Militant Woman"; and Carroll Smith-Rosenberg, *Religion and the Rise of the City* (Ithaca, N.Y., 1971).

25. A Butt Ender, *Prostitution Exposed,* 4.

26. Ibid., 3, 5–6, 20, 8, 29. Adeline Miller was also an early financier of the flash press.

27. New York constitution of 1777, Article 35; New York constitution of 1821, Article 7, sec. 13.

28. William Blackstone, *Commentaries on the Laws of England: A Facsimile of the First Edition of 1765–1769,* 4 vols. (Chicago, 1979), 4:167–169.

29. *Knowles v. State of Conn.,* 3 Day 103 (1808); Broadside, *Destruction of Indecent Prints* (1835), held at the American Antiquarian Society; *Phalen v. Virginia,* 49 U.S. (8 How.) 163, 168 (1850).

30. Horace G. Wood, *A Practical Treatise on the Law of Nuisances in Their Various Forms; Including Remedies Therefor at Law and in Equity* (Albany, N.Y., 1875), 32. On the usual necessity of proving that a criminal nuisance affected the general public, nor just a few individuals, see *People v. Roger Prout* (1819) in Rogers, *The New York City Hall Recorder* (New York, 1819), 4:87. For a general discussion of the importance of nuisance law in nineteenth-century morals regulation, see William J. Novak, *The People's Welfare: Law and Regulation in Nineteenth-Century America* (Chapel Hill, N.C., 1996), chap. 5.

31. For valuable background on the English law of obscenity, see Colin Man-

chester, "A History of the Crime of Obscene Libel," *Journal of Legal History* 12 (1991): 36–57; Frederick F. Schauer, *The Law of Obscenity* (Washington, D.C., 1976), 3–8; and Marjorie Heins, *Not in Front of the Children: "Indecency," Censorship, and the Innocence of Youth* (New York, 2001), 15–29.

32. *Rex v. Curll* (1727), 2 Str. 788; Mudge, *The Whore's Story,* 164–172; Peter Wagner, *Eros Revived: Erotica of the Enlightenment in England and America* (London, 1988), chap. 2; *Regina v. Read* (1708), *Fortescue's Reports* 98.

33. M. J. D. Roberts, "The Society for the Suppression of Vice and Its Early Critics, 1802–1812," *The Historical Journal* 26 (1983): 159–176; M. J. D. Roberts, "Making Victorian Morals? The Society for the Suppression of Vice and Its Critics, 1802–1886," *Historical Studies* 21 (1984): 157–173; Schauer, *The Law of Obscenity,* 6.

34. Francis Ludlow Holt, *The Law of Libel* (London, 1816), 73.

35. *People v. Ruggles,* 8 Johns. 290 (1811).

36. Ibid., 297. For discussion of *Ruggles,* see Leonard W. Levy, *Blasphemy: Verbal Offense against the Sacred, from Moses to Salman Rushdie* (Chapel Hill, N.C., 1995); Robert C. Post, "Cultural Heterogeneity and Law: Pornography, Blasphemy, and the First Amendment," *California Law Review* 76 (1988): 297–335; and Sarah Barringer Gordon, "Blasphemy and the Law of Religious Liberty in Nineteenth Century America," *American Quarterly* 52 (2000): 682–720.

37. *Commonwealth v. Sharpless,* 1 S. & R. (Pa.) 91 (1815), reprinted in Edward De Grazia, *Censorship Landmarks* (New York, 1969), 35–40.

38. Ibid., 35, 36.

39. Blackstone, *Commentaries,* 4:41–42.

40. *Commonwealth v. Sharpless,* reprinted in De Grazia, *Censorship Landmarks,* 37.

41. Ibid., 38–39.

42. *Commonwealth v. Holmes,* 17 Mass. 335 (1821), reprinted in De Grazia, *Censorship Landmarks,* 40–41. On a technical point, Holmes also argued that the court in which he was convicted lacked criminal jurisdiction.

43. For a summary of state statutes banning obscenity that were enacted in the antebellum era, see Elizabeth Bainum Hovey, "Stamping Out Smut: The Enforcement of Obscenity Laws, 1872–1915" (Ph.D. diss., Columbia, 1998), 422–423.

44. My conclusion about the lack of significant municipal concern over obscene publications before 1840 is based on my review of all extant indictments between 1790 and 1840 in the Court of General Sessions for New York County. On the Court of General Sessions, see Mike McConville and Chester Mirsky, "The Rise of Guilty Pleas, New York, 1800–1865," *Journal of Law and Society*

22 (1995): 443–474; and Mike McConville and Chester Mirsky, *Jury Trials and Plea Bargaining: A True History* (Oxford, 2005), 18–43.

45. Colette Colligan, "Obscenity and Empire: England's Obscene Print Culture in the Nineteenth Century" (Ph.D. diss., Queen's University, 2002), 7.

46. Joseph Chitty, *A Practical Treatise on The Criminal Law*, vol. 2, *Containing Precedents of Indictments &c. with Comprehensive Notes on Each Particular Offence, the Process, Indictment, Plea, Defence, Evidence, Trial, Verdict, Judgment, and Punishment* (London, 1816), 42–44. The only changes in the language involve the substitution of references to the people and the state of New York for references to the king and the crown.

47. For the outcome of the Bonfanti and McLelland prosecutions, see CGS Minutes, Dec. 15, 1824, 154, and Dec. 18, 1824, 180. Over the next several years, Bonfanti appears from time to time in indictment records to complain about a theft of jewelry at his store, but never again in connection with selling obscene books. *People v. Levi Fitcher*, Nov. 7, 1826 (petit larceny); *People v. William Greenough*, Sept. 11, 1828 (petit larceny) (both in Indictment Papers, CGS).

48. Bailey's indictment is missing from the CGS Indictment Papers, but his trial and sentence are recorded in the CGS Minutes, June 10, 1834, 194, and June 14, 1834, 213.

49. This comparison of obscenity prosecutions to enforcement of other morals offenses is based on my review of the indictment records for the New York County Court of General Sessions for the relevant period.

50. On the prevalence of private prosecutions in nineteenth-century law enforcement, see generally Allen Steinberg, *The Transformation of Criminal Justice: Philadelphia, 1800–1880* (Chapel Hill, N.C., 1989). On private prosecution of crime in antebellum New York, see McConville and Mirsky, *Jury Trials and Plea Bargaining;* and McConville and Mirsky, "The Rise of Guilty Pleas," 448–459. On the percentage of morals prosecutions, see Jacob D. Wheeler, *Reports of Criminal Law Cases* (Albany, N.Y., 1854), 11–12; and McConville and Mirsky, *Jury Trials and Plea Bargaining*, 23.

51. McConville and Mirsky, *Jury Trials and Plea Bargaining*, 182.

52. The need to have an identifiable victim to pursue morals prosecutions was itself the product of a prior shift in American legal culture away from theocracy and toward secularization. As Lawrence Friedman has explained, in the colonial era, "since crimes were sins, and sins crime, there was no sharp line between 'victimless crimes' and crimes of predation or violence . . . An offense against God was an offense against society, and a positive threat to the social order." Lawrence M. Friedman, *Crime and Punishment in American History* (New York, 1993), 34.

53. Holt, *The Law of Libel*, 72

54. *Documents of the Board of Aldermen of the City of New York*, no. 88 (1836–1837), 567.

55. Ibid., 582–583.

56. Ibid.

2. Flash Weeklies

1. On forms of salacious New York commerce, see Timothy Gilfoyle, *City of Eros: New York City, Prostitution, and the Commercialization of Sex, 1790–1920* (New York, 1992). On the decline of deference politics and the rise of machine politics, see Amy Bridges, *A City in the Republic: Antebellum New York and the Origins of Machine Politics* (New York, 1984).

2. The use of "flash" as a slang word for urban male rakishness had transatlantic origins, as illustrated by the title of a London "gentlemen's" magazine from 1827, Edward Duncombe's *Original Rambler's Magazine; or, Annals of Gallantry; an Amusing Miscellany of Fun, Frolic, Fashion, and Flash: Amatory Tales & Adventures, Memoirs of the Most Celebrated Women of Pleasure, Trials for Crim. Con. and Seduction, Bon Ton, Facetiae, Epigrams, Jeu d'Esprit, &c . . . Enriched with Elegant Engravings.* On "flash men" see J. E. Lighter, ed., *Historical Dictionary of American Slang* (New York, 1994), 1:770 (defining "flash man" as a "man who is a member of the underworld or demimonde, esp. a thief, pimp, or swindler"); and George W. Matsell, *Vocabulum; or, The Rogue's Lexicon* (New York, 1859), 82 (defining "flash-man" as a "fellow that has no visible means of living, yet goes dressed in fine clothes, exhibiting a profusion of jewelry about his person"). On the association of "flash" with "dashing" and "swaggering" males as well as "thieves, tramps, and prostitutes" and "gamblers and patrons of the 'ring,'" see entry for the word "flash" in *Oxford English Dictionary Online*, 2d ed. (Oxford, 1989) at http://www.oed.com.

3. My understanding of the flash press and the sporting culture it chronicled has been informed by Elliot J. Gorn, *The Manly Art: Bare-Knuckle Prize Fighting in America* (Ithaca, N.Y., 1986); Gilfoyle, *City of Eros*, 92–116; Amy Gilman Srebnick, *The Mysterious Death of Mary Rogers: Sex and Culture in Nineteenth-Century New York* (New York, 1995), 53–54; Patricia Cline Cohen, *The Murder of Helen Jewett: The Life and Death of a Prostitute in Nineteenth-Century New York* (New York, 1998); Helen Lefkowitz Horowitz, *Rereading Sex: Battles over Sexual Knowledge and Suppression in Nineteenth-Century America* (New York, 2002), chaps. 6, 8; Elliot J. Gorn, "'Good-Bye Boys, I Die a True American': Homicide, Nativism, and Working-Class Culture in Antebellum New York City," *Journal of American History* 74 (1987): 388–410; Patricia Cline Cohen, "Unregulated Youth: Masculinity and Murder in the 1830s City," *Radical History Review* 52 (1992): 33–52; Philip Howell, "Sex and the City of Bachelors: Sporting Guidebooks and Urban Knowledge in Nineteenth-Century

Britain and America," *Ecumene: A Journal of Environment, Culture, Meaning* 8 (2001): 20–50; James W. Cook, "Dancing across the Color Line," *Common-Place* 4 (October 2003); and Helen Lefkowitz Horowitz, "Another 'American Cruikshank' Found: John H. Manning and the New York Sporting Weeklies," *Proceedings of the American Antiquarian Society* 112 (2004): 93–126. The most recent contribution to this literature is an anthology of excerpts from the flash press, together with a valuable scholarly introduction: Patricia Cline Cohen, Timothy J. Gilfoyle, and Helen Lefkowitz Horowitz, eds., *The Flash Press: Sporting Male Weeklies in 1840s New York* (Chicago, 2007).

4. On changing conceptions of masculinity and manhood in Victorian America, see Mary P. Ryan, *Cradle of the Middle Class: The Family in Oneida County, New York, 1790–1865* (New York, 1981); Mark C. Carnes, *Secret Ritual and Manhood in Victorian America* (New Haven, Conn., 1989); Mark C. Carnes and Clyde Griffen, eds., *Meanings for Manhood: Constructions of Masculinity in Victorian America* (Chicago, 1990); and E. Anthony Rotundo, *American Manhood: Transformations in Masculinity from the Revolution to the Modern Era* (New York, 1993).

5. Gorn, "'Good-Bye Boys.'"

6. Donald J. Gray, "Early Victorian Scandalous Journalism: Renton Nicholson's *The Town* (1837–1842)," in *The Victorian Periodical Press: Samplings and Soundings,* ed. Joanne Shatlock and Michael Wolff (Toronto, 1982), 317–348; Howell, "Sex and the City of Bachelors," 31–36; Iain McCalman, *Radical Underworld: Prophets, Revolutionaries, and Pornographers in London, 1795–1840* (Cambridge, 1988), 220–221, 225; Pisanus Fraxi [Henry Spencer Ashbee], *Catena Librorum Tacendorum* (London, 1885), 323–343.

7. Horowitz, "Another 'American Cruikshank' Found," 102–107; "Sketches of Characters—No. 11: Females in Masquerade," *Whip,* Mar. 5, 1842, 1; "Sketches of Characters—No. 22: The French Barmaid," *Whip,* May 21, 1842, 1.

8. On the innovations of the New York penny press and the origins of popular print media in the antebellum United States, I have especially benefited from Michael Schudson, *Discovering the News: A Social History of American Newspapers* (New York, 1978), 12–60; Dan Schiller, *Objectivity and the News: The Public and the Rise of Commercial Journalism* (Philadelphia, 1981), 12–75; Paul Starr, *The Creation of the Media: Political Origins of Modern Communications* (New York, 2004), 130–139; James L. Crouthamel, *Bennett's New York Herald and the Rise of the Popular Press* (Syracuse, N.Y., 1989); John D. Stevens, *Sensationalism and the New York Press* (New York, 1991); Andie Tucher, *Froth and Scum: Truth, Beauty and the Ax Murder in America's First Mass Medium* (Chapel Hill, N.C., 1994); William Huntzicker, *The Popular Press, 1833–1865* (Westport, Conn., 1999); Isabelle Lehuu, *Carnival on the Page: Popular Print*

Media in Antebellum America (Chapel Hill, N.C., 2000); and Alexander Saxton, "Problems of Class and Race in the Origins of the Mass Circulation Press," *American Quarterly* 36 (1984): 211–234.

9. Saxton, "Problems of Class and Race," 211–212.

10. Schiller, *Objectivity and the News*, 12–75, argues that the principal audience for the early penny press consisted of artisans and mechanics.

11. Walter Isaacson, *Benjamin Franklin: An American Life* (New York, 2003); Norman Rosenberg, *Protecting the Best Men: An Interpretive History of the Law of Libel* (Chapel Hill, N.C., 1986).

12. On sexual sensationalism in the penny press, see Cohen, *The Murder of Helen Jewett;* Stevens, *Sensationalism and the New York Press;* Tucher, *Froth and Scum;* and Lehuu, *Carnival on the Page.* The passage from *Martin Chuzzlewit* is quoted in Lehuu, *Carnival on the Page,* 49.

13. Crouthamel, *Bennett's New York Herald,* 35–36.

14. *New York Herald,* May 28, 1835.

15. Starr, *The Creation of the Media,* 135; Saxton, "Problems of Class and Race," 219–223; Schudson, *Discovering the News,* 33–34.

16. "From Our Office Window," *Weekly Rake,* July 23, 1842, 2.

17. "The Battery Spy," *Whip,* June 9, 1842, 2.

18. "A Street View," *Weekly Rake,* July 9, 1842, 1.

19. "Nuisances," ibid.

20. "The Thing's So Plain the Blind May See!" *Flash,* July 10, 1842, 1.

21. Frederick Hudson, *Journalism in the United States from 1690 to 1872* (New York, 1873), 546.

22. The earliest extant copy of a flash weekly is issue no. 6 of the *Sunday Flash,* dated September 12, 1841, which is held at the American Antiquarian Society. For the birth and death dates of the editors, see "Tom Quick," *Brooklyn Eagle,* Dec. 9, 1868, 2 (on Wooldridge's death); and Cohen, Gilfoyle, and Horowitz, *Flash Press,* 230, n. 18 (other dates). For circulation figures and a list of the flash weeklies, their editors, and their print runs, see Cohen, Gilfoyle, and Horowitz, *Flash Press,* 50, 223.

23. For background on Snelling, see Cohen, Gilfoyle, and Horowitz, *Flash Press,* 28–32; and Horowitz, *Rereading Sex,* 164–165.

24. Dale Cockrell, *Demons of Disorder: Early Blackface Minstrels and Their World* (New York, 1997), 12, 96. See, on blackface minstrelsy in antebellum America, ibid; Eric Lott, *Love and Theft: Blackface Minstrelsy and the American Working Class* (New York, 1993); and Robert C. Toll, *Blacking Up: The Minstrel Show in Nineteenth-Century America* (New York, 1974).

25. Cockrell, *Demons of Disorder,* 115. Early issues of the *Polyanthos* have not survived, but we can surmise the tenor of the paper from extensive coverage

of Dixon's prosecutions for libel in other newspapers of the day and from court records of his indictments.

26. Alexander Saxton, "George Wilkes: The Transformation of a Radical Ideology," *American Quarterly* 33 (1981): 437–458. Dan Schiller, "From Rogues to the Rights of Men: Crime News and the *Police Gazette* (1845–47)," *Media, Culture, and Society* 2 (1980): 377–388; Schiller, *Objectivity and the News;* "George Wilkes," *Dictionary of American Biography.* On Walsh, see Sean Wilentz, *Chants Democratic: New York City and the Rise of the American Working Class, 1788–1850* (New York, 1984), 326–335.

27. "The Ellsler Saloon," *Flash,* Dec. 11, 1841, 2; Horowitz, *Rereading Sex,* 465, n. 29; Cohen, Gilfoyle, and Horowitz, *Flash Press,* 41.

28. Wooldridge's testimony was reported in "Court of Sessions," *New York Daily Express,* Jan. 15, 1842, 2, and "Trial of Editors of the Sunday Flash," *New York Herald,* Jan. 15, 1842, 1. On Adeline Miller's role, see Horowitz, *Rereading Sex,* 465, n. 32; and Marilynn Wood Hill, *Their Sisters' Keepers: Prostitution in New York City, 1830–1870* (Berkeley, Calif., 1993), 39. For background on Miller's business endeavors and personal wealth, see Hill, *Their Sisters' Keepers,* 37–40.

29. "The Ellsler Saloon," 2.

30. "Big Levy," *Sunday Flash,* Oct. 17, 1841, 1; *Longworth's American Almanac, New-York Register, and City Directory, 1840–41* (New York, 1841), 391.

31. The *Sunday Flash* indictment is missing from the Court of General Sessions records, but it is recorded in the minutes of the Court of General Sessions. CGS Minutes, Oct. 22, 1841, 447. See also Horowitz, *Rereading Sex,* 179–186.

32. "Lives of the Nymphs, No. 11. Amanda Green," *Sunday Flash,* Oct. 17, 1841, 3.

33. Cockrell, *Demons of Disorder,* 130; Horowitz, *Rereading Sex,* 166. Dixon's indictment is missing from the district attorney's files, but it is recorded in the CGS Minutes, Nov. 19, 1841, 536.

34. An issue of *Dixon's Polyanthos* dated November 7, 1841, reprints portions of *Prostitution Exposed.*

35. *People v. Joseph Bonfanti,* June 9, 1824 (Indictment Papers, CGS); *People v. Joseph McLelland,* June 9, 1824 (Indictment Papers, CGS); CGS Minutes, May 17, 1834, 153 (Bailey indictment).

36. Mike McConville and Chester L. Mirsky, *Jury Trials and Plea Bargaining: A True History* (Oxford, 2005), 35.

37. Whiting served as New York County district attorney from 1838 to 1844. D. T. Valentine, *Manual of the Corporation of the City of New York* (New York, 1866), 525. On Whiting's background, and opposition to his appointment, see "District Attorney," *New York Herald,* June 5, 1838, 2; "Trouble . . . the Lion and

the Four Bulls," *New York Herald,* June 11, 1838, 2; and Horowitz, *Rereading Sex,* 182. After Whiting's death in 1870, credit reporters estimated the value of his estate at between one and two million dollars. Credit report for "Est. of James R. Whiting," New York, vol. 383, p. 729, R. G. Dun & Co. Collection, Baker Library Historical Collections, Harvard Business School (entry dated Sept. 8, 1874).

38. Grand jurors were required to be worth at least $250 of personal or $150 of freehold property. *Documents of the Board of Aldermen of the City of New York,* no. 53 (1844), 706–707; Schiller, *Objectivity and the News,* 140–143 (quoting *National Police Gazette,* Nov. 14, 1846).

39. "Scurrilous Prints," *Sunday Flash,* Oct. 17, 1841, 2 (reprinting article of the same name from the *New York Sun*).

40. Horowitz, *Rereading Sex,* 173–174; "Trial of Editors of the Sunday Flash," *New York Herald,* Jan. 15, 1842, 1. On the occupations of Marsh and Jones, see *Longworth's . . . City Directory, 1840–41,* 430, 356.

41. At the time, New York law contained a provision against extortion, but it encompassed only threats of physical injury or harm to tangible property, rather than threats to reputation alone. Oliver L. Barbour, *The Magistrate's Criminal Law* (Albany, N.Y., 1841), 140. After the Civil War, the New York legislature passed a law providing that extortion could be committed by exposing or imputing "any deformity or disgrace" to an individual or his family members or exposing "any secret affecting him or any of them." George R. Donnan, ed., *Annotated Code of Criminal Procedure and Penal Code of the State of New York* (Albany, N.Y., 1884), 232. On the history of blackmail and extortion in the nineteenth-century United States, see Angus McLaren, *Sexual Blackmail: A Modern History* (Cambridge, Mass., 2002), 45–62; Lawrence M. Friedman, *Guarding Life's Dark Secrets: Legal and Social Control over Reputation, Propriety, and Privacy* (Stanford, Calif., 2007), chap. 5; and Friedman, "Name Robbers: Privacy, Blackmail and Assorted Matters in Legal History," *Hofstra Law Review* 30 (2002): 1093–1132, 1110–1114.

42. George Thompson, *New-York Life: or, The Mysteries of Upper-Tendom Revealed* (New York, n.d.), 72–73, quoted in Paul Joseph Erickson, "Welcome to Sodom: The Cultural Work of City-Mysteries Fiction in Antebellum America" (Ph.D. diss., University of Texas, Austin, 2005), 198, n. 93.

43. *People v. George W. Dixon,* Jan. 17, 1839 (Indictment Papers, CGS), quoting article in indictment. The offending story was also printed in a theater journal published by Dixon, *The Critic and New-York Theatrical Register,* Dec. 13, 1838, 4.

44. *New York Herald,* Dec. 21, 1838; *People v. George W. Dixon,* Jan. 17, 1839 (Indictment Papers, CGS).

45. Article 7, sec. 8, New York constitution of 1821.

46. "General Sessions—Yesterday: The Dixon Libel Case," *New York Daily*

Express, Apr. 16, 1839, 2; "Court of Sessions," *New York Herald,* Apr. 16, 1839, 4; "Dixon's Trial—Its Developments and Consequences," *New York Herald,* Apr. 19, 1839, 2.

47. See, for example, the following articles in the *New York Daily Express:* "General Sessions—Yesterday: The Dixon Libel Case," Apr. 16, 1839, 2; "General Sessions—Yesterday: Dixon Case—Continued," Apr. 17, 1839, 2; "General Sessions—Yesterday: Continuation of the Libel Case," Apr. 18, 1839, 2; and "The Trial of Dixon for a Libel on the Character of Minturn," Apr. 19, 1839, 2.

48. "Court of Sessions, April 16th," *New York Herald,* Apr. 17, 1839, 2.

49. This argument was reminiscent of Blackstone's vigorous defense of libel prosecutions as a protection for liberty of the press. William Blackstone, *Commentaries on the Laws of England: A Facsimile of the First Edition of 1765–1769,* 4 vols. (Chicago, 1979), 4:153: "So true will it be found, that to censure the licentiousness, is to maintain the liberty, of the press."

50. Cockrell, *Demons of Disorder,* 119.

51. "Dixon's Trial—Its Developments and Consequences," *New York Herald,* Apr. 19, 1839, 2.

52. Ibid.

53. Ibid.

54. Thomas Starkie, *A Treatise on the Law of Slander and Libel . . . from the Second English Edition of 1830, with Notes and References to American Cases and to English Decisions since 1830* (West Brookfield, Mass, 1852), 2:255.

55. *People v. George B. Wooldridge,* July 14, 1842 (Indictment Papers, CGS), with attached copy of the *Whip,* dated July 9, 1842.

56. *People v. Thaddeus W. Meighan,* July 14, 1842 (Indictment Papers, CGS), with attached copy of the *Weekly Rake,* dated July 9, 1842.

57. "More Arrests for Vending Obscene Prints and Books," *New York Tribune,* Aug. 18, 1842, 2.

58. "Not Stopped Yet," *New York Sun,* Aug. 24, 1842, 2.

59. On antebellum conflict between middle-class and working-class uses of the streets of New York, see Christine Stansell, *City of Women: Sex and Class in New York, 1789–1860* (New York, 1986), 168–216. For upper-class anxieties about control of public spaces, see Sven Beckert, *The Monied Metropolis: New York City and the Consolidation of the American Bourgeoisie, 1850–1896* (New York, 2001), 47–48.

60. In contrast, Walter Kendrick, in *The Secret Museum: Pornography in Modern Culture* (New York, 1987), has interpreted the rise of sexual censorship in England and the United States as a response by elite males to the democratization of print culture, which made erotic materials accessible to working-class men, women, and children for the first time.

61. Presentment, CGS Minutes, Oct. 19, 1841, 436 (emphasis in the original);

"General Sessions," *New York Herald,* Oct. 20, 1841, 2 (which reprints the presentment).

62. "Sunday Papers," *Flash,* Oct. 31, 1841, 2.

63. "Lives of the Nymphs, No. 11, Amanda Green," 3; "Kept Mistresses," *Weekly Rake,* July 9, 1842, 2.

64. "Presentment," CGS Minutes, Oct. 19, 1841, 436. Similar complaints had appeared in the grand jury's presentment the month before. CGS Minutes, Sept. 23, 1841, 355.

65. "The Flash," *Flash,* Oct. 31, 1841, 2. On Boggs's profession, see Horowitz, *Rereading Sex,* 183.

66. CGS Minutes, Nov. 1, 1841, 472. On the Tombs, see Charles Sutton, *The New York Tombs: Its Secrets and Mysteries* (New York, 1874).

67. "Mr. Snelling's Letter to Judge Noah," *Flash,* Nov. 20, 1841, 3; "Query," *True Flash,* Dec. 4, 1841, 1.

68. George Wilkes, *The Mysteries of the Tombs, a Journal of Thirty Days Imprisonment in the New York City Prison; for Libel. . .* (New York, 1844), 10.

69. The antebellum fascination with the fraudulent nature of moral reform is perceptively explored in David S. Reynolds, *Beneath the American Renaissance: The Subversive Imagination in the Age of Emerson and Melville* (New York, 1988), 86–88.

70. "Our Intention—Hypocrisy," *Weekly Rake,* July 23, 1842, 2.

71. "Our Indictment," *Flash,* Oct. 31, 1841, 2.

72. "Adultery and Fornication," *Flash,* Oct. 31, 1841, 2.

73. Wilkes, *Mysteries of the Tombs,* 2. Modern critics of the persistence of obscenity prosecutions as an exception to the protections the First Amendment provides for freedom of speech have seized on the paradox first perceived by Wilkes. See David Cole, "Playing by Pornography's Rules: The Regulation of Sexual Expression," *University of Pennsylvania Law Review* 143 (1994): 111–177, 114; and John Tehranian, "Sanitizing Cyberspace: Obscenity, Miller, and the Future of Public Discourse on the Internet," *Journal of Intellectual Property Law Association* 11 (2003): 1–27, 4.

74. "Nuisances," *Weekly Rake,* July 9, 1842, 1; "Newspapers," *Whip and Satirist of New-York and Brooklyn,* Apr. 23, 1842, 2.

75. "Our Work," *Flash,* Dec. 25, 1841, 2.

76. "Justice," *New York Sporting Whip,* Jan. 28, 1843, 2.

77. "Adultery and Fornication," 2.

78. On female moral reformers and their use of tools of shaming and exposure to punish male sexual license, see Carroll Smith-Rosenberg, "Beauty, the Beast, and the Militant Woman: A Case Study in Sex Roles and Social Stress in Jacksonian America," in *Disorderly Conduct: Visions of Gender in Nineteenth-Century America* (New York, 1985), 110–118; and Stephen Robertson, "Seduc-

tion, Sexual Violence, and Marriage in New York City, 1886–1955," *Law and History Review* 24 (2006): 331–373, 339–340.

79. *Advocate of Moral Reform*, Nov. 15, 1838. On women's campaign for a seduction law, see Robertson, "Seduction, Sexual Violence, and Marriage," 339–342; and Hill, *Their Sisters' Keepers*, 140–144.

80. "The Libertine," *Whip and Satirist of New York and Brooklyn*, Apr. 23, 1842, 2.

81. "The Whip's CUTS at Matters and Things in General—No. 3," *New York Sporting Whip*, Feb. 18, 1843, 1.

82. Wooldridge owned a saloon that sometimes served as a brothel and may have been married to a prostitute. George Washington Dixon was engaged to a brothel madam. Cockrell, *Demons of Desire*, 135–137.

83. "Interesting to Christians," *Sunday Flash*, Oct. 17, 1841, 2 (emphasis added).

84. On the use of criminal libel charges against antebellum newspaper editors, see Rosenberg, *Protecting the Best Men*, 130–140.

85. Wilkes, *Mysteries of the Tombs*, 2.

86. For evidence of commitment to freedom of speech and freedom of press among abolitionists in the same time period, see Michael Kent Curtis, *Free Speech, "The People's Darling Privilege": Struggles for Freedom of Expression in American History* (Durham, N.C., 2000), 216–240.

87. Article 7, sec. 8, of the New York constitution of 1821.

88. On the moral underpinnings of nineteenth-century republican theory, see Sarah Barringer Gordon, "Blasphemy and the Law of Religious Liberty in Nineteenth-Century America," *American Quarterly* 52 (2000): 682–720.

89. "The Whip's CUTS at Matters and Things in General—No. 3," 1.

90. CGS Minutes, Jan. 14, 1842, 60; "The Flash *Is* Out," *Flash*, Nov. 20, 1841, 1.

91. "The Flash *Is* Out," 1.

92. Entry "Frederick Augustus Tallmadge," in David McAdam et al., eds., *History of the Bench and Bar of New York* (New York, 1897), 495; Horowitz, *Rereading Sex*, 181. Tallmadge served as recorder from 1841 to 1846 and again from 1849 to 1852. D. T. Valentine, *Manual of the Corporation of the City of New York* (New York, 1866), 529. On the Astor Place riots, see Ivan Bernstein, *The New York City Draft Riots: Their Significance for American Society and Politics in the Age of the Civil War* (New York, 1990), 148–151.

93. On Noah and Lynch, see Horowitz, *Rereading Sex*, 182; and Jonathan D. Sarna, *Jacksonian Jew: The Two Worlds of Mordecai Noah* (New York, 1981).

94. CGS Minutes, Jan. 21, 1842, 79; Horowitz, *Rereading Sex*, 184.

95. Entry "James Topham Brady," in McAdam, *Bench and Bar of New York*, 266–267. See also entry "James Topham Brady," in *Dictionary of American Bi-*

ography, 2:583; and *In Memoriam: James T. Brady: Report of Proceedings at a Meeting of the New-York Bar Held in the Supreme Court Room on Saturday, February 13, 1869* (New York, 1869).

96. "Trial of Editors of the Sunday Flash," *New York Herald*, Jan. 15, 1842, 1; CGS Minutes, Jan. 15, 1842, 64.

97. "Trial of Editors of the Sunday Flash," 1.

98. "Court of Sessions—Yesterday," *New York Weekly Sun*, Jan. 15, 1842, 2; "Trial of Editors of the Sunday Flash," 1; "Court of Sessions," *New York Daily Express*, Jan. 15, 1842, 2 (noting that the holdout was a talesman).

99. "General Sessions: The Flash Again," *New York Herald*, Apr, 20, 1842, 2; "Court of General Sessions—Tues. April 19—before the Recorder and Judges Lynch and Noah," *New York Sun*, Apr. 20, 1842, 2.

100. Ibid.

101. "General Sessions—Sept. 9," *New York Daily Express*, Sept. 10, 1842, 2; CGS Minutes, Sept. 9, 1842, 32.

102. "Court of Sessions—Trial for Publishing an Obscene Paper," *New York Sun*, Sept. 10, 1842, 2; CGS Minutes, Sept. 9, 1842, 32.

103. "Trial for Publishing an Obscene Paper," *New York Herald*, Sept. 15, 1842, 1; "Trial for Publishing Another Obscene Paper," *New York Sun*, Sept. 15, 1842, 2.

104. The three others concerned an issue of the *Whip* dated July 9, 1842, and two issues of the *Whip & Satirist of New-York and Brooklyn* from April 1842. CGS Minutes, Sept. 14–15, 1842, 40, 49, 53, 54.

105. On Wooldridge's trial, see "General Sessions: Another of the Same Kidney," *New York Herald*, Sept. 15, 1842, 1; "City Intelligence: Trial for Publishing Another Obscene Paper," *New York Tribune*, Sept. 15, 1842, 4; and "General Sessions—Sept. 14," *New York Daily Express*, Sept. 15, 1842, 2.

106. "General Sessions: Another of the Same Kidney," 1.

107. Ibid. The *Herald* report refers to one of the prostitutes as both Kate Hall and Kate Horn. For consistency, I have used the former name.

108. Ibid.

109. "Pleas of Guilty," *New York Sun*, Sept. 16, 1842, 2; *People v. George B. Wooldridge*, July 14, 1842 (Indictment Papers, CGS)—the guilty plea on Sept. 15, 1842, is noted on the cover sheet.

110. "Court of Sessions," *New York Sun*, Sept. 29, 1842, at 2; CGS Minutes, Sept. 14–15, 1842, 40, 49, 53, 54.

111. CGS Minutes, Mar. 11, 1843, 531; CGS Minutes, Mar. 15, 1843, 544; CGS Minutes, Mar. 23, 1843, 583.

112. "Our Enlargement and Future Course," *New York Sporting Whip*, Jan. 28, 1843, 2.

113. "Madame Trust," *New York Sporting Whip,* Feb. 11, 1843, 3, attached as exhibit to *People v. George B. Wooldridge and George Colburn,* Mar. 22, 1843 (Indictment Papers, CGS).

114. Cockrell, *Demons of Disorder,* 155.

115. Stuart M. Blumin, ed., *New York by Gas-Light and Other Urban Sketches by George G. Foster* (Berkeley, Calif., 1990 [1850]), 116; Lambert A. Wilmer, *Our Press Gang; or, A Complete Exposition of the Corruptions and Crimes of American Newspapers* (Philadelphia, 1859), 173; *Brooklyn Eagle,* Aug. 17, 1855, 2.

116. "General Sessions," *New York Herald,* Nov. 22, 1843, 3; Horowitz, *Rereading Sex,* 190–191.

117. For Camp's admission, see CGS Minutes, Mar. 13, 1843, 533. On the popularity of the *National Police Gazette* throughout the nineteenth century, see Elliot J. Gorn, "The Wicked World: The *National Police Gazette* and Gilded-Age America," *Media Studies Journal* 6 (1992): 1–15.

118. "Obscene Books," *National Police Gazette,* Nov. 15, 1845, 99; "Obscene Publications," *National Police Gazette,* Feb. 21, 1846, 212.

119. "Incest Case," *National Police Gazette,* Apr. 25, 1846, 285. For additional testimony in this case, see "Incest Case," *National Police Gazette,* May 23, 1846, 316.

120. See, for example, issues of the *National Police Gazette* dated March 3, 1849, and April 7, 1849.

121. Schiller, *Objectivity and the News,* 99–102.

122. McConville and Mirsky, *Jury Trials and Plea Bargaining,* 197–198.

123. "Along the Hudson River at New York," *Atlantic Monthly,* July 1868, 1–9, 9; "Literary Poisons," *Godey's Lady's Book,* Apr. 1870; "The Mayor's Man Friday," *New York Times,* May 23, 1873, 4. On the post–Civil War connection between censorship of obscenity and the stated need to protect children from corruption, see Edward De Grazia, *Girls Lean Back Everywhere: The Law of Obscenity and the Assault on Genius* (New York, 1992); Nicola Beisel, *Imperiled Innocents: Anthony Comstock and Family Reproduction in Victorian America* (Princeton, N.J., 1998); and Marjorie Heins, *Not in Front of The Children: "Indecency," Censorship, and the Innocence of Youth* (New York, 2001).

124. George Wilkes, *The Lives of Helen Jewett and Richard P. Robinson* (New York, 1849).

3. Fancy Books and Racy Pamphlets

1. Ronald J. Zboray, *A Fictive People: Antebellum Economic Development and the American Reading Public* (New York, 1993), 12.

2. See the appendix, "Titles of Books Named in New York Obscenity Indictments, 1840–1860."

3. On the American publishing practice of stereotyping texts, see Michael Winship, "Printing with Plates in the Nineteenth Century United States," *Printing History* 5 (1983): 15–27.

4. "Genuine Fancy Books: Beautifully Illustrated with Colored Plates" (New York, 186–) [hereafter Genuine Fancy Books circular]. On the copy held at the American Antiquarian Society, discounted prices have been marked by hand on the printed circular.

5. This figure represents Peter Wagner's count. Wagner, introduction to John Cleland, *Fanny Hill; or, Memoirs of a Woman of Pleasure*, ed. Peter Wagner (New York, 1985), 28.

6. *People v. Edward Thomas*, May 17, 1847 (Indictment Papers, CGS).

7. For discussion of sexual difference, domesticity, and bourgeois class formation, see especially Nancy F. Cott, *The Bonds of Womanhood: 'Woman's Sphere' in New England, 1780–1835*, rev. ed. (New Haven, Conn., 1997); Kathryn Kish Sklar, *Catharine Beecher: A Study in American Domesticity* (New Haven, Conn., 1973); Barbara Leslie Epstein, *The Politics of Domesticity: Women, Evangelism and Temperance in Nineteenth-Century America* (Irvington, N.Y., 1981); Mary P. Ryan, *Cradle of the Middle Class: The Family in Oneida County, New York, 1790–1865* (New York, 1981); and Nancy F. Cott, "Passionlessness: An Interpretation of Victorian Sexual Ideology, 1790–1850," *Signs* 4 (1978): 219–236. Note, however, that a significant body of historical literature has challenged the hegemony of the ideology of domesticity in antebellum America. See especially Karen Lystra, *Searching the Heart: Women, Men, and Romantic Love in Nineteenth-Century America* (New York, 1989); and Christine Stansell, *City of Women: Sex and Class in New York, 1789–1860* (New York, 1986).

8. *People v. Richard Hobbes*, Sept. 28, 1842 (Indictment Papers, CGS).

9. Grand Fancy Bijou Catalogue of the Sporting Man's Emporium For 1870, 5.

10. *People v. Richard Hobbes.* The quoted scene can be found, with small differences, in Cleland, *Fanny Hill*, 67. Up to this point in the story, Fanny has had sex only with a female brothel mate.

11. *People v. Richard Hobbes.* The quoted passage can be found, with small differences, in Cleland, *Fanny Hill*, 152.

12. In eighteenth- and nineteenth-century pornography, "cyprian" was a common term for a prostitute. The title named in the Hobbes indictment is similar to an extant English translation of a seventeenth-century sex manual by Sinibaldus (Giovanni Benedetto), which was first published in London in 1657. But the subtitles of the two works are different.

13. Pisanus Fraxi [Henry Spencer Ashbee], *Catena Librorum Tacendorum* (London, 1885), 305–306.

14. Peter Wagner, *Eros Revived: Erotica of the Enlightenment in England and*

America (London, 1988), 47–67. For bibliographical information on *The Amorous History and Adventures of Raymond de B- and Father Andouillard,* see Ashbee, *Catena Librorum Tacendorum,* 154–157; and Peter Mendes, *Clandestine Erotic Fiction in English, 1800–1930: A Bibliographical Study* (Hants, England, 1993), 429.

15. On English flagellation literature, see John Chandos, *Boys Together: English Public Schools, 1800–1864* (New Haven, Conn., 1984); Sigel, *Governing Pleasures,* 74–79; and Ian Gibson, *The English Vice: Beating, Sex, and Shame in Victorian England and After* (London, 1992).

16. The exclusion of allegedly obscene material in order to preserve the "chastity" of court records was a recognized exception to the requirement that indictments specify the nature of the offensive language or conduct with precision. *Commonwealth v. Holmes,* 17 Mass. 335 (1821).

17. The excerpts appear in *People v. James Jones,* Sept. 28, 1842, and *People v. Charles Heustis,* Sept. 28, 1842 (both in Indictment Papers, CGS).

18. A London copy of *The Curtain Drawn Up; or, The Education of Laura* is held at the Kinsey Institute for Research in Sex, Gender, and Reproduction in Bloomington, Indiana. The title page indicates it was translated "from the French of the Comte Mirabeau" and published in 1818. The place of publication is bawdily described as "London Putitin, Rogers and Co., Nineinch Street."

19. *People v. James Jones*; *People v. Charles Heustis.*

20. *People v. Henry R. Robinson,* Sept. 28, 1842 (Indictment Papers, CGS).

21. Indeed, two of the titles, *The Curtain Drawn Up* and *The Confessions of a Voluptuous Young Lady of High Rank,* turned up in Anthony Comstock's early prosecutions of New York pornography dealers for obscenity. See *People v. James McDermott,* Mar. 14, 1872; and *People v. William Brooks and Charles Brooks,* Mar. 14, 1872 (both in Indictment Papers, CGS).

22. See, for example, Genuine Fancy Books circular. It advertises European works such as *Fanny Hill, The Lustful Turk, The Curtain Drawn Up,* and *The Cabinet of Venus Unlocked.*

23. [Paul de Kock], *Mary Ann Temple: Being an Authentic and Romantic History of an Amorous and Lively Girl; of Rare Beauty, and Strong Natural Love of Pleasure!* (New York, n.d.). A yellow-covered copy held at the American Antiquarian Society contains an advertisement for Henry S. G. Smith & Co. on the back cover, which lists *Mary Ann Temple* for twenty-five cents.

24. De Kock, *Mary Ann Temple,* 7–9.

25. Jean Dubois, M.D., *The Secret Habits of the Female Sex* (New York, 1848), 3.

26. On the "great vogue" for erotic sensational fiction in the 1840s and 1850s, see David S. Reynolds, *Beneath the American Renaissance: The Subversive Imagination in the Age of Emerson and Melville* (New York, 1988), 211.

27. See Kimberly R. Gladman, "Upper Tens and Lower Millions: City Mysteries Fiction and Class in the Mid-Nineteenth Century" (Ph.D. diss., New York University, 2001), which discusses the European sources of city mysteries.

28. Michael Denning, *Mechanic Accents: Dime Novels and Working-Class Culture in America* (London, 1987), 85.

29. Elizabeth Haven Hawley, "American Publishers of Indecent Books, 1840–1890" (Ph.D. diss., Georgia Institute of Technology, 2005), 169.

30. Reynolds, *Beneath the American Renaissance,* 212.

31. Ibid., 223.

32. *Joseph V. Ridgely,* "George Lippard's *The Quaker City:* The World of the American Porno-Gothic," *Studies in the Literary Imagination* 7 (1974): 77–94. A subgenre of "American porno-gothic" literature focused on the secrets and horrors of urban life, especially in major centers like New York. Scholars generally refer to these mid-nineteenth-century novels as "city mysteries." On city mysteries in Europe and America, see especially Gladman, "Upper Tens and Lower Millions"; and Paul Joseph Erickson, "Welcome to Sodom: The Cultural Work of City-Mysteries Fiction in Antebellum America" (Ph.D. diss., University of Texas, Austin, 2005).

33. "Rich, Rare, and Racy Reading," *Venus' Miscellany,* May 23, 1857, 2.

34. David S. Reynolds and Kimberly R. Gladman, introduction to George Thompson, *Venus in Boston and Other Tales of Nineteenth-Century City Life,* ed. David S. Reynolds and Kimberly R. Gladman (Amherst, Mass., 2003), xi–xii.

35. According to his autobiography, Thompson was born in New York in 1823. Ibid., 315 (reprint of George Thompson, *My Life; or, The Adventures of Geo. Thompson* [1854]). For a full discussion of Thompson's life and work, see Reynolds and Gladman, introduction to *Venus in Boston,* ix–liv. See also Reynolds, *Beneath the American Renaissance,* 219–222.

36. Ashbee, *Catena Librorum Tacendorum,* 219; Reynolds and Gladman, introduction to *Venus in Boston,* xi–xii.

37. The epigraph from *Don Juan* and the first chapter of "Greenhorn," *Jack Harold; or, The Criminal's Career: A Story with a Moral. Tracing a Life of Villainy from the Cradle to the Gallows; and Showing the Awful Effects of Crime, the Consequences of Vice, the Power of Beauty, the Seductive Influences of Voluptuousness, the Blighting Results of Passion, and the Mysteries of City Life* appeared in a Boston flash paper called *Life in Boston and New England Police Gazette* on May 18, 1850, 1.

38. George Gordon, Lord Byron, *Don Juan,* ed. T. G. Steffan, E. Steffan, and W. W. Pratt (London, 2005), Canto 12, stanza 40, p. 430. Thompson also inverted two words from the original, which reads: "But now I'm going to be immoral, now / I mean to show things really as they are, / Not as they ought to be."

39. *Jack Harold*, as excerpted in *Life in Boston and New England Police Gazette*, May 18, 1850, 1.

40. "Editorial Salutation," *Weekly Whip*, Feb. 12, 1855, 1.

41. Reynolds and Gladman, introduction to *Venus in Boston*, xxxv, liii.

42. Ibid., xi.

43. George Thompson, *City Crimes*, reprinted in Reynolds and Gladman, *Venus in Boston*, 248.

44. George Thompson, *The Delights of Love; or, The Lady Libertine. Being the Adventures of an Amorous Widow*, quoted in Ashbee, *Catena Librorum Tacendorum*, 208–209.

45. Indeed, Karen Halttunen has argued that the sadomasochistic tendencies of American popular fiction arose precisely because middle-class reformers, such as antislavery advocates, were developing new humanitarian sensibilities that made representation of pain immoral and revolting. In this sense, the grotesque violence featured in racy novels flew in the face of all that bourgeois moral reformers were trying to achieve. Karen Halttunen, *Murder Most Foul: The Killer and the American Gothic Imagination* (Cambridge, Mass., 1998), 60–90.

46. *Confessions and Experience of a Novel Reader* (Chicago, 1855), 27, 62, 66–67.

47. *Home Evangelization: A View of the Wants and Prospects of Our Country, Based on the Facts and Relations of Colportage* (New York, c. 1850), 30–31.

48. Anthony Comstock, "Vampire Literature," *North American Review* 153 (1891): 160–71; "Satanic Literature," *National Magazine: Devoted to Literature, Art, and Religion* 2 (1853): 23–25 (quotations p. 25). Note that discourse about moral reform could itself sometimes function as sensational "porno-gothic" literature, by luridly drawing attention to licentious books and behavior. For insightful analysis of the relation between sensationalism and what the author labels dark reform, see Reynolds, *Beneath the American Renaissance*, chap. 2.

49. Reynolds, *Beneath the American Renaissance*, 222–223.

50. It should be noted that legal concerns were not the only factors influencing the proliferation of racy sensational novels in the late antebellum period. The international publishing success of Eugène Sue's *Mysteries of Paris* (1843) and G. W. M. Reynolds's *Mysteries of London* (1844), which served as models for the city mysteries genre in the United States, also helps account for the commercial appeal of sensational fiction to New York publishers. Nonetheless, writers, publishers, and critics of racy pamphlet fiction in the United States all believed that a key attribute of such fiction was its capacity to evade existing legal prohibitions on obscenity.

51. On the pervasiveness of prostitution in 1850s New York, see Timothy Gilfoyle, *City of Eros: New York City, Prostitution, and the Commercialization of Sex, 1790–1920* (New York, 1992), 119–178.

52. William Sanger, *The History of Prostitution: Its Extent, Causes, and Effects throughout the World* (New York, 1859), 522.

53. George Thompson, *The Delights of Love; or, The Lady Libertine,* quoted in Ashbee, *Catena Librorum Tacendorum,* 204.

54. George Thompson, *The Housebreaker,* 20–21, quoted in Christopher Looby, "George Thompson's 'Romance of the Real': Transgression and Taboo in American Sensation Fiction," *American Literature* 65 (1993): 651–672 (quotation p. 658).

55. On the relation between censorship and literary allusion, see Annabel M. Patterson, *Censorship and Interpretation: The Conditions of Writing and Reading in Early Modern England* (Madison, Wisc., 1984).

56. George Thompson, *The Mysteries of Bond Street; or, The Seraglios of Upper Tendom,* excerpted in Helen Lefkowitz Horowitz, ed., *Attitudes toward Sex in Antebellum America: A Brief History with Documents* (New York, 2006), 148; George Thompson, *The Ladies' Garter; or, The Platonic Marriage* (c. 1851), 14, quoted in Erickson, "Welcome to Sodom," 306; Thompson, *City Crimes,* in Reynolds and Gladman, *Venus in Boston,* 214.

57. "A Publishing Establishment Broken Up," *New York Tribune,* Sept. 16, 1857, 5; "The Seizure of Obscene Literature—Letter of George Akarman to the Editor of the Herald," *New York Herald,* Sept. 20, 1857, 8.

58. On the appeal that sensational fiction held for working-class urban audiences, see Denning, *Mechanic Accents.* After the Civil War, the price of such books fell to a dime, thus giving rise to the phrase "dime novel."

59. Frederick Hollick, M.D., *The Marriage Guide; or, Natural History of Generation; A Private Instructor for Married Persons and Those about to Marry, Both Male and Female: In Every Thing concerning the Physiology and Relations of the Sexual System and the Production or Prevention of Offspring—Including All the New Discoveries Never Before Given in the English Language . . . with Numerous Engravings and Colored Plates* (New York, 1850); T. L. Nichols, M.D., *Esoteric Anthropology: A Comprehensive and Confidential Treatment on the Structure, Functions, Passional Attractions and Perversions, True and False Physical and Social Conditions, and the Most Intimate Relations of Men and Women* (New York, 1854). On the wide range of marriage and sex manuals discussing contraception and abortion, see Janet Farrell Brodie, *Contraception and Abortion in Nineteenth-Century America* (Ithaca, N.Y., 1994), 180–203.

60. Brodie, *Contraception and Abortion,* 180–203.

61. Ibid.; Kathleen L. Endres, "'Strictly Confidential': Birth-Control Advertising in a 19th-Century City," *Journalism Quarterly* 63 (1986): 748–751.

62. Brodie, *Contraception and Abortion,* 194.

63. *People v. Charles Lohman alias Dr. A. M. Mauriceau,* Sept. 15, 1847 (Indictment Papers, CGS). The full title of Lohman's work reads: *The Married*

Woman's Private Medical Companion: Embracing the Treatment of Menstruation, or Monthly Turns, during Their Stoppage, Irregularity, or Entire Suppression, Pregnancy, and How It May Be Determined, with the Treatment of Its Various Diseases. Discovery to Prevent Pregnancy: Its Great and Important Necessity Where Malformation or Inability Exists to Give Birth. To Prevent Miscarriage or Abortion When Proper and Necessary. To Effect Miscarriage When Attended with Entire Safety. Causes and Mode of Cure of Barrenness or Sterility (New York, 1847; repr. New York, 1974). The city directory of New York for 1847 identifies Lohman's occupation as "publisher." *Doggett's New-York City Directory for 1847 and 1848* (New York, 1847), 251.

64. On Lohman and *The Married Woman's Private Medical Companion*, see Brodie, *Contraception and Abortion*, 231; Amy Gilman Srebnick, *The Mysterious Death of Mary Rogers: Sex and Culture in Nineteenth-Century New York* (New York, 1995), 100–102; Helen Lefkowitz Horowitz, *Rereading Sex: Battles over Sexual Knowledge and Suppression in Nineteenth-Century America* (New York, 2002), 209; and Linda Gordon, *The Moral Property of Women: A History of Birth Control Politics in America* (Urbana, Ill., 2002), 110.

65. For background on Restell, see Clifford Browder, *The Wickedest Woman in New York: Madame Restell the Abortionist* (Hamden, Conn., 1988); and Eric Homberger, *Scenes from the Life of a City: Corruption and Conscience in Old New York* (New Haven, Conn., 1996), 86–140. On class-based antipathy to Restell, see Horowitz, *Rereading Sex*, 200–208.

66. For Restell's indictment, see *People v. Caroline Lohman alias Ann Lohman alias Madame Restell*, Sept. 7, 1847 (Indictment Papers, CGS).

67. *People v. Charles Lohman alias Dr. A. M. Mauriceau.* According to Janet Brodie, the pills were to be used as a douching solution. Brodie, *Contraception and Abortion*, 231.

68. Entry "John McKeon," in David McAdam et al., eds., *History of the Bench and Bar of New York* (New York, 1897), 2:409–410. For Lohman's plea, see *People v. Charles Lohman alias Dr. A. M. Mauriceau.*

69. *People v. Charles Lohman alias Dr. A. M. Mauriceau* (emphasis added).

70. The minutes of the Court of General Sessions reflect no resolution of the indictment. See also Horowitz, *Rereading Sex*, 209; and Browder, *The Wickedest Woman*, 77, 103.

71. For subsequent editions of Lohman's work, see Brodie, *Contraception and Abortion*, 231. Brodie refers to nine editions, but an advertisement in the *New York Atlas*, May 20, 1855, suggests there were twenty by 1855. On the demand for information about contraception and abortion, see Brodie, *Contraception and Abortion*.

72. *New York Atlas*, May 20, 1855, 3.

73. Letter to the editor, *Brooklyn Eagle*, Aug. 30, 1849, 3, complains about

advertisements for *The Married Woman's Private Medical Companion* in the city's leading newspapers.

74. *Commonwealth v. Tarbox,* 55 Mass. (1 Cush.) 66 (1848); Andrea Tone, *Devices and Desires: A History of Contraceptives in America* (New York, 2001), 56.

75. April Haynes, "The Trials of Frederick Hollick: Obscenity, Sex Education, and Medical Democracy in the Antebellum United States," *Journal of the History of Sexuality* 12 (2003): 543–574; Brodie, *Contraception and Abortion,* 116.

76. Frederick Hollick, M.D., *The Origin of Life,* 20th ed. (New York, 1845), xix.

77. Haynes, "The Trials of Frederick Hollick," 552.

78. Ibid., where Hollick's philosophy is characterized as "sex-positive."

79. "Criminal Miscellany: Obscene Book," *National Police Gazette,* May 2, 1846, 290.

80. Haynes, "The Trials of Frederick Hollick," 557. On the conflict between "regular," mainstream allopathic physicians and "irregular," "eclectic," populist physicians like Hollick and later on Edward Bliss Foote, see also Gordon, *The Moral Property of Women,* 107–115.

81. Haynes, "The Trials of Frederick Hollick," 559.

82. Hollick, *The Origin of Life,* xxxv, quoted in Haynes, "The Trials of Frederick Hollick," 573–574. Though it first appeared in 1845, *The Origin of Life* went through ten editions in one year. Brodie, *Contraception and Abortion,* 360.

83. On the popularity of *The Marriage Guide,* see Brodie, *Contraception and Abortion,* 181.

84. Quoted in Haynes, "The Trials of Frederick Hollick," 563.

85. Hollick, *The Marriage Guide,* xiv, xvi–xvii, 20, 332–340.

86. *People v. John Farrell,* Mar. 12, 1855 (Indictment Papers, CGS): *People v. Frederic Brady,* Feb. 12, 1858 (Indictment Papers, CGS).

87. *Criterion: Art, Science, and Literature* 1, no. 2 (Nov. 10, 1855): 24; Walt Whitman, *Walt Whitman's Leaves of Grass,* ed. David S. Reynolds (New York, 2005), 159.

88. William B. Lockhart and Robert C. McClure, "Literature, the Law of Obscenity, and the Constitution," *Minnesota Law Review* 38 (1954): 295–395, esp. p. 325; Albert Mordell, *Notorious Literary Attacks* (New York, 1926), 122–137, which reprints an 1851 denunciation of *The Scarlet Letter.*

89. "Satanic Literature," 25.

90. In 1882, supporters of Anthony Comstock succeeded in suppressing the publication of a new edition of *Leaves of Grass* in Boston by using the threat of obscenity prosecution. Nicola Beisel, *Imperiled Innocents: Anthony Comstock and Family Reproduction in Victorian America* (Princeton, N.J., 1998), 164–167.

Even then, as Beisel astutely notes, the censorship campaign backfired: "Whitman took his book to Philadelphia, where the furor aroused by its suppression in Boston made it an enormous financial success" (165).

91. "The Immoral Literature of the Day," *National Police Gazette*, Dec. 8, 1866, 2.

4. The Publishers

1. 5 *Statutes at Large* 466 (Aug. 30, 1842); James C. N. Paul and Murray L. Schwartz, *Federal Censorship: Obscenity in the Mail* (New York, 1961), 12. In 1857 the prohibition was amended to include daguerreotypes, photographs, images, figures, and all other "obscene articles." The Tariff Act did not bar obscene books until 1873, when it was incorporated into the Comstock Act. Paul and Schwartz, *Federal Censorship*, 17, 23.

2. *United States v. Three Cases of Toys*, 28 Fed. Cas. 112 (SDNY 1843 no. 16499).

3. *United States v. Two Packages of Books Marked J.P. 112 & 113*, 1845, case A-3-366, box 49, Admiralty Case Files, 1828–1913 (Federal Archives, SDNY, 1845).

4. *Brooklyn Eagle*, Jan. 11, 1847, 2.

5. *Edw. Scofield v. Francis Kerrigan, Cornelius Ryan, Hiram Cure, James Jones, Charles Huestis, Childs, and William Bradley*, affidavits dated Aug. 16 and 18, 1842 (Indictment Papers, CGS). On Crolius, see Tyler Anbinder, *Five Points: The Nineteenth-Century New York City Neighborhood that Invented Tap Dance, Stole Elections, and Became the World's Most Notorious Slum* (New York, 2001), 156.

6. *Edw. Scofield v. Francis Kerrigan, Cornelius Ryan, Hiram Cure, James Jones, Charles Huestis, Childs, and William Bradley*, affidavits dated Aug. 16 and 18, 1842 (Indictment Papers, CGS).

7. *People v. Cornelius Ryan* (Obscene Prints), Sept. 28, 1842 (Indictment Papers, CGS); affidavit of James Craft, in *People v. Henry R. Robinson*, Sept. 20, 1842 (Indictment Papers, CGS). For the 2007 value of 1842 dollars, see the Inflation Calculator at http://www.westegg.com/inflation/infl.cgi.

8. *Edw. Scofield v. Francis Kerrigan, Cornelius Ryan, Hiram Cure, James Jones, Charles Huestis, Childs, and William Bradley*, affidavits dated Aug. 16 and 18, 1842 (Indictment Papers, CGS); "City Intelligence: Police Office—Arrest for Vending Obscene Books, Prints, &c.," *New York Daily Tribune*, Aug. 17, 1842, 3; "City Intelligence: More Developments in Wall Street, &c.," *New York Herald*, Aug. 18, 1842, 2; *People v. Charles Huestis*, Sept. 28, 1842 (Indictment Papers, CGS); *People v. William Bradley*, Sept. 28, 1842 (Indictment Papers, CGS).

9. Peter C. Welsh, "Henry R. Robinson: Printmaker to the Whig Party,"

New York History 53 (1972): 25–53; "City Intelligence: More Developments in Wall Street, &c.," *New York Herald*, Aug. 18, 1842, 2; "More Arrests for Vending Obscene Prints and Books," *New York Tribune*, Aug. 18, 1842, 3.

10. *People v. Henry R. Robinson*; *People v. Francis Kerrigan*, Sept. 28, 1842; *People v. Cornelius Ryan* (Obscene Books), Sept. 28, 1842; *People v. Cornelius Ryan* (Obscene Prints); *People v. Hiram Cure*, Sept. 28, 1842; *People v. James Jones*, Sept. 28, 1842; *People v. Charles Huestis*; *People v. William Bradley*, Sept. 28, 1842; *People v. Richard Hobbes*, Sept. 28, 1842 (all in Indictment Papers, CGS). For the original sample indictment, see Joseph Chitty, *A Practical Treatise on the Criminal Law*, vol. 2: *Containing Precedents of Indictments &c. with Comprehensive Notes on Each Particular Offence, the Process, Indictment, Plea, Defence, Evidence, Trial, Verdict, Judgment, and Punishment* (London, 1816), 42–44. The first American edition of this work appeared in 1819.

11. *People v. Henry R. Robinson*. On Dugdale, see Iain McCalman, *Radical Underworld: Prophets, Revolutionaries, and Pornographers in London, 1795–1840* (Cambridge, 1988), chap. 10; Lynda Nead, *Victorian Babylon: People, Streets and Images in Nineteenth-Century London* (New Haven, Conn., 2000), 178–182; Lisa Z. Sigel, *Governing Pleasures: Pornography and Social Change in England, 1815–1914* (New Brunswick, N.J., 2002), 16–23; and Colette Colligan, "Obscenity and Empire: England's Obscene Print Culture in the Nineteenth Century" (Ph.D. diss., Queen's University, 2002). On *The Auto-Biography of a Footman*, see Sigel, *Governing Pleasures*, 46.

12. On stereotyping, see Michael Winship, "Printing with Plates in the Nineteenth-Century United States," *Printing History* 5 (1983): 15–27; and Paul Starr, *The Creation of the Media: Political Origins of Modern Communications* (New York, 2004), 128–129.

13. On Robinson's prints, see Helen Lefkowitz Horowitz, *Rereading Sex: Battles over Sexual Knowledge and Suppression in Nineteenth-Century America* (New York, 2002), 214–217.

14. CGS Minutes, Jan. 9, 1843, 360 (failure to appear); CGS Minutes, Mar. 10, 1843, 524 (surrender by surety).

15. *Brooklyn Eagle*, Mar. 10, 1843, 2 (emphasis in the original). On the Whig party and moral reform, see Daniel Walker Howe, *The Political Culture of the American Whigs* (Chicago, 1979).

16. Affidavit of James Craft, in *People v. Henry R. Robinson*. Craft is identified as a publisher in the city directory for 1841–1842. *Longworth's American Almanac, New-York Register, and City Directory, 1841–42* (New York, 1841), 198.

17. "City Intelligence: Obscene Print Seller Surrendered," *New York Herald*, Mar. 10, 1843, 2 (describing Robinson as a "great manufacturer" of obscene prints); Horowitz, *Rereading Sex*, 222–223.

18. "Obscene Pictures," *New York Sporting Whip,* Feb. 11, 1843, 4.

19. *People v. Adam Hartman and Charles Lee,* Oct. 18, 1848 (Indictment Papers, CGS); CGS Minutes, Oct. 20, 1848, 157 (trial and conviction); CGS Minutes, Oct. 21, 1848, 163 (sentence).

20. *People v. Michael Sullivan,* June 12, 1849 (Indictment Papers, CGS). Sullivan may have had some connection with the *National Police Gazette,* because one of its publishers, Enoch Camp, posted his bail. Indicted by the grand jury, Sullivan pleaded guilty and received a suspended sentence. CGS Minutes, June 21, 1849, 156.

21. In the first volume of Henry Mayhew, *London Labour and the London Poor* (London, 1851), the author described a "sham indecent street-trade," wherein men would stand outside shops that displayed "shameless publications" in their windows and pretend to sell the publications at a discount in sealed packages to passers-by. When the customers opened their packages, they found Christmas carols or sermons, instead of smutty pictures. Colligan, "Obscenity and Empire," 9. For a New York example of a similar swindle, see "An Old Man Taken In," *New York Weekly Herald,* Nov. 18, 1848, 166.

22. Five hand-colored indecent prints (1850), attached to complaint of A. Furnald against John Sweeney, dated June 27, 1850, held at the American Antiquarian Society in uncatalogued Leo Hershkowitz collection.

23. "City Intelligence: More Developments in Wall Street, &c.," *New York Herald,* Aug. 18, 1842, 2.

24. Affidavit of Charles Huestis, in *People v. Richard Hobbes.*

25. "Arrest of Hobbes," *New York Herald,* Aug. 18, 1842, 2; *People v. Richard Hobbes,* Sept. 28, 1842 (Indictment Papers, CGS); CGS Minutes, Jan. 9, 1843, 360.

26. CGS Minutes, Jan. 11, 1843, 370, 374; "General Sessions," *New York Herald,* Jan. 21, 1843, 2.

27. The cover page of Ryan's indictment for selling obscene books contains this notation: "Nol. Pros. by order of the court. Jany 16, 1843." Ryan pleaded guilty to the obscene prints indictment the same day. *People v. Cornelius Ryan* ("Obscene Books"); *People v. Cornelius Ryan* ("Obscene Prints"). For Ryan's sentence and his poverty, see CGS Minutes, Jan. 16, 1843, 389; "General Sessions," *New York Herald,* Jan. 21, 1843, 2; and *New York Tribune,* Jan. 21, 1843, 3; on the forfeiture of recognizances, see CGS Minutes, Jan. 9, 1843, 360 (entries for Kerrigan and Jones).

28. Pisanus Fraxi [Henry Spencer Ashbee], *Index Librorum Prohibitorum* (London, 1877), xxxi. The three volumes of Ashbee's bibliography, all published under the pseudonym Pisanus Fraxi, consist of *Index Librorum Prohibitorum*; *Centuria Librorum Absconditorum* (London, 1879); and *Catena Librorum Tacendorum* (London, 1885). They have been reprinted as *The Encyclopedia*

of Erotic Literature (New York, 1962). The last volume in the series devoted a significant section to American erotic and semierotic works. In nineteenth-century sources, the spelling of William Haines's name varied widely, often appearing as Hain, Haine, or Haynes. But both Ashbee, who was the most knowledgeable nineteenth-century bibliographer of erotica, and several contemporaneous newspapers record the mysterious publisher's last name as Haines. I therefore adopt that spelling throughout this book, except when quoting from sources that record his name differently.

29. For other accounts of Haines's preeminence as a pornographer, see Anthony Comstock, *Frauds Exposed; or, How the People Are Deceived and Robbed, and Youth Corrupted, Being a Full Exposure of Various Schemes Operated through the Mails, and Unearthed by the Author in a Seven Years' Service as a Special Agent of the Post Office Department and Secretary and Chief Agent of the New York Society for the Suppression of Vice* (New York, 1880), 388; and entry "William Haynes and Mary E. Haynes," in "Names and Description of Persons Dealing in Obscene Literature, Not Arrested, but from Whom Stock Was Seized during the Year 1872. Also Those Forced to Give Up, and Get out of the Business, during the Same Year" [hereafter 1872 YMCA Log of Persons Not Arrested] in the Papers of the New York Society for the Suppression of Vice, held in the Manuscript Division, Library of Congress; "Obscene Books: Their Publishers and Profits," *Pomeroy's Democrat*, Oct. 28, 1871, 2; Gustav Lening, *The Dark Side of New York Life and Its Criminal Classes from Fifth Avenue down to the Five Points* (New York, 1873), 652.

30. Comstock, *Frauds Exposed*, 388.

31. Lening, *The Dark Side of New York Life*, 652. Given the repetition of the year, 1846, and the identity of "W. Haines," it is likely that Ashbee relied on Lening's account for his own chronology.

32. Comstock, *Frauds Exposed*, 388; entry "William Haynes and Mary E. Haynes," in 1872 YMCA Log of Persons Not Arrested.

33. Comstock, *Frauds Exposed*, 388.

34. Michael Winship, *Literary Publishing in the Mid-Nineteenth Century: The Business of Ticknor and Fields* (New York, 1995); Winship, "Printing with Plates in the Nineteenth Century United States"; Elizabeth Haven Hawley, "American Publishers of Indecent Books, 1840–1890" (Ph.D. diss., Georgia Institute of Technology, 2005).

35. "The Seizure of Obscene Literature," *New York Herald*, Sept. 17, 1857, 5.

36. Lening, *The Dark Side of New York Life*, 652. See also Comstock, *Frauds Exposed*, 388.

37. Haven Hawley's bibliography of nineteenth-century American erotica shows no surviving imprints by Haines. Hawley, "American Publishers of Indecent Books," 421–422.

38. *People v. William Hain,* July 17, 1846 (Indictment Papers, CGS).

39. "Trial for Vending Obscene Books, &c.," *National Police Gazette,* July 25, 1846, 388; *New York Herald,* July 23, 1846, 2; *People v. William Hain,* July 17, 1846 (Indictment Papers, CGS).

40. "Obscene Books," *National Police Gazette,* June 2, 1849, 3, quoted in Horowitz, *Rereading Sex,* 224.

41. "Police Items: Selling Obscene Books," *National Police Gazette,* Apr. 17, 1847, 251.

42. *People v. Edward Thomas,* May 17, 1847 (Indictment Papers, CGS). Though the indictment referred to Edward Thomas, the *National Police Gazette* story identified the defendant as Edward Thomas Scofield.

43. Ronald Zboray, *A Fictive People: Antebellum Economic Development and the American Reading Public* (New York, 1993), 11.

44. CGS Minutes, Jan. 9, 1843, 359. On the practice of detaining material witnesses, see Wesley Oliver, "The Rise and Fall Of Material Witness Detention in Nineteenth-Century New York," *New York University Journal of Law and Liberty* 1 (2005): 726–781.

45. *People v. Edward Thomas;* "General Sessions," *National Police Gazette,* May 29, 1847, 302 (sentence).

46. Horowitz, *Rereading Sex,* 224.

47. *People v. Albert Gazeley,* Sept. 22, 1853 (Indictment Papers, CGS).

48. For an early sale of this work, see *People v. Richard Hobbes,* Sept. 28, 1842 (CGS Indictment Papers).

49. It is also possible that Gazeley avoided further prosecution by bribing the authorities. For an early charge that the police used obscenity indictments both to obtain bribes and to force cooperation, see George Wilkes, *The Mysteries of the Tombs, a Journal of Thirty Days Imprisonment in the New York City Prison; for Libel . . .* (New York, 1844), 1.

50. *People v. William Hain,* July 17, 1846 (Indictment Papers, CGS).

51. *People v. William Haynes,* Oct. 18, 1853 (Indictment Papers, CGS). On Dugdale's fictitious imprint, see Peter Mendes, *Clandestine Erotic Fiction in English, 1800–1930: A Bibliographical Study* (Hants, England, 1993), 205. On the plot of *La Rose d'Amour,* see Ashbee, *Catena Librorum Tacendorum,* 161–163. Ashbee surmised that *La Rose d'Amour* was an original American work from 1849, but recent scholars have persuasively disputed this assertion and have assigned it English provenance. Colligan, "Obscenity and Empire," 97–100, esp. n.67.

52. *The Life and Adventures of Cicily Martin* (New York, 1846). For a comprehensive analysis of the authenticity of the text and illustrations in the volume held by the American Antiquarian Society, see Hawley, "American Publishers of Indecent Books," 181–183.

53. *People v. William Haynes,* Oct. 18, 1853 (Indictment Papers, CGS).

54. "Obscene Books: Their Publishers and Profits," *Pomeroy's Democrat,* Oct. 28, 1871, 2; entry "William Haynes and Mary E. Haynes," in 1872 YMCA Log of Persons Not Arrested. For additional evidence that 1850s pornography dealers tried to "settle" cases against them by bribing police, see *People v. William Wilson,* May 19, 1854 (Indictment Papers, CGS).

55. Entries "William Haynes and Mary E. Haynes," "Edward M. Grandin," and "E. Snowden," in 1872 YMCA Log of Persons Not Arrested.

56. On the audience for blackface minstrelsy in antebellum New York, see Eric Lott, *Love and Theft: Blackface Minstrelsy and the American Working Class* (New York, 1993).

57. "Another Alleged Obscene Publisher Arrested—Cartloads of Books and Prints Found," *New York Times,* Sept. 29, 1857, 1.

58. For instance, Brady produced George Thompson's *The Ladies' Garter,* a suggestive but sexually inexplicit sensation novel of the sort that did not trigger indictments for obscenity, under the Henry S. G. Smith & Co. imprint.

59. Credit report for "Frederick A. Brady, Publisher," New York, vol. 192, p. 581, R. G. Dun & Co. Collection, Baker Library Historical Collections, Harvard Business School (entry dated Sept. 30, 1859). *People v. John Farrell* (attaching list of titles sold by Henry S. G. Smith & Co.), Mar. 12, 1855 (Indictment Papers, CGS).

60. Ashbee, *Catena Librorum Tacendorum,* 121–124.

61. Credit report for "Frederick A. Brady, Publisher," New York, vol. 192, p. 581, R. G. Dun & Co. Collection, Baker Library Historical Collections, Harvard Business School (entry dated Jan. 25, 1858). When I quote from the Dun Collection, material in brackets represents my interpretation of the abbreviations used by the credit reporter. A list of common R. G. Dun & Co. abbreviations prepared by Professor Robert C. Kenzer of the University of Richmond, which is available at the Baker Library, provided valuable assistance.

62. "Obscene Publications and Pictures," *New York Times,* Sept. 18, 1855, 2.

63. *People v. Arthur Crown,* Mar. 12, 1855; *People v. John Farrell,* Mar. 12, 1855; *People v. Terence Morris,* Mar. 12, 1855 (all in Indictment Papers, CGS).

64. CGS Minutes, Mar. 12, 1855, 554 (sentences for Morris, Farrell, and Crown). On Crown's 1858 arrest, see "Mayor's Office—Tuesday," *New York Times,* Aug. 13, 1858, 8. This article suggested that the defendant in question, Arthur Crown, was involved in a pornography ring that bought religious tracts at the Bible House in order to peddle them with obscene prints hidden in their leaves.

65. The raid on Akarman's firm is discussed in detail in Chapter 5.

66. "Another Alleged Obscene Publisher Arrested."

67. "Letter of F. Brady to the Editor of the Herald," *New York Herald,* Oct. 1, 1857, 8.

68. Affidavits of John Hackett and John W. Reynolds, in *People v. Frederick Brady alias Henry S. G. Smith* (Selling Obscene Publications), Feb. 12, 1858 (Indictment Papers, CGS).

69. "Police Intelligence: Selling Obscene Books," *New York Times,* Jan. 26, 1858, 5.

70. Credit report for "Frederick A. Brady, Publisher," New York, vol. 192, p. 581, R. G. Dun & Co. Collection, Baker Library Historical Collections, Harvard Business School (entry dated Jan. 25, 1858).

71. On Sweeny's party affiliation, see "Political," *New York Times,* Oct. 17, 1857, 5. For the indicted works, see *People v. Frederick Brady alias Henry S. G. Smith* (Selling Obscene Publications).

72. *People v. Frederick Brady alias Henry S. G. Smith,* Feb. 12, 1858 (Having Obscene Publications) (Indictment Papers, CGS).

73. CGS Minutes, Mar. 17, 1858, 357.

74. "The Charges against Officers of the Mayor's Squad," *New York Times,* Mar. 5, 1859, 1.

75. Credit report for "Frederic A. Brady, Publisher," New York, vol. 192, p. 581, R. G. Dun & Co. Collection, Baker Library Historical Collections, Harvard Business School (entry dated Sept. 30, 1859).

76. Horowitz, *Rereading Sex,* 245–246; Hawley, "American Publishers of Indecent Books," 446–447.

77. Credit report for "Frederic A. Brady, Publisher," New York, vol. 192, p. 581, R. G. Dun & Co. Collection, Baker Library Historical Collections, Harvard Business School (entry dated Jan. 8, 1867, and June 15, 1870).

78. Edward Zane Carroll Judson [Ned Buntline], *The Mysteries and Miseries of New Orleans* (New York, 1851).

79. *People v. Thomas Ormsby and John Atcherson,* Feb. 23, 1855 (Indictment Papers, CGS).

80. The masthead of the first issue of the *Weekly Whip* reads: "Weekly Whip, George Thompson, Editor, Gillen & Co., Office 122 1/2 Fulton Street, Publishers, Vol. 1—no. 1, New-York, Monday, February 12, 1855. Price Two Cents"; "Circular to the Million," *Weekly Whip,* Feb. 12, 1855.

81. *Edward Rice v. Thomas Gillen, a.k.a. Ormsby* (Selling Obscene Works), Mar. 22, 1856 (Police Court Papers, box 7955). For unknown reasons, the grand jury declined to indict Ormsby.

82. *People v. Thomas Ormsby, alias Gillen,* CGS Minutes, May 21, 1858, 531. Though Ormsby gave five hundred dollars in bail and promised to appear for trial, there is no record of a trial or plea. See also "Selling Vile Books," *New York*

Times, Apr. 12, 1858; "City Items," *New York Times,* Apr. 14, 1858, 4; and "Police Intelligence," *New York Herald,* Apr. 12, 1858, 1.

83. Credit report for "Thomas Ormsby," New York, vol. 196, p. 918, R. G. Dun & Co. Collection, Baker Library Historical Collections, Harvard Business School (entry dated June 14, 1865, mentioning Ormsby's date of death as June 13, 1865).

84. Circular for "Thomas Ormsby's Commission Bureau," copy held at the American Antiquarian Society; *People v. Frederick Brady alias Henry S. G. Smith* (Selling Obscene Publications).

85. On praise of activism and the entrepreneurial spirit in the Dun reports, see Scott A. Sandage, *Born Losers: A History of Failure in America* (Cambridge, Mass: Harvard University Press, 2005), 84. In many ways, Ormsby and other pornographers fit the nineteenth-century prototype of a dynamic, risk-taking capitalist described in the landmark work by James Willard. Hurst, *Law and the Conditions of Freedom in the Nineteenth-Century United States* (Madison, Wisc., 1956).

86. Credit report for "Thomas Ormsby," New York, vol. 196, p. 918, R. G. Dun & Co. Collection, Baker Library, Harvard Business School (entry dated June 21, 1864).

87. On Dugdale's fusion of sexual and political radicalism, see Sigel, *Governing Pleasures,* 10, 15–27; and Nead, *Victorian Babylon,* 178–182. In addition to William Dugdale, radical British pressmen who published pornography in the first half of the nineteenth century included John Dugdale (William Dugdale's brother), George Cannon, John Benjamin Brookes, and John and Edward Duncombe. Sigel, *Governing Pleasures,* 18.

88. Robert Darnton, *The Forbidden Best-Sellers of Pre-Revolutionary France* (New York, 1995), 21. On censorship, erotic writing, and political radicalism in the French Enlightenment, see also Lynn Hunt, ed., *Eroticism and the Body Politic* (Baltimore, 1991); and *The Invention of Pornography: Obscenity and the Origins of Modernity, 1500–1800* (New York, 1993); Robert Darnton, *The Literary Underground of the Old Regime* (Cambridge, Mass., 1982); and *Revolution in Print: The Press in France, 1775–1800,* ed. Robert Darnton and Daniel Roche (Berkeley, Calif., 1989).

89. Ashbee, *Index Librorum Prohibitorum,* xxviii.

90. On the promotional function of law and its vital role in creating the conditions for economic development in nineteenth-century America, see Hurst, *Law and the Conditions of Freedom.*

5. Venus in the Mail

1. Anthony Comstock, *Frauds Exposed; or, How the People Are Deceived and Robbed, and Youth Corrupted, Being a Full Exposure of Various Schemes Oper-*

ated through the Mails, and Unearthed by the Author in a Seven Years' Service as a Special Agent of the Post Office Department and Secretary and Chief Agent of the New York Society for the Suppression of Vice (New York, 1880), 388.

2. Credit report for "Geo. Akerman," New York, vol. 268, p. 554, R. G. Dun & Co. Collection, Baker Library Historical Collections, Harvard Business School (entry dated Sept. 29, 1852). In nineteenth-century sources, Akarman's name appears variously as Akerman, Ackerman, and Akarman. Because the publisher signed his name Akarman in a letter he wrote to the *New York Herald* in 1857 and was listed as Akarman in city directories for the early 1850s, I adopt that spelling throughout, except when quoting from sources that record his name differently.

3. Credit report for "Geo. Akerman," New York, vol. 268, p. 554, R. G. Dun & Co. Collection, Baker Library Historical Collections, Harvard Business School (entry dated Sept. 29, 1852). For Ormsby's obscenity arrests, see *People v. Thomas Ormsby and John Atcheson,* Feb. 23, 1855 (Indictment Papers, CGS); *Rice v. Gillen, a.k.a. Thomas Ormsby,* Mar. 22, 1856 (Police Court Papers, box 7955); and *People v. Thomas Ormsby, alias Gillen,* CGS Minutes, May 21, 1858, 531. The city directory for 1851–1852 lists Akarman and Ormsby as publishers at 102 Nassau Street. *Rode's New York City Directory, 1851–1852* (New York, 1851), 24.

4. Credit report for "Garrett & Co.," New York, vol. 188a, p. 84, R. G. Dun & Co. Collection, Baker Library Historical Collections, Harvard Business School (entry dated Apr. 5, 1852); "Obituary," *New York Times,* Oct. 12, 1881, 5.

5. Credit report for "Geo. Akerman," New York, vol. 268, p. 554, R. G. Dun & Co. Collection, Baker Library Historical Collections, Harvard Business School (entry dated Sept. 29, 1852). "Obituary," *New York Times,* Oct. 12, 1881, 5.

6. Credit report for "Geo. Akerman," New York, vol. 268, p. 554, R. G. Dun & Co. Collection, Baker Library Historical Collections, Harvard Business School (entry dated Sept. 29, 1852).

7. Credit report for "Geo. Akerman," New York, vol. 268, p. 554, R. G. Dun & Co. Collection, Baker Library Historical Collections, Harvard Business School (entries dated Feb. 6, 1853, and Oct. 12, 1853).

8. Trow's *New-York City Directory* for 1853–1854, for instance, stated: "Akarman George, books, 82 Nassau." Trow's *New-York City Directory . . . for 1853–54* (New York, 1853), 25. Similarly, Charles Rode's *New York Directory* for 1854–1855 contained an entry for "Akarman George, publisher, 17 Beekman." Charles R. Rode, *The New-York City Directory, for 1854–1855* (New York, 1854), 30.

9. Comstock's notes from 1872 state that Akarman had been in the "business of manufacturing obscene books for 22 to 25 years," which would date his entry into the field around 1850. Entry "George Ackerman," in 1872 YMCA Log of Persons Not Arrested.

10. The information in this paragraph was obtained from lengthy articles about Akarman's various businesses that appeared in the *New York Herald*, the *New York Times*, and the *New York Tribune* on September 16 and 17, 1857.

11. The earliest known issue, dated Jan. 31, 1857, is numbered vol. 1, no. 12. The numbering suggests that publication began in November 1856.

12. For examples of this approach in historical scholarship on pornography, see Joan Hoff, "Why Is There No History of Pornography?" in *For Adult Users Only: The Dilemma of Violent Pornography*, ed. Susan Gubar and Joan Hoff (Bloomington, Ind., 1989), 30; and Steven Marcus, *The Other Victorians: A Study of Sexuality and Pornography in Mid-Nineteenth-Century England* (New York, 1966).

13. See "Rosina's Dream of Real Bliss," *Venus' Miscellany*, May 16, 1857, 1; and "Donna Inez—The Wanton Bather," *Venus' Miscellany*, May 9, 1857, 1.

14. On the nineteenth-century contraception business, see Janet Farrell Brodie, *Contraception and Abortion in Nineteenth-Century America* (Ithaca, N.Y., 1994); and Andrea Tone, *Devices and Desires: A History of Contraceptives in America* (New York, 2001).

15. *Venus' Miscellany*, May 23, 1857, 2.

16. *People v. Ackerman*, Sept. 25, 1857 (Indictment Papers, CGS); Five Hand-Colored Indecent Prints (1850), attached to Complaint of A. Furnald against John Sweeney, dated June 27, 1850. The prints are held at the American Antiquarian Society in the uncatalogued Leo Hershkowitz collection.

17. *Venus' Miscellany*, May 16, 1857, 2. I reached this conclusion by comparing the titles in the advertisements with the bibliography of Thompson novels in George Thompson, *Venus in Boston and Other Tales of Nineteenth-Century City Life*, ed. David S. Reynolds and Kimberly R. Gladman (Amherst, Mass., 2002), 379–384.

18. *Venus' Miscellany*, May 16, 1857, 2.

19. "Stray Thoughts," *Venus' Miscellany*, July 11, 1857, 2. On the national drama concerning polygamy in the 1850s, see Sarah Barringer Gordon, *The Mormon Question: Polygamy and Constitutional Conflict in Nineteenth-Century America* (Chapel Hill, N.C., 2002).

20. Even Akarman later conceded that the material in the letters may have been legally obscene. "The Seizure of Obscene Literature—Letter from George Akarman, to the Editor of the Herald," *New York Herald*, Sept. 20, 1857, 8.

21. Sigmund Freud, *The Most Prevalent Forms of Degradation in Erotic Life* (1912) in Freud, *Collected Papers*, trans. Joan Riviere (New York, 1959), 4:203.

22. Georges Bataille, *Erotism: Death and Sensuality*, trans. Mary Dalwood (San Francisco, 1986 [1957]), 63; Jessica Benjamin, *The Bonds of Love: Psychoanalysis, Feminism, and the Problem of Domination* (New York, 1988).

23. Judith Butler, *Excitable Speech: A Politics of the Performative* (New York,

1997), 117; Michel Foucault, *The History of Sexuality: An Introduction*, trans. Robert Hurley (New York, 1990), 158.

24. Foucault, *History of Sexuality*, 114. For discussion of Foucaultian and other theoretical insights on censorship, see Robert C. Post, "Censorship and Silencing," in Robert C. Post, ed., *Censorship and Silencing: Practices of Cultural Regulation* (Los Angeles, 1998).

25. David S. Reynolds, *Beneath the American Renaissance: The Subversive Imagination in the Age of Emerson and Melville* (New York, 1988), 214–219.

26. "Mr. Editor," *Venus' Miscellany*, May 9, 1857, 3.

27. "To Maria C.," *Venus' Miscellany*, May 16, 1857, 3.

28. For background on the free love movement, see Hal D. Sears, *The Sex Radicals: Free Love in High Victorian America* (Lawrence, Ks., 1977); Taylor Stoehr, ed., *Free Love in America: A Documentary History* (New York, 1979); and John C. Spurlock, *Free Love: Marriage and Middle-Class Radicalism in America* (New York, 1988).

29. "My Dear Sir," *Venus' Miscellany*, July 11, 1857, 3.

30. The free love cause was also deployed as an erotic plot device in George Thompson, *Fanny Greeley; or, Confessions of a Free-Love Sister Written by Herself*, published by Henry S. G. Smith & Co. sometime in the 1850s. For an excerpt from this now lost novel, see Pisanus Fraxi [Henry Spencer Ashbee], *Catena Librorum Tacendorum* (London, 1885), 210–217.

31. On female "passionlessness," see Nancy F. Cott, "Passionlessness: An Interpretation of Victorian Sexual Ideology, 1790–1850," *Signs* 4 (1978): 219–236.

32. "Immense Seizure of Obscene Works—Ackerman Again in Trouble," *New York Times*, Sept. 16, 1857, 5; Virginia Penney, *How Women Can Make Money* (New York, 1971 [1863]); J. Luther Ringwalt, ed., *American Encyclopaedia of Printing* (Philadelphia, 1871), xii.

33. "Immense Seizure of Obscene Works," 5.

34. On Mary Haines's role, see the entry "William Haynes and Mary E. Haynes," in 1872 YMCA Log of Persons Not Arrested. On Mrs. Simpson's role, see Affidavit of Anthony Comstock, dated Jan. 26, 1874, in *United States v. William Simpson*, indictment filed Oct. 7, 1873 (Federal Archives, SDNY).

35. Several historians of sexuality have ably advanced this point, with a corresponding critique of the notion of a "repressive" nineteenth century. See especially Carl N. Degler, "What Ought to Be and What Was: Women's Sexuality in the Nineteenth Century," *American Historical Review* 79 (1974): 1467–1490; Peter Gay, *The Bourgeois Experience: Victoria to Freud* (New York, 1984–1998); Karen Lystra, *Searching the Heart: Women, Men, and Romantic Love in Nineteenth-Century America* (New York, 1989); and Christine Stansell, *City of Women: Sex and Class in New York, 1789–1860* (New York, 1986).

36. Brodie, *Contraception and Abortion in Nineteenth-Century America*, 102.

37. On the popularity of sexual massage and hydrotherapy among bourgeois women in the nineteenth century, see Rachel P. Maines, *The Technology of Orgasm: 'Hysteria,' the Vibrator, and Women's Sexual Satisfaction* (Baltimore, 1999), 72–81.

38. George Thompson, *New-York Life: The Mysteries of Upper-Tendom Revealed* (1849), 78, quoted in Reynolds, *Beneath the American Renaissance,* 219.

39. Metropolitan Museum of Art, *Art and the Empire City, New York, 1825–1861* (New York, 2000), 165.

40. "Palmer's White Captive," *New York Times,* Dec. 30, 1859, 2.

41. See, for example, "The Free-Lovers' Troubles," *New York Times,* Oct. 20, 1855, 2.

42. For one account of sexual passion between American women in the period in which *Venus' Miscellany* was published, see Lisa Merrill, *When Romeo Was a Woman: Charlotte Cushman and Her Circle of Female Spectators* (Ann Arbor, Mich., 1999), 205–242 (describing intense "sapphic desire" between the actress Charlotte Cushman and a young admirer, Emma Crow).

43. T. L. Nichols, M.D., *Esoteric Anthropology: A Comprehensive and Confidential Treatise on the Structure, Functions, Passional Attractions and Perversions, True and False Physical and Social Conditions, and the Most Intimate Relations of Men and Women* (New York, 1854), 201.

44. For a now classic account of how social actors operate within the "shadow of the law," see Robert H. Mnookin and Lewis Kornhauser, "Bargaining in the Shadow of the Law: The Case of Divorce," *Yale Law Journal* 88 (1979): 950–997. See also Michael Grossberg, *A Judgment for Solomon: The d'Hauteville Case and Legal Experience in Antebellum America* (New York, 1996), 2, in which Grossberg applies the concept of bargaining in the shadow of the law to a nineteenth-century child custody dispute.

45. "The Seizure of Obscene Literature—Letter from George Akarman, to the Editor of the Herald."

46. "The Police Descent upon the Obscene Literature," *New York Herald,* Sept. 17, 1857, 4; "The Moral Condition of the Country," *New York Herald,* Sept. 18, 1857, 4; "The Obscene Literature Again—Effects of Fourierism," *New York Herald,* Sept. 20, 1857, 4.

47. "A Model Love Paper," *Venus' Miscellany,* Jan. 31, 1857, 3.

48. "Our Story," *Venus' Miscellany,* May 9, 1857, 3.

49. "To Subscribers" *Venus' Miscellany,* May 30, 1857, 3.

50. "My Dear Venus," *Venus' Miscellany,* July 4, 1857, 3.

51. "A Publishing Establishment Broken Up," *New York Tribune,* Sept. 16, 1857, 5.

52. "To Subscribers."

53. "Boston Morality," *Venus' Miscellany,* May 23, 1857, 3.

54. "Editorial: $100 Reward—Philadelphians Take Notice," *Venus' Miscellany,* May 30, 1857, 3.

55. "Postmasters," *Venus' Miscellany,* Jan. 31, 1857, 3 (emphasis in the original).

56. "Great Seizure of Obscene Literature," *New York Herald,* Sept. 16, 1857, 8.

57. "Not Stopped Yet," *New York Sun,* Aug. 24, 1842, 2 (for the quotation "thrust in the face").

58. Stansell, *City of Women,* 41, xii.

59. "Great Seizure of Obscene Literature."

60. Ibid; "A Publishing Establishment Broken Up," *New York Tribune,* Sept. 16, 1857, 5; "The Moral Condition of the Country."

61. "News of the Day," *New York Times,* Sept. 14, 1857, 4; "Great Seizure of Obscene Literature"; "A Publishing Establishment Broken Up."

62. "Great Seizure of Obscene Literature."

63. "A Publishing Establishment Broken Up."; "Great Seizure of Obscene Literature."

64. "A Publishing Establishment Broken Up"; "The Seizure of Obscene Literature," *New York Herald,* Sept. 17, 1857, 8.

65. On Akarman's business records, see "The Seizure of Obscene Literature," *New York Herald,* Sept. 17, 1857, 8; "Great Seizure of Obscene Literature"; "Immense Seizure of Obscene Works—Ackerman Again in Trouble"; and "A Publishing Establishment Broken Up." For the 2007 value of 1857 dollars, see the Inflation Calculator at http://www.westegg.com/inflation/infl.cgi.

66. *People v. Ackerman,* Sept. 25, 1857 (Indictment Papers, CGS).

67. For an example, see the ad in *Venus' Miscellany,* May 23, 1857, 2.

68. The publishers Henry Robinson and Richard Hobbes had been indicted, for instance, for selling *Memoirs of a Woman of Pleasure* and *Memoirs of the . . . Celebrated Mademoiselle Celestine* back in 1842. *People v. Henry Robinson,* Sept. 20, 1842; *People v. Richard Hobbes,* Sept. 28, 1842 (both in Indictment Papers, CGS).

69. "The Seizure of Obscene Literature"

70. Akarman's letter appeared as "The Seizure of Obscene Literature—Letter from George Akarman, to the Editor of the Herald." It was reprinted in the city's other major dailies.

71. Under the constitutional law of his day, Akarman would not have had a valid argument under the First Amendment. In 1833 the U.S. Supreme Court held that the Fifth Amendment to the U.S. Constitution did not apply to state action, a ruling that was widely perceived to extend to the Bill of Rights as a whole. *Barron v. Baltimore,* 7 Pet. 243 (U.S. 1833). But the New York constitution contained protections for freedom of speech and freedom of the press—

though in more qualified language than its federal counterpart—that Akarman might have invoked if he had wanted to defend himself on the grounds of free speech. Specifically, it provided: "Every citizen may freely speak, write, and publish his sentiments on all subjects, being responsible for the abuse of that right; and no law shall be passed to restrain or abridge the liberty of speech or of the press." Article I, § 8, New York constitution of 1846.

72. *Wynehamer v. People,* 13 N.Y. 378, 386, 398 (1856) (emphasis added).

73. "The Seizure of Obscene Books and Prints," *New York Herald,* Sept. 23, 1857, 5.

74. Just that summer, a justice of the New York Court of Appeals had reached a similar conclusion: "The city of New-York is the commercial metropolis of this continent; its port is filled with shipping from every clime; its streets crowded with residents and sojourners, intent on business, pleasure and crime." *People ex rel. Wood v. Draper,* 15 N.Y. 532, 556 (1857) (Shankland, J., concurring).

75. Akarman died in May 1873. Entry "George Ackerman," in 1872 YMCA Log of Persons Not Arrested.

6. The Triumph of Pornography

1. On business failures during the Civil War, see Scott A. Sandage, *Born Losers: A History of Failure in America* (Cambridge, Mass., 2005), 199–206. For the Ormsby ad, see *New York Clipper,* Apr. 13, 1861, 416.

2. *New York Clipper,* Feb. 1, 1862, 336. In the 1860s "gay" referred to the world of prostitutes and brothels. Timothy J. Gilfoyle, *City of Eros: New York City, Prostitution, and the Commercialization of Sex, 1790–1920* (New York, 1992), 157. On the extent of Farrell's involvement in the erotica trade, see Anthony Comstock, *Frauds Exposed; or, How the People Are Deceived and Robbed, and Youth Corrupted* (New York: J.H. Brown, 1880), 388.

3. "*New York Clipper,* Feb. 13, 1864, 349.

4. "Morals of Our Soldiers," *Christian Recorder,* Aug. 31, 1861.

5. "Improper Books," *New York Times,* Aug. 16, 1863, 1.

6. Capt. M. G. Tousey to Abraham Lincoln, Mar. 23, 1864, copy of typescript in Vertical File, Kinsey Institute for Research in Sex, Gender, and Reproduction.

7. Daniel P. Carpenter, *The Forging of Bureaucratic Autonomy: Reputations, Networks, and Policy Innovation in Executive Agencies, 1862–1928* (Princeton, N.J., 2001), 76–79; Wayne E. Fuller, *Morality and the Mail in Nineteenth-Century America* (Urbana, Ill., 2003), 57–58.

8. Elizabeth Anne McCauley, *Industrial Madness: Commercial Photography in Paris, 1848–1871* (New Haven, Conn., 1994), 161–162. The first appearance of photography in an obscenity indictment in the New York County Court of General Sessions occurred in 1863. *People v. James Murray,* Feb. 13, 1863 (Indictment Papers, CGS).

9. On *cartes de visite* and pornography in Paris, see McCauley, *Industrial Madness,* Chap. 4; quotation p. 158.

10. On stereoscopic views, see generally McCauley, *Industrial Madness,* 97–98; and Edward W. Earle, ed., *Points of View: The Stereograph in America—A Cultural History* (Rochester, N.Y., 1979). On stereoscopic views and pornography in Paris, see McCauley, *Industrial Madness,* chap. 4.

11. *New York Clipper,* Aug. 15, 1863, 144.

12. McCauley, *Industrial Madness,* 162.

13. *People v. James Hanley,* June 23, 1865 (Indictment Papers, CGS); Publisher's Prospectus for "'Venus' Library;' or Tales of Illicit Love," held at the American Antiquarian Society.

14. *New York Clipper,* Feb. 13, 1864, 349.

15. *The Libertine Enchantress; or, The Adventures of Lucinda Hartley* (New Orleans, 1863). A copy of *The Libertine Enchantress* is held at the Kinsey Institute for Research in Sex, Gender, and Reproduction. Its title page attributes the novel to the same author as *The Confessions of a Washington Belle, The Beautiful Creole of Havana,* and the other books in the Venus' Library series.

16. *The Libertine Enchantress,* 48–49.

17. On the importance of the Fourdrinier machine, see Shelly Streeby, *American Sensations: Class, Empire, and the Production of Popular Culture* (Berkeley, Calif., 2002), 11. For a list of the titles in the Cupid's Own Library series, see Pisanus Fraxi [Henry Spencer Ashbee], *Catena Librorum Tacendorum* (London, 1885), 200; *People v. Thomas O'Connor,* June 15, 1869 (Indictment Papers, CGS), with circular attached as an exhibit; and Grand Fancy Bijou Catalogue of the Sporting Man's Emporium for 1870, 5.

18. Ashbee, *Catena Librorum Tacendorum,* 199–200.

19. Ibid.

20. For pricing differentials, see *People v. Thomas O'Connor;* and Grand Fancy Bijou Catalogue, 3–5.

21. [Philocomus], *The Love Feast; or, A Bride's Experience. A Poem in Six Nights* (n.p., 1865). The Kinsey Institute copy was rebound in leather at a later date and has the title embossed in gold on the spine.

22. On the flourishing commerce in contraception during the Civil War and Reconstruction eras, see generally Janet Farrell Brodie, *Contraception and Abortion in Nineteenth-Century America* (Ithaca, N.Y., 1994); Andrea Tone, *Devices and Desires: A History of Contraceptives in America* (New York, 2001), which emphasizes entrepreneurship; and Kathleen L. Endres, "'Strictly Confidential': Birth-Control Advertising in a 19th Century City," *Journalism Quarterly* 63 (1986): 748–751. On specific types of contraceptives sold ("condoms, douching syringes"), see Tone, *Devices and Desires,* 14. For statement by Reverend Todd,

see John Todd, *Serpents in the Dove's Nest* (Boston, 1867), quoted in Tone, *Devices and Desires,* 15.

23. For Foote's birth control advertisements, see Edward B. Foote, M.D., *Medical Common Sense; Applied to the Causes, Prevention and Cure of Chronic Diseases and Unhappiness in Marriage* (New York, 1864), 378–380. On Foote's medical practice and publishing business, see Michael Sappol, *A Traffic of Dead Bodies: Anatomy and Embodied Social Identity in Nineteenth-Century America* (Princeton, N.J., 2002), 241–273; Helen Lefkowitz Horowitz, *Rereading Sex: Battles over Sexual Knowledge and Suppression in Nineteenth-Century America* (New York, 2002), 333–338; and Janice Ruth Wood, *The Struggle for Free Speech in the United States, 1872–1915: Edward Bliss Foote, Edward Bond Foote, and Anti-Comstock Operations* (New York, 2007).

24. *Venus' Miscellany,* May 23, 1857, 2; *New York Clipper,* Feb. 13, 1864, 349; *Sunday Mercury,* Sept. 22, 1867, 1; *People v. Thomas O'Connor,* with circular attached as exhibit; Grand Fancy Bijou Catalogue, 6–7.

25. On the draft riots, see Iver Bernstein, *The New York City Draft Riots: Their Significance for American Society and Politics in the Age of the Civil War* (New York, 1990). On the Tweed Ring's corruption, see Alexander B. Callow, Jr., *The Tweed Ring* (New York, 1965).

26. Herbert Asbury, *The Gangs of New York: An Informal History of the Underworld* (New York, 1928), 158–159.

27. Timothy J. Gilfoyle, "The Moral Origins of Political Surveillance: The Preventive Society in New York City, 1867–1918," *American Quarterly* 38 (1986): 637–652; Sven Beckert, *The Monied Metropolis: New York City and the Consolidation of the American Bourgeoisie, 1850–1896* (New York, 2001).

28. On the populist aspects of the New York Democratic machine, see Bernstein, *The New York City Draft Riots,* 6; and Leo Hershkowitz, *Tweed's New York: Another Look* (New York, 1977). On the ideology of municipal Republicans in the 1860s, see Bernstein, *The New York City Draft Riots,* esp. chap. 3.

29. On the tradition of free thought in America, see Albert Post, *Popular Freethought in America, 1825–50* (New York, 1943); Sidney Warren, *American Freethought, 1860–1914* (New York, 1966). On Democratic resistance to state-driven moral reform, see Marvin Myer, *The Jacksonian Persuasion: Politics and Belief* (New York, 1960); and Harry L. Watson, *Liberty and Power: The Politics of Jacksonian America* (New York, 1990), 194. On the Whig predilection for morals regulation, see Daniel Walker Howe, *The Political Culture of the American Whigs* (Chicago, 1979); Richard Gerring, "Party Ideology in America: The National Republican Chapter, 1828–1924," *Studies in American Political Development* 11 (1997): 87–96. On cultural and political conflict over alcohol in 1850s New York, see Paul O. Weinbaum, "Temperance, Politics, and the New York City Riots of 1857," *New-York Historical Society Quarterly* 59 (1975): 246–270.

30. James C. Mohr, *The Radical Republicans and Reform in New York during Reconstruction* (Ithaca, N.Y., 1973).

31. "New York," in *Appleton's Annual Cyclopaedia and Register of Important Events* (1865), quoted in Morton Keller, *Affairs of State: Public Life in Late Nineteenth-Century America* (Cambridge, Mass., 1977), 50.

32. *New York World*, Mar. 7, 1865, quoted in Keller, *Affairs of State*, 50.

33. *People v. Henry S. Harris*, Mar. 23, 1860; *People v. James Murray; People v. James Hanley; People v. Thomas O'Connor; People v. David J. Gomperts*, July 12, 1869; *People v. David J. Gomperts*, July 29, 1869 (all in Indictment Papers, CGS). A recent study has found that starting in 1860, the Court of Special Session became swamped with morals prosecutions, "principally prostitution, bawdy house and liquor law violations." Mike McConville and Chester Mirsky, *Jury Trials and Plea Bargaining: A True History* (Oxford, 2005), 247, n. 68. Rather than indicating an increase in municipal attention to morals regulation, this evidence suggests a reduction in the seriousness of morals prosecutions as they shifted from General Sessions to Special Sessions, and a simultaneous increase in opportunities for graft among lower-level magistrates and police officers. In any event, obscenity cases were few and far between in both General and Special Sessions. A survey of the "Law Reports" column of the *New York Times* reveals only six additional arrests for obscenity during the entire decade.

34. "Court of Oyer and Terminer," *New York Times*, Mar. 10, 1863, 5. On the pervasiveness of judicial and political corruption in the 1860s, particularly at the lower-court levels, see Kenneth T. Jackson, ed., *The Encyclopedia of New York City* (New Haven, Conn., 1995), 292; "The Judiciary of New York City," *North American Review* 105 (1867): 148–176; and Anna M. Kross and Harold M. Grossman, "Magistrates' Courts of the City of New York: History and Organization," *Brooklyn Law Review* 7 (1937): 133–179, 146–148.

35. See especially William J. Novak, *The People's Welfare: Law and Regulation in Nineteenth-Century America* (Chapel Hill, N.C., 1996), 149–189; and Herbert Hovenkamp, "Law and Morals in Classical Legal Thought," *Iowa Law Review* 82 (1997): 1427–1465.

36. Joel Prentiss Bishop, *Commentaries on the Criminal Law* (Boston, 1865), cited in Novak, *The People's Welfare*, 150.

37. For one example, see "The Demi-Monde of New York," *National Police Gazette*, Dec. 28, 1867, 2.

38. George Akarman reportedly bragged that he had enough money to buy up all the police justices in the city. "Great Seizure of Obscene Literature," *New York Herald*, Sept. 16, 1857, 5. The bookseller William Simpson boasted that he was immune from incarceration for dealing in obscenity because he paid his politically well-connected landlord twice the going rate for rent. "A Filthy Depot in the Heart of the City—How the Morals of Our Youth Are Corrupted," *New*

York Times, Jan. 15, 1872, 2; "Obscene Books: Their Publishers and Profits," *Pomeroy's Democrat,* Oct. 28, 1871, 2.

39. On the identification of law with orthodox Protestant morality, see Sarah Barringer Gordon, *The Mormon Question: Polygamy and Constitutional Conflict in Nineteenth-Century America* (Chapel Hill, N.C., 2002); and Gordon, "Blasphemy and the Law of Religious Liberty in Nineteenth-Century America," *American Quarterly* 52 (2000): 682–720.

40. For valuable discussions of the motivations of businessmen–moral reformers in this era, see Paul S. Boyer, *Urban Masses and Moral Order in America, 1820–1920* (Cambridge, Mass., 1978); and Nicola Beisel, *Imperiled Innocents: Anthony Comstock and Family Reproduction in Victorian America* (Princeton, N.J., 1998).

41. On state police power to protect public morality, see generally Novak, *The People's Welfare,* 149–89; and Hovenkamp, "Law and Morals in Classical Legal Thought." For the YMCA resolution and subsequent report, see YMCA, *Fourteenth Annual Report* (New York, 1866); YMCA, *A Memorandum Respecting New-York As a Field for Moral and Christian Effort among Young Men; Its Present Neglected Condition; and, The Fitness of the New-York Young Men's Christian Association As a Principal Agency for Its Due Cultivation* (New York, 1866).

42. Junius Henri Browne, *The Great Metropolis: A Mirror of New York* (Hartford, Conn., 1869), 314.

43. Ibid., 314–315, 94.

44. Ibid., 94–95, 314.

45. Gustav Lening, *The Dark Side of New York Life and Its Criminal Classes from Fifth Avenue Down to the Five Points* (New York, 1873), 655–656.

46. On the general surge in state laws criminalizing abortions between 1860 and 1880 and the role of licensed physicians in putting these laws in place, see James C. Mohr, *Abortion in America: The Origins and Evolution of a National Policy, 1800–1900* (New York, 1978), chap. 8; and "State Medical Society," *New York Times,* Feb. 7, 1868, 5 (on the New York Medical Society campaign to prohibit unlicensed practitioners from selling nostrums or medicines to induce abortions).

47. To avoid the appearance of a conflict of interest, the newly created New York Society for the Suppression of Vice asked the legislature to eliminate this provision as applied to its own investigators in 1873.

48. In 1858 a New York court had approved the permanent confiscation and destruction of obscene publications on the ground that they were criminal nuisances, but only *after* conviction of the owner. *Willis v. Warren,* 5 Barb. 590, 594–595 (New York Court of Common Pleas 1858).

49. Keady had been president of the New York Practical Housepainters' Association. On Keady, see Bernstein, *The New York City Draft Riots,* 188; and

David Montgomery, *Beyond Equality: Labor and the Radical Republicans 1862–1872* (New York, 1967), 210–211.

50. "Obscene Literature—Its Radical Origin and Propagators," *Sunday Mercury*, Apr. 26, 1868, 4. By way of example, the article predicted: "During the Presidential campaign next fall, any criticism on amalgamation would be considered obscene, and the journal indulging in it entitled to be extinguished." Ibid. On the New York Democratic Party's penchant for racist harangues against the pro-black policies of the Republican Party in Reconstruction New York, see Mohr, *Radical Republicans and Reform*, esp. chap. 8.

51. *Journal of the Senate of the State of New York at Their Ninety-first Session* (Albany, N.Y., 1868), 768–769.

52. "The Obscene Literature Bill," *New York Tribune*, Apr. 24, 1868, 5. Only Assemblymen McKlever and Murphy voted against the bill in the final roll call. *Journal of the Assembly of the State of New York at Their Ninety-first Session* (Albany, N.Y., 1868), 1250; "The Obscene Literature Bill," *New York Tribune*, Apr. 23, 1868, 10.

53. During the evening session, Keady promised to introduce a resolution to "advocate in the next Democratic Convention a plank in the platform protesting against the suppression of any kind of obscenity," but there is no evidence that this ever materialized. "The Obscene Literature Bill," *New York Tribune*, Apr. 24, 1868, 5.

54. Reconsideration was defeated by a vote of 52 to 46. "Legislative Proceedings," *New York Times*, Apr. 23, 1868, 5; "The Obscene Literature Bill," *New York Tribune*, Apr. 24, 1868, 5; *Journal of the Assembly of the State of New York at Their Ninety-first Session*, 1286.

55. *Journal of the Senate of the State of New York at Their Ninety-first Session*, 810. Laws of New York, 91st sess., chap. 430, 856–857 (Apr. 28, 1868).

56. "The Obscene Democracy," *New York Tribune*, Apr. 25, 1868, 4. On the political affiliations of the *New York Tribune*, see Mohr, *Radical Republicans and Reform in New York*, 97.

57. "The Obscene Democracy."

58. "Minor Topics," *New York Times*, Feb. 15, 1868, 4.

59. Ibid. *The Black Crook*, which opened at the elite Niblo's Garden theater in 1866, featured a hundred female dancers in tights. It was an immediate sensation: "Despite criticism by clerics and moralists, the show ran for 475 performances over sixteen consecutive months, grossing over one million dollars." Gilfoyle, *City of Eros*, 128.

60. On the YMCA Committee on Obscene Literature, see Horowitz, *Rereading Sex*, 360, 363. This committee was renamed the Committee for the Suppression of Vice in 1872.

61. *People v. Thomas O'Connor;* ad for Dexter's "Sportsman's Emporium," *New York Clipper,* June 29, 1867, 93.

62. *People v. Thomas O'Connor.* For a list of twelve European titles, commonly stocked by erotica dealers, see Grand Fancy Bijou Catalogue, 4.

63. For *Kate Percival* ad, see Grand Fancy Bijou Catalogue, 4. The same catalogue advertised *La Rose d'Amour* as containing ten colored plates.

64. *People v. Thomas O'Connor.*

65. *People v. David J. Gomperts,* July 12, 1869; *Sunday Mercury,* Sept. 22, 1867, 7; *People v. David J. Gomperts,* July 29, 1869.

66. Lening, *Dark Side of New York Life,* 653.

67. "Morals of Our Soldiers" (quotation on "flimsy publications"). On Comstock's wartime experiences, see Charles Gallaudet Trumbull, *Anthony Comstock, Fighter: Some Impressions of a Lifetime of Adventure in Conflict with the Powers of Evil* (New York, 1913), 31–42. For additional biographical background on Comstock, see Heywood Broun and Margaret Leech, *Anthony Comstock: Roundsman of the Lord* (New York, 1927); Anna Louise Bates, *Weeder in the Garden of the Lord: Anthony Comstock's Life and Career* (Lanham, Md., 1995); Beisel, *Imperiled Innocents;* Horowitz, *Rereading Sex;* Paul S. Boyer, *Purity in Print: Book Censorship in America from the Gilded Age to the Computer Age* (Madison, Wisc., 2002); Richard C. Johnson, "Anthony Comstock: Reform, Vice, and the American Way" (Ph.D. diss., Univ. of Wisconsin, 1973); and Elizabeth Bainum Hovey, "Stamping Out Smut: The Enforcement of Obscenity Laws, 1872–1915" (Ph.D. diss., Columbia, 1998).

68. On Comstock's original ambition to become a merchant and his employment history, see Trumbull, *Anthony Comstock,* 43–48.

69. Broun and Leech, *Anthony Comstock,* 81; "Improper Books, Prints, etc.," Report of the YMCA Committee for the Suppression of Vice for 1872–1873, dated Jan. 28, 1874, 9 ("volunteer detective and complainant"); entry "Charles Conroy," in 1872 YMCA Arrest Records.

70. Letter of Anthony Comstock (on stationery of his employer, Cochran, McLean and Company), dated Feb. 21, 1872, to Hon. Gunning S. Bedford in *People v. William Simpson,* Dec. 5, 1871 (Indictment Papers, CGS). Comstock later described Simpson as the "worst man in New York." Entry "William Simpson," in 1872 YMCA Arrest Records.

71. For samples of Simpson's advertising, see exhibits to *United States v. William Simpson,* indictment filed Oct. 7, 1873 (Federal Archives, Southern District of New York), and *United States v. William Simpson,* indictment filed Oct. 13, 1874 (Federal Archives, Southern District of New York).

72. Affidavit of Anthony Comstock, dated Jan. 26, 1874, in *United States v. William Simpson,* indictment filed Oct. 7, 1873; letter of Anthony Comstock to Rep. Clinton L. Merriam, dated Jan. 18, 1873. *Congressional Globe,* 42d Cong.,

3d sess., Appendix, 168 (complaining about dealers who lent "vile books at ten cents per week to the youths and children of our public schools"); "Improper Books, Prints, etc.," Report of the YMCA Committee for the Suppression of Vice for 1872–1873, dated Jan. 28, 1874, 6 ("The retail dealers also loan out the books at a small sum per week, and in this way any boy, or girl even, can have access to the whole list").

73. "A Filthy Depot in the Heart of the City."

74. For evidence of Simpson's mail-order trade, see *United States v. William Simpson*, indictment filed Oct. 7, 1873; and *United States v. William Simpson*, indictment filed Oct. 13, 1874.

75. Affidavit of William Fitzmorris, dated Mar. 9, 1872, in *People v. William Simpson.*

76. *United States v. William Simpson*, indictment filed Oct. 13, 1874, which resulted in a ten-year sentence.

77. *People v. William Simpson;* "A Filthy Depot in the Heart of the City."

78. Trumbull, *Anthony Comstock*, 52–53.

7. The Comstock Act

1. Comstock quoted the *Sunday Mercury*'s charge in his letter to Rep. Clinton L. Merriam, dated January 18, 1873, which called for stricter federal legislation against obscene literature. *Congressional Globe*, 42d Cong., 3d sess., Appendix, 168. On Comstock's complaint and the police officer's dismissal, see Charles Gallaudet Trumbull, *Anthony Comstock, Fighter: Some Impressions of a Lifetime of Adventure in Conflict with the Powers of Evil* (New York, 1913), 53.

2. "Dealers in Obscene Literature Arrested," *New York Tribune*, Mar. 4, 1872, 8; "Arrest of Dealers in Obscene Literature," *New York Times*, Mar. 4, 1872, 2.

3. Entries "Patrick J. Bannon," "Richard Elmore," and "John Bannon," in 1872 YMCA Arrest Records.

4. Grand Fancy Bijou Catalogue of the Sporting Man's Emporium for 1870, 4.

5. See the entries "William Barkley" and "Charles Barkley," in 1872 YMCA Arrest Records; *People v. William Brooks and Charles Brooks*, Mar. 14, 1872 (Indictment Papers, CGS).

6. On the case against McDermott, see *People v. James McDermott*, Mar. 14, 1872 (Indictment Papers, CGS); entry "James McDermott," in 1872 YMCA Arrest Records. On McDermott's clerk, see entry "Thomas Ward," in 1872 YMCA Arrest Records.

7. Richard H. Rovere, *Howe & Hummel: Their True and Scandalous History* (1947; New York, 1985); *People v. William Brooks and Charles Brooks*, Mar. 14, 1872 (Indictment Papers, CGS); entries "William Barkley" and "Charles Bark-

ley," in 1872 YMCA Arrest Records; *People v. James McDermott*, Mar. 14, 1872 (Indictment Papers, CGS); entry "James McDermott," in 1872 YMCA Arrest Records.

8. 1872 YMCA Arrest Records, entries no. 1–44; "The Prevention of Vice," *New York Times*, Feb. 6, 1878, 2; Fourth Annual Report of the New York Society for the Suppression of Vice (presented at New York, Jan. 28, 1878), 8. For an example of the refusal of New York County juries to convict despite strong evidence of the defendant's guilt, according to Comstock, see entry "Peter F. Weill," in 1875 Arrest Records of the New York Society for the Suppression of Vice.

9. "Improper Books, Prints, etc.," Report of the YMCA Committee for the Suppression of Vice for 1872–1873, dated Jan. 28, 1874, 5; Anthony Comstock, *Traps for the Young*, ed. Robert Bremner (1884; Cambridge, Mass., 1967), 141; Anthony Comstock, *Frauds Exposed; or, How the People are Deceived and Robbed, and Youth Corrupted* (New York, 1880), 388. On Farrell's acquisition of Brady's stock, see Helen Lefkowitz Horowitz, *Rereading Sex: Battles over Sexual Knowledge and Suppression in Nineteenth-Century America* (New York, 2002), 245–246. On Brady's death, see credit report for "Frederick A. Brady, Publisher," New York, vol. 192, p. 581, R. G. Dun & Co. Collection, Baker Library Historical Collections, Harvard Business School (entry dated June 15, 1870).

10. Comstock put the names of Haines, Akarman, and Farrell in a special section at the front of his 1872 arrest log under the caption "Names and description of Persons . . . forced to give up, and get out of the business." See entries "William Haynes and Mary E. Haynes," "George Ackerman," and "Jeremiah H. Farrell," in 1872 YMCA Log of Persons Not Arrested.

11. Entry "William Haynes and Mary E. Haynes," in 1872 YMCA Log of Persons Not Arrested; entries "James McDermott" and "Edward M. Grandin," in 1872 YMCA Arrest Records.

12. Trumbull, *Anthony Comstock*, 62–63.

13. On Comstock's early relations with the YMCA and for background on Jesup, see Horowitz, *Rereading Sex*, 371–374 (quotation from Comstock's letter to McBurney p. 373); Trumbull, *Anthony Comstock*, 63–65; Wayne E. Fuller, *Morality and the Mail in Nineteenth-Century America* (Urbana, Ill., 2003), 104; "The Society for the Suppression of Obscene Literature," *New York Times*, May 9, 1872, 3; "An Offense against Decency," *New York Times*, Nov. 29, 1872, 4; and Tenth Annual Report of the New York Society for the Suppression of Vice (presented at New York, Jan. 22, 1884), 14.

14. Trumbull, *Anthony Comstock*, 65–69; entry "William Haynes and Mary E. Haynes," in 1872 YMCA Log of Persons Not Arrested.

15. *People v. Adolph Beer*, Apr. 17, 1872 (Indictment Papers, CGS); entry "Adolph Beery," in 1872 YMCA Arrest Records. The picture in Beer's indictment may have been pirated from an eighteenth-century British source. In 1773

a defendant was indicted in London for selling an obscene anticlerical print, "The Parson Receiving Tithes in Kind," in a periodical called *The Covent Garden Magazine, or Amorous Repository, Calculated Solely for the Entertainment of the Polite World.* John Frederick Archbold, *A Summary of the Law Relative to Pleading and Evidence in Criminal Cases; With Precedents of Indictments, &c.* (New York, 1824), 30.

16. Entry "John Ulm," in 1872 YMCA Log of Persons Not Arrested; entry "Riehl," ibid.

17. Entry "E. Snowden," in 1872 YMCA Log of Persons Not Arrested.

18. Entry "George Ackerman," in 1872 YMCA Log of Persons Not Arrested; Trumbull, *Anthony Comstock,* 70–77; entry "Thomas Timpson," in 1872 YMCA Log of Persons Not Arrested.

19. On the encounter between Akarman and Comstock, see Trumbull, *Anthony Comstock,* 76–77.

20. Ibid. Comstock identified the source of the funds he used to purchase Akarman's stock as J. Salmon of South Bergen, New Jersey. Entry "George Ackerman," in 1872 YMCA Log of Persons Not Arrested. For Comstock's attempt to take credit for the deaths of Akarman, Haines, and Farrell, see letter of Anthony Comstock to Rep. Clinton L. Merriam, dated Jan. 18, 1873.

21. Though Comstock records Farrell's age in 1872 as forty, Farrell's 1872 death certificate indicates that he was only thirty-five. Elizabeth Haven Hawley, "American Publishers of Indecent Books, 1840–1890" (Ph.D. diss., Georgia Institute of Technology, 2005), 557, n. 56. For quotations in the text, see credit report for "Jeremiah H. Farrell," vol. 196, p. 919, R. G. Dun & Co. Collection, Baker Library Historical Collections, Harvard Business School (entries dated Aug. 27, 1864, Dec. 21, 1867, Jan. 31, 1871, and July 12, 1871).

22. Comstock, *Frauds Exposed,* 388; entry "Jeremiah H. Farrell," in 1872 YMCA Arrest Records.

23. "Improper Books, Prints, etc.," report of the YMCA Committee for the Suppression of Vice for 1872–1873, dated Jan. 28, 1874, 5; Comstock, *Frauds Exposed,* 388; Trumbull, *Anthony Comstock,* 77.

24. Pisanus Fraxi [Henry Spencer Ashbee], *Catena Librorum Tacendorum* (London, 1885), 149–150; "Works of Wit, Fancy, and Humor" (publisher's advertisement appended to back of Henry S. G. Smith & Co. edition of *The Lady in Flesh Colored Tights!*); *People v. Jeremiah H. Farrell,* Apr. 30, 1872 (Indictment Papers, CGS).

25. Entry "Jeremiah H. Farrell," in 1872 YMCA Arrest Records; Hawley, "American Publishers of Indecent Books" (for date of Farrell's death); entries "Thomas Bleiner," "James Foley," and "Thomas Holman," in 1872 YMCA Records. On use of religious disguises by pornographers, see Trumbull, *Anthony Comstock,* 78–79.

26. Entry "Thomas Holman," in 1872 YMCA Arrest Records; "Improper Books, Prints, etc.," 6–7 (describing Farrell's network without identifying the publisher by name).

27. Entries "Charles Darrow" and "Joseph Darrow," in 1872 YMCA Arrest Records. On the prevalence of female laborers in bookbinding, see J. Luther Ringwalt, ed., *American Encyclopaedia of Printing* (Philadelphia: Menamin & Ringwalt, 1871), xii.

28. Entry "Arthur Brown," in 1872 YMCA Log of Persons Not Arrested.

29. Entries "Thomas Holman," "Charles Darrow," and "Joseph Darrow," in 1872 YMCA Arrest Records.

30. Entry "Louis Beer," in 1872 YMCA Log of Persons Not Arrested; Grand Fancy Bijou Catalogue, 6.

31. "Measures for the Suppression of Obscene Literature," *New York Times,* May 10, 1872; Trumbull, *Anthony Comstock,* 101. The YMCA committee later officially hired Comstock and awarded him an annual salary of $3,000. Horowitz, *Rereading Sex,* 374.

32. For analysis of Woodhull's life and career, see Richard Wightman Fox, *Trials of Intimacy: Love and Loss in the Beecher-Tilton Scandal* (Chicago, 1989); Horowitz, *Rereading Sex,* chap. 15; and Amanda Frisken, *Victoria Woodhull's Sexual Revolution: Political Theater and the Popular Press in Nineteenth-Century America* (Philadelphia, 2004).

33. Trumbull, *Anthony Comstock,* 103; Elizabeth Bainum Hovey, "Stamping Out Smut: The Enforcement of Obscenity Laws, 1872–1915" (Ph.D. diss. Columbia, 1998), 63; *Laws of New York,* 96th sess., chap. 527, 828 (May 16, 1873).

34. *Laws of New York,* 96th sess., chap. 527, 828.

35. Paul S. Boyer, *Purity in Print: Book Censorship in America from the Gilded Age to the Computer Age* (Madison, Wisc., 2002), 5–7; Nicola Beisel, *Imperiled Innocents: Anthony Comstock and Family Reproduction in Victorian America* (Princeton, N.J., 1998), 49–53.

36. Hovey, "Stamping Out Smut," 63.

37. Comstock, *Frauds Exposed,* 389, 391 (emphasis in the original).

38. *Congressional Globe,* 38th Cong., 2d sess., 660–661 (Feb. 8, 1865).

39. 5 *Statutes at Large* 466 (1842); James C. N. Paul and Murray L. Schwartz, *Federal Censorship: Obscenity in the Mail* (New York, 1961), 12.

40. The floor debate in the Senate is reported at *Congressional Globe,* 38th Cong., 2d sess., 660–661. For discussion of the Senate debates, see Paul and Schwartz, *Federal Censorship,* 17–18, 254–255; and Fuller, *Morality and the Mail,* 100–101.

41. *Congressional Globe,* 38th Cong., 2d sess., 660–661. On Reverdy Johnson, see David Montgomery, *Beyond Equality: Labor and the Radical Republicans, 1862–1872* (New York, 1967), 53. On the political conflict over the proposal to

ban antislavery literature in the mail, see Michael Kent Curtis, *"The People's Darling Privilege": Struggles for Freedom of Expression in American History* (Durham, N.C., 2000); and Curtis, "The Curious History of Attempts to Suppress Antislavery Speech, Press, and Petition in 1835–37," *Northwestern University Law Review* 89 (1995): 785–870.

42. *Congressional Globe,* 38th Cong., 2d sess., 661. On classes of mail, see Dorothy Ganfield Fowler, *Unmailable: Congress and the Post Office* (Athens, Ga., 1977), 55.

43. *Ex parte Jackson,* 96 U.S. 727, 733 (1878).

44. *Congressional Globe,* 38th Cong., 2d sess., 661; 13 *Statutes at Large* 507 (1865).

45. For early use of sealed mail to distribute erotica, see advertisements by "C. S. Wood" and "Day's Purchasing Agency," in *New York Clipper,* Feb. 13, 1864, 349. On ordering by number, see circular captioned "Genuine Fancy Books. Beautifully Illustrated with Colored Plates," held at the American Antiquarian Society; *People v. Thomas O'Connor,* June 15, 1869 (Indictment Papers, CGS), with circular attached as exhibit; "Improper Books, Prints, etc.," Report of the YMCA Committee for the Suppression of Vice for 1872–1873, Jan. 28, 1874, 6.

46. "Private Circular, for Gentlemen Only," nos. 1–4. The print and broadside specialists at the American Antiquarian Society, which holds copies of the circulars, estimate the date of their publication as 1870, when color printing became common. For the contemporaneous description of *The Roue's Pocket Companion,* see Grand Fancy Bijou Catalogue, 3. On Akarman's specialty in French transparent playing cards, see Comstock, *Frauds Exposed,* 388.

47. "Private Circular, for Gentlemen Only," no. 2.

48. Ibid.; *People v. Thomas O'Connor,* June 15, 1869 (Indictment Papers, CGS), with circular attached as exhibit; 29 *Statutes at Large* 52 (1897); Fuller, *Morality and the Mail,* 185–186.

49. "Private Circular, for Gentlemen Only," nos. 3–4. On the admission of parcels in the mail, see Richard R. John, *Spreading the News: The American Postal System from Franklin to Morse* (Cambridge, Mass., 1995), 39.

50. Grand Fancy Bijou Catalogue, 1–2.

51. On the exhibits, see Heywood Broun and Margaret Leech, *Anthony Comstock: Roundsman of the Lord* (New York, 1927), 131. On Strong's role in revising the Comstock Act, see Gaines M. Foster, *Moral Reconstruction: Christian Lobbyists and the Federal Legislation of Morality, 1865–1920* (Chapel Hill, N.C., 2002); 51; Trumbull, *Anthony Comstock,* 85–86.

52. *The Days' Doings,* Apr. 20, 1872, 15. On use of customer lists, see letter of Anthony Comstock to Rep. Clinton L. Merriam, dated Jan. 18, 1873; and "Improper Books, Prints, etc.," Report of the YMCA Committee for the Suppression of Vice for 1872–1873, dated Jan. 28, 1874, 5.

53. Act for the Suppression of Trade in, and Circulation of, Obscene Literature and Articles of Immoral Use, 17 *Statutes at Large* 598 (1873).

54. *Laws of New York,* 91st Session (Apr. 28, 1868), chap. 430, 856–857.

55. *The Days' Doings,* Sept. 7, 1872, 15.

56. Andrea Tone, *Devices and Desires: A History of Contraceptives in America* (New York, 2001), 16–17.

57. On the social, economic, and political influence of the New York YMCA and the soon-to-be-incorporated New York Society for the Suppression of Vice, see Boyer, *Purity in Print;* and Beisel, *Imperiled Innocents.*

58. Tone, *Devices and Desires,* 18. As Tone explains: "Remonstrations against contraceptives in public should not be confused with their frequent use in private, which contributed to the steadily falling birthrate in America after 1820 and turned the contraceptive industry into the 'hydra-headed monster' Comstock deplored." On women seeking illegal abortions in the last quarter of the nineteenth century, see Leslie Reagan, *When Abortion Was a Crime: Women, Medicine, and Law in the United States, 1867–1973* (Berkeley, Calif., 1997).

59. 17 *Statutes at Large* 598 (1873). The minimum and maximum sentences under the provision banning the manufacture and sale of obscene materials in the District of Columbia were half of those for sending obscenity through the mail.

60. The money for this new position was earmarked in a separate postal appropriations measure. Comstock's selection for this office was then arranged in private discussions between the bill's Republican sponsors in Congress and the Postmaster General. Horowitz, *Rereading Sex,* 381–382.

61. Register of Arrests for Offenses against Postal Laws, 1864–1897. Record Group 28, National Archives, Washington, D.C.

62. For valuable discussions of Comstock's enforcement efforts as an inspector of the Post Office and as secretary of the Society for the Suppression of Vice, see Broun and Leach, *Anthony Comstock;* Trumbull, *Anthony Comstock,* Hovey, "Stamping Out Smut"; Beisel, *Imperiled Innocents;* Horowitz, *Rereading Sex;* Daniel P. Carpenter, *The Forging of Bureaucratic Autonomy: Reputations, Networks, and Policy Innovation in Executive Agencies, 1862–1928* (Princeton, N.J., 2002); Fuller, *Morality in the Mail;* and Craig L. LaMay, "America's Censor: Anthony Comstock and Free Speech," *Communications Law and Policy* 19 (1997): 1–59.

63. Broun and Leech, *Anthony Comstock,* 128.

64. Third Annual Report of the New York Society for the Suppression of Vice (presented at New York, Jan. 4, 1877), 6–7 (emphasis in the original).

65. For examples of Comstock's aliases, see *United States v. William Simpson,* indictment filed Oct. 7, 1873 (Federal Archives, Southern District of New York) ("Harry Ketchem"); and *United States v. Robert Noak,* indictment filed

Oct. 13, 1874 (Federal Archives, Southern District of New York) ("Ketcham & Co.").

66. Second Annual Report of the New York Society for the Suppression of Vice (presented at New York, Jan. 27, 1876), 7–8.

67. Comstock devoted sections of his first two books, *Frauds Exposed* (1880) and *Traps for the Young* (1883), to legal defenses of his investigative methods: Comstock, *Traps for the Young*, 231–237; Comstock, *Frauds Exposed*, 526–539, both defending his use of decoy letters and undercover operatives.

68. Comstock, *Traps for the Young*, 236–237 (emphasis added by Comstock).

69. The discussion of the Camp case is based on *United States v. Henry Camp*, indictment filed Oct. 1, 1872 (Federal Archives, Southern District of New York), and the entry "Henry Camp," in the 1872 YMCA Arrest Records.

70. On the federal prosecution of Simpson, see entry "William Simpson," in 1874 Arrest Records of the New York Society for the Suppression of Vice; D. M. Bennett, *Anthony Comstock: His Career of Cruelty and Crime* (1878; New York, 1971), 1025; and *United States v. William Simpson*, indictment filed Oct. 13, 1874 (Federal Archives, Southern District of New York).

71. Comstock's success in federal cases and the support he received from federal law enforcement officials are evidenced in the Arrest Records of the YMCA and the New York Society for the Suppression of Vice, as well as the case files of federal prosecutions in the Southern District of New York. On the composition of federal juries in the Southern District of New York, see Hovey, "Stamping Out Smut," 136, n. 50.

72. For analysis of historiography on the Comstock Act, see Donna I. Dennis, "Obscenity Law and the Conditions of Freedom in the Nineteenth-Century United States," *Law and Social Inquiry* 27 (2002): 369–399. On the customary prerogatives of local and state governments to regulate morality in nineteenth-century America, see William J. Novak, *The People's Welfare: Law and Regulation in Nineteenth-Century America* (Chapel Hill, N.C., 1996), 149–189. On expansion of national power over morals regulation in the post–Civil War period, see Sarah Barringer Gordon, *The Mormon Question: Polygamy and Constitutional Conflict in Nineteenth-Century America* (Chapel Hill, N.C., 2002); Foster, *Moral Reconstruction;* Carpenter, *Forging of Bureaucratic Autonomy*.

8. New Frontiers

1. The Twenty-sixth Annual Report of the New York Society for the Suppression of Vice (presented at New York, Jan. 30, 1900), 8.

2. Ibid.

3. The Second Annual Report of the New York Society for the Suppression of Vice (presented at New York, Jan. 27, 1876), 5–7.

4. Entry "Charles E. Meackey," in 1872 YMCA Arrest Records; Helen

Lefkowitz Horowitz, *Rereading Sex: Battles over Sexual Knowledge and Suppression in Nineteenth-Century America* (New York, 2002), 326 (for quotation of ad from August 1870).

5. Entry "Charles E. Meackey," in 1872 YMCA Arrest Records; *People v. David T. Shaw,* May 20, 1873 (Indictment Papers, CGS).

6. Entry "James Bryan," in 1873 YMCA Arrest Records.

7. Entries "Solomon R. Solomon" and "Benjamin Bryant," in 1874 Arrest Records of the New York Society for the Suppression of Vice. See also *People v. Solomon Solomon and Benjamin Bryant,* Jan. 26, 1874 (Indictment Papers, CGS).

8. *People v. Edward Murray,* Sept. 8, 1875 (Indictment Papers, CGS), with poem attached as exhibit.

9. Entry "Stephen Schall," in 1876 Arrest Records of the New York Society for the Suppression of Vice; *People v. Stephen Schall,* July 7, 1876 (Indictment Papers, CGS), with poem attached as exhibit; "Convicted of Circulating Obscene Literature," *New York Times,* Sept. 23, 1876, 3.

10. Second Annual Report of the New York Society for the Suppression of Vice (presented at New York, Jan. 27, 1876), 7.

11. Fourth Annual Report of the New York Society for the Suppression of Vice (presented at New York, Jan. 28, 1878), 12, 7; "The Prevention of Vice," *New York Times,* Feb. 6, 1878, 2.

12. Tenth Annual Report of the New York Society for the Suppression of Vice (presented at New York, Jan. 22, 1884), 15. 5.

13. Timothy Gilfoyle, *City of Eros: New York City, Prostitution, and the Commercialization of Sex, 1790–1920* (New York, 1992), 287.

14. *People v. Elena Del Varto,* Sept. 25, 1884 (Indictment Papers, CGS), with statements by Del Varto attached; 1884 Artifacts File (Indictment Papers, CGS), containing photographic exhibits from the Del Varto case.

15. Bookseller catalogues of J. W. Bouton (1881–1886), held at the Grolier Club Library in New York City; bookseller catalogues of David G. Francis (1867–1878), ibid.

16. Pisanus Fraxi [Henry Spencer Ashbee], *Index Librorum Prohibitorum* (London, 1877), 71.

17. Lisa Z. Sigel, *Governing Pleasures: Pornography and Social Change in England, 1815–1914* (New Brunswick, N.J., 2002), 50–80; Ashbee, *Index Librorum Prohibitorum,* 174.

18. Ashbee, *Index Librorum Prohibitorum,* 238–248; J. W. Bouton, Catalogue of Rare and Standard Books (New York, 1881), 15. On the English tradition of flagellation literature, see John Chandos, *Boys Together: English Public Schools, 1800–1864* (New Haven, Conn., 1984); Ian Gibson, *The English Vice: Beating, Sex, and Shame in Victorian England and After* (London, 1992); and Sigel, *Governing Pleasures,* 74–79.

19. J. W. Bouton, A Connoisseur's Private Collection: Catalogue of a Rare and Interesting Collection of Illustrated Works (New York, n.d.), 25, 27; Bouton, A Catalogue of Sterling Second-Hand Books Ancient and Modern . . . (New York, 1886), 40; David G. Francis, Catalogue of New and Second-Hand Books, no. 33 (New York, 1874), 15; Francis, Catalogue of Cheap and Valuable Books, no. 36 (New York, 1875), 14.

20. On the late nineteenth-century movement of pornographic publishers from London to Paris and on *The Romance of Lust,* see Sigel, *Governing Pleasures,* 84, 93–95. For the turn-of-the-century U.S. circular, see "Erotica: A Priced bibliography" [n.p., 189?], copy held at New York Public Library.

21. *People v. Robert T. Sabin and William W. Sabin,* June 14, 1880 (Indictment Papers, CGS); "Comstock Makes Another Raid," *New York Times,* May 25, 1880, 3. For extensive bibliographic information on *The Merry Muses of Caledonia* and Hotten's 1872 edition, see Gershon Legman's "Erotic Folksongs and Ballads," at http://www.drinkingsongs.net/html/bibliography/1990-legman-bibliography/index.htm.

22. Entries "William Sabin" and "Robert Sabin," in 1880 Arrest Records of the New York Society for the Suppression of Vice. For background on Joseph Sabin, see entry "Joseph Sabin," in *Dictionary of American Biography;* and "Death of Joseph Sabin," *New York Times,* June 6, 1881, 5.

23. *People v. Robert T. Sabin and William W. Sabin,* June 14, 1880 (Indictment Papers, CGS); entries "William Sabin" and "Robert Sabin," in 1880 Arrest Records of the New York Society for the Suppression of Vice; "Death of Joseph Sabin," *New York Times,* June 6, 1881, 5.

24. *People v. Rudolph Geering, John Archie (aka Achille Verdalle) and George C. Mass,* Oct. 6, 1887 (Indictment Papers, CGS), with testimony of Oram attached.

25. The Fifth Annual Report of the New York Society for the Suppression of Vice (presented at New York, Jan. 29, 1879), 16. For a Comstock prosecution involving sales of the *Decameron,* see entry "Newell Campbell," in 1879 Arrest Records of the New York Society for the Suppression of Vice.

26. *People v. Rudolph Geering, John Archie, and George C. Maas,* Oct. 6, 1887 (Indictment Papers, CGS), with testimony of Britton attached.

27. Ibid.

28. Ibid. Sentences are noted on the cover sheet of the indictments and in a letter of Anthony Comstock that is included in the case file.

29. On the Knoedler case and public opposition to prosecution of upscale art dealers, see Nicola Beisel, *Imperiled Innocents: Anthony Comstock and Family Reproduction in Victorian America* (Princeton, N.J., 1998), chap. 7. On the fines, see Elizabeth Bainum Hovey, "Stamping Out Smut: The Enforcement of Obscenity Laws, 1872–1915" (Ph.D. diss. Columbia, 1998), 166.

30. *In re Worthington Co.*, 30 N.Y.S. 361 (Sup. Ct. N.Y. Co. 1894), reprinted in Edward De Grazia, *Censorship Landmarks* (New York, 1969), 44–45 (emphasis added). Throughout his career, Comstock vigorously rejected any distinction between art and obscenity, and he devoted a whole book to refuting the idea. Anthony Comstock, *Morals versus Art* (New York, 1887). On twentieth-century debates over art versus obscenity, see Morris L. Ernst and Alan U. Schwartz, *Censorship: The Search for the Obscene* (New York, 1964); Edward De Grazia, *Girls Lean Back Everywhere: The Law of Obscenity and the Assault on Genius* (New York, 1992); and Rochelle Gurstein, *The Repeal of Reticence: America's Cultural and Legal Struggles over Free Speech, Obscenity, Sexual Liberation, and Modern Art* (New York, 1996).

31. Remarks of Senator Vest, *Congressional Record*, 50th Cong., 1st sess., 7661 (Aug. 17, 1888).

32. On perceived limits on congressional power to exclude merchandise from interstate commerce, see *Ex parte Jackson*, 96 U.S. 727, 735 (1878). On the 1897 ban against the transmission of obscenity by common carriers, see 29 *Statutes at Large* 512 (1897); and Wayne E. Fuller, *Morality and the Mail in Nineteenth-Century America* (Urbana, Ill., 2003), 185–186. In 1903 the U.S. Supreme Court affirmed the power of Congress to exclude lottery material (and, by extension, obscene publications) from interstate commerce. *Champion v. Ames*, 188 U.S. 321 (1903).

33. For the Chicago dealer's circular, see box 147, no file number, Records of the Post Office Department, Bureau of Chief Inspector, National Archives, cited in Fuller, *Morality and the Mail*, 230 (emphasis in the original). See also box 114, file no. 277, Records of the Post Office Department, Bureau of Chief Inspector, National Archives (offering to ship catalogue containing sexually explicit pictures by express for fifty cents).

34. Fuller (quoting assistant attorney general), *Morality and the Mail*, 213. The 1892 decision was *Ex parte Rapier*, 143 U.S. 110 (1892).

35. For informative discussions of the constitutional advocacy of social reformers such as the free love advocate Ezra Heywood, the birth control proponent Edward Bliss Foote, and the freethinker D. M. Bennett, see David M. Rabban, *Free Speech in Its Forgotten Years* (New York, 1997), 23–44, aptly characterizing such thinkers as "libertarian radicals"; Beisel, *Imperiled Innocents*, chap. 4; Horowitz, *Rereading Sex*, chap. 19; Janice Ruth Wood, *The Struggle for Free Speech in the United States, 1872–1915: Edward Bliss Foote, Edward Bond Foote, and Anti-Comstock Operations* (New York, 2007).

36. Anthony Comstock, *Traps for the Young*, ed. Robert Bremner (1884; Cambridge, Mass., 1967), 184–207. See also Anthony Comstock, *Frauds Exposed; or, How the People are Deceived and Robbed, and Youth Corrupted* (New York, 1880), 392–393.

37. Edward Bliss Foote, *A Step Backward* (New York, 1877), 3–4; E. H. Heywood, *Cupid's Yokes: The Binding Forces of Conjugal Life* (Princeton, Mass., 1876). The constitutional scholar Robert Post has observed the way in which "all discursive practices establish themselves through the marginalization and suppression of competing practices." Robert C. Post, "Censorship and Silencing," in *Censorship and Silencing: Practices of Cultural Regulation*, ed. Robert C. Post (Los Angeles, 1998), 6.

38. [T. B. Wakeman], *The Comstock Laws Considered as to Their Constitutionality; Being T. B. Wakeman's Faneuil Hall Speech, Letter from James Parton, Replies to the Index, etc.* (New York, 1878), 21.

39. See "Arrested for Disseminating Obscene Literature," *New York Times*, July 12, 1874, 1, for an example of a bribe to avoid arrest; entry "William Sabin," in 1880 Arrest Records of the New York Society for the Suppression of Vice, for an example of a forfeiture of bail and subsequent escape to Europe; entry "Albina Marchal," in 1885 Arrest Records of the New York Society for the Suppression of Vice, for another forfeiture of bail and escape to Europe; *People v. Rudolph Geering, John Archie, and George C. Maas*, Oct. 6, 1887 (Indictment Papers, CGS), for a light sentence meted out to a defendant with political influence; entry "Edward [Gould]," in 1883 Arrest Records of the New York Society for the Suppression of Vice, for a suspended sentence for defendant with political influence; and entry "John Crozer," in 1883 Arrest Records of the New York Society for the Suppression of Vice, for a suspended sentence on account of family circumstances.

40. For a claim by moral reformers that pornography dealers had internalized moral and legal sanctions, see Third Annual Report of the New York Society for the Suppression of Vice (presented at New York, Jan. 4, 1877), 7. On the importance of covert as well as overt strategies of resistance, see George Chauncey, *Gay New York: Gender, Urban Culture, and the Making of the Gay Male World, 1890–1940* (New York, 1994), 5; and James Scott, *Weapons of the Weak: Everyday Forms of Peasant Resistance* (New Haven, Conn., 1985).

41. "Convicted of Circulating Obscene Literature," *New York Times*, Sept. 23, 1876, 3; *People v. Stephen Schall*, July 7, 1876 (Indictment Papers, CGS).

42. See *People v. Elena Del Varto*, Sept. 25, 1884 (Indictment Papers, CGS); and D. R. M. Bennett, *Anthony Comstock: His Career of Cruelty and Crime* (1878; New York, 1971), describing charges of perjury and blackmail by Comstock in individual cases.

43. *United States v. Grimm*, 156 U.S. 604 (1895).

44. "Anti-Criminal Societies," *New York Times*, Jan. 30, 1881, 6.

45. Ibid.

46. See Arrest Records of the New York Society for the Suppression of Vice,

1875–1900; Records of the Post Office Department, Bureau of Chief Inspector, National Archives; and Fuller, *Morality in the Mail,* chap. 10.

47. Gilfoyle, *City of Eros,* chap. 12.

48. Ibid., 261–265.

49. On the flourishing of commercial sexual recreation in early twentieth-century New York, see especially Lewis A. Erenberg, *Steppin' Out: New York Nightlife and the Transformation of American Culture, 1890–1930* (Westport, Conn., 1981); Kathy Peiss, *Cheap Amusements: Working Women and Leisure in Turn-of-the-Century New York* (Philadelphia, 1986); Chauncey, *Gay New York;* and Marybeth Hamilton, *When I'm Bad, I'm Better: Mae West, Sex, and American Entertainment* (Berkeley, Calif., 1997). On debates about obscenity in New York in the first half of the twentieth century, see Andrea Friedman, *Prurient Interests: Gender, Democracy, and Obscenity in New York City, 1909–1945* (New York, 2000).

50. On the resurgence of erotic publishing and distribution in New York between World War I and World War II, see Jay Gertzmann, *Bookleggers and Smuthounds: The Trade in Erotica, 1920–1940* (Philadelphia, 1999).

Acknowledgments

This book has come about with the help of a great number of wonderful family members, friends, colleagues, and teachers. I have benefited especially from a remarkable group of mentors. As an undergraduate at Yale, I first studied with David Brion Davis, who introduced me to what would become an enduring fascination with nineteenth-century culture and society. I found equally outstanding teachers, as well as good friends, while a doctoral student in Princeton's History Department. The program there was an unusually nurturing and inspiring environment in which to begin a scholarly career, and I feel tremendously fortunate to have been a part of it.

Several scholars deserve special acknowledgment for their support and guidance. Robert Post of Yale Law School offered rigorous analysis and much-appreciated enthusiasm at an early stage of this project. Elizabeth Lunbeck, then at the Princeton History Department, provided essential theoretical grounding. I am deeply grateful to Stanley Katz for his sage advice on many matters related to this study and for his kindness and encouragement throughout. Christine Stansell's work on New York City was an inspiration from the outset and provided a model for the creative possibilities of cultural history.

No one has had a greater impact on this work than Hendrik Hartog. I feel exceptionally fortunate to have found my way to legal history under his mentorship. A superb critic and scholar, Dirk has always generously gone the extra mile as an adviser. His astute readings have improved this book in ways that are too numerous to list, and his unflinching support of my career has been a great gift. Those of us who have had the benefit of his guidance know how lucky we are. Perhaps best of all, Dirk is an outstanding friend.

Many thanks go to the archivists, curators, and librarians at the American Antiquarian Society; the New York City Municipal Archives and Record Center; the National Archives and Records Administration; the Library of Congress; the Baker Library of the Harvard Business School; the Kinsey Institute for Research in Sex, Gender, and Reproduction at Indiana University; the Grolier Club Library; the New York Public Library; the New York Historical Society; the Museum of the City of New York; the Firestone Library of Princeton University; and the Beinecke Rare Book and Manuscript Library at Yale University who helped to make this project possible. I offer special thanks to Georgia Barnhill, Joanne Chaison, and Dennis Laurie at the American Antiquarian Society; Steven Ferguson at the Department of Rare Books and Special Collections of Princeton's Firestone Library; Kenneth Cobb at the New York City Municipal Archives; and the terrific librarians at Rutgers School of Law in Newark, New Jersey. In addition, thanks to my former students at Rutgers, Kris Brewer and Chad Wolf, for stellar research assistance.

Early in this project, I was lucky to discover a lively group of fellow researchers, especially Kimberly Gladman, Paul Erickson, and Haven Hawley, who shared their findings, exchanged drafts, and helped to organize panels on indecent literature and obscenity in nineteenth-century America. A special note is owed to George Thompson of New York University's Bobst Library, whose extensive collection of articles on cultural life in antebellum New York enabled me to piece together vital information about the life of George Akarman at a very early stage of my research.

I am also grateful to my editor at Harvard University Press, Joyce Seltzer, for her wise editorial judgment and engaging conversation. I am likewise thankful for the comments of the anonymous reviewers and other readers at Harvard University Press, which helped improve the manuscript in important respects, the gracious assistance of Aria Sloss, and the excellent editorial work of Susan Abel during the copyediting process.

I have benefited greatly from comments I received when presenting earlier versions of portions of this book to Princeton University's Center for Arts and Cultural Policy Studies; the Fellowship of Woodrow Wilson Scholars at Princeton; annual meetings of the American Society for Legal History, the Law and Society Association, and the American Studies Association; the Program in Book History and Print Culture at the University of Toronto; the Law and Humanities Junior Scholar Interdisciplinary Workshop (special thanks to David Rabban and Reva Siegal for their detailed comments); the Yale Law School Legal History Forum; the UCLA Legal History Workshop; and faculty colloquia at my home institution, Rutgers School of Law–Newark. Earlier versions of some of the material in this book also appeared in "Obscenity Law and the Conditions of Freedom in the Nineteenth-Century United States," *Law and Social Inquiry* 27 (2002): 369–399; and "Obscenity Law and Its Consequences in Mid-Nineteenth-Century America," *Columbia Journal of Gender and Law* 16 (2007): 43–95.

I deeply appreciate the financial support and fellowships I received over the years from the Princeton History Department, the Princeton

Center for Arts and Cultural Policy Studies, the Princeton Fellowship of Woodrow Wilson Scholars, and the Mrs. Giles Whiting Foundation. I also thank Stuart Deutsch, dean of Rutgers School of Law–Newark, and the Dean's Fund of Rutgers School of Law for valuable financial assistance and research leave. At Rutgers I am fortunate to be in the company of a number of excellent colleagues who work in the field of legal history, including Mark Weiner, Greg Mark, Jim Pope, and George Thomas. Mark Weiner, who generously read the entire manuscript on very short notice at a critical point, deserves particularly warm acknowledgment.

I am especially indebted to my parents, Elle Dennis and David Paul Dennis, who nurtured my love of history at a very early age.

Finally, it is difficult to express the depth of my gratitude to Nancy Louden, to whom this book is dedicated. Her love, generosity, and all-around sanity, not to mention her discerning editorial eye, have improved this book, and life in general, immeasurably. Throughout this long project, her companionship has brought me immense happiness.

Index

Index

www.ingramcontent.com/pod-product-compliance
Lightning Source LLC
Chambersburg PA
CBHW030641150426
42811CB00076B/1995/J
* 9 7 8 0 6 7 4 0 3 2 8 3 5 *